ISBN: 9781290944755

Published by:
HardPress Publishing
8345 NW 66TH ST #2561
MIAMI FL 33166-2626

Email: info@hardpress.net
Web: http://www.hardpress.net

A. F. Cohn

THE LIBRARY
OF
THE UNIVERSITY
OF CALIFORNIA
LOS ANGELES

MALINGERING
AND FEIGNED SICKNESS

BY

SIR JOHN COLLIE, M.D., J.P.

MEDICAL EXAMINER, LONDON COUNTY COUNCIL: CHIEF MEDICAL OFFICER, METROPOLITAN
WATER BOARD: CONSULTING MEDICAL EXAMINER TO THE SHIPPING FEDERATION;
MEDICAL EXAMINER TO THE SUN INSURANCE OFFICE; CENTRAL INSURANCE
COMPANY; LONDON, LIVERPOOL AND GLOBE INSURANCE COMPANY; AND
OTHER ACCIDENT OFFICES; LATE HOME OFFICE MEDICAL REFEREE
WORKMEN'S COMPENSATION ACT

ASSISTED BY
ARTHUR H. SPICER, M.B., B.S.Lond., D.P.H.

ILLUSTRATED

LONDON
EDWARD ARNOLD
1913

[All rights reserved]

THIS BOOK IS DEDICATED

TO MY FRIEND

THE BRITISH WORKMAN

TO WHOM I OWE MUCH

PREFACE

THE sympathy of everyone is naturally with the sick and suffering, and anything which may, at first sight, appear to deny that feeling, is liable to misconstruction. So that no misapprehension may exist as to the object of this book, this foreword is penned. Many deserving cases do not receive proper consideration because unworthy persons have had expended upon them the sympathy and help which are the legitimate right of the true sufferer. Those who by law are responsible for the results of accidents, in the causation of which they have had no part or lot, should not be subjected to greater burdens than those which their misfortunes have imposed. True it is that in many instances the loss is made good by an insurance company; but, though corporations may have " no soul to be saved or body to be kicked," it is to be remembered that they are composed of individuals to whom the ultimate loss is a serious consideration. The cost of insuring against accidents to industrial workers is now far in excess of the actuarial estimates upon which the Compensation Acts were based; and a study of the statistics in relation to non-fatal accidents shows an increase in the number of those accidents since the advent of this legislation, which cannot be accounted for even by the speeding-up of machinery and the conditions of modern labour. Malingering and dishonesty must have had an influence in raising the figures to their present abnormal height. Naturally the amount of compensation paid is reflected in the premiums demanded, therefore, unless unjust claims are sternly repressed, the burden upon the community will be greater than it legitimately should be.

To those who may think that being acute to detect fraud, and to prevent lapses into a species of fraud, are not within

v

PREFACE

the province of a medical man, I would put the question : Are not the confining of sympathy and benefits to their proper channels, the prevention of improper claims against innocent persons, and the restoration to useful occupation of those who might otherwise become parasites of society, services which deserve well of the community ? Very often this service can only be rendered by a medical man, and surely when such cases present themselves it is a duty which must be performed. The medical attendant's first consideration is certainly due to his patient, but we quasi-public servants owe a duty to a wider constituency, in the performance of which we probably do the best service to our immediate patients.

This work deals with a very dark side of human nature, and does not admit of the display of that sympathy which I trust all genuine cases receive. Having met with all types of working men, the brighter side of the picture has at times been presented, and I gladly recall many acts of unostentatious heroism which have reflected credit not only on the individual, but also on the class to which he belongs. Deeds of fine independence, and sufferings nobly borne, remain in my memory ; but with such this work necessarily has no concern. I am tempted, however, to relate an instance which came to my notice quite recently. A young man was at work in a bunker of " slack " coal, trying to clear the shoot which had become blocked ; suddenly the obstacle gave way, and he was sucked down by the rush of coal. As the coal closed over his head, he called out " Good-bye " to his fellow-workmen. After fourteen men had dug for three-quarters of an hour, he was rescued from beneath tons of coal. The next day but one he voluntarily returned to work !

In 1836 a prize essay by Gavin, in the Class of Military Surgery at the University of Edinburgh, entitled " Feigned and Factitious Diseases, chiefly of Soldiers and Sailors," was published. Since then only one small similar treatise has appeared ; there have been French and German works on the subject, which, although suggestive, have not been very helpful. For obvious reasons, therefore, the conclusions arrived at, and the cases cited, are those with which I have had to wrestle. In the illustrative cases great pains have been taken to avoid giving any particulars which might lead to the identification of the cor-

PREFACE

vii

porations, insurance companies, solicitors, or medical men concerned ; so they need have no fear of being recognized. Some of my friends have hinted that the cases quoted are somewhat one-sided, in that they are mainly restricted to those in which I have been successful. I plead guilty, and shall mend my ways when they " hold a candle to their shame "—in public. The wise admit (to themselves) their errors, and profit more by them than by their successes. We all make mistakes, and no one knows this better than those who specialize in the difficult branch of professional work with which this book deals. It is in consequence of the mistakes of which I am conscious that the many danger-signals have been erected as this book progressed.

That much of the phraseology is of a more or less popular nature arises from the fact that all the reports quoted were written for public bodies or insurance companies, and this also is why such simple tests as Romberg's are explained. The profession will, I hope, pardon these elementary definitions found in the histories of several cases, for they were interpolated solely to make the reports intelligible to the layman to whom they were addressed. Further, I hope the lapses into non-technical language will be excused by medical men when it is pointed out that to some extent this work may be of use to members of the legal profession and those who are responsible for the administration of the National Insurance Act. My thanks for much assistance are due to an eminent legal friend who insists upon remaining anonymous.

I am indebted to Dr. Christine Murrell for writing the chapter on Electrical Testing ; it proves her thorough knowledge of the subject. I interested myself in its progress and intervened with suggestions, and the fact that we are still friends testifies to her forbearance.

I am also indebted to Messrs. Baillière, Tindall and Cox for their permission to reprint many of the cases quoted in my book on " Medico-Legal Examinations and the Workmen's Compensation Act, 1906," published by them.

J. C.

Porchester Terrace,
Hyde Park, W.
1913.

CONTENTS

CHAPTER		PAGE
PREFACE		v
LIST OF ILLUSTRATIONS		xi
I. WHAT IS MALINGERING ?		1
II. PREVENTION OF MALINGERING		14
III. THE MEDICAL EXAMINATION		31
IV. THE EXAMINATION OF THE NERVOUS SYSTEM		61
V. FUNCTIONAL NERVE DISEASES, INCLUDING NEURASTHENIA, HYSTERIA, AND TRAUMATIC NEURASTHENIA		81
VI. THE EXAMINATION OF THE EYE		109
VII. THE EXAMINATION OF THE EAR		118
VIII. THE EXAMINATION OF THE BACK		126
IX. THE EXAMINATION OF THE UPPER AND LOWER EXTREMITIES		146
X. ASYMMETRY		167
XI. EXAMINATION BY X-RAY PHOTOGRAPHY		175
XII. THE USE OF ELECTRICITY IN ALLEGED MALINGERING		182
XIII. HERNIA AND MALINGERING		189
XIV. EPILEPSY, APOPLEXY, HEATSTROKE AND MALINGERING		204
XV. INSANITY AND MALINGERING		211
XVI. HÆMORRHAGE AND MALINGERING		216
XVII. ACCIDENTS WHERE PRE-EXISTING DISEASE IS PRESENT		219
XVIII. REPORTS ON PROBABLE CAUSES OF DEATH AFTER THE EVENT		222
XIX. THE MEDICAL MAN'S POSITION AS REGARDS LIBEL AND SLANDER		236

CONTENTS

CHAPTER	PAGE
XX. CONDUCT OF THE MEDICAL WITNESS IN COURT - - -	239
XXI. MEDICAL ASPECT OF THE WORKMEN'S COMPENSATION ACT, 1906	242
XXII. MEDICAL ASPECT OF THE WORKMEN'S COMPENSATION ACT, 1906 *—continued* - - - - - -	265
XXIII. THE NATIONAL INSURANCE ACT, 1911 - - - -	280
XXIV. LEGAL AID SOCIETIES - - - - - -	286
XXV. EPONYMIC SIGNS - - - - - -	292
XXVI. ELECTRICAL TESTING - - - - - -	298
GENERAL INDEX - - - - - -	323

LIST OF ILLUSTRATIONS

FIGS.   PAGES

1. HUMAN SKELETON : FRONT VIEW WITH BONES NAMED - - 58

2. HUMAN SKELETON : BACK VIEW WITH BONES NAMED - - 59

3. BABINSKI'S SIGN (EXTENSOR PLANTAR REFLEX) - - 68

4. GAIT OF HYSTERICAL HEMIPLEGIA - - - - 85

5—8. DIAPHRAGM TEST FOR BINOCULAR VISION (HARMAN) 110-112

9. THE AUTHOR'S STETHOSCOPE TEST - - - - 124

10, 11. THE TRAPEZE TEST - - - - - - 149

12. THE DYNAMOMETER - - - - - - 153

13. THE HAND-GRIP TEST - - - - - - 160

14—19. DIAGRAMS DEMONSTRATING MEASUREMENTS FOR SYMMETRY
AND ASYMMETRY - - - - - 168-173

20, 21. RADIOGRAMS OF FRACTURED FIBULA - - - 177

22, 23. THE AUTHOR'S APPARATUS FOR DEMONSTRATING RADIOGRAMS
IN COURT - - - - - - - 180

24. TESTING ELECTRODE HANDLE WITH BREAK KEY - - 183

25, 26. DIAGRAMS SHOWING HOW HERNIA OCCURS - - 194, 195

27, 28. MOTOR POINTS OF UPPER LIMB (ERB) - - 304, 305

29. MOTOR POINTS OF LEG (ERB) - - - - - 306

30. MOTOR POINTS AT BACK OF THIGH AND LEG (ERB) - - 307

31. MOTOR POINTS OF ANTERIOR THIGH MUSCLES (ERB) - - 308

32. AREA OF LOSS OF SENSATION FOLLOWING LESION OF MEDIAN
NERVE (HEAD) - - - - - - - 309

33. ULNAR PARALYSIS FROM A WOUND OF THE NERVE BEHIND THE
INTERNAL CONDYLE OF THE HUMERUS - - - 310

34. AREA OF LOSS OF SENSATION FOLLOWING A LESION OF THE ULNAR
NERVE (HEAD) - - - - - - 311

LIST OF ILLUSTRATIONS

FIGS.   PAGE

35. AREA OF LOSS OF SENSATION FOLLOWING LESION OF BOTH THE ULNAR AND MEDIAN NERVES (HEAD) -   -   -   - 311

36. LEFT-SIDED MUSCULO-SPIRAL PARALYSIS SHOWING DROP-WRIST AND ATROPHY OF SUPINATOR LONGUS   -   -   - 312

37. AREA OF LOSS OF SENSATION FOLLOWING LESION OF RADIAL AND EXTERNAL CUTANEOUS NERVES (HEAD)   -   -   - 313

38. BATTERY FOR FARADIC CURRENT ONLY -   -   -   - 316

39—41. SCHEMA OF FARADIC BATTERY   -   -   -   - 317

42. TESTING ELECTRODE HANDLE WITH MAKE KEY -   -   - 318

43. BATTERY FOR CONTINUOUS CURRENT ONLY   -   -   - 319

44. BATTERY FOR COMBINED CONTINUOUS AND FARADIC CURRENTS 320

MALINGERING

CHAPTER I

WHAT IS MALINGERING ?

Malingering.—The many provisions made by the Legislature in recent years for securing benefits to injured workpeople have, undoubtedly, given rise to a large number of cases of malingering. Not many years ago it was practically only in naval and military circles that one heard the term used, where the ingenious Jack or Tommy feigned all sorts of ailments in order to evade an unpleasant duty or get discharged from the Service. Chewing cordite or rubbing gunpowder into self - inflicted wounds were among their more drastic means of giving an air of verisimilitude to otherwise unconvincing symptoms. The workhouses and prisons probably provided other examples.

The Common Law of England, which gave the right to obtain monetary compensation from negligent people, whether employers or otherwise, undoubtedly gave the first impetus to a more general adoption of the practice of making much out of little ; the various Workmen's Compensation Acts have still further enlarged the field ; and, with the advent of the National Insurance Act, it is practically certain that, so far from malingering being a subject which rarely comes within the purview of the general practitioner, it will become a matter for which all medical men must always keep their eyes open.

The Necessity for Recognition.—I have found the methods of the conscious deceiver so ingenious, and the mental outlook of the unconscious exaggerator so difficult to deal with, that, having in view the fact that now it will be necessary for all medical men to look for the possibility of deceit or exaggeration in many cases that come before them, I propose to formulate

1

2 MALINGERING

certain theories with regard to these matters, exemplifying them with typical cases from my own experience, and offer certain tests for discovering, and remedies for dealing with, them. One may have a case which justifies the gravest suspicion, but, without previously having had a similar experience, one hesitates to condemn it as fraudulent ; it is therefore my hope that the cases quoted hereafter may be of assistance in helping the profession to perform the very serious duty that will be upon them of protecting the State, the Approved Societies, and Employers, from the unjust and improper demands which doubtless will be made upon them.

It is seldom that so gross and deliberate a fraud is perpetrated as the following instance, which occurred in the practice of a personal friend of mine :

Dr. F. was asked to examine A. A., a man of the shopkeeping class, who informed him that his life was insured, that he had allowed his policy to lapse through non-payment of the premiums, that he desired to resuscitate his policy, and that the insurance company had agreed to his doing so on condition that he sent a cheque for arrears of premiums, accompanied by a medical certificate stating that he was in good health. He therefore appealed to my friend to give him the necessary certificate, which Dr. F. expressed himself quite willing to do after, and only after, he had thoroughly examined him. In vain did the patient point out that the fee allowed by the company was a very small one, that the certificate was only a matter of form, and that, as a matter of fact, he was in perfect health. The examination was undertaken ; indeed, it was done with some thoroughness, for the applicant was stripped to the waist, and his lungs and heart carefully examined. Whilst thus undressed, placing his hands on his hips, or in that neighbourhood, he struck an attitude, saying, with some emphasis : " Now, doctor, are you satisfied ? Am I not a fine fellow ?" My friend's reply was that he did not think so, but, as he could find nothing wrong, he supposed he would have to give him a certificate, and he did.

Six months afterwards an insurance company communicated with the doctor, asking why he had given a certificate of good health to one of their assured who had just died of cancer of the rectum, and who had had an inguinal colotomy performed *antecedent* to the date of his examination.

The brave words, the dramatic attitude, the hands on the hips, were all a piece of consummate acting, designed to cover the tell-tale scar of a colotomy wound.

Relative Extent of Malingering.—Cases of gross deception, in which serious illness or injury is feigned, based upon the

WHAT IS MALINGERING ?

slightest physical symptoms (or, it may be, upon none at all), are readily and accurately described as cases of " malingering "; but there are other cases to which the expression cannot be so easily applied. The undue prolongation of illness, the unwillingness to return to work, and the exaggeration of symptoms, are all matters which may well fall under the same classification ; and it is not necessary that deliberate fraud should alone be present in order to make a person a malingerer. Only a comparatively small proportion of the vast number of sick people are out-and-out malingerers, but it must be remembered that, although the number is a relatively small one, there is, in the aggregate, a large number of working-class men and women who, in returning, linger on the threshold of work.

I am aware that in a large number of cases workmen do not share the opinion expressed by the medical man who examines on behalf of the employer. Apart altogether from attempts to postpone return to work, by deliberate malingering, there is a large number of men who put off the return to laborious work merely because they do not appreciate that complete recovery is always a gradual process, and that stiffness, and even some slight degree of pain, seldom entirely disappear until an injured part has been subjected to a certain amount of movement and exercise—such, indeed, as they might reasonably be expected to put up with, having regard to the fact that it can only be of a temporary nature. I am convinced that this is the real explanation of a large number of cases which find their way to the Arbitration Courts.

Statistics relating to this particular class of cases are practically non-existent, for until recently attention has not been drawn to the matter ; I am therefore, in dealing with this subject, forced to draw mainly from my own experience. Two large public bodies and some fifteen to twenty insurance companies send sick and injured workpeople to me for my opinion as to their fitness or otherwise for work. For some years past I have seen approximately 2,000 such cases a year, and 25 per cent. (*one in every four*) were reported to be fit for work. The majority of these were not typical malingerers, but they would, nevertheless, from various causes, have unduly prolonged their illnesses. It is impossible to examine so large a number of cases and not come to certain definite conclusions

MALINGERING

as to the psychical and other conditions engendered by the tendency of present-day legislation.

On the whole, I have little to complain of apparent unwillingness of workmen in the Public Service to return to duty on the date when I report they should do so.

Not so, however, with cases which are sent to me by insurance companies. These stand on a different footing, for they are as a rule cases which have already been seen by other medical men, and come for a final opinion prior to an action at common law or arbitration proceedings being instituted.

The trouble in dealing with cases which ought really to be termed " fraudulent " is not so much the difficulty of recognizing the fraud as of determining its gravity in relation to each individual concerned, because what would amount to a fraudulent statement if made by a fairly educated working man, must be treated as a mere exaggeration when proceeding from the mouth of an East End alien tailor. There is, however, no difficulty, once the facts are ascertained, in classifying such a case of gross fraud as the following :

A. B. injured his right ankle in October, 1909, whilst trucking a case at the Royal Albert Docks.

He was asked by the Shipping Federation to attend at my house for medical examination in April, 1910, but absolutely declined. Indeed, he had refused to receive half-wages, which were being paid to him regularly, because the agent of his employer had declined to take the money to the top of the house where he happened to be at the moment. The weekly payments were stopped, and the case came before the County Court the same month. Not having examined the applicant, I was not present at the hearing ; but a doctor who had previously seen him on behalf of his employers was called, and gave evidence to the effect that, in his opinion, A. B. was well and fit for work.

Evidence was given by two doctors as to his total incapacity for work, and an award of twelve shillings per week was made in his favour. The medical referee did not sit with the Judge.

Two months after getting his award he was sent to me for examination.

Examination.—He complained that his right ankle was too painful to use in consequence of the previous accident, and that he now had pain in his right hip.

From the moment this man entered my room his manner impressed me unfavourably. He insisted on his wife being present as a witness. He was a burly, muscular fellow, who assumed a blustering, insolent attitude, and it struck me that he would be very easily provoked to violence. His mental attitude was shown

WHAT IS MALINGERING ?

by the following little incident : In order that I might examine his ankle thoroughly, it was necessary for him to take off his boot and stocking. When this was done, as the trouser-leg interfered with my view, I politely asked him to pull up his trousers ; he expressed great reluctance, glaring at me in a defiant manner. However, I quietly insisted upon his doing so, and baring the other leg also. A portable thirty-candle-power bell-lamp was brought within a few feet of his legs, and before I had commenced the examination, or had time to turn on the electric light, he at once said : " That is the battery ; this is enough for me. I will not let you examine me any more !" He forthwith put on his boots and stockings. When he had finished I switched on the electric light, and requested him to take them all off again. Seeing the mistake he had made, he changed his tactics, saying he would " not be pulled about " ; but upon my pointing out that I had not yet touched him, he became more reasonable.

The ankle was absolutely normal in every particular. His suggestion of acute pain was evidently feigned. He resolutely declined to allow me to manipulate the ankle-joint ; he refused to have the foot X-rayed, protesting that he " would not be burned." When it was pointed out to him that he would feel no more inconvenience than if he were having his portrait taken, he changed his ground, stating that he would have nothing done until he had seen his own doctor, whom he stated he was in the habit of consulting once a fortnight.

With regard to the hip, when he was asked to touch the spot, without being allowed to look at his hip, great difficulty was experienced in getting him to commit himself to anything so precise, but ultimately he consented. Five separate times he indicated the painful spot with his finger, and on each occasion I marked it with coloured chalk ; on four of these occasions different spots were pointed to, two of them being $4\frac{1}{2}$ inches apart. It was noticeable that on leaving my house he walked with his foot turned outwards—an unnatural attitude, which would necessarily strain the muscles at the hip.

I had no hesitation in reporting this man to be a rank impostor, a deliberate malingerer. The company then informed me that for some time they had regarded him as a malingerer, and had been more than usually surprised that the Judge had held that he was partially disabled. The secretary to the company stated that they appreciated my remark that he looked a violent man, for he had, in fact, attempted to assault the doctor who had examined him prior to his being sent to me, but that it had only resulted in his putting one of his own fists through a window !

An X-ray examination was arranged, but nothing would induce the man to attend.

Result.—Three months later, at the trial, I was subjected to a very severe cross-examination when I stated that he was a malingerer, but it was proved that *at the time of the first trial*, when he got compensation for continuing disability (sworn to by two doctors), he was doing heavy work, and that for several months after his award (of 12s.

MALINGERING

a week) he had continued to do it ; he had, in fact, got a day off from his work to attend the Court at the first hearing by stating to his employer that he had been summoned for arrears of rent !

This, of course, settled the case, and the Judge sent the papers to the Public Prosecutor with a view to criminal proceedings, which, however, were not taken.

Malingerers of this type can only be dealt with by strong measures. It may be said that such cases are exceptional, but recently, on my advice, at least eighteen consecutive cases of a similar, if less pronounced type, have been taken to the Law Courts for decision, and the result in each case has justified the advice given.

It is not often that an absolutely uncomplicated case of malingering pure and simple occurs :

History.—A. C., whilst at sea, fell down the stokehole. Fracture of the left collar-bone and bruising of the muscles of the corresponding arm were the alleged result. First-aid was rendered by the crew. He stated that on reaching port, seventeen days later, a doctor examined him, and had him removed to hospital, where the collar-bone was " reset " under an anæsthetic. The story appeared highly improbable, for fracture of the clavicle is not a serious affair, and even had the union not been quite satisfactory, as was alleged, most surgeons would hesitate to reset a collar-bone, for good results are often obtained from the most unskilled treatment of this common accident.

Medical Examination.—Four months after the alleged accident he was sent to me, still alleging inability to work. Six weeks is a reasonable period for recovery from fracture of the clavicle. Nothing amiss could be discovered. He was obviously acting a part ; under examination he wriggled, making violent contortions, and assumed an agonized expression of countenance when the shoulder, which was the only part of his anatomy he complained of, was moved. It was apparent, however, that not only could he use the muscles of the shoulder, but that he did use them, for they were not wasted, as they must have been if disused. At a subsequent interview with his doctor it transpired that in his opinion the trouble was not really in the shoulder, but in the hand ! The doctor volunteered the information that if the claimant were paid his wages up to the date of my examination, *and a little over*, he would return to work !

Two months later, no settlement having been effected, at my suggestion an X-ray photograph was taken. The negative showed that the collar-bone had never been fractured. Another examination confirmed my previous diagnosis that A. C. was an undoubted malingerer. He pretended that when the arm was raised to more than a right angle with the body, intense pain was produced ; but it was noticeable that pain was complained of when the arm was elevated sometimes to one level. and sometimes to another. On one occasion when the arm was

WHAT IS MALINGERING ?

raised at right angles with the body, his expression of intense suffering was pitiful to see ; yet when his attention was directed elsewhere, the expression of pain passed away. It was amusing to note that when his own doctor raised his patient's arm, it did not seem to cause pain. A. C. would not work, and the shipping company would not pay, so the case came before an Arbitration Court.

Result.—At the hearing of the arbitration I demonstrated to the Court that the claimant was obviously shamming. He now complained he had lost sensation in the fingers of the left hand. In the presence of the Judge I instructed him to close his eyes and hold up both his hands. He was told to say at once " Yes " when he felt a pin-prick, and " No " when he did not. This ridiculous instruction he carried out. The fingers of the two hands were pricked alternately, and A. C. recorded many times " Yes " on the right, and a large number of " No's " on the left. Why should " No " ever have been given ? If there was, as he alleged, no sensation, there obviously should have been no answer.

Notwithstanding this, the decision was given in *favour* of the claimant. The Judge stated, however, that he thought the plaintiff was " grossly exaggerating " ! Although a considerable weekly allowance was ordered to be paid to this worthy soldier, wounded in the industrial warfare, for reasons which were not apparent, he returned to sea in a few weeks, proving himself a little ungrateful to the arbitrators who had given him the award ! I wrote to the medical referee informing him of the man's ingratitude. The Judge will probably remember the case.

Psychology of the Fraudulent Mind.—Malingering is much more common in connection with accidents than with disease, probably because of the legal liability involved ; it has, therefore, to be anxiously watched for and considered. Everyone is liable to exaggerate symptoms if doing so may operate to his advantage or excite sympathy. For instance, pain in the back following an accident is a condition which is often caused by suggestion—auto-suggestion. It does not necessarily mean malingering ; but pain in the back after an accident, be it caused by a wealthy railway company or by a mishap in one's own garden, is, much more often than not, accompanied by no serious pathological change. The pain is often only psychic.

Experience teaches that closely similar injuries attributable to like accidents present one kind of clinical picture, and run one kind of course, amongst those who make no claim for compensation ; but they present a very different picture and run a very different course amongst those who embark upon the troubled sea of litigation. This difference is highly signifi-

8 MALINGERING

cant of the influence of litigation in magnifying pain and perpetuating incapacity.

In a large number of cases which eventually come before the Courts, introspection and subjective sensations are unwittingly fostered.

The problem frequently presents itself for solution : Is the patient a wilful malingerer, or the victim of psychical conditions consequent upon an accident ?

Psychologists tell us that we conceive only that partial aspect of a thing which the individual regards, for *his* purpose, as its essential aspect. What is considered essential varies, of course, with the point of view of the individual. For instance, the substance chalk is looked upon by different people according to the use to which it is put ; the geologist thinks of it as the cemetery of millions of animalcula ; the schoolmaster, as a messy but useful aid to imparting knowledge ; the chemist, as carbonate of calcium. In short, the essential quality of a thing is its worth to the individual, and its value to him is its power to serve his private ends.

One often has much sympathy with victims of an accident, who, by morbid contemplation of their condition, have exaggerated their subjective consciousness and made themselves slaves of every abnormal sensation.

It is a mistake to think that all malingering is the outcome of deliberate wickedness. Because a man does not return to work as soon as one thinks he ought, it is harsh to assume that he is a shammer, and should be branded as a wilful malingerer. Such a view is not only unjust, but demonstrates a poor knowledge of human nature. Great allowance has to be made for the personal equation. Moral responsibility, even amongst the highly educated, is a variable quantity ; indeed, it varies almost as much with different individuals as do the features. We cannot always fully appreciate the mental processes taking place in each individual mind, and, as long as unregenerate human nature is being dealt with, so long are we bound to weigh all the circumstances of each case, if we wish to be fair. The mental attitude of workmen with regard to recovery after sickness is a very complicated one, and it is only by studying and fully understanding it that such cases can be successfully dealt with.

WHAT IS MALINGERING ?

Those who do much medico-legal work are constantly coming across cases of strong, healthy, able-bodied people who are absolutely well and fit for work, and are suffering from no pathological condition, but who have become self-centred, and, having a lively appreciation of the supposed benefits of obtaining money which they do not earn, have become victims of the operation of the Workmen's Compensation Act and other Acts conferring benefits in the event of illness or injury.

Now, what are the circumstances directly affecting the working-classes when ill ? In considering this question I omit all reference to the pitiable lack of individual comfort and remedial means (worthy of the name) which is often the lot of the toilers of the community when laid on a bed of sickness, and I confine myself for the moment to the sick man's mental influences and surroundings.

It must be remembered that sick and injured workmen belong to a class whose education is incomplete, and that they are peculiarly unfit to take a detached view of themselves, especially when ill. Too often the essential aspect of *their* case is the value unconsciously put upon their abnormal sensations in so far as they influence the continuance of sick pay. In the case of an insurance claim, the value of a symptom to the claimant is its power of obtaining either a lump sum or weekly payments.

In this connection I always find it of value to ascertain, as far as possible, the circumstances of the particular individual I am examining. For instance, it is of the utmost importance to know if A. B. (who is in receipt of half-wages, say 15s. a week, under the Workmen's Compensation Act) happens to be in receipt of 18s. a week from the Hearts of Oak Benefit Society, 10s. a week from a yard club, and another 10s. from a slate club, making an income in all of £2 13s. when sick, as compared with his wages of £1 10s. a week when hard at work. Or, as an alternative, that A. B. is in no club at all, but his wife is engaged in laundry-work or goes out charing, and he has two or three children at work. It is not an unreasonable deduction to draw that, so long as a man's circumstances are more comfortable when he is on the sick-list, he will have no inducement to " declare off " the sick-fund.

It is well known that the first stimulus for work in all classes

MALINGERING

of the community, and more especially when dealing with the working-classes, comes from the knowledge of the necessity of earning daily bread. It is this which keeps many men at work to whom labour is distasteful, and this applies not only to hard manual labour, but also to mental effort.

Perhaps it is not much to be wondered at that needy toilers become self-centred, exaggerate disturbances of function, and seize upon slight aches following accident as a means of temporary escape from the humdrum of manual labour. It must be remembered that the fixation of attention upon internal organs, or upon a back supposed to be strained, does, in fact, reflexly, if it does not actually, produce the condition looked for ; it certainly augments abnormal sensations.

We are all familiar with cases where a fixed desire and determination to take his place in the activities of life helps to pull a man through a critical illness, and, on the other hand, who does not know of cases where loss of all interest in life, either from mental, emotional, or physical causes, has turned the scale and precipitated a fatal issue ?

The stricken soldier in the industrial warfare is, because of distrust, too often over-anxious, at all hazards, to guard himself against the possibility of future incapacity arising out of his disability. He assumes that the State, or the insurance company by which his master is protected, will minimize his illness, and therefore he must exaggerate ; he considers that, in any case, the fullest demand he makes must be as nothing compared with the vast sums at the command of the Government or insurance company.

It is unfortunately the experience of most physicians that nervous people, who are generally given to self - examination, unconsciously foster subjective sensations which their stronger and better balanced neighbours would ignore. The idea of illness or of an injury and its possible consequences obsesses them. Their pains are real, but often only psychic. Such people are victimized by their unstable nervous systems. Too often they make no stand against introspection. It is small wonder, then, if, by repeated medical examinations at the instance of a third party, a man's attention is concentrated on the condition of his body, the desire for sick allowance is encouraged, and gradually a vague feeling of having been wronged is first

WHAT IS MALINGERING ?

created and then fostered. Frequent gossips with others who have found themselves in similar circumstances, continual rehearsals of the details of the illness or accident, and the oft-repeated recital of sensations, all act as co-operating factors in bringing about a condition of auto-suggestion, in the diagnosis and treatment of which the medical profession is lamentably backward.

If an introspective, self-centred workman is unfortunate enough to find himself entitled, when sick, to the material advantages before mentioned, he is much to be pitied ; for he is subjected to temptation that many succumb to, even in a class whose antecedents and traditions are not his. It is impossible for him to think impartially. Consciously or unconsciously he is influenced not only by his immediate environment, but by his individual mental outlook.

When a poor man is idle, and in consequence forfeits the benefits of labour, he is looked upon as merely vicious. The vicious idle man is as yet not amenable to the law ; but when, in addition to being idle, he is healthy, and claims an allowance from the funds accumulated by a section of the community for the use of invalids, it is obvious that his conduct tends to cause the disintegration of that section of the community. Hence the malingerer must be seriously dealt with, for not only does he eat the bread of idleness, but he does so at the expense of the community, some of whom will resent, while others imitate, his vicious conduct.

It is unfortunate, in this respect, that many medical men who have looked to a club practice as the staple factor of their income have been dependent upon their popularity with the working-men for the security of the tenure of their office, because it is well known that a doctor who freely certifies for sick benefits is considered a " kind " man, and his appreciation by the working-classes is undoubted. That there is cruelty in this kindness, and that compulsory return to work on recovery is a real service, cannot be gainsaid.

There is one mental peculiarity of all classes of the community which has always struck me as being inexplicable, and that is that so many people do not seem to think it a wrong to rob a company. Many otherwise honest people do not consider it a mean thing to travel first-class with a third-class ticket,

12 MALINGERING

and rejoice over an evasion of the income tax. In discussing this matter with perfectly reputable members of society, I have often been surprised at the prevalent idea that an insurance company is fair game. I suppose it is the same spirit which stimulates a schoolboy to raid an orchard, when he would disdain to rob a fruit-stall, a situation which is well commented upon in " Tom Brown's School Days."

My own experience of insurance companies (and it embraces many) is that in all their dealings they have been exceedingly fair to claimants ; and it does not strike one as unreasonable that a corresponding fairness should be demanded for them, and steps taken to insure it.

The Penalty for Malingering.—There is little doubt that, in a large number of cases of accident where a workman is in receipt of compensation from his employer and is receiving, in addition, in consequence of the accident, allowances from other sources, serious charges of malingering can be brought. It is, however, always a most difficult matter to prove, and an arbitrator not unnaturally requires incontestable proof before taking the strong line necessary.

A point which does not appear often to arise in the mind of the malingering workman is the considerable risk he runs of coming into conflict with the criminal law, apart altogether from his conduct in endeavouring to obtain money which he is not justly or legally entitled to.

The serious aspect of the case is, that if in the witness-box a workman knowingly makes statements that are untrue, he comes within the meshes of the law, and renders himself liable to be charged with perjury.

The question whether a workman could be convicted for perjury arising out of evidence given in the course of proceedings under the Workmen's Compensation Act came before the Court of Criminal Appeal in 1909, when the Court unanimously held that an indictment charging a man in such circumstances with perjury was properly laid. The following is a short statement of the case referred to :

> A workman, who was concerned in proceedings under the Workmen's Compensation Act, was convicted at the Liverpool Assizes in 1908 on an indictment charging him with perjury at common law. The perjury alleged was the wilful and corrupt giving of false evidence in an arbitration under the Act before a County Court Judge. The

WHAT IS MALINGERING ?

man appealed against the conviction on the ground that an arbitration under the Act was not a proceeding to which the law of perjury applied.

The Lord Chief Justice, in delivering judgment, said that, in the opinion of the Court, arbitration proceedings before a County Court Judge under the Act of 1906 constituted a judicial proceeding. The fundamental question was whether or not such arbitration was a judicial proceeding. If so, there was no doubt that perjury at common law could be committed at such a proceeding. The consequences would be very serious if there was no power to punish perjury committed in proceedings of that kind. In the opinion of the Court, those proceedings being judicial proceedings, the indictment for perjury was properly laid. The appeal was therefore dismissed (Rex *v.* Crossley [1909], 1 K.B., 411).

The framing of indictments is a legal matter, and the exact charge which might be brought does not concern us ; but I feel confident I have seen many cases which would render workmen liable to a charge of obtaining money by fraud or by false pretences, the punishment for which is, I take it, no light matter. Indeed, a shipping company consulted me recently with regard to making two such charges in connection with cases I had examined for them.

In February, 1912, a workman was summoned before the magistrates of the Borough of Tamworth, at the instance of his employers, for having committed wilful and corrupt perjury in the evidence he gave on oath in an application to the County Court for compensation under the Workmen's Compensation Act, in respect of injuries alleged to have been sustained by him whilst at work. A further summons for attempting to obtain money by false pretences arising out of the same claim for compensation was also preferred against him, but this charge was withdrawn.

Evidence was given to the effect that the man had himself purposely caused injury to one of his eyes just prior to the case coming before the County Court Judge, and that the condition of the eye at that time was not the result of the accident which he had sustained, and for which he had for a time received compensation.

The man, who was defended, gave evidence to the effect that he had been under hospital treatment, and that the treatment was always administered properly as directed ; also that he had never tampered with his eye, nor allowed anyone else to do so except for proper treatment, and denied that he had committed perjury in the course of the proceedings for compensation. The magistrates, after consultation, unanimously decided to commit the man for trial for wilful and corrupt perjury. He was subsequently tried on this charge at the Assizes for the county, and sentenced to six months' hard labour.

CHAPTER II

PREVENTION OF MALINGERING

In order that the preventive measures I propose discussing may be fully appreciated, I shall first consider the causes which are responsible for many of the labouring class seeking to postpone their return to work.

It is abundantly apparent to those of us who have much to do with working-men that there are certain persons who deliberately set class against class, who day by day breed discontent, who prolong the period of incapacity caused by illness, and debase honest working-men; but with these harpies this work does not deal.

The Dependent Position of the Club Doctor.—As long as medical men who attend the working-classes are dependent on the working-men themselves and the club officials for the security of their tenure of office, so long will gross exaggeration and malingering be rampant.

Medical men doing this class of work have said to me that it is not in their interest to tell members of the club that the time has come when it is their duty to declare off the sick-fund.

If the employee's doctor had the courage he would, at a very early stage, cause the morbid growth of ideas to abort by resolutely declining to be party to exaggeration and self-examination. If this is not done at an early stage, it is hopeless to attempt it later on. Surely it is the duty of medical men to help the State to count amongst her citizens the maximum number of units capable of working.

A. D. fractured his fibula, a condition which, most surgeons will agree, wholly recovers in from six to eight weeks. He drew compensation for two years, limped badly with a stick, *but sometimes*

14

PREVENTION OF MALINGERING

forgot to do so. He was very indignant when told that the time had come when he should resume work, and it required the lengthy procedure of the Law Courts to induce him to return to work.

A. E. met with an accident, and took to his bed. He groaned piteously when asked to turn, and assumed the attitude of one thoroughly exhausted. At the end of the examination, having left the room, I suddenly returned, and found him, with a smiling countenance, sitting up in bed detailing to a friend how exceedingly clever he had been !

The position of the medical man is rendered more difficult if he lives in the near neighbourhood of his working-class patients. The rule is not absolute, but it is generally found that the better a man is paid, the better he does his work ; it is always true that the more independent the position of the medical man, the less biassed is his judgment.

Medical Certificates of Unfitness too easily Obtained.—Medical certificates of unfitness for duty are too easily procurable from some general practitioners, with the inevitable result that sick-pay, by the various benefit societies to which so many working-men belong, is unnecessarily prolonged. Actions for damages carry in their train, in a large proportion of cases, a moral degradation to the working-man which is truly pitiable. Most of us are frequently in the position of having small disabilities oppressing us, in spite of which we do our ordinary duties, and thus, by ignoring those petty physical troubles, prevent them from getting the mastery over us.

To most medical men simulation of disease or malingering presents a difficult, almost insoluble puzzle. It is not hard to understand the reason. In ordinary medical practice feigned illness seldom occurs; whereas the examiner to a large municipal corporation or insurance company has to keep an open mind as to the possibility of deceit and exaggeration (conscious or unconscious) in every case that comes before him.

In a considerable number of cases where work is not resumed when recovery has taken place I believe the cause to be failure to procure an independent and reliable medical certificate. In many cases prolonged absence from work might be avoided if employers took a more personal interest in those of their employees who meet with accidents at their works.

The Workmen's Compensation Act has practically compelled employers to insure against their legal liability for accident

16 MALINGERING

claims of every description, and thus has necessarily displaced the human interest employers took in their servants when injured, and has substituted for it the purely economic interest of the insurance companies, which, of course, must be run on business lines.

I feel confident that in these circumstances constant watchfulness, and not infrequently much firmness, on the part of medical examiners is absolutely necessary in the interests of employees themselves, apart altogether from the business aspect of the " sick - pay " system. Such a line in the early stages of all cases of attempted malingering is the truest kindness to the workman, for the moral degradation which inevitably follows months of misspent time and unearned income *must* have far-reaching effects on character and conduct, both in the home and subsequently in the workshop.

History.—A. F., a porter, aged twenty-four, stated that whilst moving timber he sprained his right ankle by getting the foot between two pieces of wood. *Eight months after,* when he was sent to me for examination, he declared he was still unable to work. as the ankle constantly doubled over, and that he was unable even to walk far, because it began to swell.

Examination.—He was asked to take off both boots and stockings and walk about my consulting-room. He at once replied that he could not walk without limping. When told that it did not signify whether he limped or not, he walked, but obviously intentionally turned the right foot so that he walked wholly upon its outside edge ; yet when firmly told to put his foot down flat on the ground he did so in a perfectly natural manner !

He told me that he often stumbled, but it was difficult to believe this. When asked to stand upon his toes, whilst I balanced him with my hands, he did so at first with both feet, and then on the right foot alone.

He was, in fact, a deliberate malingerer, and he knew it. He told me that he was receiving no medical treatment—obviously none was necessary—but he *obtained from a doctor, in exchange for sixpences, certificates of disability as often as he wanted them.*

As he left my house he asked me what I thought of his case, and I told him. I advised that compensation should be stopped at once.

This was done from the date of my examination. A. F. placed his case in the hands of a solicitor, but the legal representatives of his employers took a firm attitude, and nothing further was heard of the matter.

The Duty of Medical Men not to countenance Exaggerated Claims.—The difficulties which defendants have in refuting unjust or exaggerated claims are enormous. A plaintiff assumes

PREVENTION OF MALINGERING 17

that the defendant will minimize his alleged injuries, and—consciously or unconsciously—is led to exaggerate them. Not unnaturally, he looks to his own family doctor to support him against what he assumes to be a large and wealthy corporation, and in my experience he is seldom disappointed.

By self-observation, the encouragement of every morbid sensation, and a complete surrender of his better *ego*, he tutors himself into a condition in which his aches and pains—assuming them to be present—run riot.

Litigants of this class should be taught that a firm determination to turn a deaf ear to their distorted sensations really makes for happiness, and that self-control, self-respect, and a return to work when able, are of more service and more lasting value than many coins of the realm.

Now, the best treatment, from a patient's point of view, for a case of this sort is a little plain speaking by his own doctor very early in the case. But what is the position of the family doctor ? Can he do this, or anything approaching to it ? Too often, I fear, if he did so, it would mean the sacrifice of his position as medical attendant. I have on more than one occasion, when in consultation with the family doctor, been asked by him to *give my views quite candidly to the patient*. Not long ago I sent a man, who had been bedridden for six months and appeared to be paralyzed, back to work within a week by means of a few well-chosen sentences !

Medical Reports are Privileged Documents.—With regard to legal responsibility, the medical examiner need have no fear, for his position is absolutely privileged, so far as libel or slander is concerned ; but, of course, privilege could not be pleaded if the examiner had been guilty of malice. Anything said in the witness-box is, of course, covered by the protection extended to witnesses, as well as any report written by him on the case, and any statement given to proper persons for the purpose of his proof of evidence.

When asking for a medical report, an insurance company would do well to state that the report, whatever its nature—provided only it be given without animus—is privileged, and that they will indemnify the doctor in respect of all the possible consequences arising therefrom. By adopting this course they would obtain reports of more real value. Unsatisfactory re-

2

18   MALINGERING

ports are often sent in by medical men who are afraid of committing themselves on paper, and thereby, as they think, possibly exposing themselves to the loss of much or all of their hard-earned capital in an action for libel or slander. The question of privilege is so important, from the medical man's standpoint, that a full reference to the subject will be found on p. 237.

Medical Defence Union.—A large number of medical practitioners, by mutual co-operation, have already freed themselves from the trouble and expense incident to defending their professional reputation against attack. Many years ago the Medical Defence Union was formed for this purpose. For a limited entrance-fee, and a small annual subscription, the costs of any action taken up for a member by the Council are defrayed, and, if a small additional annual premium is paid, any member can· insure himself up to some two or three thousand pounds against " the costs of the other side and damages," if any, even in lost actions. By a payment of some nineteen shillings per annum, any registered medical practitioner can relieve himself of all personal trouble and expense in connection with actions which may be brought against him involving professional principle, provided only that he can satisfy the Council of the Defence Union as to his good faith in the matter at issue.

Medical Evidence is with much Difficulty appreciated by Lay Tribunals.—Arbitrators, judges, and juries cannot, in the nature of things, properly appreciate medical matters, which are always technical and necessarily perplexing, as the following case illustrates :

A. G., a painter, aged forty-five, made a claim for half-wages on the ground that in the course of his work whilst holding a ladder it slipped, and he fell flat on his back.

Examination.—He was sent for examination sixteen days after the alleged accident. The details of the accident were very carefully gone into, and the following interesting history was elicited :

He stated that he felt some inconvenience at the time of the alleged accident, but very little afterwards, and continued work for *four* days. He then had, apparently, an attack of influenza, being suddenly seized with pains everywhere ; he felt cold and shivery ; his eyes were sensitive to light ; he had a headache, backache, felt giddy, and was sick. His statement was that he remained in bed for three days, then got up, called upon his doctor, who lived near by, and obtained a certificate of unfitness for work. Three days later he

PREVENTION OF MALINGERING 19

again called on his doctor. It appears that then, and not till then, he told the doctor about the accident, alleging that his illness was caused by it, and got another certificate to that effect.

He was very breathless on coming up the short flight of stairs to my consulting-room. On examination I found no trace of an injury. He was manifestly suffering from marked anæmia, due to constitutional causes, although he appeared to have made himself believe that the fall was the cause of all his symptoms. He was apparently determined not to work if he could help it. He complained of a constant drumming noise in his ears " like a locomotive," obviously the result of extreme anæmia. He told me that he was suffering from " shock," but it is obvious that a man could not sustain " shock " by merely falling from his feet on to his back.

On applying the faradic current to his back on two or three occasions, he stated he felt the electricity over the alleged painful area, when, in fact, although the coil was still buzzing loudly, I had, unknown to him, cut the current off, so that it could not reach him. Repeatedly he said he felt the current more as it approached his loins, although on each occasion I had switched off the current before it reached the pole applied to his loins. When I carefully pointed this out to him, and how he had given himself away, he was good enough to say, in a somewhat patronizing way : " I like your style ; you speak very plain."

I noticed that when he was putting on his clothes he bent his back quite freely. As he was an employee of the London County Council, it was my duty to tell him that he was able to return to work; but he said he was about to consult a " professor." Eventually, however, he agreed to go back to light work, if it were provided for him.

Three months later, as he had not resumed work, I examined him again in conjunction with another medical man. He was still obviously anæmic, and complained of various symptoms, such as blood-spitting, hæmorrhoids, giddiness, all of which were manifestly produced by his general condition of health, with which the accidental fall could have had no possible connection.

Result.—At the arbitration proceedings, nearly three weeks later, he did not attend, and the Judge postponed the hearing for a month : on the second occasion also he did not appear, and the Judge again postponed the hearing for another month. On the third occasion the plaintiff, but not his doctor, put in an appearance, and judgment was given for the defendants. This case cost the employers £60.

The Importance of Medical Examination prior to Employment.—The majority of employers insure against the risk of financial loss in case of accident, by paying a premium to an insurance company, which covers the employer's risk. The amount of the premium is, of course, regulated according to the risk, and it is practically certain that very soon the premium will be in progressive ratio to the workman's age. The em-

MALINGERING

ployer if he wishes to retain the services of the older and more experienced workman will then have to pay an enhanced premium for the privilege of doing so. This means that the older workman will inevitably be supplanted by the younger. Already large numbers of working-men who are getting on in years, but by no means inefficient, are compelled to join the ranks of the unemployed. Indeed, it has been recently stated by a Local Government Board inspector that the Workmen's Compensation Act has done more than anything else in recent years to force men between fifty and seventy years of age into the workhouse. Mr. Sidney Gladwell has pointed out that statistics are to no useful extent available as to whether old men are or are not more liable to accident than their younger brethren, but there can be no doubt that the older a man becomes, the more serious are the consequences likely to accrue from even a slight accident.

Very many of the difficulties which have to be contended with would be obviated if a thorough medical examination were made of all workpeople prior to their entering upon any employment. The advantages of such a system are almost too obvious to need enumeration. Insurance companies would certainly give more favourable terms to employers who adopted the practice. Pre-existing physical defects could not be worked in to enhance the severity of a minor accident. Casual labour, of course, presents a difficulty ; but is it too much to imagine that a system might be devised whereby even casual labourers could be examined and given a medical report, which they would retain and produce as occasion required ? Medical examination is a condition precedent to employment by most public bodies ; and, as there is nothing to prevent a contract of service being made subject to proof of physical fitness, this requirement could very well be extended to employment by private persons and firms.

Unsatisfactory Results of County Court Actions.—That the provision made for the decision of disputed claims by the County Court is not a sufficient safeguard in itself is shown by the following table, from which it will be seen that only one claim out of every 519 is successfully resisted by the employer :

PREVENTION OF MALINGERING

TABLE COMPILED FROM A BLUE BOOK WHICH WAS ISSUED BY THE HOME OFFICE IN NOVEMBER, 1912, DEALING WITH THE OFFICIAL RECORDS OF COMPENSATION UNDER THE WORKMEN'S COMPENSATION ACT, 1906.

Cases during the year 1911.
423,052.

Settled out of Court.	*Decided in Court.*
418,565 cases—that is, 98·94 per cent. of whole.	4,487 cases—that is, 1·06 per cent. of whole.

Verdict for Applicant.	*Verdict for Respondent.*
3,673 cases—that is, 81·9 per cent. of Court cases.	814 cases—that is, 18·1 per cent. of Court cases.

This means that in 98·94 per cent. of all cases the employer submits to the injured workman having his claim settled without a judicial decision. Nor is the reason far to seek. In an arbitration case where a workman is injured, the only point the Judge (who, of course, has no adequate medical or surgical knowledge) is called upon to decide is a purely surgical one, and technical points are always raised, both by solicitors and doctors who specialize in these cases, with results so unsatisfactory that 98·94 per cent. of the cases are settled apart from the Court. It costs at least from £20 to £30 to defend a County Court action of this class, and double if they lose. Workmen and their solicitors know this. Is it unreasonable to suggest that a large proportion of the cases in the 98·94 per cent. are settled by processes which might be described by an ugly word ?

The vast majority of these were, of course, not fighting cases ; but how many weeks and months of unnecessary sick-pay have been paid to lazy, skrimshanking employees rather than risk the result of disputing impudent and dishonest claims ? One large friendly society has for years been paying £10,000 a year in excess of the actuarial estimates of the amount probably required for the incidence of sickness.

It is difficult to see why defendants should have to pay damages measured by the extent of the plaintiff's capacity for practising auto-suggestion, especially when, as so often happens, the result of an arbitration cures what the physician could not.

22 MALINGERING

A. H. alleged that he met with an accident, injuring his back, which compelled him to walk with his back bent at an obtuse angle. After examination, which included X-ray photography, I satisfied myself that he was not suffering as alleged, and I told the Court so. Evidence was given by two medical men, one stating that he was suffering from functional paraplegia—that is, paralysis of both limbs—and the other that he was suffering from spinal irritation, the result of the injury. I think, however, that I must have been right, for the Court was satisfied, after hearing the evidence, that no accident had occurred !

Contracting Out.—The Workmen's Compensation Act of 1906 absolutely precludes the possibility of contracting out in any way. Prior to the passing of the Act, one occasionally recommended workmen to be accepted conditionally.

A. I., a very fine muscular man of over 6 feet, who had been a Guardsman, applied for admission into the service of the London County Council as a park-keeper. He had a hernia, and I advised his acceptance subject to the proviso that, should he be incapacitated from employment as the result of his hernia, he should receive no benefits which might otherwise accrue to him, and he was accepted for service on these terms. When, however, the last Workmen's Compensation Act came into force, it nullified this agreement, for the Act expressly forbids all contracting out.

This is a mistaken policy, for there are many cases in which contracting out for certain disabilities might well be allowed, such as where a man has monocular vision, or has some slight defect in hearing, conditions which to a greater or lesser extent predispose towards accident, but which ought not to prevent his earning a livelihood. It is obvious that if such people were allowed to contract out they would not help, as they do now, to swell the army of the unemployed.

Medical Examination Form.—The form for medical examination of candidates entering a large public body is usually divided into two parts, one to be filled up by the candidate and the other by the medical examiner.

Practical experience of a very large number of these entrance examinations, amounting to over 10,000, has proved the value of the following question : Are you *now* in good health ? In this connection a medical friend informed me of the following instructive case, which came under his observation :

PREVENTION OF MALINGERING

A. J., who appeared to be well, strong and healthy, and answered questions quite frankly, was passed as wholly satisfactory. Two months later she absented herself from work, and sent a medical certificate to the effect that she was now incapable of work, as she was the subject of neurasthenia, which had lasted some three months.

Another instance showing the advantage of inserting this question is as follows :

A. K., a clerk in the public service, stated, four months after he had been admitted into the service, that he was unfit for clerical work as he was suffering from writer's cramp, and seemed to claim as a right that he should be transferred to an outdoor occupation. When asked how long he had suffered from writer's cramp, he quite frankly, and even boldly, stated that he had had the disease for many years, and, indeed, that was the reason why he left his last occupation !

No ordinary medical examination, however carefully and searchingly conducted, would discover this condition. The copy of the candidate's medical examination form was therefore referred to, and it was pointed out to him that he had intentionally deceived, inasmuch as he now admitted that he had had the disease for years, and that some four months previously he had replied in the affirmative to the question : " Are you now in good health ?" This settled the matter.

Examination of Urine.—*Albumen.*—The mere presence of albumen in the urine is by no means an indication of nephritis, either acute or chronic. I never summarily reject candidates because albumen appears to be present in the urine when I first examine them, because frequently upon re-examination it is absent. Albumen is temporarily present in the urine much more frequently than is supposed ; it is not fair that a candidate should be finally rejected until microscopic examination of the centrifugalized deposit has been made. The examination of over 10,000 specimens of urine impresses me with the feeling that there is yet much to learn. I have repeatedly noticed that when albumen has been found in the urine, if the patient is asked to pass a second quantity for further test, albumen is not infrequently absent from the second specimen, although it was passed but a few minutes after the first. In a large number of cases I believe the first reaction was really produced by nuclear albumen obtained from a deposit lying in the urethra, probably the result of an old gleet, which, being washed

24   MALINGERING

out by the first sample examined, was therefore not present in the second.

There is, of course, no doubt that in many cases, especially in young adults, albumen is indicative of what is known as " physiological or adolescent albuminuria," and does not point to organic change in the kidneys.

The practical difficulty lies, not in the academic question as to whether functional albuminuria is a sufficient reason for rejecting a candidate who is otherwise healthy, but in settling whether in a given case the albuminuria is or is not due to definite kidney mischief. Anyone who has conducted many examinations must be satisfied that it is unjust, when considering the temporary passage of a small quantity of albumen (which, after all, is too often but a symptom of we know not what), to magnify it to the importance of an organic disease, and reject the candidate.

The problem can only be solved by repeated examinations for albumen, and microscopic examinations of the deposit at stated intervals on several consecutive days. Hyaline casts alone do not indicate disease ; I think it unwise to reject a candidate (altering, it may be, his whole career) on account of the doubtful presence even of epithelial casts, especially when one remembers that the diagnosis of the nature of a doubtful cast often depends upon the personal equation of the microscopist.

> A. L.—Some time ago I found that a specimen of urine contained albumen, and laid it aside for further testing. The next candidate could not urinate in the consulting-room, and was asked to do so alone in my laboratory. Finding he could not micturate even then, he presented me with a specimen which he had craftily poured from the one he found already there. It was only upon my telling him that I had found albumen in his urine that he confessed. The lesson was a valuable one.

Sugar.—So many substances besides glucose reduce cupric sulphate to the hydrate or oxide that I never reject a candidate unless with the phenyl-hydrazine test the crystals of glucosazone are actually seen on the field. Indeed, I have observed the presence of temporary glycosuria, accompanied by a high specific gravity, and crystals of glucosazone, induced apparently by mental and physical causes. Candidates often make long night journeys to London. They not unnaturally

PREVENTION OF MALINGERING

have considerable mental stress when appearing before selection committees, and subsequently before the medical examiner. They are not infrequently the subjects of a condition which responds to all the tests for diabetes, but which is nevertheless of a temporary nature, as I have frequently proved by one or more re-examinations. It should not, however, be forgotten that glycosuric urines often reveal the early stage of true diabetes.

A. M., a professional man whom I was examining for a public service, stated very definitely that he could not urinate when asked to do so in my presence. It is my invariable rule to insist upon this. When told that the examination could not be completed without it, he was obdurate, but later, when offered the advantage of a room to himself, he stated quite frankly that he was the subject of diabetes, and that I should most certainly find sugar in his urine !

A. N.—On one occasion a specimen of urine voluntarily brought in a bottle was found to be normal, but the urine passed in my presence contained sugar.

When a patient consults his doctor, there is no reason why he should not be absolutely frank ; indeed, the whole transaction is based on this premise. When examining candidates for important positions one has to introduce a little of the spirit expressed in the old maxim—*caveat emptor.*

Periodic and Systematic Medical Examination of Sick Employees.—At my suggestion, two of the largest Corporations in this country, both of which I serve, send to me all employees who have been on the sick-list for twenty-eight days, not for treatment, but for medical examination and report. This is also the practice of the Home Office, and has been found to work well. My experience of its adoption by the two bodies to which I have referred is eminently satisfactory.

These two Corporations retain the services of a staff of over 100 well-qualified district medical officers, whose chief duty is to furnish certificates in the case of illness of members of the staff, and, in certain sections of the work, actually to treat the sick employees.

After twenty-eight days' absence on account of sickness the case (for the purpose of certification only) passes out of the hands of the district medical officer into those of the chief medical officer, who either certifies the employee fit for duty, or gives a certificate for further leave of absence, as he thinks fit. If, however, at the end of that period the employee alleges

26   MALINGERING

that he is still unfit for duty, he is again sent to the chief medical
officer for certification and report.

Medical officers, when sending up cases, are required to com-
municate directly and privately in writing with the chief
medical officer, especially in difficult or obstinate cases. Head
officials are authorized to send to the chief medical officer at
any time suspected malingering cases, even though the employee concerned has not been absent for so long as twenty-
eight days.

There are many reasons why this system has been found to
work well.

Since there is no relationship of doctor and patient between
the chief medical officer and the employee, the former is in
every sense independent.

The district medical officers are glad to have an opportunity
of imposing upon the chief medical officer the disagreeable task
of accepting the responsibility of informing employees that
the time has come when their illness no longer prevents their
working.

When a number of district medical officers are employed it
is a definite advantage to a large public body to have one
medical officer who, on the one hand, is in touch with the
district medical officers, and, on the other, personally responsible to the head office.

There can be no question that the system is an effective
check upon malingering and unduly prolonged illness, and is
well worthy of extension.

**Figures which show a Remarkable Reduction in Sickness fol-
lowing Periodic Examination.**—In the case of a large group of
employees in a public service, all of whom had been medically
examined before entering the service, and were entitled to
medical attendance by district medical officers paid by capita-
tion grant, it was found that, prior to the institution of the independent medical inspection after twenty-eight days, the total
number of days men were on the sick-list amounted in one year
to 14,400 ; whereas, subsequent to the institution of the new
rule, this number was reduced to 9,600—a reduction, in a well-
organized and disciplined small force, of no less than 4,800 days
in one year, the percentage of reduction being 33⅓. During the
corresponding periods the total number of men sick for *more*

PREVENTION OF MALINGERING   27

than twenty-eight days was reduced by the somewhat surprising figure of 50 per cent.

> A. O., who had been drawing sick-pay for nearly two years prior to the passing of this twenty-eight-day rule, complained that he was weak and had a pain in his back, and that the weather affected it. I satisfied myself that he had no physical disability, and pointed out to him that, as he had not given notice of his injury a year ago, he could not claim under the Employer's Liability Act ; that the alleged accident happened prior to the passing of the Workmen's Compensation Act of 1906 ; that I believed he was never really ill ; and told him that he was to return to duty forthwith, otherwise I would report him unfit for duty, and he would be dismissed without compensation. He returned to work, and has never complained since of his back or any other portion of his anatomy.

Systematic Examination of Sick Employees has Other Advantages.—The twenty-eight-day rule, though by no means equal to systematic re-examination of every employee at set intervals, certainly enables one to keep an eye to some extent upon the health of the employees generally. For instance, amongst others, the following cases may be cited showing the unexpected results of medical examination.

Two tramway drivers, each with slight injury to head, were found to have locomotor ataxia.

An elderly man with fractured radius of the wrist was found to have advanced paralysis agitans.

A woman with a needle in her hand had cancer in her breast on the same side.

A man with injury to the shoulder was found to have advanced phthisis.

A man with a slight cut on his hand was found to have general paralysis of the insane.

A tramway driver with a slight injury was also found to be suffering from heart disease—aortic regurgitation.

In two cases men with sprained ankles were found to have locomotor ataxia.

The Comparative Ease with which Non-Litigious Cases can be dealt with.—The four following cases illustrate how easily such cases may be handled when they are dealt with by representatives of the employers, and when, presumably, they are not contemplating litigation.

MALINGERING

A. P. had an accident ; seen after having been treated for myelitis for thirteen months ; full pay most of the time ; bedridden ; ordered to hospital for observation, where he had " fits " ; blackened his face to give them a realistic effect. I sought and obtained a private interview with him, and ventured upon some exceptionally straightforward plain speaking. He walked to my house, distant a mile, next day, and resumed work within a week.

A. Q., a pensionable officer, had malingered for thirteen months ; complained of obscure pains ; examined by eleven doctors during his supposed illness. Never had any objective symptoms ; kept under observation in hospital for nine weeks ; charged with malingering before employers ; ordered to be dismissed and forfeit pension if work not resumed. Commenced work forthwith.

A. R., who covered a wound $\frac{1}{8}$ inch broad with ointment, lint, three bandages, and a large gout-boot, was obviously surprised, and I fancy not a little indignant, when most of his dressings were put in the fire, and he was told to resume work that day.

A. S., who had been on the sick-list for three weeks, was sent to me as he complained of a sprained right thumb. I discovered he had made the journey to my house from his home—a considerable distance—on his bicycle. As there was nothing apparently wrong with his thumb, he was told that as he was able to ride his bicycle he was able to resume work at once, which he did.

I should like to mention a case in which some strong measures were necessary to restore the workman to self-respect.

A. T. was confined to his bed, the result of an injury. He complained of intense pain when I touched the dorsal region of his back. His case reminded me very forcibly of one in which, but an hour before, I had given evidence in the High Court. The injury in that case, where the claimant was awarded nearly £100, was not so severe as it appeared to be in the case before me, and I made up my mind to bow to the inevitable and report accordingly, when I suddenly bethought me of my trusty friend, the electric battery. There is a popular, but of course erroneous, idea that an electric current is not felt even in minor injuries of the spinal column. I applied the battery. The claimant said he did not feel it over the painful area. I made the current considerably stronger, and he tried to bear it manfully. At last, with a howl, he fell in a heap on the ground. There was no one in the room to sympathize, so I told him to get up and not make a fool of himself, explaining that I now knew what was the matter with him, and that he was to go back to work at once.

His wife, who was downstairs, hearing the yell, entered the room, and I explained to her that he was now well, as I had cured him with the battery. I said I was very pleased ; he said he was, and the wife agreed with both of us. He said he would go back to work forthwith, and he did so.

PREVENTION OF MALINGERING

A System of Lay-Inspection as a Means of checking Malingering.—It has been suggested that large employers of labour should have on their staff a number of inspectors, who would assist the examining medical officer by visiting workmen suspected of malingering at their own homes, and otherwise obtaining information about them. Such inspectors have, in fact, been already appointed by friendly societies and mine-owners, with good results.

It must be remembered that the examining medical officer is often entirely unacquainted with the claimant. He has to rely for the history of the case almost exclusively on the claimant's statement, or that of interested friends. Such histories are, of course, often very unreliable, so much so that an experienced medical officer practically always ignores them. A man suffering from a stiff shoulder will state that he has been, and is, attending the hospital daily for massage, or, conversely, a man with an ulcerated leg supposed to be confined to his room is really attending hospital daily, or, still worse, going to and from the neighbouring public-houses. In either case we have only the man's word for it, and the corroboration or disproof of his statement obtained by the unexpected visit of an inspector would be most valuable. Or, again, a man may state that his wife and children are starving, and he is only too anxious to go back to work, whereas as a matter of fact the former is keeping a small shop, and some of the latter are earning weekly wages. Or, yet again, he may be receiving sufficient sick-pay from various friendly societies and slate clubs to render him better off when ill than when well.

The subjoined case illustrates the advantage that may be obtained from an unexpected visit :

A. U. detained me a suspiciously long time at his front-door. Thinking that he had probably been getting into bed whilst I waited, I ventured to look below the table, which was covered with a table-cloth, and there found his clothes, which he had evidently just taken off. I have no doubt that, had I followed the example of the late Mr. Rose, and put my hands into his boots, I should have found them warm.

The following fraud would scarcely have been attempted had a regular system of lay-supervision been in vogue :

A. V. was recently sent to me by a solicitor for examination and report. An appointment was made, and a man giving the correct

MALINGERING

name attended. He was duly examined ; he had the usual pain in his back, tenderness, giddiness, incapacity for work, etc. He said he was a boxer, and looked one. I was about to write my report, and state that he was a malingerer, when the solicitor rang me up on the telephone and asked me to describe him. I did so. It then appeared that this scoundrel was counterfeiting and assuming the name of another. He was detained, under some pretext, while a detective who knew him was sent to my house. They were brought together by a subterfuge, and he was, as we had expected, an impostor. This man and a friend made a living by periodically having accidents !

A Summary of the Best Means of preventing Malingering.— The principal means by which to check malingering may be briefly stated thus :

1. A system of organized lay-inspection.

2. Repeated, periodical, independent medical supervision.

3. Complete independence of the medical attendant.

4. Some system of registration which shall make apparent what is the full amount of sick-pay, and other benefit, if any, that the patient is in receipt of.

CHAPTER III

THE MEDICAL EXAMINATION

The Special Difficulty of Medico-legal Examinations.—The task of examining a patient who alleges disability as the result of an accident is by no means an easy one. In ordinary medical practice it can safely be assumed, at any rate in the vast majority of cases, that a patient who presents himself for examination does so with the sole object of getting well as soon as possible. He is unlikely intentionally to keep anything back or make any false statements. The cases under consideration, however, are by no means so simple.

When an employee is sent by a solicitor for examination, it often means that the medical man may have to substantiate his opinion in Court in face of the slings and arrows of opposing counsel, and the too often partisan evidence of members of his own profession.

A claimant often has much which he wishes to conceal, much which he is prone to exaggerate.

> *History.*—A. W., a labourer, aged twenty-two, alleged that whilst near Wandsworth Bridge a tramcar collided with the tramcar in which he was a passenger, and that the impact caused the opening up of an old abscess.
>
> *Examination.*—A fortnight after the alleged occurrence he was sent to me for examination and report. On examining the alleged injury, and inquiring into the facts of the case, I ascertained that twenty days previous to the "accident" he had been operated upon for fistula. The operation wound was still unhealed, and no objective symptoms of an accident being discoverable, it was considered that the claim was fraudulent.
>
> *Result.*—The defendants refused to pay any damages, denying liability, and the claim was dropped.

The full unravelling of these cases demands on the part of the examiner a number of somewhat special qualities. He should, in the first place, have had a wide experience of accidents

31

32   MALINGERING

and their results ; he should also be conversant with the conditions under which the working-classes live ; he should know something of the work entailed in the various kinds of employment ; and club practice itself should not be unknown to him.

The detection of malingering is not always so much a question of scientific knowledge as of the personal equation of the examining medical officer. He must be independent and fearless, and his general alertness' must be past all telling. Large experience of this class of work gives one a sort of instinct when dealing with the malingerer.

> A. X., a lady who had met with a trifling accident some three or four years prior to my seeing her, had, from first to last, been examined by no less than nine doctors. I was called in consultation a few days before the trial, with a view to giving evidence in the High Court. I reported that she was obviously ill medically, but was not suffering as the result of any accident. A few days later the case was settled out of Court, and the lady wrote me saying that now the claim was settled she would like to know if I had been astute enough to see through her case, kindly adding that she believed I had done so. My curiosity was aroused, and I took the unusual course of calling upon her, when she confessed that at the date of my examination she was convalescing from typhoid fever, the knowledge of which she had suppressed from everyone but her own doctor.

In the following cases, in which the inability to work was alleged to follow traumatism, examination showed that the incapacity was due to a cause wholly unconnected with any accident.

> *History.*—A. Y., a labourer, alleged that, after lifting seventeen heavy cases on to a van, he suddenly felt a pain at the right groin, dropped unconscious, and was taken to a hospital. He was fitted with a truss at the expense of his employers, placed on compensation for seven weeks, and then resumed light work as messenger. Three and a half months later he was transferred to his old work, but after a day and a half he said he could not lift even a light package without pain in his back, and refused to continue work.
>
> *Medical Examination.*—Nine and a half months after the alleged strain he was sent to me by his employers for an opinion as to whether, when wearing a truss, it was safe and proper for him to work as a labourer.
>
> The inguinal canal on both sides was large, but no bowel protruded. He was asked to cough and jump on his heels (both of which actions as a rule bring down herniæ which are only temporarily replaced) ; not only did no hernia descend, but on inserting the finger into the canal no bulging of the bowel, and therefore no tendency towards

THE MEDICAL EXAMINATION

hernia, could be felt. This, of course, did not conclusively demonstrate that no hernia had ever descended, but the physical appearances made me suspicious; for even if one admitted that at one time the man had had a hernia, it was obvious it was not present now, and I was at a loss to understand why he should insist he was unfit for work on account of hernia.

I subjected him, therefore, to further examination, in the hope of finding the real reason of his refusal to work. He turned out to be practically blind, owing to nystagmus. On careful examination of his eyes, I discovered that with each eye separately he could only read letters three-quarters of an inch in height at a distance of a foot and a half, and that with both eyes he read letters of this size no farther than a yard! He was, in fact, wholly unfit for any work except that performed in an asylum for the blind.

Result.—Proceedings were instituted by the claimant, but the Judge dismissed the claim on hearing my evidence.

A. Z. claimed under the Workmen's Compensation Act against his employers, a Metropolitan Borough Council, on the ground that whilst repairing a valve attached to a flushing-cart the horse started, throwing him off, so that he fell on his back and loins. He continued his work for half an hour, but had done no work since.

Examination.—Three months after the accident I was asked by the Borough Council to examine him in the presence of his own doctor, in conjunction with another medical man who had previously examined him.

He told me he was unable to work on account of the injury to his back, complaining that the whole of his back from the neck to the hips was affected.

During the course of careful examination I asked him to indicate, with one hand only, the area of the back that was still painful, and, although uncertain at first, he eventually located a definite area, which I marked on the flesh with a red pencil; later, when again asked to indicate the same spot with the other hand, he pointed to a different area, which I marked with a blue pencil. Upon further examination he complained bitterly when the lightest touch was applied many inches away from either of the spots originally marked.

When the spine is diseased or injured, Nature tries to repair it by keeping the spinal joints stiff, movement being injurious and painful. A. Z. was asked to stoop several times, and as he raised himself on each occasion I pressed deeply between the successive spinal vertebræ, with the result that I found they all moved freely, showing that pain did not exist at the areas alleged.

When asked to stand with his feet close together, whilst the upper part of his body was twisted from side' to side, he complained of no pain. All reflexes were normal; therefore, as far as spinal injury was concerned, he was perfectly fit for work.

Examination of his heart showed old-standing disease of both the aortic and mitral valves, with enlargement of the heart. One of the medical men present remarked that he had attended A. Z. for this

MALINGERING

condition twelve years previously. Although the cardiac condition was well marked, it did not appear probable that it was solely on this account he wished to make the happening of the accident a reason for not returning to work, because the condition showed no evidence of recent increase, and obviously he had been working for many years with his heart in its crippled state.

This was a difficult man to examine, for he was of the aggressive type—indeed, early in the examination he tried to browbeat me when ordinary tests were applied ; but it was pointed out to him that, in accordance with the terms of the Workmen's Compensation Act, under which he had been receiving a weekly allowance for three months, he was bound to submit himself to medical examination, and that if he obstructed the examination his half-wages would cease in accordance with the provisions of the Act. He therefore allowed me to proceed with the examination, until I asked him to divest himself of his trousers. This at first he absolutely refused to do. Ultimately, after considerable waste of time, and after I had appealed to his medical man, A. Z. exposed to view a condition of affairs which fully explained his mental attitude with regard to return to work. His left leg was deformed, the condition being what is known as talipes equino-varus, and on the shin there was a large, ulcerating, discharging wound, obviously connected with diseased bone. This was ample explanation of his alleged inability to work. Being assured that he was a deliberate malingerer (as far as his back was concerned), I advised the Borough Council to repudiate all liability in connection with the alleged accident.

Result.—Four months later I was informed that the claimant was taking his case to Court, and I was asked to give evidence at the arbitration proceedings, fixed to take place in ten days' time. However, three days before the date fixed the applicant withdrew his claim.

The foregoing was a mixed case of " suppressio veri " and " suggestio falsi." The next is a pure case of " suppressio veri."

B. A., an employee in a large public body, was sent to me to consider the question of the termination of his engagement on account of alleged incapacity, caused by an ulcer in his leg which would not heal. At the examination he pulled down the stocking from his *left* leg, showing me a large healed ulcer ; he protested that it had not, and did not, prevent his doing his work, and he seemed quite pleased and relieved when he was told that there was no necessity to take any action. As I bent over him, however, I recognized a peculiar musty smell, characteristic of an old-standing ulcer, and he was told to expose the whole of his *right* leg, when the largest unhealed ulcer I have ever seen was exposed to view ! It covered an area of between a quarter and half a square foot, and he admitted it had been unhealed for twenty-two years. It must obviously for a long time have prevented him doing his work efficiently.

THE MEDICAL EXAMINATION

It is most important that the examiner should be absolutely unbiassed and judicial in his attitude towards the case, and while he should always be alive to the possibility of malingering, he should be equally on the lookout for every indication of organic disease. He should hold the balance fairly between employee and employer, or insurance company, for it is unseemly that any medical man should be biassed in favour of insurance companies and allege malingering where it does not exist, or *minimize disabilities that do exist.* Even when convinced that a man is malingering, it is always unwise to make a definite accusation unless one is prepared to substantiate it with weighty evidence ; but, having formed an opinion, the medical witness should have the courage of his convictions, and when he has once given an honest opinion, or has made a statement which he knows to be true, no amount of forensic craft should cause him to contradict himself in the witness-box.

I think there is ample scope for the evolution of a class of medical men who would specialize in medico-legal work, and who, from long experience and observation of these cases, would become really qualified to deal with them—an evolution which has already taken place in Germany.

Some little time ago a young consultant told me that a friend of his had been asked to advise a general practitioner in the following circumstances. With the help of an abortionist a woman had criminally procured abortion. Her husband was very angry, and evidently had some suspicion of what had occurred. In order to divert his suspicions, the woman said that she believed the miscarriage was caused by an accident that had happened to her a short time before. My friend informed me that the family doctor was much concerned, inasmuch as the woman had confessed the real facts of the case to him, but had not told her husband, who, in ignorance of the truth, was bringing an action against the people who would be liable for any such accident as that alleged. A few weeks later I was requested to examine a young married woman, and the facts at once struck me as having a remarkable resemblance to those just narrated.

B. B. stated that, being in a crowded vehicle, some slight collision occurred, and she was knocked up against someone near her, and had rather a fright. Immediately after the so-called accident she

MALINGERING

appears to have walked to a friend's house at some distance. Ten days after this she had the miscarriage. She was emphatic in stating that she did not think it was physical injury which had produced the miscarriage, but the fright to which she had been subjected by the crowd. She also said that the accident did not upset her, and that she had not thought of it again except when she entered an omnibus or car, or spoke to someone about it.

Apparently she did not tell her husband anything about the miscarriage, and when he discovered what had taken place she declined to send for a doctor. It was not until three days later, when the husband insisted upon having a doctor, that she sent for Dr. X. After a few days in bed she went to stay with friends.

When about to make my examination, I wrote asking the doctor to meet me at the patient's house at a certain hour, but he did not do so, although his house was quite near. On my visiting the lady alone, she told me that her husband was bringing an action (*against her wish*), because he could not account for the miscarriage in any other way than by the accident. The claim was for quite a small sum.

I had a good deal of difficulty in securing an interview with the family doctor, and when at last I succeeded in meeting him, I put it to him that he " had received a confidence " from the lady, and he admitted it, adding he would be very glad of help. Later in the interview, however, I found that he was prepared to swear that *the lady* attributed the miscarriage to the jostling and fright which she had suffered ten days before, and that he knew no more about the matter. From this position nothing could dislodge him. As I left the house he remarked : " When Scot meets Scot . . ."

The salient points to be remarked in this case were—

1. The lady expressed no regret at the miscarriage, although it was her first pregnancy.

2. She had not any of the usual spirit of revenge which would actuate most women under similar circumstances.

3. She admitted that at first she did not tell her husband anything about it.

4. It was her husband who insisted upon having the doctor.

5. She only remained in bed a few days, and then went to stay with some friends.

6. Her husband was angry, but was only making a small claim.

7. The lady remarked to me when I entered the room that she " did not like claims."

8. Her doctor endeavoured to avoid meeting me, but when escape was impossible he tried hard to have the woman present at the interview.

9. The doctor's attitude and admissions were very significant, especially his allusion to " When Scot meets Scot."

Result.—The obvious inference to be drawn and insisted upon was that the case was a suspicious one ; and upon the claim being resisted it was abandoned.

THE MEDICAL EXAMINATION

It is not always an easy task to maintain a judicial attitude, for patients often come with the preconceived idea that the examiner is their enemy, and they are accordingly either mulish and stubborn to a most exasperating degree, or insulting and refractory in their demeanour. If not as bad as this, they are often so garrulous as to severely try the patience of the examiner; and, again, are sometimes so stupid that it is difficult to get them to take any intelligent interest in the tests to which they are subjected.

In setting out to examine a case the patient should be carefully noted from the moment he comes under observation. It is a good plan, when possible, to watch his approach to the place where he is going to be examined, so that his gait and demeanour can be seen before he is aware that he is under observation. The way he enters the room, the way he sits down, removes his clothes, and so forth, should all be very carefully watched.

Before commencing the examination of a case which may eventually be of medico-legal interest, and more especially in cases sent by insurance companies and other corporations, where the question of fitness or otherwise for work may arise, it is always expedient to courteously but firmly insist upon friends or relations of the examinee withdrawing. In the event of it being found necessary to report that no such illness as alleged does in fact exist, allegations of unfair treatment and harshness are not unlikely to be made; and, however groundless and unjust such statements may be, it would add to the embarrassment of the medical examiner if such statements were supported, as they sometimes are, by a friend or relative who had ostensibly attended, to give moral support to the applicant. The author recalls an occasion when a third person was incautiously allowed to be present during the interview; subsequently it transpired that this individual was a clerk in the employ of the claimant's solicitor, and he supported the claimant's perjured evidence. The precautions indicated are of still more importance when it is proposed that the examination shall take place in the presence of a paid agent of the trade union to which the examinee belongs, or of the solicitor who may be conducting the claim for compensation under the Workmen's Compensation Act of 1906.

38 MALINGERING

After a large experience of medico-legal examinations and evidence in Court, I urge the extreme importance of those engaged in this work making it an absolute rule on all occasions to exclude third parties.

In workmen's cases the applicant is by Section 14 of the First Schedule of the Workmen's Compensation Act bound to submit himself for medical examination.

> "Any workman receiving weekly payments under this Act shall, if so required by the employer, from time to time submit himself for examination by a duly qualified medical practitioner provided and paid by the employer. If the workman refuses to submit himself to such examination, or in any way obstructs the same, his right to such weekly payments shall be suspended until such examination has taken place."

It will be observed that no mention is made of the presence of a third party.

It is obvious that the applicant should be encouraged to arrange for the presence of his own medical attendant, and in workmen's compensation cases this has been expanded to include the medical nominee of the solicitor who has taken up his case when, as occasionally happens, the injured man has long ceased to employ a medical man. This arrangement cannot be objected to ; for obviously the plaintiff would prefer the presence of a medical attendant, and *his* attendance at these interviews is occasionally helpful.

It should be carefully noted that these remarks apply only to the Workmen's Compensation Act, and have no bearing on actions brought under Common Law, or on what are known as third party claims, nor on actions under the Employers' Liability Act. In these cases the Legislature does not arrange for a medical examination, and all sorts of conditions are sometimes imposed by solicitors employed in actions of this kind.

In such cases my practice has been, where the plaintiff insists upon being examined in the presence of his own solicitor, to do so only when the defendant is also represented by a solicitor. If the plaintiff's doctor is present, it is generally sufficient, except in the case of the most aggressive of the legal profession, to point out that the plaintiff is abundantly protected by the presence of his own medical man, and that the presence of two solicitors is uncalled for, and is more likely to embarrass than expedite the examination.

THE MEDICAL EXAMINATION

It is no part of the duty of a medical examiner to trespass on the legal aspect of the case. The question of liability is one in which he should have no interest, and with which he certainly has no business.

At a medical examination, therefore, only such questions as will assist in forming an opinion as to the condition of the patient should be asked. It is of the first importance to conduct every case in an impartial spirit, and it is almost of as great importance to let all parties concerned see that such is one's intention. In this way only can confidence be inspired.

As an example of how sometimes a doctor may by mistake treat a man who really had no injury, the following may be of interest :

B. C., a fireman, aged thirty-seven, stated that whilst "slicing" fires on board ship, he slipped, felt something grip, as it were, at the lower part of his back, fell down, and was picked up by his mates. In view of the ultimate issue of this case, the history of his subsequent dealings with the medical profession is of interest, and may therefore be related in some detail. He stated that he finished the morning watch, but was unable to work in the evening, and reported the matter to the Captain, who told him he had sciatica. He did no more work till the ship reached the first port of call, where he consulted a doctor, who gave him medicine. He resumed work until the ship reached the next port, when he again told the Captain he could not work. The Captain sent for a doctor, who examined him and told him he would be better at work. He continued work till the ship reached the third port, when he again consulted a doctor, who also said he would be better at work. At the next three stopping-places he did not consult a doctor. On the return voyage he went to the medical man he had seen before at the third port, who a second time told him not to stop work. At future stopping-places he consulted no doctor. Four and a half months after the alleged accident the ship reached London, and the claimant went to a medical man, who diagnosed injury to the spine, gave him oil to rub in his back, and saw him twice a week for some weeks.

Examination.—Seven months after the alleged accident, when he was sent to me, he stated he was unfit for work on account of pain in his back, caused by his fall. He was well nourished, with no evidence of muscular wasting. He explained that the pain radiated horizontally in front of, and then vertically down the outside of, each thigh— a practical impossibility, because this direction follows no group of nerves. He persistently held himself stiff (except when he was lacing up his boots) until the end of the examination, when he straightened his back in a comparatively nimble manner. An X-ray photograph

MALINGERING

of the portion of the spine where pain was alleged showed nothing abnormal.

I told him to strip, and kneel with his hands, elbows, and knees on the floor, putting his clothes below his elbows, and arranging his back so that it was perfectly level. This position, equivalent to the erect position when standing, he assured me, caused him no pain. On applying faradism to his back, he asserted he could not feel a strong current in the neighbourhood of the alleged painful area, although I distinctly observed the muscles involuntarily contracting under the force of the current, and that he was alive to this usually painful sensation was evidenced by his distorted facial expression. It was obvious that he considered that with his disability he should not feel anything, and bore the current manfully.

When picking up his clothes he stretched out his right leg behind him, and bent upon the left side, which he had alleged to be painful. He walked away with his back bent, but I came to the conclusion that he was fit for work, and if not actually malingering, was under an obsession that he could not work.

Result.—The shipping company stopped paying compensation on receipt of my report, and when the matter subsequently came before the Court, the shipping company proved that the alleged accident had never, in fact, occurred. Judgment for defendant.

Claimants are very apt, in giving a history, to mix up symptoms from which they *have been* suffering, with those from which they *are* suffering at the date of examination. The examiner should keep very clearly before him the fact that he is called upon to examine and to report on the physical and mental condition of the applicant *at the time* of his examination. If any attempt be made to report on the condition of the claimant from his *ex parte* statements prior to the examination, it inevitably leads to confusion. It should be borne in mind that those who have the conduct of the case may have intentionally allowed time to elapse, for reasons best known to themselves, before submitting the applicant to a thorough medical examination. Indeed, it not infrequently happens—and in one insurance company I am acquainted with it is the rule—that several medical opinions are sought, at intervals, prior to action being taken which may lead to Court proceedings. It is always to be remembered that those who want the report are business men, and they expect—indeed, they can only understand—a statement which is business-like.

There is only one way of getting at the facts systematically, and that is by first asking the patient for the history of the accident (letting him understand that only such details as

THE MEDICAL EXAMINATION 41

will assist in forming an opinion from a medical point of view are desired), then insisting upon his stating categorically his *present* complaints. Everything that the patient says in his history should be carefully written down at the time, as nearly as possible in his own words, for future reference.

Where, as sometimes happens, the Statement of Claim is submitted to the medical examiner, a careful note should be made of the different allegations as to the effect of the accident, *and* of the discrepancies, if any, between the patient's statement as to his disabilities and that put forward by his solicitor. There is often a marked difference between the condition of the claimant on the date of his medical examination and that which he presumably was in, when the lawyer was furnished with the details of how the accident had affected him.

The difference may, of course, be accounted for by the interval of time which has elapsed, improvement probably having taken place meanwhile ; but my experience is that Statements of Claim in ordinary " running down " cases are often grossly exaggerated. On the other hand, it should not be forgotten that a solicitor takes his client's " instructions," and one can well understand that after pain and suffering have been experienced—the result, it may be, of culpable carelessness on the part of the defendant—a feeling of resentment, or even a desire for revenge, takes possession of the plaintiff, and he is tempted to exaggerate when pouring the details of his symptoms into the sympathetic ear of a solicitor's clerk.

The following case illustrates the necessity of having a detailed statement of alleged disabilities, of taking up each point in its proper order, of thoroughly investigating it, and setting out the result of the examination systematically.

History—B. D.—A firm of solicitors requested me to examine, on behalf of the defendants, a boy aged eleven years, who seven months previously had been run down by a cart ; the shaft had struck his left cheek, and the horse trampled on him. The examination took place in the presence of the boy's family doctor and a well-known surgeon.

Examination.—The Statement of Claim set out that the lad was still suffering, as the result of the accident, from the following ailments : *Physical :* (1) Small abrasion on · left cheek ; (2) loss of second incisor tooth on left side, causing permanent disfigurement ; (3) depression at angle of the jaw ; (4) injury to left forearm ; (5) inter-

MALINGERING

mittent swelling of the knees ; (6) discharge from the left ear. *Mental :* (1) Nervousness ; (2) preoccupation and restlessness ; (3) headache ; (4) sleeplessness ; (5) dreaming and fear of the dark ; (6) loss of memory.

The examination lasted considerably over an hour.

Physical Disabilities.—(1) The abrasion on the cheek was a trifling red scar about the size of a split pea ; (2) the doctor was very emphatic that the incisor tooth was broken by the accident, but I was able to point out to him that the teeth were absolutely normal. The lad's milk-tooth had obviously been on the point of falling out at the time of the accident, and may have been helped out by the fall, but had been replaced by the permanent tooth by the time I saw him. The incident was therefore of no value from the plaintiff's point of view, but might have been very telling in cross-examination at the trial had not the plaintiff's solicitor decided to abandon his claim for the disfigurement ! (3) There was a slight depression at the angle of the jaw, of no serious import. (4) A swelling and discoloration, the remains of some inflammation of the left forearm, was apparently rapidly disappearing. The lad asserted, and his doctor supported him, that there was loss of power in the left hand. He certainly did not grasp so firmly with this hand as with the other. All the muscles of the left hand were softer than those of the right, evidently from want of use after the accident ; this probably accounted for any difference in power of grasp. (5) He obviously suffered from knock-knees, a common result of rickets, which, admittedly, could have no connection with the accident. (6) The father informed me the boy had a discharge from his ear, which came on with, but dried up a few hours after, the headache. This was not correct, for on examining the ear with the otoscope the drum was found to be perfectly normal.

Mental Ailments.—(1) I had observed that in the waiting-room before the examination the lad showed no symptoms of nervousness. (2) There were no signs of preoccupation and restlessness in his manner. (3) It was difficult to affirm or deny the presence of headache (a subjective symptom), but from careful questioning it appeared that he was subject to "sick headaches" (migraine) prior to the accident. (4) He told me he slept continuously from 8 p.m. to 8 a.m. (5) It was probably true that he had dreams and was afraid of the dark ; this must, however, have been suggested to him in the first instance, for, on being asked if he ever dreamt, he at once stated, with evident satisfaction, that he had dreamt of lions. On my suggesting that a lad of his age should not be afraid of the dark, he stoutly asserted that he was, and obviously considered it the right condition to be in after an accident. (6) After dismissing the boy and his father, I suggested to the doctor and the surgeon that the lad was acting his part, and the latter admitted that this was true to a certain extent. The question of the alleged loss of memory, therefore, was a difficult one to deal with. My impression was that he did not suffer from loss of memory as the result of the accident.

THE MEDICAL EXAMINATION 43

Result.—Six and a half months later, in the High Court, a verdict for the defendants with costs was returned; this, however, was upon grounds other than medical.

In eliciting the history of the accident, great care should be taken to avoid giving information to the claimant. A very great deal of mischief is done by doctors, unused to these cases, who put leading questions; who, for example, ask a man who alleges " slipped cartilage " whether his knee was locked; or trace out the course of a nerve, and ask whether the pain radiates along it. They supply the dishonest man with material for bolstering up his case, and furnish the true hysteric or neurasthenic with a list of new complaints; for to *suggest* new symptoms to such patients is tantamount to causing them to experience them. *Under no circumstances, therefore, should leading questions be put.*

In getting out the history, it is of value to notice whether the series of events and the evolution of symptoms follow a course which experience shows one might fairly expect them to follow after the injury in question.

It should always be remembered that the patient is at a great disadvantage compared with the doctor, in that he has not the latter's special knowledge; and if he is lying and endeavouring to make up symptoms which he thinks suitable to the case, he will produce a picture so distorted, so lacking in verisimilitude, that its artificial production is manifest. It should also be noticed whether the symptoms complained of are such as can be successfully imitated, for obviously the malingerer will select these for his purpose, and will ignore those which either cannot be reproduced at all, or can only be imitated with pain and difficulty. Indeed, I often feel that the contest between a medical man and the class of patient being dealt with here is really *in some respects* a very unequal one, and it is fortunate that it is. Your exaggerator or malingerer, as the case may be, is sadly deficient in the proper equipment for a successful issue. He is ignorant of anatomy and physiology, and pretends symptoms which in his imperfect knowledge he assumes should be present in his particular pet disease. He may often, in fact, be exposed by asking whether he experiences symptoms which might appear to the lay mind likely to occur, but which the expert knows are utterly foreign to the ordinary sequences of the accident in question. As has

44 MALINGERING

been well remarked, "sometimes the whole symptomatology is so unreal as to amount, constructively, to malingering."

In putting questions, allowance must be made for the particular degree of mental alertness of the individual. It is obviously unfair to brand a man as deceitful, when he has not understood a question which has been propounded in a manner not clear enough for his limited intelligence to comprehend.

When a patient complains of symptoms which appear bizarre, unlikely, and not conforming to any known type of disease, it must not be assumed too readily that they are false. It will well repay the medical examiner in these difficult cases to institute a searching, and, if necessary, prolonged examination (in the interests of all concerned) before writing his report.

It is a safe rule never to think lightly of a group of symptoms which, however extraordinary in themselves, are nevertheless compatible with one another.

Having elicited the history of the accident, and ascertained if any light is likely to be gleaned from it, the patient should next be asked to state what his present complaints are. It will be noted that it is not suggested that the history of previous illnesses or the family history should be inquired into, for the very sufficient reason that a medico-legal examination is not a game in which either party puts all his cards on the table.

The physical examination of the patient should then be proceeded with, and this should be as thorough as possible. Never was the old instruction of " eyes first, ears second, hands third," and so forth, more necessary than in dealing with these cases. The patient should be carefully watched as he undresses, as he takes off his boots, and clothes ; all dressings should be removed, for it will often be found that the most portentous dressings cover the most insignificant wounds ; crutches and sticks, if used, should be taken away. He should be sufficiently stripped for thorough examination, and the light should be the best possible, for in these days of aseptic operations it is very easy to miss the delicate scar of an appendicitis or a gastro-enterostomy operation, or such things as the marks made by the pressure of a truss.

THE MEDICAL EXAMINATION

If it is a question of an injury to a limb, its healthy fellow should *always* be compared with it. Actual measurements of both sides at corresponding points should be taken. If it is a question of the limitation of the movement of a joint, the actual degree of movement which the patient declares possible should be noted. If it is a question of pain, the patient should indicate the exact spot where he feels the pain, and the exact lines upon which it radiates; all these should be put on a diagram for future reference.

It will generally be found that the more honest the patient is, the more clear-cut are his statements and his description; whereas, if he is trying to deceive, it will be found difficult to pin him down clearly to any definite statement. If asked, for example, where the pain is felt, he will move his whole hand vaguely over a wide area, and will only with difficulty be induced to put one finger on the spot. A feature of lying is that it requires a very good memory, and, knowing this, the malingerer naturally tries to make his tale as indefinite as possible, so as to lessen the strain on his memory. He will, moreover, always try to look at the spot complained of; this should be avoided either by making him turn his eyes away, or, more safely, by bandaging them.

It is advisable in all cases, after going over the symptoms of which the patient complains, to make sure that there is nothing grossly wrong with the chief organs of the body: the lungs, heart, etc.; to test the urine, and in all cases to run over the chief reflexes—the pupil, knee-jerk, Babinski, and so forth. Sugar and albumen are not infrequently found at these examinations, and albuminuria and diabetes, as the result of an accident, are frequently alleged; discomfiture of the examiner in the witness-box will be caused if the urine has not been examined.

Finally, the patient should be watched as he dresses himself, and the examiner will often be amused at bandages discarded and dressings forgotten.

When employees are sent for medical examination with a view to a consideration of the question whether they are or are not now fit for duty, a great deal can be learned from very small matters, not only by carefully listening to their statements, but also by observing their manner. For instance, the deliberate malingerer will not commit himself to anything

46　MALINGERING

approaching a definite statement as to when he even hopes
he may be well. He invariably says that he will return to
work when he feels able, or when his doctor says he is fit.
Now, if a man is suffering pain, it is perfectly obvious that he,
and not his doctor, is the best judge as to when the pain ceases.
It is equally clear that if he chooses stoutly to assert that the
pain continues to be present, he knows that his own private
medical attendant will find difficulty in denying its presence.

The following case illustrates the important bearing that
apparently minor points have upon the ultimate result. It was
the aggressive and ostentatious way in which the workman
asserted his complete inability to undress and dress himself
which first aroused my suspicion.

History.—B. E., a stevedore, sixty-three years of age, while engaged,
seven and a quarter years ago, stowing bales of jute on board ship,
was injured by one of the bales striking him on the left leg ; he also
dislocated his left thumb. Four weeks later the doctor reported he
was suffering from a bruise on the calf of the left leg, that the joint of
the thumb was swollen and stiff, and the man would probably be well
and fit to return to work in about eight weeks. In the same month
an agreement was made between the man and the agents of the
owners of the steamer that he should receive fifteen shillings a week
during total incapacity. Apparently no improvement took place in the
man's condition, and six months later he was again examined by the
same doctor, who expressed the opinion that the man was exaggerating
his injuries ; the only sign of injury he could find was a slight thickening of the left thumb-joint. Eight weeks later he was again examined, and the doctor reported that, beyond the slight thickening of
the left thumb-joint, there were no objective symptoms, and he was
still of opinion that the man was exaggerating the pain which he stated
he felt. Six months later his own doctor stated that the illness for
which he was then attending him was totally unconnected with the
accident. Some negotiations for a lump-sum settlement took place
about this time, but ultimately the weekly payments continued.

Five months later the man was examined by another doctor, who
reported that he was incapacitated from working, and recommended
certain massage and electrical treatment. The claimant was told
that the owners were prepared to pay for the treatment suggested,
provided he and his doctor approved. Further negotiations for a
lump-sum settlement took place, and ultimately an offer of £150
was made, but it was declined, and therefore the weekly payments
continued.

A year later the doctor for the shipping company reported that the
man was in the same condition as when previously seen—viz., that
there were no objective signs of injury to the leg, and that he seemed to
have a poor grip with the left hand, the thumb of which he kept

THE MEDICAL EXAMINATION

rigid. In the face of this report, the payments were continued; but the owners began to be doubtful as to the genuineness of the man's complaints, and he was sent to me for examination.

Examination.—He was a thick-set, healthy-looking workman, of superior appearance, with all his muscles in excellent condition. He walked with a decided limp, whether he used a stick or not. He insisted in an aggressive manner that his son should remain with him for the purpose of helping him undress. Indeed, had B. E. been an old man of ninety and his son his valet, his dependence could not have been more complete. I mention this, as it is of considerable interest in view of subsequent disclosures.

His complaints, seven and a quarter years after the accident, were— (1) that he was never out of pain; (2) that he did not sleep well; (3) that he had pain from the left heel up the back of the left leg right into the fork; (4) that every now and then his left leg was drawn up, that he had pins and needles in the legs, and that he "dropped all of a lump"; (5) that he was "all of a shake" very often.

His left leg, with which he limped badly, showed not an $\frac{1}{8}$th of an inch difference of measurement when compared with the right leg. It was obvious that if the pain, which he described as being "agonizing," were present, he would not have used the leg as freely as the right, that, in consequence, the muscles would have wasted, and this wasting would have been shown by measurement. It was noticeable that the complaint of agonizing pain was always mentioned in order to prevent any special examination; yet when, in spite of protest, the examination was carried out, there was no evidence, judging from his facial expression, that he was suffering. He was very unwilling to locate the exact position of the pain, but finally described it as running in a direction anatomically inconsistent with the course of the nerves; indeed, no known surgical or medical complaint could produce pain such as described.

On asking him to stand on tiptoes, he did so quite easily at first; but later, when I insisted upon his standing on the tiptoes of his left foot alone, he described the pain as excruciating, and said: "You may as well put a knife into me and end my troubles." He was asked to lie on his back while an attempt was made to examine the hip-joint, but he completely frustrated the examination by keeping the joint absolutely stiff. He described the manipulation as "inhuman," and I therefore desisted, though I was assured there was nothing wrong with him.

He described the pain in his arm as running in a direction in which there are no nerves or sinews which could possibly give rise to this, and on attempting to examine his shoulder he kept the joint so stiff that I had to relinquish the desired examination. His left hand he had kept stiff so long that possibly the fingers did move with difficulty, but he gave me no facility for testing this. He said it pained him very much when he tried to move the left thumb, and yet the muscles of this thumb were not wasted, as they must have been had the thumb been genuinely stiff for even six months, not to speak of seven years. In

MALINGERING

short, there was no evidence of wasting or disease in the whole arm.

When I put my hand in his and asked him to squeeze it, at the same time placing my other hand upon the muscles of his forearm, I discovered that he was deliberately not using these muscles. This, therefore, was an attempt to impress me with the fact that he had lost the power of the muscles of the forearm. Careful examination of the nervous system gave negative results. There was tremor of his hands, but this disappeared when they were held, suggesting that it was purely functional.

Now, what was this man's history during the last seven and a quarter years ? He said he had attended hospital for three years and a half, and there was ample evidence of his having done so. During this period he must have seen dozens of house-surgeons ; he had received 176 bottles of medicine, all those given for internal use being quart bottles. This constant attendance of necessity gave him the official stamp of an invalid. On looking at his hospital cards (which he allowed me to inspect), I noticed that, so far back as three and three-quarter years before, there was a note, " no improvement under massage," and a further note by an eminent electrician to the effect, " muscles react normally ; unsuitable for electricity."

He stated he had eight children, some of whom were at home and helped to keep the house going, and that he had a wealthy relative in America who was in the habit of sending him two or three hundred dollars at a time. Here was a man of sixty-three, who had had an accident, had received compensation for many years, was well dressed, and obviously comfortably off, and very naturally did not wish to begin stevedore's work again after such a lapse of time. The opinion I formed was that he was suffering either from functional nervous disease, in which case he had tutored himself into the genuine belief that his left leg and left arm had at one time been injured and were still useless, or that he was a rank impostor. Difficult as it is to believe that a man of his respectable appearance and of his age would deliberately and intentionally pretend illness which he had not, yet I came to the conclusion that it was so in this case, and that B. E. had been imposing on his employers for years.

After the examination, prior to his leaving, he handed me an envelope containing seven postcards, with some printed matter on each about himself. The photographs depicted him in various attitudes of diving and swimming. As the letterpress indicated that B. E. did this daily, I elicited the fact that as recently as the previous day he had enjoyed his daily bath and swim, it being his practice to take a header from the edge, and to swim 50 feet across the bath, and presumably back again. One of the illustrations showed him swimming on his side, and when I pointed this out to him he explained—seeing presumably that his admissions were a mistake—that he really only used his left hand very little. The suggestion, of course, was preposterous, but, assuming for the sake of argument that it were true, if his left hip was anything like as stiff as it appeared at my examina-

THE MEDICAL EXAMINATION

tion, he must indeed have been an expert swimmer to keep himself afloat.

Shortly afterwards, at my instigation, his left shoulder, left elbow, left and right hips, were all X-rayed and found normal. During the examination he moved more than once in an endeavour to prevent a proper photograph being taken. His medical attendant informed me that, in his opinion, there was nothing organically wrong with the claimant. There was a history of his having some ten years previously obtained a considerable sum of damages in the Law Courts for an alleged injury to the same leg, his complaint then being the same as on the present occasion.

On receipt of my report, his employers told me it was " a revelation " to them, and expressed surprise at the consistent manner in which he had for so long a period been able to produce certificates of inability from so many medical men.

It was ascertained that B. E. was in the habit of going to a bath in the East End to swim, and accordingly he was watched, and as a result the detective reported that he had *seen him diving and swimming, and, moreover, that he both dressed and undressed himself !*

In view of the above facts, the owners stopped the weekly payments. Accordingly the man applied to the Court for leave to issue execution against the owners for non-payment of the weekly amounts due under the agreement already referred to ; but meanwhile the owners had filed an application to the Court for leave to terminate on the ground that the man was not suffering as he alleged, and therefore the man's application was postponed. On the matter going before the Judge at the County Court, the above facts were proved, the owners' case being that the man was a malingerer ; but at the instigation of the claimant's counsel an adjournment was allowed for the man's son, and also the attendant at the swimming-baths, to be called on his behalf. At the adjourned hearing the owners were able to show satisfactorily that not only did this man swim, but on three occasions he had been seen riding a bicycle ; on one of these occasions, some months previously, he was knocked down by the motor-car belonging to a medical man, and had been medically attended by this doctor, for the injury then received, for many weeks. The Judge, who was assisted by a medical referee, decided that the man wilfully misrepresented and exaggerated, not only his symptoms, but the various facts connected with this case ; that the limp, which he alleged resulted from the accident on board ship, was a habit, and that the man had in fact recovered. He therefore made an award, terminating the weekly payments as from the date of my examination. He had received from the date of accident to the time of the decision about £290 !

A knowledge of the number of friendly societies from which a sick man is receiving assistance is often of very great value. Whilst every working-man should be encouraged to make adequate provision for the inevitable rainy day, it is

50 MALINGERING

the duty of the examiner to very carefully scrutinize the case of the employee whose total income when ill exceeds his earnings when at work. One may be excused for viewing such a case with considerable suspicion, especially when an attempt is made, as is so often the case, to conceal the number of clubs and minimize the benefits received therefrom.

A return to work at the earliest possible moment is almost more than can be expected of human nature when one finds oneself in the position of being better off when not working than when engaged in the hard and laborious work of the artisan classes.

It is inadvisable to allow a working-man to quote the opinion of either the authorities of the hospital he may be attending, or his own medical man. There can be no question that assistance from those members of the profession who are in daily attendance upon the case would be of much value ; but the difficulty is, that a poorly educated man can rarely repeat accurately his doctor's remarks, and his not unnatural desire to magnify the seriousness of his case inevitably ends in one's being, intentionally or unintentionally, misled by his statements. *It should be an invariable rule to decline to listen to any opinion said to have been given by any other medical examiner.* This attitude has the additional advantage of impressing the examinee with the fact that the examiner is forming an impartial and wholly independent opinion, and is likely to have the courage of his opinion. Much experience helps one instinctively to suspect those who are attempting to exaggerate their complaints. In the case of the malingerer there is often a want of frankness, an inability to look one straight in the face, an indefiniteness as to the alleged disabilities, and a superabundant indication of the alleged agonizing pain by the groaning which accompanies it—manifestations which, curiously enough, can often be stopped by a little firmness on the part of the examiner.

It is characteristic of the true malingerer that he is often taciturn. He very well understands his position when he meets the medical examiner. He commits himself to very little, but he is very positive with regard to his complaint, which is generally a subjective symptom.

The claimant should first of all be asked for an account of the accident, and not only this, but the events prior to and

THE MEDICAL EXAMINATION 51

succeeding the accident should be carefully gone into, for it is obvious in a head injury, for example, if the patient remembers everything right up to the time of the accident, the probabilities are that he has not suffered from concussion of the brain. Next, one tries to elicit how seriously he was damaged by the accident—whether he was able to get up without assistance and go on with his work ; whether he could walk to his home or the hospital, or whether he was carried ; if he went to the hospital, whether he was detained, and if so, for how long ; whether he continued to attend as an out-patient, and for how long, and so forth.

The history of the treatment he has received is a very important one, for while the honest workman will generally be found to have endeavoured to obtain the best treatment possible, and, having obtained it, to follow it out rigorously and conscientiously, the malingerer will make every effort to avoid adequate treatment. If, by what he considers mischance, he has been taken to a hospital, he will speedily take his discharge therefrom, and his subsequent attendances as an out-patient will be either nil or at very infrequent intervals, and he will generally be content to present himself for a certificate of disablement at stated periods at the surgery of some poorly-paid and hard-worked club doctor, who in all probability will not take the trouble to examine him thoroughly.

The following case is related in its entirety, as it exemplifies many important points in the examination of a malingerer :

History—B. F.—The previous history of the man was briefly as follows : He had had an accident, and was examined by several well-known physicians for alleged traumatic neurasthenia. The insurance company concerned, after paying compensation for a time, declined to continue payment, and the case was brought before the County Court Judge, who with some hesitancy decided in the man's favour, awarding the applicant £1 a week. Subsequently, during the course of the next two years, he was seen by various doctors on behalf of the defendants ; all had their suspicions, but decided there was insufficient evidence to ask for a review.

The fact that this man declined to allow his own doctor to examine him and report on behalf of the company, without first obtaining the formal permission of his solicitors, was indicative of his mental outlook. The case was submitted to me two years after the accident, and, after reading the whole of the papers and taking careful

MALINGERING

notes of special points, I called upon the claimant without giving previous notice of the visit.

Examination.—He opened the door himself, and at once expressed surprise, and I think regret, that I had not given him notice. When he opened the door he was in his shirtsleeves. It may be remarked here that, after examining him, I made an excuse to enter his kitchen, and found that my visit had interrupted his cleaning the fender and fireirons—that, in fact, he was engaged in housework. He had obviously cooked a somewhat savoury supper, and seemed exceedingly annoyed at my referring to this fact ; indeed, he intimated (perhaps with some truth) that my business was to examine him and not his circumstances, by which he meant I was to conduct a formal physical examination, without having any regard to the suspicions to which he had laid himself open.

He stated that his age was forty-four, the same age that he had given two years previously.

The circumstances of the accident having already been fully detailed by several medical men who had examined him, I inquired into them, but it appears unnecessary to set them out here. There was, however, this variation in his story—that he now said that his assistant witnessed the accident, whereas previously he had made no mention of this fact.

He was asked to strip, and I carefully examined his heart, lungs, liver, and stomach, all of which were perfectly healthy. His pulse was regular, his tongue was normal, perhaps a little white. Early in my examination he began to groan, but when I sharply called him to order he desisted. When the examination had lasted for ten minutes, whilst the examination of the front of his chest was taking place, his right hand began to shake visibly. I told him to stop, but he would not ; yet when I turned him round and examined the back of his chest, it was noticed the shaking at once ceased. At intervals during my examination he again resorted to this shaking, but as the examination progressed it gradually ceased.

Three times during the examination he deliberately attempted to make himself sick, and towards the end of the examination the sickness came on. He did not become pale, and it was not the sickness of disease, for after much retching the only result was a little watery fluid. This sickness was hysterical or intentional, for upon my steadily plying him with questions, even when he was retching, and showing him no sympathy, it rapidly subsided ; indeed, I was fully persuaded it was not genuine, but a very clever piece of acting.

He stated that he never took " any food," but, upon my pressing him, he said he only took milk and eggs, and never touched meat. He said that he was often sick, and still had much diarrhœa, and that he was so nervous that if sometimes a piece of paper flew past him in the road it produced diarrhœa and sickness !

He was a strong, well-developed, muscular, somewhat plump individual, and after an examination which lasted an hour I could find no physical disease of any sort whatever ; but there was the most

THE MEDICAL EXAMINATION

abundant evidence that he was playing a part, and posing as an invalid in order that he might live in idleness. In short, my belief was that if this man had ever suffered from traumatic neurasthenia, he did not then so suffer, and that he was, in fact, a rank impostor.

He complained of extreme tenderness on both sides of his chest. On the right side he located it at a spot which he covered with the point of his thumb ; the spot was marked. He was told to look in a different direction, and then asked to locate the spot again, but he failed to hit the same mark. The experiment was repeated a third time, and he again indicated a different locality.

On the left side of his chest he complained of pain over an area of 1 by 2 inches, warning me that very great care must be taken when that side of his body was touched, as it was so painful ; and when the most superficial touch, *not pressure,* was applied, he complained bitterly. He did not notice, and he was not told, that only a few minutes before, when examining his lungs, I had percussed very firmly the whole area he would now hardly let me touch. On endeavouring to ascertain if both sides expanded equally, I asked him to draw a long breath, and he pretended he could not without pain, although he had done so frequently before when I was using the stethoscope.

He had no nystagmus, no loss of pupil reflexes, and no ankle clonus. His plantar reflexes were normal, which was also a negative sign. His knee reflexes were normal, but he somewhat naïvely pointed out that I should not be able to get the reflex from the right knee (remembering, no doubt, the observation of a former medical examiner that at the time of his examination that knee-jerk was absent) ; I was, however, able to demonstrate that on the occasion of my visit it was, in fact, present.

Romberg's test, it will be remembered, consists in asking the patient to stand with the feet close together and the eyes shut, and in observing whether he sways. This test had, of course, been tried on this man before, and when it was applied by me he immediately began to fall directly forwards ; but upon my telling him that I should let him fall, he promptly pulled himself back without opening his eyes. Later, when the experiment was repeated, he pretended to fall backwards. While examining his eyes, he was for a third time placed under similar conditions, and, his attention being directed away from all questions of Romberg's test, he stood quite firmly. It was obvious he had no organic nerve disease.

With regard to his habits, he said he took very little alcohol, and only occasionally smoked a cigar.

He somewhat ostentatiously marked the time when my examination ceased, and, upon my drawing him out upon the subject, I found he took notes of everything.

He mentioned the name of his medical attendant, but upon my asking when he had last seen the doctor, he seemed to have no idea of the date.

It appeared that his wife went to work daily, whilst he, apparently, acted as housekeeper ; he declined to give any further information

54 MALINGERING

with regard to her working capacity, but added that she had often lost her situation through having to stay at home to nurse him, which I suspected she would have been doing if he had had notice of my visit.

This man seemed very comfortably off, and told me that he had been away in Yorkshire for some months. He informed me that he wondered how many more doctors were coming to examine him; and when I told him that he would be examined from time to time, as the insurance company were entitled to insist upon such examinations under the provisions of the Workmen's Compensation Act, 1906, he suggested that the company would soon get tired of it, as they probably had to pay me very well for what I was doing!

He told me that he had many medical certificates to the effect that he would " probably never work again."

Shortly after this examination he was induced by the defence to enter a metropolitan hospital as an in-patient, but was not permitted by the authorities to stay any length of time.

Result.—A physician to a metropolitan hospital subsequently saw him in consultation, and entirely agreed with my opinion, and corroborated my evidence in Court. At the trial, after my evidence, the plaintiff was asked to give evidence in his own behalf, but he declined. The Judge, in giving judgment for the insurance company, said it was the most serious case he had ever had before him ; that it was the grossest case of deliberate, fraudulent imposition he had ever seen ; and he suggested that there ought to be some means of obtaining a return of the money which had been paid to the claimant.

As I have shown, a great deal can often be learned from watching the patient dressing and undressing, but the whole value of an observation of this sort will be entirely negatived if steps are not taken to prevent the examinee observing that any interest is taken in this part of the proceeding. As a rule, the malingerer is particularly ceremonious with regard to details, especially of this nature, and he will with much ostentation almost demand assistance in the removal of his clothes. The moral effect, however, of a searching examination is, as a rule, so beneficial that the process of dressing is carried out unaided. On two occasions, when it was perfectly obvious that confirmed malingerers were being dealt with, assistance to dress was flatly declined, and the unfortunate examinees, finding themselves in an awkward position, were compelled to throw up the sponge, accept the inevitable, and put on their clothes.

Straws show how the wind blows. On two separate occasions, after examining plaintiffs, with the medical assessor, before the Judge in his private room after a trial, I have given the necessary turn in favour of the defendant by pointing out that,

THE MEDICAL EXAMINATION

whilst the man declared he had a limp, the soles of his shoes were equally worn.

One of the most frequent pitfalls for those who are not accustomed to dealing with cases of medico-legal interest is the class of cases in which there is a genuine but trifling injury which is so exaggerated that the matter amounts to malingering. The contrast between the insignificance of what is actually present and the gross deception attempted by the claimant not infrequently ends in the trifling disability being entirely ignored, while the fraud is ruthlessly exposed. This is a fatal error. If the case comes to Court, the accident will be proved; subsequent attendance at the out-patients' department of a hospital will, with very little difficulty, be established; the man's conduct immediately after the accident will be testified to by his friends; and, to crown all, the fact that his employer was paying him half-wages at the time of, and after, the medical examination, will satisfy the Court that there was at some time an injury of some sort. Assuming, in these circumstances, that the medical examiner *was* correct in saying that the plaintiff was malingering at the time of the examination, yet if he ignores the fact that the claimant even then had still some slight disability, what chance will that examiner have of establishing his case if the above chain of evidence is completed against him?

In a case of this sort there is only one safe line of action, and that is frankly to admit that some sort of injury may have, or did, exist, stating that at the time of the medical examination practically all traces save the memory of it had disappeared, and that the fact that the patient had had an accident so influenced him at the time of the examination that he was attempting to deceive by magnifying what could not be more than a trifle.

Medical Examination of Women the Subjects of Accidents.— The physiology and psychology of her sex often makes the medical examination of a woman peculiarly difficult. When she is ill, or thinks so, she is apt to be hypersensitive, sometimes loses her sense of perspective and proportion, while occasionally she is almost irresponsible.

The feminine nervous system is much more unstable, and can stand strain less than that of men. Physically there is less reserve; as a result, when injured, the feminine method of ex-

56 MALINGERING

pressing sensations and emotions is not always easily understood. Most men, for instance, intuitively understand the connection between cause and effect, but many women seem to blind themselves to this, and think things must turn out as they hope ; hence the necessity for great care, infinite patience, and an impenetrable reserve during the medical examination.

Youthful Claimants.—In considering the value of a history, the influence of age is important. I have invariably found that children are by far the most honest claimants.

When an insurance company sends me a little boy or girl to examine and report on, I am always pleased, for they seldom lie to a doctor, or, should they do so, are easily caught out—especially if their parents are resolutely forbidden to interfere or to coach at the interview.

> B. G.—I well remember a fine little fellow whose parents were claiming £1,400 for serious injuries done to the boy's head. He was supposed to be mentally defective in consequence of the head injury, for which he had been trephined. I tried him with vulgar fractions ; this, apparently, was his *forte*. His spelling he was proud of. He distressed his mother by the way he showed off his general intelligence. Finally, when I asked him which eight had won the Boat Race this year and the year before, he fairly scoffed at my ignorance. I verily believe he knew the last Derby winner. The mother was very angry—but she accepted £250.

Examination of Claimants under Influence of Alcohol.—As a final remark, I would warn medical men of the dangers of examining a person who is under the influence of alcohol.

Workmen, especially when they have been in receipt of compensation for prolonged periods, and when they are conscious that the claim is either based on deception or on gross exaggeration, sometimes fortify themselves for the medical examination by recourse to alcohol.

The amount taken, I believe, is not always large, and the effect produced is not infrequently the joint result of a scanty and hurried breakfast, followed by a visit to a public-house. It should be made an invariable rule, *if there is any suspicion that the examinee has lost his sense of responsibility and of proportion of things on this account, that the examination should be absolutely declined.* The danger of conducting an examination in such circumstances is that the examinee, when partially under the influence of alcohol, is abnormally frank,

THE MEDICAL EXAMINATION 57

and makes statements or admissions which he absolutely denies at a later stage. Further, it is not fair to a candidate in these circumstances to apply, for instance, the delicate tests for sensibility, fine co-ordination of muscles, etc. It may be difficult under the circumstances to decline to examine a man whose presence has been obtained after much trouble, and a mass of correspondence, or where both he and his solicitors have raised all but insuperable difficulties. . Nevertheless, the examination should be firmly declined. I urge this with much emphasis as being the only safe line of conduct under the circumstances. To conduct an examination under these conditions is unfair to the examinee, and is equally unfair to the examiner.

A brief statement in writing to the effect that the examination had, in the man's own interests, been declined owing to his condition, will invariably pave the way for his attending on a subsequent occasion with amazing alacrity, for both he and his solicitor know well the prejudicial effect which further postponement might have should any judicial proceedings follow.

The Writing of the Medical Report.—It must be remembered that when our opinion is sought, the medical report must be clear, decided, accurate, unbiassed, and expressed in nontechnical language. All the facts should be set out ; there should be no redundancy ; and, other things being equal, the shorter and more concise the report the better. It should never be forgotten that any statement may be challenged in the witness-box when under cross-examination, and that, therefore, in stating opinions one must be prepared to give the grounds on which they are formed.

We must always bear in mind that we are not partisans, and that our mental attitude must be a judicial one.

As already stated, a medical report, provided it is given without malice, is privileged. There is therefore no reason why the full facts as found should not be stated frankly and freely. The author has found it useful to have the following formula printed at the head of paper used for writing reports :

"This Report is made in the *bona-fide* belief that litigation may ensue, and solely for that reason, and for the purpose of furnishing to the Manager, Solicitor, or Secretary to the Corporation or Company information which may lead to the obtaining of evidence to be used

T Temporal Bone
8 Lower Jaw
12 Clavicle (or collar bone)
13 Scapula (or blade bone)
S Sternum (or breast bone)
14 Humerus
2—10 Ribs (the two floating ribs are not seen in front)
18 Sacrum
19 Coccyx
16 Ulna.
15 Radius
25 Carpus (or wrist)
26 Metacarpals
27 Phalanges
17 Ilium (or haunch bone)
30 Trochanter
26 Neck of Thigh bone.
21 Thigh bone.
A, B, C, D, E, Lumbar Vertebræ.
22 Patella (or knee cap)
24 Fibula (or brooch bone).
S Seat of Potts Fracture.
40 Metatarsals.
41 Phalanges.
23 Tibia.

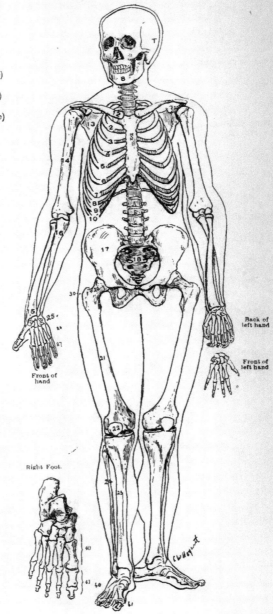

Fig. 1.

THE MEDICAL EXAMINATION

7 Scapula (Shoulder blade).

2 Humerus (arm bone)

1, 5, 7, 9, 11, Ribs.

3 . Olecranon.

A, B, C, D, E, Lumbar (loin) vertebræ.

4 Ulna.

5 Radius

6 Wrist bones.

F Ilium (haunch bone)

K Neck of thigh bone.

H Thigh bone.

N N Condyles of thigh bone.

Q Fibula (brooch bone).

P Tibia (shin bone).

S Seat of Potts fracture in brooch bone.

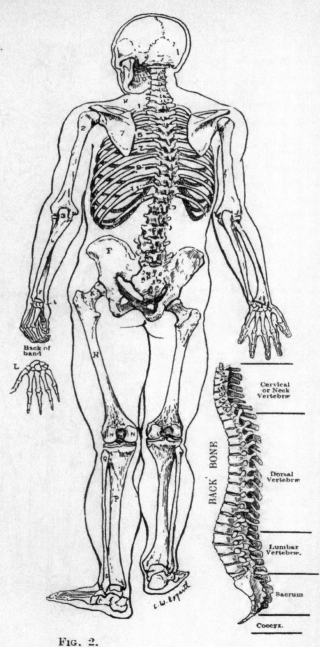

Fig. 2.

MALINGERING

in anticipated litigation, and to enable him to conduct such litigation, and to advise the Corporation or Company whether to defend such litigation, and otherwise advise the Corporation or Company in reference thereto."

The difficulty of helping the laity to visualize the exact situation and character of an injury or the position of alleged pain is best got over by a rough drawing on the Report form. The author has, when writing Reports, been in the habit of using outlines of the human body in which the more important bones, joints, etc., are numbered ; the numbers correspond to their names set out in the margin (see Figs. 1, 2). This guide is especially useful when one happens inadvertently to be betrayed into using technicalities.

When the medical examiner is asked to conduct an examination away from his own consulting-rooms, it is well for him to have with him a few of the instruments necessary for diagnosis. The following list comprises those I have found most useful, and which I always take with me when called upon to examine a medico-legal case away from home.

1. Small faradic battery, with break key in one of the electrodes.
2. Stethoscope.
3. Ophthalmoscope.
4. Plain mirror for retinoscopy.
5. Aural specula.
6. Tuning-fork.
7. A treble-wick candle.
8. Ordinary tape measure.
9. Nasal specula.
10. Sheet of Snellen's test-types for distant vision, unmounted.
11. Test-types for near vision (Professor E. Jaeger's or Snellen's).
12. Set of red, blue, and green pencils for marking the skin.
13. Bottle of biniodide soloids.
14. India-rubber finger-stall for vaginal examination.
15. Tube of sterile vaseline.
16. Notebook and pencil.

CHAPTER IV

THE EXAMINATION OF THE NERVOUS SYSTEM

ONE of the most frequent complaints alleged to be the consequence of an accident is an injury to the nervous system. The symptoms most frequently are those that are found in functional disease, but not a few simulate organic mischief of either the brain or spinal cord. The diagnosis of organic and functional nerve disease is always difficult, and particularly so to those who have not made a special study of this subject. The difficulty is by no means diminished when, as is so often the case, functional nerve disease is inextricably mixed up with malingering, and where a candid outspoken statement of symptoms is not to be expected from the patient. The pitfalls are indeed numerous, and, as might be expected, litigants are too often given the benefit of the doubt, when the doubt represents only the line of least resistance on the part of the examiner in a subject which he finds to be extremely difficult.

> B. H. had an accident, and was said to have injured his back. He complained of persistent pain in his back, which he kept bent when out of doors. He walked with an awkward shuffling gait, which was not characteristic of any known nerve disease. For months he stayed indoors, and was said to be confined to his bed. After he had received full pay for over a year, I was asked to see him. His doctor, who had been in regular attendance, stated that he believed B. H. was suffering from myelitis. A very few weeks of separation from home, firm treatment, and a due proportion of plain speaking, restored this man to his work with a rapidity which was inconsistent with organic or even functional disease. He was, in fact, a malingerer of the most pronounced type, and was astute enough to see that his doctor could not differentiate between feigned and real nerve disease.

For some years the accident laws have revealed to the unscrupulous the infinite possibilities of fraud, and I feel confident that, unless this fact is recognized by those who will have the

61

62　MALINGERING

responsibility of working the Insurance Act, " the moral currency " of the working-classes will be much debased.

On the other hand, it must be remembered that it is fatal to believe too readily that a patient under examination is a malingerer, either because the essential features of his alleged injury are not apparent, or because he is making too much of some obviously functional nervous sign. The more experience the examiner has the better will he be able to interpret the symptoms alleged by the patient. Highly strung, neurotic people not infrequently simulate unconsciously a symptom which is not unlikely to mislead, or, at any rate, is not viewed in its proper perspective, by those who have not a deep knowledge of human nature, or who have had little opportunity of gaining experience in the examination of a class of cases which bristles with difficulties. It is always a serious matter to assume that, in spite of his protestations, the patient under examination is, in fact, not suffering as he alleges ; indeed, it has been well said, " There is only one thing more painful than missing deceit, and that is to deny the existence of disease in a case where a more careful expert, or one who is better informed, would have diagnosed it."

But it is also neither good for the patient nor just to those who ask for an independent report, to shut one's eyes to either gross exaggeration of symptoms or highly coloured manifestations of alleged physical disabilities, even when, as so often happens, these exaggerations have a neurotic basis. A very fair test in most cases is to try, as it were, to take the picture from its setting, and to ask oneself : If there were no Insurance Act, or Compensation Laws, would the clinical aspect of this case be as it is? The fact that so many cases of so-called " traumatic neurasthenia " following accident, for which someone else pays, are rapidly cured when damages are awarded, or the patient removed from the sympathetic environment of his own home, suggests that some of these cases are the result of conscious or unconscious exaggeration, and some are undoubtedly sheer cases of malingering.

With a view to assisting those who are not in daily contact with these problems, the following pages upon the examination of the nervous system have been penned ; for it is in connection with the nervous system that symptoms are most frequently

THE EXAMINATION OF THE NERVOUS SYSTEM 63

feigned or exaggerated, and I have endeavoured, as far as possible, to set out the different tests which indicate abnormalities in the nervous system, and to indicate as nearly as may be the distinctions between functional and organic nerve disease.

Before dealing with the routine examination of the nervous system in medico-legal cases, I would draw the reader's attention to, the extreme importance of being ever on the lookout for grave nervous disease, such as general paralysis of the insane and locomotor ataxia. A large proportion of that class of the community which most frequently suffers from the ordinary accidents incidental to industrial occupations have at some time in their lives had syphilis, and not infrequently the medical examination which follows the accident exposes for the first time the presence of the disease when it manifests itself in the nervous system. It is obvious that the presence of either general paralysis of the insane or locomotor ataxia predisposes to accident. I have seen many cases in which these diseases have been diagnosed for the first time when some comparatively trifling accident has been brought under my notice.

Now, nothing can be more embarrassing or unfortunate for the reputation of a medical man than to have suddenly sprung upon him irrefutable evidence that he had reported on a case of accident without having discovered that the patient was, at the time of his examination, suffering from grave nervous disease. The difficulty of these cases is that the plaintiff may quite honestly say that he noticed none of the symptoms prior to the accident, and, believing it, will stoutly maintain that the whole of the symptoms of either of these diseases are the direct result of some trifling injury.

The following case is illustrative of one of the many pitfalls which at every turn lie in the way of those in medico-legal practice :

B. I. had been employed as a carman, and, being found by his employer to be too weak for his ordinary work, was, without having been submitted to medical examination, given work which involved his presence in a busy thoroughfare. In the course of time he met with an injury to his head ; the wound was dressed at one of the large Metropolitan hospitals. The symptoms, although not diagnosed by the medical officer there, evidently aroused his suspicions, for questions were admittedly put to the patient ; they were not, however, followed up by an efficient physical examination at the time. A few days later the man was sent to me with a view to his being certified as fit or unfit to resume duty. He was then slow and apathetic, his speech was slurring, his pupils irregular, and his knee-jerks were absent. He was, in fact, a typical general paralytic; indeed, within a few weeks he found his way to the insane ward of a Poor Law infirmary, and, judging from his condition when re-examined, there was no doubt he would end his days under institutional treatment.

If this man had resumed work without being subjected to a complete medical examination, the probability is that he would have gone on until his condition necessitated his removal to an asylum, and it might have been difficult then to say definitely that the disease was of such long standing that it must have existed prior to the head injury.

These cases are difficult, and their difficulty is twofold: firstly, there is the recognition of a double condition; and, secondly, the difficulty of proving that the accident did not cause, but followed, a pre-existing constitutional condition. Claimants often try to make the employer liable for a graver and pre-existing disease, failing which the plea is set up that, admitting the presence of the serious nerve disease, the accident aggravated it, and by precipitating the fatal issue rendered the employer liable.

These cases are therefore of the utmost importance, and the following illustration may be helpful:

B. J.—Not very long ago I was asked to examine a man who had injured his right foot whilst at work. He had a soundly healed scar on his instep. The accident had evidently been a trivial one, and he had obviously wholly recovered therefrom. But the man's manner struck me as being foolish, and upon examining his mental condition it was not difficult to discover that he had much deteriorated. Upon further physical examination he was found to be suffering from general paralysis of the insane, a condition which is very slow and insidious at its onset. Judging by the stage of the disease from which he was suffering, he must have been ill for from six to twelve months. His wife positively asserted that he had not had a single symptom until a fortnight *after* the accident. The case was very important from the insurance point of view, for it was quite evident that this man would never work again; indeed, he could not possibly live for more than two years, and, if any admission were made, his widow would, on his death, be entitled to a sum of £300, less the weekly payments made during her husband's lifetime. With the consent of the insurance company, I interviewed the foreman of the works in which the man was engaged at the time of the accident, who informed me that he had

THE EXAMINATION OF THE NERVOUS SYSTEM 65

not found anything wrong with the claimant, who was a perfectly intelligent, able-bodied, good workman, and that he never had any fault to find with him. I suspected that the foreman appreciated the position, and was not telling the truth. I therefore interviewed the master, who had a different tale to tell. He had noticed that for some time the man was dreamy, slow, and strange in his manner ; indeed, he was so strange that he was often suspected of being under the influence of alcohol. Further, the master informed me that prior to his commencing work with him, three months previously, he had, in fact, been dismissed from his former situation for incapacity, and that he owed his present position to the foreman whom I had just interviewed. Syphilis being the usual cause of general paralysis of the insane, I had a Wasserman blood test made, with the result that the presence of the disease was established. This, then, was the last link in the chain, and I advised the insurance company to stop payment, as the injured foot had recovered. This was done, and the claim was not pursued.

The course to be adopted in that case was plain ; but with somewhat similar conditions different considerations may lead to another conclusion. The following is an example :

B. K., whilst engaged in mending the permanent way, was knocked down by a tramcar. He was injured somewhat, but not very severely. Recovery from the immediate shock of the accident was at once followed by acute maniacal symptoms. I saw him in an asylum within a few weeks, a typical general paralytic, with less than two years to live. He had undoubtedly had syphilis. I advised that it was a case of permanent incapacity due to the accident, for I never raise ethical or controversial questions where public bodies are concerned, or it would have been useless to attempt to resist the claim in a Court of law.

The Pupil Reflexes.—These are very important, and I always make it a rule in the preliminary examination of a patient to take note of the size and mobility of the pupils. A slight inequality, an irregularity, more especially a very contracted pupil, may put one on one's guard and cause one to search carefully for nervous disease which might otherwise be very easily missed. Before coming to the conclusion that the pupil reflex is abnormal, care should be taken to eliminate actual disease in the eye itself, such as iritis, old adhesions, or glaucoma, and the effects of drugs such as atropin and eserine. The chief points to be tested for are—

1. Loss of light reflex alone—*i.e.*, the Argyll-Robertson pupil as found in tabes and general paralysis of the insane.

2. Loss of contraction of pupil during accommodation, and

MALINGERING

of light reflex, which are usually found in tabes, and sometimes after diphtheria.

3. Loss of all reflex movements of the pupil, usually due to syphilis.

4. Inequality of the pupils, as found in tabes, general paralysis of the insane, aortic aneurism, glaucoma, a unilateral lesion of the third nerve or cervical sympathetic, and found also when the refraction of one eye differs considerably from that of the other.

In addition to testing the pupil, the various movements of the eye—up, down, in, and out—should be observed, and the size of the field of vision should also be noted when there is any suspicion of a hysterical element being present.

The movements of the tongue and soft palate should also be tested.

The Knee-Jerk—Tendon Reflex.—The usual method, as is well known, of obtaining the knee-jerks is by getting the patient to cross his knees whilst sitting on a chair. The knee-jerk can, however, be obtained with more certainty if the quadriceps extensor femoris is just sufficiently stretched to give it the necessary tonus and the calf muscles kept absolutely flaccid. Many patients find it absolutely impossible to produce this relaxation at will, and the best results, certainly the most uniform, can be obtained when the patient is lying on a couch, or in bed, with the hips slightly flexed and the knees at an angle of about 150 degrees. The knees should be separated, but not too widely, and the heels should rest on the couch. A sharp tap over the ligamentum patellæ with the hand, or the binding of a stiff book, or a wooden stethoscope, will certainly elicit the knee-jerk if present. One often sees the knee-jerks tested when the patient is dressed, and this is a perfectly legitimate procedure; but it should never be forgotten that, if the knee-jerk is not elicited under these conditions it must not be assumed to be absent, and to make the test conclusive the patient must be undressed. It is a very common experience, especially with nervous people, to find that when asked to cross their knees it is extremely difficult for them to let the muscles of the lower extremities relax, and not infrequently the more they try the less they succeed, with the result that the muscles are all so rigid that although a healthy mechanism is

THE EXAMINATION OF THE NERVOUS SYSTEM 67

undoubtedly present the knee-jerk cannot be elicited therefrom. Much assistance is often obtained by asking the patient not to look at his knee, but at the ceiling, or to lock the fingers of the hands firmly together and pull hard upon them. This method of what is called " reinforcement " is sometimes successful.

The reason why reinforcement helps to elicit a knee-jerk is explained by the fact that the reflex tonus of the quadriceps extensor femoris muscle is controlled by the reflex arc in the lumbar region of the spinal cord, and some of the normal inhibitory influence which is being constantly exerted on the spinal cord by the brain is, by the suggested method of reinforcement, diverted from the lumbar reflex arc to the cervical region of the cord, and the removal of some inhibition from the lumbar centres increases the reflex excitability of the quadriceps extensor femoris.

Another method is to make the patient press the point of his toe against the observer's hand, his heel being off the ground and the knee flexed. If a knee-jerk is obtainable at all, it will certainly be called forth under these conditions.

Exaggeration of the knee-jerk by itself may be of little importance, as it is met with in most debilitated persons, and merely means that the control of the higher centres is more or less diminished. If, however, it is associated with extensor reflex of the big toe and absence of the abdominal reflexes, it points to organic change in the pyramidal tract or in the motor cells of the brain.

The knee-jerk is very easily simulated and exaggerated, but if this is attempted a shammer can be induced to give himself away by asking him to shut his eyes, or distracting his attention in some way or other, and then tapping, not over the tendon, but at the side of it.

Babinski's Sign.—This is a very important reflex, as it may be said with certainty that if the Babinski sign is definitely persistent in the adult, then the lesion must be of an organic nature.

Babinski's sign consists in an extension, instead of flexion, of the great toe when the sole of the foot is tickled—that is to say, the great toe bends upwards towards the instep instead of downwards towards the sole of the foot.

It is a curious fact that if the foot be cold or damp the more delicate reflexes are not obtained readily; so, to obviate any difficulty arising from this cause, I get the patient to warm his feet at the fire just before I apply the test.

The patient should lie on a comfortable couch with his feet rotated outwards, so that they are supported on the couch. The ankle should be grasped to prevent movement of the whole foot, and the sole of the foot should then be stroked on the outer side from the heel forwards with a pencil or a blunt-pointed instrument, and one's attention should be directed entirely to the big toe; the movements of the other toes may be ignored. Normally, the big toe should under these circumstances be flexed, but if Babinski's sign is positive the toe will be definitely turned up. Sometimes the sign is elicited from one foot more

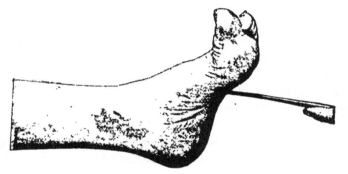

FIG. 3.—BABINSKI'S SIGN (EXTENSOR PLANTAR REFLEX).

definitely than from the other. If the result of the Babinski test is negative, it by no means necessarily follows that there is no organic disease present. The sign is not found, for example, in locomotor ataxia, peripheral neuritis, infantile paralysis, and the peroneal type of progressive muscular atrophy. It must always be remembered that the sign is unreliable in young children; indeed, all infants normally have a decided tendency to extend their great toes.

Ankle-Jerk.—To obtain this, the patient should be instructed to kneel on a chair with his feet at right angles to his legs. The tendo-Achillis is then tapped. This reflex is as important as the knee-jerk, and its absence sometimes precedes that of the knee-jerk, this of course being dependent upon which nerve roots are attacked.

THE EXAMINATION OF THE NERVOUS SYSTEM 69

Ankle Clonus.—This is often said to be present when, as a matter of fact, it is absent. Not every jerky movement of the foot produced by flexing it on the leg is necessarily true clonus. If true clonus is really present, its characteristics will be as follows : the patient's knee being flexed and the foot forcibly flexed on the leg, a series of jerky movements of the foot take place, and *continue as long as the pressure is maintained.* If jerky movements commence when the foot is at a right angle with the leg, and cease when it is more strongly flexed, then the condition is known as false ankle clonus. An increased knee-jerk and ankle clonus should be accompanied by Babinski's sign and the absence of contraction of the plantar muscles of the foot.

The absence of Babinski's sign does not count for very much, but its presence would strongly emphasize the value of a doubtful ankle clonus or increased knee-jerk. Babinski's test is much more delicate than ankle clonus, and is therefore of special value when, as sometimes happens, a false ankle clonus is obtained.

Tremor.—Tremor is often present at examinations following accidents. Fine fibrillary tremor in isolated muscle groups cannot be simulated. Simulated tremors always come on during the course of a prolonged examination. Tremor which is accompanied by increased rapidity of breathing, or rise in the pulse-rate, leads to the suspicion of simulation.

Paralysis agitans is a disease which is characterized by an involuntary shaking of the whole body, sometimes starting at a single limb and extending all over the body. A peculiar mask-like expression of settled sadness is also characteristic of the disease. Further, a poking forward of the head and shoulders is almost invariably found in this disease.

Romberg's Test.—In order to minimize the possibility of deception when this test is applied, it is a good plan, after a patient has brought his feet together and closed his eyes, to insist repeatedly upon his shutting his eyes *very tightly.* This instruction should be repeated again and again with some emphasis, for when the patient's attention is thus directed from the test no attempt at simulation of swaying is likely to be made.

Another way of distracting the patient's attention is to

MALINGERING

apply at the same time some other test ; for example, after the examinee has put his feet together and closed his eyes, he is asked to say whether he feels certain pin-pricks in different parts of his body. It will be found that many people who sway, or attempt to sway, will maintain their equilibrium when their minds are directed away as indicated above.

There need be no fear that an injustice will be done under these conditions, because the tendency to sway and fall due to organic disease cannot be overcome by this procedure. Indeed, the length of time taken in testing for loss of sensibility gives abundant opportunity for swaying, etc., if the case is genuine.

Vertigo.—The dull or less imaginative person may merely complain of giddiness or an indeterminate pain in some part of his anatomy, because it does not, apparently, require much skill or knowledge to successfully persist in the allegation.

In order to assist in the unmasking of any fraudulent attempt in this connection, the tests to be applied, and the matters to be taken into consideration, will now be dealt with.

When giddiness is alleged, it is, of course, impossible to deny or affirm that the symptom is present, because there may be nothing to go upon except the patient's word. If during an examination in which he is made to bend and touch his toes, then suddenly assume an erect position, put his heels and toes together, and shut his eyes, he stands perfectly steady, it is not absolutely incompatible with alleged giddiness at a different time, but it certainly goes a long way towards proving that on the occasion of the examination there was physical evidence of a condition inconsistent with the presence of giddiness.

It must not be assumed, because we cannot find an objective reason for alleged giddiness, that, therefore, it does not exist. It is well known that long after *head* injuries a sensation of vertigo will persist. But where no objective symptoms whatever can be discovered (in the entire absence of kidney, heart, cerebellar, or ear disease, etc.), one must to a large extent be guided, in considering the case as a whole, by the likelihood and reasonableness of the alleged subjective symptoms, and, above all, by the examinee's truthfulness, as demonstrated by certain tests which will readily occur to anyone accustomed to dealing with such people.

THE EXAMINATION OF THE NERVOUS SYSTEM   71

True vertigo is accompanied by a certain amount of congestion of the facial capillaries, and sometimes of the conjunctivæ, and, after repeated stooping, some failure of co-ordination of the muscles of the legs. Later the face becomes pale, the pulse loses force, and sometimes there is sweating.

Subjective sensations, which from their nature cannot be demonstrated, are the sheet-anchor of the fraudulent claimant. If I assert that at this moment I suffer from pain in the head and giddiness, who can deny it ? If I happen to be a house-painter, and say that in consequence of the pain and giddiness I am afraid to go up ladders, how can I be declared fit for my work as a painter ? There are dozens of painters now living fairly comfortable lives at the expense of insurance companies, which, after arbitration proceedings, have had to continue weekly payments, or commute them for lump sums, because the claimants have asserted (and it amounts to nothing more than assertion) that going up a ladder would make them giddy.

The following case is interesting in this connection :

B. L.—Recently I examined a man who had done no work for six and a half years, and whose alleged disability was "giddiness." When he came into my consulting-room, he staggered in a manner which, before I had spoken to him, gave me the impression that he was either very giddy or was pretending. I asked him to walk up and down, first in my consulting-room, then in my hall, and he swayed in a way which experience has shown me was not genuine. I therefore sharply called him to order, and the sway altered in character. I next told him to run up the stairs in my house ; this he at first declined to attempt, but upon my insisting he did so, at first supporting himself by both the wall and the banisters. When told to turn at the top of the stairs and come down, in full sight he deliberately stumbled and sat on the stairs. The action was, without any shadow of doubt, deliberate, so I directed him to go up to the top of the stairs, and come down again without holding on to anything. This he did. I then brought him into my consulting-room, and asked him to stand, heels and toes together, and shut his eyes. The object of this was to test whether he swayed, as some people with advanced nerve disease do. The moment he shut his eyes, he deliberately let his body fall backwards. I pointed out to him that it was quite obvious that this was a pretence, and he was not to do it. On repeating the experiment, he boldly and deliberately let himself fall straight back, and, losing his equilibrium, would have fallen flat on his back had not a medical friend (who the claimant knew was behind him) caught him under the armpits. My friend, recognizing what was happening, said, " I shall leave the room," and, opening a door behind the patient, closed it again, pretending that he had left the room, and remained motionless behind the man. I repeated the experiment. This time the claimant went backwards, but fell in a sitting position—that is to say, he let himself down gently, thinking that there was no one to catch him !

The importance of excluding physical causes for what are apparently subjective sensations is well illustrated in the following case, where the alleged giddiness might very well have arisen from one of two physical causes, both of them remedial, but for which no curative steps had been taken.

History.—B. M., a dock labourer, aged forty-five, was struck on the head by a crane. He was at first prepared to accept three weeks' pay as compensation in full, but consulted a firm of solicitors, and then preferred to continue receiving weekly payments. One doctor had recently seen him on behalf of the employers, and reported him fit for work. Another doctor came to the conclusion that he was suffering from catarrh of the auditory canal, not caused by accident, and that he would be fit for work after having wax removed from his ear. The man himself maintained he was still suffering from the effects of the accident. Four and a half months after the accident, the shipping company sent him to me for an opinion prior to taking the case into Court.

Examination.—His present complaints were giddiness in the head, trouble with the right ear, and indistinctness of vision after reading the newspaper for a little while.

This claimant told me he attended hospital for six weeks after his accident, wearing a dressing on his head all the time. This appeared improbable, since it was only with a strong lens that I was able to discover the scar of a wound on his head, less than an inch in length, which from its appearance had evidently healed by " first intention."

His complaint of giddiness was not supported by any physical signs. All his organs seemed healthy, and there were no symptoms of neurasthenia, with which giddiness is so often associated after head injuries.

His complaint with regard to his sight was very easily explained. He had different strengths of sight in the two eyes, the right being normal and the left only half the normal range. With Jaeger's test-types for near vision, the focal distances of the two eyes were found to be quite different, which naturally would lead to considerable confusion when attempting to read. The condition was produced by myopia, and at his age the presbyopia of advancing years would make it impossible for him to read with comfort without the aid of suitable lenses. This condition had no connection with the accident.

The history of the condition of his ears was interesting. His solicitor had sent him to a certain medical man, whom I had met before in medico-legal cases. It appeared that the doctor had looked at the ears, said wax was present, did not remove it, and allowed the

THE EXAMINATION OF THE NERVOUS SYSTEM   73

man to attend at his surgery once a week for some time merely to
have drops put in his ears.

The feelings of numbness, deafness, etc., which this man complained
of were those usually produced by the pressure of wax, more especially
if, as in this case, the wax was in one ear only. With his consent, I
removed the whole of the wax, so that he could have no further complaint. He was, in fact, quite well, and had practically been so for
six weeks. One could, however, understand how this man, having
strange sensations in his head, due solely to accumulation of wax,
might ignorantly attribute them to the blow he had received. But
it was difficult to understand, from a purely medical point of view,
why he did not have proper treatment long before.

Result.—The shipping company made application to Court for
termination of payments. I gave evidence at the hearing, and the
Judge decided in favour of the company.

Alleged excessive sensibility, which is often hysterical or
fraudulent, is usually found to be annular in its distribution,
instead of following the anatomical distribution of the nerves.
It must not be forgotten that the exact areas of skin supplied
by nerves vary in different persons, but as a rule they are
more or less definite. These cases should be approached from
a psychological rather than a physical point of view.

Pain.—One of the most frequent questions the examiner
has to decide is whether an alleged pain is real, exaggerated,
or wholly absent. This is a very difficult task, and every
possible help is required if mistakes are to be avoided. Anyone
who has had much experience of medico-legal cases soon
acquires an instinctive perception of the truth about alleged
pains; but it is one thing to be convinced in one's own mind,
and quite another thing to be able to adduce such tangible
evidences of shamming as would bring conviction to the minds
of Judge and jury.

The attitude of the malingerer at the very commencement of
the examination will often show what course he is going to
pursue. He shrinks away before he is touched. When he is
induced to submit to examination, he complains bitterly
long before he can possibly have been really hurt. He can,
in fact, be seen making his preparations for complaint, and it
will often be remarkably difficult to keep him from looking at
the part which is being manipulated, for, knowing that he
cannot really feel pain from the passive movement which is
taking place, he desires to fall back upon the sense of sight for
information as to the exact time when his protest may best

74 MALINGERING

be made. It is therefore one of the first essentials in an examination to make the patient keep his face turned away from the part which is being manipulated. The way in which he indicates that he is feeling pain often gives him away, for he does so by the most ludicrous contortions, grimaces, cries, and groans, such as a man who is geniuinely feeling pain would not make use of. One of the first things to do is to localize exactly the seat of the alleged pain in the way described on p. 129, and to see whether it remains constant or shifts its position during the examination or at subsequent examinations. The next thing to do is to distract the patient's attention by one of the methods already described, and see whether some given stimulus then provokes less expression of pain than it does when the patient is allowed to direct his attention to what is being done.

In true neuralgia there are often tender points to be felt, as, for instance, where nerves emerge from canals ; but the nerve trunk itself is not sensitive to touch. When one remembers that the laity are ignorant of the anatomical distribution of the nerves, methods of detecting a malingerer will at once occur to the examiner.

A very important thing to observe is whether there is any interval between the movement alleged to be painful and the expression of pain on the part of the patient. In true pain the wince or the cry, or whatever indication is being made that pain is felt, follows almost instantaneously on the stimulus causing the pain, and is involuntary. If there is an *appreciable* interval, however short, it indicates that the patient has had to think whether or not he is really suffering, and such delayed expression gives rise to the suspicion that no pain is really felt.

There are also certain objective symptoms which may be present. These are flushing of the face on the one hand, or pallor and sweating on the other, dilatation of the pupil, and increased rapidity of the pulse. If any or all of these are present, it may fairly be supposed that pain is being felt ; if absent, their absence goes a long way towards showing that the pain is simulated. For the proper observation of these indications, it is almost essential that the examiner should have the services of a skilled assistant to carefully examine the pupil in a good light when the alleged pain is produced. Coppioli states that

THE EXAMINATION OF THE NERVOUS SYSTEM   75

the pupil will sometimes be found to dilate rapidly when pain is really felt. In examining the pulse, an idea must be obtained as to its rate when the patient is free from pain. In many cases, as soon as pain is felt it will promptly jump up 20 or 30 beats a minute.

Admirers of Scott will remember that in " Peveril of the Peak " that consummate master of English literature portrays with dramatic effect the discovery that Fenella was malingering when she assumed the rôle of a deaf mute.   The following is the passage referred to :

Said the King :

" I will instantly convince you of the fact, though the experiment is too delicate to be made by any but your ladyship.   Yonder she stands, looking as if she heard no more than the marble pillar against which she leans.   Now, if Lady Derby will contrive either to place her hand near the region of the damsel's heart, or at least on her arm, so that she can feel the sensation of the blood when the pulse increases, then do you, my Lord of Ormond, beckon Julian Peveril out of sight. I will show you in a moment that it can stir at sounds spoken."

The Countess, much surprised, afraid of some embarrassing pleasantry on the part of Charles, yet unable to repress her curiosity, placed herself near Fenella—as she called her little mute—and, while making signs to her, contrived to place her hand on her wrist.

At this moment the King, passing near them, said : " This is a horrid deed—the villain Christian has stabbed young Peveril !"

The mute evidence of the pulse, which bounded as if a cannon had been discharged close by the poor girl's ear, was accompanied by such a loud scream of agony as distressed, while it startled, the good-natured monarch himself.   " I did but jest," he said ; " Julian is well, my pretty maiden.   I only used the wand of a certain blind deity called Cupid to bring a deaf and dumb vassal of his to the exercise of her faculties."

" I am betrayed !" she said, with her eyes fixed on the ground— " I am betrayed ! and it is fit that she whose life has been spent in practising treason on others should be caught in her own snare.   But where is my tutor in iniquity ?   Where is Christian, who taught me to play the part of spy on this unsuspicious lady, until I had wellnigh delivered her into his bloody hands ?"

It is a good plan to count the pulse-rate at the commencement of a medico-legal examination and again at the end, and to judge of the condition of the nervous system by a comparison of the two rates.

Of the two other signs previously mentioned, the dilatation of the pupil is the more important.   It has often been noted that in patients suffering from such painful affections as pleurisy,

MALINGERING

rheumatic fever, neuralgia, appendicitis, and so forth, the pupil can be readily seen to dilate when pressure is applied to the affected part.

One of the best and simplest means of forming a rough idea as to whether pain is as persistent and severe as is alleged, is to observe whether it does or does not cause sleeplessness.

In conclusion, although none of these signs taken by themselves are conclusive, a general consideration of the whole of them will leave the examiner in little doubt as to his diagnosis. Alleged pain in a healthy, able-bodied workman which is not constant, which varies from day to day, and which pressure accentuates only when the attention is directed to the spot, may well arouse suspicion.

The following case is typical of a large class of cases which many will readily recognize :

History.—B. N., aged forty-four, employed as a donkeyman, walked into the hatchway of the engine-room, slipped and fell, injuring his right side. Within forty-eight hours, when the ship reached port, he had medical attendance, and resumed work after a month. But on reaching this country some weeks later he put himself on the sicklist again, under the care of a doctor who saw him once a week for the purpose of furnishing a certificate of unfitness for work, but who prescribed no treatment whatever. After continuing compensation for several weeks, the shipping company stopped payment, two medical men of standing having certified the man fit for duty.

Examination.—After an interval of three and a half months, I was asked to examine the plaintiff, with a view to giving evidence at the arbitration proceedings fixed to take place a few days later.

When B. N. came to me, he informed me with evident relish that his doctor had told him he would be unable to do any work for a long time ; but when asked on what grounds his doctor made this assertion, B. N. said : " I don't know ; I suppose he said so because I still complain of pain !"

He complained of pain in the chest at three places : A, near the middle of the ninth rib on the right side ; B and C, at the attachments to the breastbone of the third and fifth right ribs respectively.

With regard to the pain at A, I pressed very firmly on the *back* of his ribs near the spine, and also at the same time near the breast-bone in front, and by compressing his chest bent all his ribs. If there had been any pain at A, this procedure would have caused it to become apparent ; but he complained of no pain, except at the spots where my hands were pressing him. Again, on directing his attention to the area of his heart and pressing meantime firmly on A, I asked him if he had pain at his heart (on the left side), and he did not notice the very considerable pressure upon A on the *right* side. Further, I asked him

THE EXAMINATION OF THE NERVOUS SYSTEM   77

to indicate, without looking, the exact position of the pain in the area A ; three times he indicated different spots, two of them being 1½ inches apart.

With regard to the alleged pain at B and C, although he complained only of pain at these spots in *front*, I noted that at the time of the accident he had complained only of injury to his *side*. It was quite obvious he had no pain at any of these spots, for the following reasons : Whilst examining his lungs (which were healthy), I firmly percussed this region, and, his attention being directed away, he did not complain of pain. Whilst using the stethoscope, I pressed firmly on his chest without eliciting complaint. When asked to take long breaths, whilst I used the stethoscope, the movement of his chest everywhere was perfectly free, which would not have been the case had there been any genuinely painful region. Further, on applying the faradic current, he told me quite truthfully when he felt the current and when he did not. I took advantage of his attention being directed to this method of testing to press very firmly over the alleged painful regions, but he made no complaint. While dressing and undressing, it was quite obvious that no movement was painful.

Result.—At the arbitration proceedings, I gave reasons for stating that this man was an impostor, and was making a fraudulent claim. The case was referred to a medical referee, who decided in favour of the employers. The referee stated he found no objective signs of illness, and expressed the opinion that the man had been able to do his work on and from the date on which compensation had been stopped, three and a half months previous to the trial.

Areas of Anæsthesia.—A good method of exposing pretended loss of feeling is to bandage the eyes, map out with a pin the alleged anæsthetic area, mark the circumference of it with a blue pencil, and repeat this proceeding at short intervals, when the area will be found to vary.

The rank malingerer, especially if he is unintelligent, may occasionally be caught out by a very simple test. If loss of sensation is alleged—say, in the leg—both legs are bared, the patient is blindfolded, and the legs pricked. He is asked to say definitely and at once " Yes " each time he feels the pricks, and " No " when he does not. Occasionally, but by no means always, an amusing result is obtained, the patient correctly saying " Yes " when pricked in the sound leg, and on each occasion when the leg alleged to be anæsthetic is pricked giving the answer " No."

In using this test it is well not to prick the legs alternately, but to vary the sequence of the pricks, for it has been alleged, after a successful application of this device, that the patient,

78 MALINGERING

assuming that each leg was to be touched alternately, gave the correct answer ; but a satisfactory explanation cannot be forthcoming of why the answer " No " was ever given, seeing that if there was no sensation there should have been no answer at all, and evidence of fraud is thus obtained. This condition is also found in Hysteria.

Functional and Organic Nerve Disease.—It is of the utmost importance to be able to distinguish between functional and organic nerve disease. The diagnosis of functional disease has been well said to be the " positive affirmation of a universal negative."

It must not be forgotten that organic disease is often very insidious, and it may be months before physical signs show themselves.

It is a good and safe clinical rule not to give a diagnosis of functional disease as the result of a single examination. However useful this rule may be in general and consulting practice, it is, for obvious reasons, an extremely difficult one to adhere to in medico-legal cases. Although, as a rule, an opinion must be given after a single examination, one occasionally has to admit that one cannot form a definite opinion on the data obtained from the first examination, and should ask for the opportunity of seeing the case a second time. Indeed, in extremely difficult cases it is my custom to have the patient under hospital observation prior to taking a strong line.

The following signs are inconsistent with functional nerve disease :

1. Absence of the knee-jerks. It is stated that very rarely do cases occur where in health the knee-jerks are absent.

2. Babinski extensor response.

3. An Argyll-Robertson pupil. Inequality of the pupils is not necessarily indicative of disease, especially if mobile. It must be remembered that the iris is sometimes adherent to the lens capsule, owing to an old inflammatory attack.

4. Hemianopia.

5. Incontinence of urine and fæces.

6. Optic neuritis and optic nerve atrophy.

7. Marked muscular wasting, especially when localized and associated with the reaction of degeneration. Such wasting is uniform, and affects groups of muscles. It is an interesting

THE EXAMINATION OF THE NERVOUS SYSTEM 79

observation that the nerves of the face, tongue, and eye are very rarely affected with functional disease.

A paralysis which after continuing for months does not become spastic, and is not associated with wasting, is very suggestive indeed of functional nerve disease ; but, on the other hand, spasticity does not actually *prove* that the disease is organic.

It is well to keep ever in mind that one has in disseminated sclerosis a disease which is very likely to cause one to trip. The mental and physical manifestations so closely resemble those of hysteria that mistakes are often made. At the early stage, when the disease is being gradually established, the symptoms fluctuate ; they become at one time pronounced, and then seem almost to disappear, and it is well to be on one's guard when meeting with a group of symptoms similar to the following : weakness, spasticity and ataxia of the lower limbs, alteration in the speech, and a tendency to nystagmus, especially when these symptoms present themselves one at a time, and are combined with some alteration in the mentality of the patient.

The anæsthesia of functional nerve disease is not always deep. It never maps out the nerve-roots, but is generally of the stocking or glove type. Anæsthesia which is functional extends to the mucous membrane, which is rarely the case with that due to organic changes.

The following brief but comprehensive report was given by a well-known consultant in the case of a man who was ultimately proved to be making a false claim, and may be useful as showing the thoroughness with which it is necessary to carry out these examinations :

X. Y. shows no signs of any organic disease of the nervous system. All his cranial nerves are normal.

He has no inco-ordination or weakness in the upper or lower limbs. No Rombergism.

No loss of sense of position.

No alteration of sensation.

The triceps and supinator jerks are normal, and equal on the two sides.

The knee-jerks and Achilles jerks are normal.

There is a double flexor response on stimulating the soles of the feet.

No ankle clonus is present.

MALINGERING

The spinal column is normal, and shows no bony irregularity or deformity.

There is no tenderness along the spine, all the movements of the back are good, and there is no muscular spasm.

He walks well, and all the movements of his joints are full and free.

No active disease in the lung can be made out, and the heart is normal.

Nothing abnormal can be found in the abdomen, nor can anything abnormal be found *per rectum.*

I cannot find any signs to bear out this man's statement that he is unable to work, and I believe he can work if he is made to do it.

CHAPTER V

FUNCTIONAL NERVE DISEASES, INCLUDING NEURASTHENIA, HYSTERIA, AND TRAUMATIC NEURASTHENIA

I. NEURASTHENIA

NEURASTHENIA may follow immediately on an accident, or there may be an interval of a few days or weeks before its onset. It is by no means necessary that severe actual bodily injury should have been sustained by the patient ; indeed, cases are on authentic record where merely witnessing an accident has induced the condition.

> B. O. was in a recent accident. He himself admittedly received but slight injury, nor was he concussed. The mental effect of the scene, which was in broad daylight, so took possession of him that shortly afterwards he was seized with violent spasmodic hiccough. This continued at intervals of a few seconds during his waking hours for over a year, but ceased when asleep. This patient was seen and examined by me in a London hospital.

That many cases are psychic in their origin is shown, in my experience, by the fact that incidents, which at the time have achieved considerable notoriety, and have had the most strenuous efforts of the sensational Press expended on them, such as big fires and affairs like the Sidney Street battle, are often followed by a number of cases of neurasthenia in which the actual traumatism has really been *trifling.* An engine-driver who sees an apparently inevitable accident before him has been known to suffer from bad neurasthenia, even when the accident has at the last moment been averted. In fact, generally speaking, although the rule has many exceptions, it may be said that the more the accident results in actual physical injuries, such as broken bones and so

82 MALINGERING

forth, the less likelihood is there of serious nervous sequelæ, especially if the case is wisely treated from the first.

It is a well-known fact that in railway accidents passengers who at the time happen to be asleep or tipsy do not suffer so much subsequently from mental symptoms as those who are in full possession of their senses.

The symptoms of neurasthenia are multifarious, but there are certain signs or stigmata which are very generally constant, and should always be searched for.

DIMINUTION OF BOTH MENTAL AND PHYSICAL CAPACITY.

The neurasthenic is unable to fix his attention for any length of time, or to follow any prolonged intellectual labour : on the other hand, the pretended neurasthenic, who in the witness-box is able to stand a prolonged cross-examination without getting tired and confused, gives himself away. The true neurasthenic is irritable, he avoids loud sounds, bright lights, the noise and chatter of society, and it is significant that these symptoms are ameliorated by rest and food. Just as he is incapable of prolonged mental exertion, so is he of physical work. His muscles are easily tired, he is unable to walk or bicycle the distances he formerly could, his whole muscular system lacks tone ; his heart beats quickly and with diminished force, so that his blood-pressure is low ; he suffers from atony of the stomach and bowel, so that he is a martyr to indigestion. Another example of his muscular weakness is that he cannot read for any length of time, owing to accommodative asthenopia.

Hyperæsthesia of various portions of the body is one of the commonest features of neurasthenia, and neuralgias of all sorts are frequent.

The typical headache of neurasthenia is the well-known feeling of weight on the top of the head. Another common symptom is pain along the course of the occipital nerve or over the temples. Sleeplessness is a very usual symptom, and takes two forms : one—the more general—where the patient is unable to get off to sleep ; the other where, after a few hours' sleep, he wakes and is unable to get to sleep again. Many neurasthenics suffer from giddiness, which is

FUNCTIONAL NERVE DISEASES

occasionally so severe as to lead those unaccustomed to seeing much of neurasthenia to suspect Ménière's disease. Loss of weight is the rule, though a certain proportion of neurasthenics become fat. The knee-jerks are exaggerated, and are somewhat characteristic in that the swing of the leg is a long one, and it is brought back with a jerk. The patient usually starts violently when the knee-jerk is being tried.

Cardiovascular symptoms, such as palpitation of the heart, are very common. The abdominal aorta usually pulsates violently, giving the unwary the impression that there must be an aneurism present. Vasomotor disturbances are very frequent.

On the mental side we have the various " states of anxiety " —the familiar fear, on the one hand, of open spaces ; on the other, of closed confined spaces, of solitude, of crowds, of being buried alive, and of impending ruin. Another feature of the disease is that the patient is quite unable to make up his mind as to any particular course of action, and will vacillate to and fro, first inclining to one road and then to another, until he reduces himself to a condition of complete impotence.

Gastro-intestinal dyspepsia of the nervous type is a common complaint, and is distinguished by the fact that it is independent of food, and can be cured by such drugs as phenacetin.

II. HYSTERIA

The question of the presence or absence of hysteria in a medico-legal case is one of the thorniest problems which beset the path of the medico-legal expert, for, broadly speaking, it may be said that the malingerer and the hysterical patient present symptoms which are so closely similar that a differentiation of the two may be difficult. Such a differentiation, however, is perfectly possible, as will be shown later, and must, indeed, be made ; for in these days it is impossible to regard hysteria as on all fours with malingering, and to be treated as such. When it is remembered that in some cases of hysteria breasts have been removed, limbs have been amputated, and in others there has been such a repulsion to food that the patients have become mere skeletons, it is impossible to doubt

84 MALINGERING

that the conditions are of such gravity as to amount to a distinct disease.

One is often asked for a definition of hysteria, and a satisfactory one has yet to be framed. Perhaps the best is that of Mobius. He describes it as a state in which ideas control the body, and produce morbid changes in its function. The hysteric is forced by this disease to play a part, in which one of the rules is that one or more of his normal bodily functions should be considered to be absent; for example, that one of his eyes is blind, that one of his limbs cannot feel, and so forth. He is extraordinarily consistent in remembering these rules, never forgetting his part except during sleep or under the influence of an anæsthetic.

Symptoms.—I do not propose to go into all the protean forms in which hysteria may manifest itself, but only to deal with those which are most closely associated with traumatism and most nearly resemble malingering, and of these perhaps the most common, and at the same time the most important, are the sensory manifestations.

Loss of Sensation.—This is a very common complaint of the hysteric, and its area does not follow anatomical lines. He does not describe a loss of feeling which happens to be limited to the distribution of any particular nerve, but he says that the whole of one hand, or of one arm, or of one side of the body, is insensible; hence, we have such phrases as " glove " and " stocking " anæsthesia. That ordinary sensation is not lost in the parts affected can readily be shown, for while he is indifferent to being pricked or hurt by the examiner, he nevertheless never injures himself or burns himself on the insensitive areas in the way that a sufferer from organic anæsthesia, such as syringomyelia, may do. Moreover, the pupil will be seen to dilate on the side which is being pricked; an insensitive hand will close round a walking-stick presented to it, and so forth. He can be waked from sleep by pinching him in the anæsthetic area, and reflexes will still occur in the area which is involved.

It is noteworthy, however, that in the region of anæsthesia needle-pricks will often fail to draw blood, and the temperature is in some cases lower than that of the other side. Another feature is the extreme variability of the areas declared insensitive. If accurately mapped out at one sitting, at a subsequent examination they will often be found to have markedly changed their site. There is here, of course, a close resemblance to malingering, but, nevertheless, this is a usual feature in hysteria.

Diminution or retraction of the field of vision, though not so common in this country as in France, should always be looked for. Here, again, it is quite easy to prove that the area of the retina declared insensitive can, nevertheless, react to impressions. The hysteric, although displaying a marked retraction of the field of vision, will walk and turn about in a room in a fashion which a patient suffering from organic retraction of the field is quite unable to do. A striking case is recorded by Janet. The case was that of a hysteric, the starting-point of whose disease had been a fire. The sudden presentation of a lighted candle always produced in him a hysterical seizure, and it was noted that when a lighted candle was presented to a portion of the retina declared to be insensitive he immediately had a hysterical fit.

FIG. 4.—GAIT IN A CASE OF LEFT-SIDED HYSTERICAL HEMIPLEGIA.

The marks on the left leg are scars of self-inflicted burns. (From Purves Stewart's "Diagnosis of Nervous Diseases.")

Paralyses. — Of these, paraplegia and crossed paralysis are more common than hemiplegia, or one-sided paralysis; and as a rule the leg suffers more than the arm. The loss of power is rarely absolute; certain groups of muscles are not affected, but the whole limb is declared to be more or less powerless. The gait of the hysterical leg is very characteristic. In walking, the whole limb is dragged behind, as if it were a dead weight, and no effort of circumduction is made, as in the organic palsies. It is noteworthy that often, in the early stages of

86　　　　　　　　　　　MALINGERING

the administration of an anæsthetic, the paralyzed limb will be forcibly flung about by the patient.

Contractures and Spasms.—These are most commonly seen in the arm, the elbow and wrist joint often being affected. These contractures frequently disappear during sleep, under an anæsthetic, or after the application of an Esmarch bandage.

POINTS WHICH ARE COMMON TO MALINGERING AND HYSTERIA.

First, in both conditions the symptoms are very variable, being different in character every time the patient is seen ; second, they are all functional in character ; third, there is an absence of any anatomical basis ; fourth, the hysteric almost always reacts to tests in exactly the same way as the malingerer. If, for example, the complaint is loss of sight of one eye, the hysteric will, in every test designed to show that both eyes are capable of sight, react in exactly the same way as the malingerer. His contractures and his paralyses also disappear under chloroform. How, then, are we to differentiate the cases ? Before coming to the opinion that the case is one of malingering, the possibility of hysteria should always be kept in mind, and search should be made for the presence of other stigmata of hysteria, such as have been described above. Take, for example, the case of a hysterical woman who says she cannot see out of one eye. She will readily react to every test (such as the use of prisms, the binocular test, the coloured-glass test, and all the others which are described in the chapter devoted to the simulation of eye diseases) in exactly the same way as the malingerer would, but with this important difference: the hysteric, believing herself genuinely blind in one eye, will answer the tests without any hesitation, without contradicting herself, and is easily caught out every time ; whereas the malingerer, knowing that she can really see, will react to some tests and not to others, will contradict herself, will be suspicious in her manner, and her behaviour will be very different from that of the hysterical patient.

In some cases of hysteria many of the symptoms would be readily terminated if the patient were younger and could be subjected to the rational punitive methods of the nursery.

FUNCTIONAL NERVE DISEASES 87

Now, as this is a disease which is essentially one of suggestion, to say the least of it, it seems to me hard upon the insurance company if a claimant who has been injured has continuing incapacity suggested to her—I care not whether by her lawyer, her doctor, or herself—more especially if, as the result of the insurance policy, she is placed in a position in which it is a distinct advantage to allege disability.

The following case shows how intimate and how delicate the connection between hysteria and a fraudulent claim for damages may be, and how fine is the line that may separate them.

B. P.—I was asked by an insurance company to examine and report on the case of a girl who was said to be totally incapacitated for her work in consequence of her hand having been bitten by a dog five and a half months previously.

Examination.—The wound had healed in due course. The girl's self-control was obviously affected, and she was suffering from marked hysteria. Physical examination of the reflexes, and the usual tests for nerve disease, revealed no sign of organic complaint. The case was not one of traumatic neurasthenia, but of hysteria. I considered that she was not consciously exaggerating her condition, but that the happening of the accident had brought about that loss of self-control which is well known to be the main feature of hysteria.

As her relations evidently did not in the least understand the appropriate treatment for her condition—*i.e.*, firmness, and an apparent lack of sympathy—and in her then environment she was never likely to get well, I induced her to enter a hospital for nervous diseases. After an appropriate course of treatment, she was discharged cured, and at my suggestion went to a convalescent home for a fortnight. The insurance company paid for both the hospital and convalescent home treatment.

Four months later she was sent to me again, her statement being that, as soon as she began to work, the hand swelled up and became "black." I found the hand enveloped in ointment, lint, plaster, bandages, and a sling, and it was only upon my assuring her that I would take full responsibility for my action that she was persuaded to allow me to remove the dressing. The hand, when bared, proved to be in the perfectly normal condition in which it had been when I examined it first! She flinched when it was touched, but firm pressure was applied unnoticed when she was engaged in conversation.

The hospital surgeon under whose care she had been, agreed that she was fit for work. Although there were suspicious elements in the case, the want of balance, which is associated with hysteria, accounted to some extent for (what amounted to) her delusion that she could not work. An X-ray photograph was taken, which proved there was no local cause for disability ; and the fact was that, so far as the dog-bite was concerned, she had no physical basis for her incapacity for work. Surely a firm attitude on the part of the family doctor, who had been attending her regularly, would have really been the truest kindness.

Result.—Four and a half months later a County Court Judge terminated the compensation as from the date, eight months before, at which I had first reported that she was well.

It is very important that hysteria should be diagnosed early, for two reasons : First, it is an obvious injustice to brand as a malingerer anyone who is really suffering from hysteria ; and, second, because, for a speedy cure, it must be treated at once.

It is a well-known feature in the treatment of hysteria that the influence of the physician who is attending the case is at its maximum the first time he sees the patient, and gradually dwindles away from that time onwards. It is, therefore, of paramount importance that the hysteric taint should be recognized at once, and treated with the utmost promptitude and vigour, for, if not, the case may readily become one of those intractable, hopelessly incurable, neurotic wrecks with which the shores of the medico-legal world are strewn.

It is no argument that a case cannot be one of hysteria because the symptoms do not immediately follow the accident, for in many authenticated cases there has been an interval of days or weeks between the injury and the onset of the hysterical symptoms.

Chief Differences between Neurasthenia and Hysteria.

Having gone over the main features of similarity in hysteria and neurasthenia, I think it may be of use to make a résumé of the main differences between the two diseases, more especially as medical witnesses are often asked in the box to differentiate between them, and sometimes find difficulty in doing so.

It cannot be pretended that a case of pure neurasthenia or of pure hysteria is at all common, inasmuch as the two diseases gradually merge into one another, and many cases present a blend of the two diseases united in various proportions. It is important, however, to decide whether, on the whole, the case is mainly hysterical or mainly neurasthenic, for several reasons.

FUNCTIONAL NERVE DISEASES 89

One is that the larger the element of hysteria, generally speaking, the worse is the prognosis ; another, that hysterics are people on whose statements no reliance whatever can be placed. Hysteria is, therefore, in my view much more closely allied to malingering than neurasthenia. A third reason is that the treatment of the two diseases is somewhat different, for the hysteric can be treated with wise neglect far more safely than can the neurasthenic, who often requires much sympathy and much care if he is to be cured.

Neurasthenia is primarily a condition brought about by the bankruptcy of an individual's nervous force, whereas hysteria is a disease of self-suggestion. Hysteria is largely a disease of the female sex, though among males it is far more common than is generally suspected. Neurasthenia, if not actually predominant in men, is certainly fairly evenly divided between the two sexes.

The more outstanding symptoms of the two diseases are very different. The well-known hysterical seizure or fit has nothing corresponding to it in neurasthenia. A prominent feature of neurasthenia is that the patient becomes easily tired both mentally and physically, whereas the hysteric is capable of prolonged effort, as is shown by the constrained attitudes which she will take up—attitudes involving considerable muscular expenditure—and by her persistence therein for very long periods of time, more than long enough, in fact, to exhaust the powers of ordinary persons.

Another primary distinction between the diseases is as follows : In hysteria it seems as if many of the peripheral stimuli have great difficulty in reaching the higher centres. One of the commonest symptoms is loss of feeling, or anæsthesia of a portion of a limb or of a whole limb, or even of half the body. The stimuli applied to the affected regions, although as has been shown, they reach the lower centres, do not get beyond these, and are not actively perceived by the patient. Just as this applies to the skin for sensation of heat and cold, pain and touch, so does the same thing occur for the special senses. The hysteric is often deaf. Her field of vision is often so restricted that in looking across a room she will only see, for example, the handle on the door or one figure in a picture. The stimuli produced by the rays of light emanating

MALINGERING

from all the objects in the room do not get through to the higher centres, and are not perceived.

Compare this condition with that of the neurasthenic. He, on the contrary, suffers from a too great permeability of the subconscious centres, so that he not only gets more acute, but more numerous stimuli to his consciousness than the ordinary person. He suffers from hyperæsthesia of various parts of the body, from neuralgias of all sorts—occipital, frontal, intercostal, and so forth. He is acutely sensitive to a too intense light. For him the sounds of the street, the barrel-organ, the bark of a dog, which the ordinary man intent on some task can ignore, are productive of acute torture. Moreover, as has been said, he is prone to impulses which in the ordinary course should not affect his consciousness, so that often the beating of the heart, the sagging movements of the intestines, and various other activities of the visceral organs (of which normal people are unconscious), become to him a perpetual source of anxiety.

The paralyses and contractions of hysteria impose further limitations on the stimuli going to the brain of the hysteric, and are in strong contrast to the restless, irritable movements, the tapping of the foot on the ground, the constant movements of the hands, and the general jerkiness so characteristic of the neurasthenic.

Again, the sleeplessness, the increased knee-jerks, the vertigo, the various states of anxiety, and the phobias, all of which are so common in neurasthenia, are more or less unrepresented in hysteria. Finally, as has been mentioned above, the mental attitude of the two diseases is entirely different, for while the hysteric is, to put it mildly, an untruthful person, the neurasthenic is only too painfully meticulous to convey to you a truthful estimate of the multifarious sensations from which he is suffering.

The following is a good example of the fineness of the distinction which has been referred to.

History.—B. Q., a carman, aged fifty-one, brought an action against a public body to recover damages in respect of personal injuries sustained in consequence of a collision between an electric tramcar and the van he was driving. It was alleged that the plaintiff's injuries consisted of an incised wound of the scalp and severe bruising

FUNCTIONAL NERVE DISEASES

of the body, particularly the small of the back, resulting in progressive ascending degeneration of the spinal cord, and severe shock.

Examination.—Four months after the accident I was asked to visit the plaintiff and examine him in the presence of his own medical attendant, in conjunction with a medical man who had already seen him on behalf of the tramway authority.

His chief complaint was of pain across the back, and of some loss of power in all the lower part of the body.

He was confined to bed. Early in the examination I removed the bedclothes and asked him to stand on the floor, watching him closely. He turned on his face, and with a pushing, shuffling movement got on his feet with much alacrity. When asked to come forward into the middle of the room, he rapidly did so with a shuffling gait, his whole body assuming a peculiar dancing movement, similar to that which would probably be assumed if one were compelled to walk barefoot on hot bricks.

The usual tests revealed no organic disease of the nervous system. The spine was tender. He had proper co-ordination of all his muscles when his mind was directed from the fact that the muscles were being tested. He was well developed, with no muscular wasting.

There were patches of anæsthesia at different spots on his legs. He said he felt no sensation, even when deeply pricked with a sharp pin, but at other times stated very definitely that he did feel the pin when after an interval it was applied over exactly the same area. With both legs and thighs bared, and his legs supported whilst he sat on a chair, he was asked to close his eyes, and say " Yes " when he felt the pin prick him, and " No " when he did not. Both legs were pricked at first alternately, and he invariably said " Yes " when the pin was applied to the skin of the left leg, and " No " when it was applied to his right ! In case it might be contended in subsequent Court proceedings that this was an accident, he was pricked two or three times successively on the right leg only, and on each occasion he said " No."

Some years ago I should have said that such a man was a deliberate malingerer, but experience has shown me that this view would be erroneous. In the first place, he was an exceptionally good type of working-man, industrious and able-bodied, and evidently anxious to recover. He and his wife were obviously respectable people. But he was unfortunate in his surroundings ; his doctors had admittedly not appreciated the functional character of the case.

This man genuinely believed he was paralyzed from his spine downwards ; having been strong and healthy before the accident, and, having subsequently convinced himself that progressive ascending degeneration of the spinal cord was his portion, he had not unnaturally abandoned hope, and was now the victim of hysteria. He and his wife appeared to be genuinely relieved when I told him he would be all right soon. His case was not a difficult one to cure ; he required to leave his then surroundings, and to be gradually and judiciously led out of himself.

MALINGERING

Result.—A sum of money was paid into Court, and this was accepted in full settlement of the claim.

A month after my examination he was admitted to a metropolitan hospital, and discharged four weeks later, much better after massage and ward work. A fortnight later he was sent to a convalescent home for three weeks. He returned cured.

Four months after his return from the convalescent home, on personal inquiry at his house I found that he was out. It appeared that three months previously he had started looking for work as a coalheaver !

From this it will be seen that a genuinely injured man, having recovered from the physical disabilities of his accident, not infrequently allows the happening of his accident to obsess him. He has, from want of will-power, and it may be also from a keen sense of the probabilities of material advantages, lost the sense of proportion when dealing with subjective sensations. Now, such a case requires very careful handling from a medical point of view, and the first essential for the doctor's armamentarium is a clear conviction that the diagnosis that his patient's trouble is psychic, and not physical, is correct. It is essential that he should have the confidence of his patient, and, lastly, he must be possessed of much tact.

III. TRAUMATIC NEUROSES.

It does not decrease the difficulties of medico-legal work that the psychoses which may follow traumatism are generally neither pure neurasthenia nor pure hysteria, but present some of the characteristics of both diseases. A man may have the melancholy expression, the mental and physical weakness, the paralysis of will and the self-attention of the neurasthenic combined with the paraplegia or hemiplegia of the hysteric. Similarly, we may have the neurasthenic insomnia, headache and neuralgia, combined with the patches of anæsthesia which are so characteristic of hysteria. The accommodation asthenopia of the one disease may be combined with the retraction of the field of vision of the other. In fact, generally speaking, it may be said that the signs and symptoms of the two diseases will be found blended in a variety of proportions in the majority of cases. This hystero-neurasthenia was for some time described as a neurosis of distinct character, and one peculiar to

FUNCTIONAL NERVE DISEASES

traumatism, and the term " traumatic neurosis " was applied to it. But this term is too vague, as the blends are too numerous and too varied, being different in practically every case. Moreover, by a little careful sifting and analysis, the hysteric and neurasthenic portions of the disease can be separated from one another, and it is of much importance that this should be done.

When confronted with a difficult case of this kind, the first thing to do is to make as absolutely certain as one can that no organic disease is present. This is by no means easy, as certain diseases in their incipient stages closely resemble hysteroneurasthenia. Of these, the most likely to cause mistakes are disseminated sclerosis, general paralysis of the insane, tabes, the parasyphilitic nervous affections generally, tumour of the brain, and melancholia.

Having by careful examination and the usual tests put these out of the question, the next thing to be decided is how far the symptoms complained of are real, exaggerated, or assumed. This can only be done by careful questioning, by watching the way in which the patient behaves, by suggesting to him impossible symptoms, and, in short, by utilizing all the methods of examination which are detailed in other parts of this book.

The next question that arises is how far the patient's symptoms are due to the accident, and how far they are due to his own faulty mental processes. One of the first things that strikes an examiner who has to deal with the labouring classes is the great prevalence of neurasthenia among workmen. The generally accepted idea is that it is a disease of the more highly educated classes, but this is by no means the case.

In a large number of cases introspection and subjective sensations are unwittingly fostered, and a traumatic neurosis is brought into being which is of psychogenic origin, and does not rest upon the physical injury itself, but upon the idea of the injury, which in its turn is dependent upon the personal equation and the personality of those who are associated with the claimant in any claim that may be contemplated.

Automatic psychological reflexes probably have their origin in subconsciousness.

Were a truthful answer likely to be forthcoming, it would generally be found, on careful questioning, that cases of traumatic neurosis have been neurotic before the accident, and that they have neurotic relations and parentage. In fact, this condition seldom if ever occurs in people of sound constitution. The difficulty, however, of obtaining a reliable history in this class of cases is apparent.

Since the passing of the Workmen's Compensation Act, cases of this disease have multiplied with great rapidity. The reason for this can easily be seen, for, whereas in former times the victim of an industrial accident had either to get back to work as soon as possible or starve, he is now provided for by legislation, and in many cases comes to regard his accident as a valid reason for living the rest of his life at the expense of his employer. Many things contribute to this, the most potent being that in a number of cases the injured workman, what with his club pay and his compensation allowance, is as well off, or better off, when idle than when at work. Another reason is that, having been thrown out of work, he is often unable to get it again. In the case of elderly workmen, this difficulty is very pronounced. Trade unions, again, have a tendency to endeavour to save their funds at the expense of the employers. Speaking generally, it may be said that the stimulus to return to work is often either non-existent, or is very much less than it formerly was.

The following case illustrates the influence of excessive club allowance in prolonging disability :

History.—B. R., a market gardener, aged thirty-five, slipped from the thirteenth rung of a ladder, falling on the small of his back. This happened seven and a half months before the date on which I was asked by an insurance company to examine him, in consultation with a medical man who had previously seen the case.

Examination.—B. R., who had done no work since the accident, was a healthy, able-bodied, florid-looking man. He complained of a pain that went up his back and across the front of his chest, of pain in his head, and inability to sleep well.

Application of the faradic current proved that he was not truthful in his allegation of pain in the back. He said he could not stoop without difficulty ; on one occasion, whilst in the stooping position, I told him I could find nothing whatever the matter with him, at which he was so surprised and indignant that for the moment he forgot himself, and assumed very nimbly an erect position.

Examination of the spinous processes showed that there was no disease of the spinal column. From first to last, during a protracted

FUNCTIONAL NERVE DISEASES 95

examination, he exhibited no sign of disease or traumatism, except that he had the happening of the accident on his mind.

It transpired that during the first six months following the accident he was in receipt of club money which made his income two shillings a week more than when he was at work, and that he was still in receipt of only two shillings a week less than his usual income, therefore he had no pecuniary inducement to resume his occupation.

B. R.'s doctor maintained that his patient was unfit for work. The claimant's solicitors stated that their client was unable to attend at my house, so that fourteen weeks later I had to make a considerable journey to his house in order to examine him.

Examination of the nervous system showed no sign of disease ; his doctor even stated that B. R. had increased in weight. When asked to walk about, he separated his legs and bent his back, making a ridiculous feint of walking, but marched about pretty quickly when his arm was taken in a jocular way and he was made to do so.

His statement that he had not slept five hours consecutively for nearly a year was inconsistent with his appearance. Although he said he could only bend his back with very great difficulty, he stooped easily to pick up his belt which had been dropped on the floor.

He complained of pain in the top of h's head (which, being a subjective symptom, it was impossible to deny or affirm) and of involuntary micturition, which I ascertained to be untrue from an inspection of his clothes.

The alleged pain in the back existed in his imagination only. Whilst he complained bitterly when his back was pressed in the ordinary course, he allowed firm pressure with a metal electrode when his attention was directed away from himself.

The case was in some ways an exceptional one. Here was a strong, well-nourished, robust young man, who stoutly declared that he was wholly unfit for work in consequence of a comparatively slight accident which he had sustained nearly twelve months previously. He was suffering solely from an obsession that he could not work, and from the demoralizing effect that twelve months' idleness has upon healthy, full-blooded individuals of his class. The two most potent causes of his present condition were, first, the club allowance, which made his income almost as much as he could get when at work ; and, secondly, his doctor, who, whilst the best of fellows, was the club doctor, and happened not to have the knack of dealing with these difficult cases. B. R. remarked to me that in a very short time his club allowance would be reduced to the sum of seven shillings a week for life. He was not likely to get better so long as he had the prospect of this annuity and half-wages under the Workmen's Compensation Act.

Compensation was stopped immediately after my examination, and proceedings were instituted.

Result.—Some weeks later, at the County Court, I gave evidence at the hearing of the case. The Judge decided in favour of the defendants.

MALINGERING

Now take the case of a man used to a busy, occupied life, suddenly thrown into a condition of complete idleness by some accident, with no stimulus ever to resume work again, and the following familiar sequence of events will be observed. His mind being unoccupied by anything else, he goes through the details of his accident over and over again, and each time he does so he renews in some measure the original shock from which he suffered. The sympathy of friends, and repeated medical examinations, all tend to make him unhealthy and introspective. He has a very natural fear that, even if he is willing to go back to work, he will, after his weeks of idleness, be unable to do it.

It will generally be found, in watching the course of a case of this nature, that at a more or less prolonged time after the accident his symptoms will be ameliorated, and he will become almost well. It is at this stage that it is so important to take a strong line. He should be induced by every means to take up some work again, modified, if necessary, for the time being, until he is fit to resume full work. Large employers of labour would do well to keep certain classes of work of not too severe a nature for injured workmen to be employed in until their full strength has been recovered.

If, however, this favourable opportunity is allowed to slip by, if he is not induced to return to work, or if he cannot, after honest endeavour, get work, then it is practically certain that he will fall into the miserable condition of hystero-neurasthenia, which is not due at all to the accident, but partly to the man's unhealthy auto-suggestion, and partly to the unfavourable nature of his environment.

A very fine line divides traumatic neurosis from a form of nervous apprehension, which is shown in its full intensity in so-called highly-strung people. After an accident they become nervous, querulous, introspective, and complain of sleeplessness, giddiness, buzzing in the ears, and of pain almost anywhere, which has no real basis locally, but has its origin in the brain. These subjective symptoms are, as a rule, best seen when the patient happens to be a Jewess, who is unfortunate enough to live with near relations who consciously or unconsciously assist in magnifying every morbid sensation which the tyranny of her neurotic organization suggests. These cases are, from the point of view of the defendant, very serious, but when,

FUNCTIONAL NERVE DISEASES 97

in addition, the medical man of her choice happens to be un-acquainted with the nature of the case he is treating, or cannot for commercial reasons be faithful, the prospect is indeed a dreary one.

Cases of this sort are incurable in their existing environment, and they must either be sent to the seaside or country, away from their relatives, friends, and medical attendant, and placed under the care of those who have some understanding of what is required, or, better still, placed some six weeks or two months in the healthy environment of a *good* nursing-home. If neither of these alternatives is possible, or will be acceded to, a line of less resistance, and occasionally a successful method, is to introduce into the household a good nurse.

Some of these cases are pseudo-neurasthenics for medico-legal purposes ; others are hysterics, with not a little guile. All are obviously suffering from the prospect of litigation with all its possibilities. They are, in fact, professional valetudinarians, and how far they differ from real malingerers is an ethical point of great subtlety. As a rule they have a small mental banking account, little sense of responsibility, very little idea of the proportion of things, and are quite ignorant of the fact that the only true happiness in life lies in work.

FUNCTIONAL NERVE DISEASE.

It should be clearly understood that functional nerve disease is in itself not malingering, although it has in certain circum-stances a kinship to conscious or unconscious deception, especially in those cases where monetary advantages may be reasonably expected to follow disease if proven.

Too often the abnormal condition will remain until the dispute arising from an accident is settled, and generally it matters very little whether the claimant wins or loses : the settlement will effect the cure.

Experience teaches that if active steps are not taken to hurry on legal proceedings or to settle these cases out of Court, the apprehensive condition into which the plaintiff (more especially if she happens to be a woman) allows herself to drift, postpones indefinitely the date of recovery.

7

MALINGERING

History.—Miss B. S., a teacher in a Day school, was travelling inside a public conveyance, when a horse suddenly put its head through the window. She *received no physical injury*, but stated she had been so frightened she was quite incapacitated for work.

Examination.—Seventeen days after the occurrence I was asked to examine her, and found her in bed. She was evidently of a nervous temperament. I learned she had had a nervous breakdown some time previously. Her doctor had taken her to a nerve specialist, who had diagnosed neurasthenia, and ordered her to bed, where she was being assiduously attended by a trained nurse. The doctor intended to send his patient to the seaside after a few days, and I strongly urged this course as the best means to cut short the illness. The question of damages, assuming liability, being one which often looms largely in the minds of those who are the subject of accidents, I considered that the sooner the case was settled the sooner the patient would return to her duties.

Result.—No settlement, however, was arrived at, and *seven* months after the accident the case came to Court, resulting in a verdict for the defendants.

The fact that any individual happens to have met with an accident, and deliberately throws courage to the winds, is no reason why he should be permitted to welcome every abnormal sensation, and look upon them as of commercial value from the point of view of those who appeal to the Law Courts. In these cases the usual clinical tests show the absence of organic changes in the various parts of the nervous system. These people have, as a rule, the full measure of control over the power of equilibrium and muscular co-ordination, but they have a weakened self-control, and have developed a wonderful capacity for dwelling on their imaginary pains and of educating themselves into invalidism. They are so anxiously on the lookout for fresh symptoms that it is surprising they are not possessed of a better stock than they usually have. On the other hand, they have an entire absence of true neurasthenic symptoms, such as nervous tremors, the characteristic mask-like expression of indifference, and so forth.

Many of these cases are not malingerers in the first instance, but their want of pluck, combined with many months of idleness, introspection, and medical attendance, so demoralizes them that it becomes a little difficult to classify them.

It is my firm belief that nine-tenths of the subjective symptoms (not, of course, the physical signs) which I meet with in trifling accidents are the results of auto-suggestion.

FUNCTIONAL NERVE DISEASES 99

As an example of the influence of the mind on the body, I well remember the case of a young man who was submitted to me for examination after being ill for three weeks.

B. T.'s temperature appeared to range between 97·4° and 103·4° F. When the doctor took the temperature in the morning, it was always normal or subnormal ; the patient himself took it sometimes as often as six times in the day, waking occasionally in the middle of the night for this purpose. Neither the doctor nor a consultant who had been called in could form any opinion as to what was the matter with the patient. His blood was tested for typhoid.

I found that if the doctor did not call once daily he was always sent for in a hurry—that the patient was very nervous and worried. His wife was hourly expecting her baby.

I induced the doctor to take the thermometer from B. T. He did so, and called subsequently once or twice in the afternoon, when the temperature, which previously had, as a rule, been above normal, was found to be normal. From the time the thermometer was taken away from him the patient made a rapid and uninterrupted recovery !

When a man or woman neither expects nor desires to get well, has evidently an intuitive knowledge of the methods of malingering, and openly expresses strong views about the liability of his employers, the condition is psychic, not physical. Many of these claimants absolutely deny receiving assistance from more than one club, and it requires considerable fortitude and not a little knowledge of human nature to wring from them the fact that they are in receipt of what to them are considerable sums of money from more than one club.

The following is the case of a man in receipt of sufficient club money, together with half-wages under the Workmen's Compensation Act, to make his income exactly what it would have been had he been at work :

History.—B. U., a carman, aged sixty-two, whilst driving his van under an archway, was struck on the head, and also sustained a broken rib. Five months after the accident I was asked to call and examine him on behalf of the insurance company with whom his employers were insured.

Examination.—He told me he was unable to work, and complained of a feeling of weariness at his neck and the upper part of his back after walking for an hour or so.

From the history of his case and my examination, it appeared that he had never been really seriously injured, and certainly, after five months' idleness, the time had come when he should resume work. It was pointed out to him that idleness very naturally made him apt to examine his sensations, that from time to time on first returning to duty he might have some slight inconvenience in his back, but that he was now well and able to resume work. After reasoning with him in this way, he replied : "Very well ; if you say I am fit for work, I will go back." He pointed out, however, that his duties compelled him to assist sometimes in the actual moving of furniture. I told him I had no doubt his employer would make it easy for him in this particular for a week or two. In this case the point was to get the claimant back to work.

Second Examination.—Seven weeks later B. U. was sent to me again, because, although he had returned to his work, he persistently declined to do full work.

Now, this man was a cripple before the accident, his condition being what is popularly known as " hunchback," and on this account the case was a difficult one to deal with ; for a working-man with a bent spine is, even when well, seriously handicapped in his daily work. Doubtless long before the accident his daily work must at times have been unduly irksome, and he must have felt his back painful at times when assisting in the removal of furniture. At this juncture the somewhat dramatic nature of his accident, the sympathy which would be afforded to a little deformed man at hospital and convalescent home, prolonged idleness before he returned to work, the fact that when he did return he was very rightly allowed to go easy for a time, and his sixty-two years, all conspired to endow him with what appeared to be a fixed determination that he would not, as he expressed it, "take to his old job." He probably understood, moreover, that his deformed appearance alone would command success in the Law Court.

Result.—I was loth to advise the insurance company to contest this case in Court, though convinced that the man was quite as fit for his work as he had been before the accident. He was not really a malingerer, but, having all along been reluctant to resume, had convinced himself that certain feelings of weakness—which, in fact, he must have always had—were accentuated as the result of his accident.

I put myself to some considerable trouble in reasoning with this man, and was pleased to hear from the insurance company that they were able to settle with him satisfactorily without having recourse to further proceedings.

The happening of an accident too often so perverts the mental outlook of the recipient that he deliberately fosters and exaggerates every morbid sensation, which in process of time so gets possession of him that to a certain extent he genuinely believes that he is not fit for work. Physically, these men are perfectly able to work, provided they have sufficient stimulus. The Workmen's Compensation Act deprives them of this stimulus, and so, after months and years of idleness, they become unfitted for any real laborious work. The psychological moment having passed, when by a real effort they

FUNCTIONAL NERVE DISEASES 101

could have again become useful members of society, they acquire by irregular and loafing habits a mental outlook which renders them incapable of doing an honest day's work; and it follows that, in order to retain compensation, they exaggerate such symptoms as do exist, and attempt to introduce others which have no foundation whatever. Most of the alleged symptoms in these cases are subjective, and one has to depend solely on the patient's statements; and no one knows better than the malingerer how difficult is the position of the medical examiner when he has to found his disbelief in the existence of disease on grounds other than those of his own observation.

A large number of alleged illnesses in such cases practically amount to deliberate frauds. Often one is only prevented from reporting such cases as deliberate malingering because one believes that the combination of circumstances has so influenced the patient consciously or unconsciously that in the end he *cannot* exercise his will-power.

The boundary between wilful imposture on the one hand and the more or less involuntary imposture of hysteria on the other is exceedingly difficult to determine. Too often claimants seem to suffer not so much from the effect of the accident as from the memory of it. These cases are constantly labelled in the Law Courts " traumatic neurasthenia." They are, in truth, nothing more nor less than cases of hysteria, where the claimant is on the lookout for morbid sensations, and has welcomed them rather than made any attempt to ignore and suppress them. The whole burden of his complaint lies in what he *feels* and what his sensations are, the truth being he is so demoralized by idleness that he is determined he shall not work.

History—B. V.—The following is the case of a man said to be suffering from traumatic neurasthenia as the result of a fracture of the left arm and a cut on the temple received some years previously. He had obtained an award in his favour in the County Court under the Workmen's Compensation Act. It will be noticed this examination, instead of being a strictly medical one, degenerated into a battle between us to see how far he could deceive me.

Examination.—His complaints, dealing with them categorically, were as follows:

1. Pain in the upper part of his back, extending over his head to his temples.

This being an entirely subjective symptom, in the absence of any

MALINGERING

physical sign, one was dependent upon his truthfulness; but, from the anatomical distribution of the nerves in this region, its existence as alleged was extremely improbable.

When the battery was applied to his back, he said at first that the current was so intense that it seemed to be "tearing his flesh off," when, in fact, no current was running. Later he discovered what had taken place, for he said he felt nothing, which was correct, seeing that the current had been switched off.

2. He complained that he could not see so well as before the accident, and that the lines of print ran into one another when he tried to read.

Having with me test-types and lenses, a thorough examination was made of his vision. A certain amount of long-sightedness was present —a condition which in no way interfered with his ability to work, was wholly unconnected with the accident, and had, indeed, been present since birth. Covering his right eye, a certain-sized letter was placed at a measured distance in front of him; this he said he was unable to read with the left eye. When, however, two lenses were placed in front of this eye, he said he could read the letter correctly with their aid, and did so. Now, these two lenses were " plus one " and " minus one," and as they neutralized each other he was, in fact, looking through plain glass, and had, therefore, intentionally attempted to deceive me in the first instance.

3. He said that, although he could now move the left arm (which had been fractured) freely, he could not yet raise it properly above his head.

When asked to show me how far he could raise the arm, he placed it at a right angle with his body; subsequently, when asked to show me again, he raised it to *less than* a right angle; and on a third occasion, when asked to do the same thing, he raised it to considerably *more than* a right angle. He was asked to place both hands on the back of a chair, and, whilst a pretext was made of examining his back, was induced to step back from the chair, his hands still resting upon it, until his back was almost on a level with his outstretched arms. When asked if he felt pain anywhere, he replied that he did not. He did not observe that he had, in fact, raised his arms high above his head, because he had done so in a horizontal instead of the usual vertical position.

4. He said he had lost the power of grip in the left hand.

Owing to want of use, the whole of the left arm was somewhat smaller than the other. When he was asked to bend his elbow whilst I resisted the movement, it was obvious, on feeling the biceps muscle, that he was not bringing it into use. When asked to make certain movements which necessarily entailed tightening, and consequently hardening, certain muscles, he voluntarily avoided bringing these muscles into play. The arm was a perfectly useful one.

5. He complained of giddiness, and that when he went out of doors he felt " as if his heart would stop."

He was caused to stoop frequently for considerable periods during the examination, without eliciting any complaint of giddiness. Nor

FUNCTIONAL NERVE DISEASES

did he complain of giddiness or of his heart when I took him out of doors and made him walk with me. The heart and kidneys were perfectly healthy; the pulse and tongue also were normal. During the examination, he repeatedly caught hold of any chair or table near; but when these articles were removed from him, he stood firmly without their aid.

This man had been medically examined on many occasions, and had therefore been previously subjected to Romberg's test, which consists in causing the patient to stand steady, with heels and toes together and eyes shut. When asked to do this, he immediately lurched forward in an obviously assumed manner. I stepped aside, telling him he would be allowed to fall, and on each repetition of the test he fell forward in a lesser degree. When his attention was directed away from this test, and the pupils of his eyes were at first closed in order to test their contractibility (Argyll-Robertson pupil), I took the caution of seeing that he stood with heels and toes together, as in the previous experiment. This time there was no tendency to fall.

He told me that at the hospital he had last attended, the doctor told him he " could do nothing for him "—a somewhat significant statement.

This sturdy, well-nourished, though somewhat flabby man was not a traumatic neurasthenic in the ordinary sense, but one of those deliberate malingerers, who, having had a genuine illness, had become work-shy and lazy, and was rapidly developing into a confirmed loafer.

Result.—Acting on my advice, the insurance company made immediate application to the Court to stop the weekly allowance under the Act. Two months later I gave evidence in Court, and the Judge ordered termination of the award on payment of £15.

In workmen's compensation cases the keynote to the situation is often found in a desire for a lump-sum settlement. This too often becomes very apparent as time goes on. These people are, in fact, fit for work, but their unwillingness to commence is prompted by the hope of gain. Half-wages and idleness to men of this type are of much more value than full wages combined with hard work. The boundary between self-deception and malingering is not a territory but a line.

In passing, reference may be made to the views held on the Continent regarding these questions.

Germany, by means of invalidity insurance, and other schemes, pays those of her workers who suffer in the stress of industry, *but a very strict watch* is kept upon the *treatment.* They are *compelled,* if so desired, to enter a hospital for observation. I have sometimes found it very useful to adopt this method when patients can be induced to enter a hospital.

104 MALINGERING

The following case is illustrative of the value of this procedure :

B. W. was engaged in a branch of the public service to which was attached a liberal pension. Seven years previously he had been off work for a whole year, suffering from a strained back ; received full wages and the use of a cottage. On this occasion, having been off work nine months with his back (again said to be strained), he was sent for examination with a view to superannuation. I sent him to hospital for observation. After eleven days he was told he would be reported as a malingerer and lose his pension if he did not immediately resume work. He left hospital and resumed work next day.

The following is the case of a deliberate malingerer who threw up the sponge on being watched :

B. X., a seaman, when sent to me for examination, had been in receipt of compensation for nineteen months in respect of an injury to his back and shoulder caused by a piece of stone having struck his head and shoulder. For some time he was certified by the local medical examiner of the shipping company to be suffering from traumatic neurasthenia.

Examination.—This was a somewhat unusual case. The claimant, a short man, with a short circular beard and a smiling, not over-intelligent face, walked with his back at an angle of about 45 degrees, bent his body to the left side, twisted in his left leg, and supported himself with a stick.

He smiled during the whole examination, and from first to last, even when straightened out, he never showed even a passing evidence of pain, judging from his facial expression.

The nervous reflexes were all normal, save exaggerated knee-jerks, and his heart, lungs, and liver showed no signs of disease. He weighed 10 stone stripped, his muscles being well developed. When asked to lie on the floor, he lay in a hunched-up condition, with a beaming, benevolent expression. Gradually, as I insisted upon his straightening his back and putting his legs in a line with his body, he relaxed his muscles, and eventually was persuaded to lie quite straight. The moment he got up, however, he assumed the old deformed appearance, practically that of a hunchback. However, when suspended from a trapeze, he was induced, with a little persuasion, to hang absolutely straight.

There being no question, after examination, of this claimant having any nerve disease, obscure or otherwise, one had to decide whether this was a case of purely functional neurosis or deliberate malingering.

In spite of the fact that he repeatedly told me that the electric current produced intense pain over his sacrum when the current was cut off, although the battery remained in noisy action, I was (erroneously, as it turned out) of opinion that a long period of idleness, probably many medical examinations, and a clear recognition of the fact that he could live on land on half-wages without working, had

FUNCTIONAL NERVE DISEASES 105

all combined to make him believe to a certain extent that he must assume the grotesque, contorted appearance he presented.

The case being an eminently curable one, I advised that he be admitted to a hospital where the functional element in his case would be recognized, and where he would be gradually led out of his morbid mentality.

His mental attitude was demonstrated by the fact that, when asked if he wanted to be cured, he agreed ; but, when told that I knew a man who could cure him, he had not even the passing curiosity to ask who he was or how it could be done. In order to test him, after the interview I dismissed him, and it was only when I called him back, and asked him whether he would agree to my taking steps to promote his recovery, that he agreed to enter an institution—provided there was no " slaughtering " done ! It was pointed out to him that in any hospital recommended for his case no semblance of an operation would even be suggested.

Result.—After a short period of hospital treatment, he held his back quite straight, made no complaints, and stated definitely that he was prepared to return to sea, and it was arranged that on leaving the hospital he should be sent straight to his ship. This was done.

The interesting fact leaked out that, at the time he was sent for by the hospital authorities, he was at work in the hop-gardens !

A great part of the treatment received by working-men at the out-patient departments of our large London hospitals consists merely of the dressing of a wound by a student or nurse. I have known of cases where, upon my suggesting that massage would shorten an illness, I have been told that the patient *is* being massaged at such-and-such a hospital ; but upon inquiry I have found that the so-called massage consists of a certain amount of rubbing for ten minutes once, or it may be twice, a week !

For some time it has been my practice to induce insurance companies for whom I act to send their more difficult cases, such as a stiff shoulder following dislocation, or patients who are indifferent as to recovery, to a trained masseur, who for a definite sum per week applies not only massage, but also psycho-therapeutic treatment in the form of candid advice, and encouragement to use the affected joint.

It is unfair to insurance companies that a dislocated shoulder should be allowed to become stiff from want of use, and should cause incapacity for work for four, six, or even twelve months, simply because the patient has not been taken in hand from a *mental* point of view.

106　　　　　　　　MALINGERING

According to Ewald,* it appears that there are in Germany an "immense number of nervous workmen, lacking in energy, in whom the thought of compensation has become a fixed idea." My experience is that this obsession is not confined to our Teutonic neighbours. It is obvious that in that country, where 20,000,000 inhabitants are affected by the Compensation Laws, experience of the effect of these laws on the working classes must be very large. It is not surprising to find that in Germany exaggerated claims and simulation are causing a good deal of anxiety to those who administer these laws, and that there is an agitation for some alteration of the existing enactments.

Traumatic neuroses have, of course, existed as long as traumatism, but those of us who see much of this department of practice well know that the question of compensation has a great and prejudicial influence on the progress of these cases towards recovery. The slightest (peripheral) accident not infrequently starts a neurosis of a serious type, whereas the victim of a severe accident, when no compensation is payable, frequently recovers rapidly.

The German Courts recognize that predisposing causes influence traumatism, and it is held that the effect on the nervous system must bear some proportion to the nature of the accident ; and the time must come when, even in this country, special attention will have to be paid to the question of how far trauma is merely an exciting factor of predisposing conditions, and whether disability following traumatism is mainly due to pathological changes or psychical conditions. This is a difficult problem, and so long as we are ignorant of the pathological changes which arise from nervous shock, so long may those who are wont to exaggerate get the better of us.

There can be no doubt that repeated examinations and rehearsals of the details of the accident reproduce some of the effects of the shock of the accident, though, of course, in a much milder form. Every remembrance brings further injury to the nervous system, causing, as Ewald expresses it, a "summation of excitements which has a prolonged effect, and

* "Traumatic Neuroses and the Accident Laws" (Die traumatischen Neurosen und die Unfallgesetzgebung), Ewald, *Beiheft zur Med. Klinik*, 1908, H. 12. Urban and Schwarzenberg. Wien. M. 1.

FUNCTIONAL NERVE DISEASES

finds its expression in neurosis." Auto-suggestion, or what I have called " medico-legal suggestion," comes into play. It is not difficult to see how a nervous introspective man allows morbid ideas to obsess him. For instance, shock is comparatively rare after even severe operations, because the anæsthetic to a great extent prevents such impressions from reaching the higher centres, and so there is no memory of them.

By expending the mental energy on the reconstruction of such impressions, they are strengthened, and even new ones may be created, the current travelling, as it were, from the brain to the site of pain instead of in the contrary direction. When Napoleon III. was operated upon for stone, the symptoms of the disease were much discussed in the newspapers. As a result, Sir Henry Thompson stated that several gentlemen consulted him, believing that they would require operation. They had no stones. The pains, etc., which they undoubtedly felt, were purely subjective, the result of vivid imaginations.

The extra attention which is being paid to a simple man of the working class, both by his friends and his employer, impresses him with the conviction that he is the central figure of some quite extraordinary occurrence. Then, again, the idleness which must too often necessarily follow an accident encourages introspection with many of the working class, and fosters thoughts of compensation, and brings about a condition of mind in which the injured man really does not care how long his illness may last.

It is always exceedingly difficult after an accident to determine how much of the alleged disability is due to a physical condition consequent upon the accident, how much to true neurosis.

To act fairly in a case of this sort both to employer and employees is a task which can only be successfully performed by those who are constantly in touch not only with nervous disease, but also with claims for damages.

A very similar condition of affairs exists in industrial circles in France.

A. Brissaud, in the French *Journal of Neurology*, describes a condition which he states is one of the unexpected effects of the French Accident Law of 1898. It is described as a new

MALINGERING

disease, to which he has given the name of " sinistrosis." He describes it as a " psychical accident," caused by the fixed idea which takes possession of the injured workman that every accident occurring in the course of work constitutes a damage admitting of indemnity. The Fourth Chamber of the Tribunal non-suited a plaintiff workman on the ground that : " the incapacity with which the workman in this case seems to be affected results not from the accident, but from the erroneous opinion which the injured man formed of the rights to which he was entitled by persuading himself that an income was necessarily due to him. In these circumstances, he is not entitled to ask for the allocation of an allowance."

If the above judgment is jurisprudence, a contemporary naïvely remarks, there is reason to hope that sinistrosis will find in it the curative treatment that doctors have, until now, been unable to discover.

Brissaud claims that the preoccupation of the patient in still feeling his imaginary pains has become an obsession, and is in reality a disease.

This condition has nothing to do with traumatic hysteria. It is produced by neither physical nor mental shock. It is an obsession which starts from a different point, and has as its basis the fixed idea that every accident in course of work constitutes damage which necessitates indemnity.

The people referred to by Brissaud have a temperament which is highly strung and neurotic, and think that, having narrowly escaped from injury or from death, they should receive recompense in proportion to the injury threatened and the fright entailed thereby, and not merely for the tangible bodily injury received.

CHAPTER VI

EXAMINATION OF THE EYE

ALLEGED total or partial blindness is not so difficult to detect as might at first sight be imagined. The pupil of an eye which is sightless cannot be made to contract to the smallest degree, by light, even when a strong light is suddenly flashed on it. It must not, however, be forgotten that a pupil will react if but feeble vision still remains, but the persistence of a light reflex should make one suspicious.

Test Types.—In testing for lack of visual acuity, it is obviously unwise to depend upon one set only of Snellen's or other test-types. The examiner, for obvious reasons, should be in possession of a number of cards with different lettering.

It is a good plan to have two different cards, with the lettering of the test-types identical, except that the letters differ in size, one set being distinctly smaller than the other. This will be found very useful in detecting the simulator who pretends he cannot read lower than a certain line on the test-card.

Squint.—An amblyopic eye generally squints. If, therefore, it is alleged that a squinting eye has become recently and suddenly blind, the presumption is against the truth of the allegation.

Blind Eyes.—A blind eye, as a rule, deviates when the sound eye is fixed ; but this is by no means an absolute rule, depending as it does upon how long the two eyes had acted in unison before one became sightless.

A blind eye has its pupil dilated as a rule. The dilatation is always somewhat less than that produced by atropine. The pupil may be bound down by old-standing synechiæ. If a patient is blind in both eyes, the pupils are, as a rule, both inordinately dilated.

109

Everyone knows the relative positions of his hand and face. If the malingerer is asked to put his hand straight out in front of him, not infrequently he puts it to the side. His hand may be taken and placed in different positions, and he is asked to look at it; even a blind man will attempt to follow the direction. Not so the malingerer; he looks away.

Test for Alleged Blindness in One Eye.—A very simple method of testing alleged blindness in one eye is as follows: the person being examined is asked to read simple, small printed words from a book. Suddenly, whilst he reads, a pencil is placed vertically in the middle of the page of print. If he sees with both eyes, he can read straight on, for he can see round the pencil, as it were—he really reads on each side of it. If one eye is blind he stops, for one or two words are hidden by the pencil.

Another efficient method is to place a lighted candle first to the extreme right and then to the extreme left side of the head, directing the patient to look *straight* forward. Assuming the left eye is said to be sightless, and he admits he sees the candle when it is on his left, then he sees with his left eye. The more prominent the bridge of his nose, the more reliable the test.

An effective method consists of placing a trial frame on the patient's nose. Opposite the admittedly good eye, let us say the right, a high + lens, say + 12, is placed. This puts it out of action. A plain glass is put in front of the left, the alleged blind eye. Print of a good size is suddenly placed in front of both eyes. If he now reads test types of any size the attempted deception is proved.

Fig. 5.

The Diaphragm Test for Binocular Vision.—Tests for the exposure of pretended blindness of one eye cannot be too

EXAMINATION OF THE EYE 111

numerous. One that is simple, yet efficient, is afforded by the use of a small apparatus invented by Mr. Bishop Harman. This consists of a flat black wooden ruler about 18 inches long and an inch wide (Fig. 5), at one end of which is set a vertical carrier (Fig. 6, T), in which small cards, 2 by $1\frac{3}{4}$ inches can be placed. At a distance of some 5 inches from the carrier holding the cards (and consequently 13 inches from the eye)

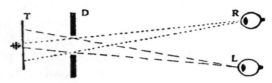

FIG. 6.—THE PATHS OF VISION.
T = Test-card ; D = screen with hole.

is placed the " diaphragm " (Fig. 6, D), after which the instrument is named. This diaphragm consists of a vertical screen pierced by a round hole $\frac{3}{4}$ inch in diameter.

In making the test, the patient is instructed to hold the ruler by the handle underneath it (Fig. 7, H), and the end of the ruler distant from the carrier is placed immediately beneath the patient's nose, upon his upper lip (Fig. 7, P). A card is inserted in the carrier (Fig. 6, T), and he is asked to look

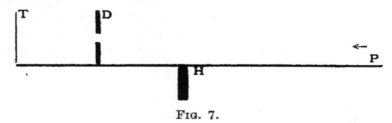

FIG. 7.

along the ruler through the hole in the screen (Fig. 6, D) to the card beyond, and describe what he sees on the card.

Test-cards of infinite variety may be used, showing printed matter, figures, paired capitals, etc. For the use of children, representations of well-known objects such as cats, dogs, birds, are provided. One very simple device consists of a card on which two small oblongs are printed, one oblong on the right, and the other on the left (Fig. 8). The oblongs are of different colours—a red and a green oblong on one card, for instance, and a blue and a yellow oblong on another. The cards are reversible, so that when fitted in the carrier, either a red or a green oblong may be uppermost, or on the left or right, as the examiner desires. Additional cards with black oblongs are provided for the use of colour-blind people.

Let us suppose the card chosen is that depicted in Fig. 8. It is obvious that the oblong of colour on the left is invisible to the left eye, but is visible to the right eye, and similarly that the oblong of colour on the right is invisible to the right eye, but is visible to the left ; so that if the patient is using both eyes, he will see both oblongs of colour. But if the patient has no sight in, say, the right eye, then the oblong of colour on the left will be invisible to him. Fig. 6 makes clear the paths of vision.

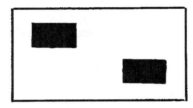

FIG. 8.—ARRANGEMENT OF TEST-CARD WITH COLOURED OBLONGS.

It is important that the patient's eyes should be under observation throughout the test. Any attempt at blinking so that he can get an idea of what he would see if one eye were really blind, can be discovered at once if the examiner stands in front of him and watches his eyes. The cards can be changed as often as required. For example, take a card with the letters *A* and *B* printed on it : if the patient is blind with the left eye he sees only the letter *A*, and this he sees with his right eye, and *vice versa*.

The instrument readily lends itself to variations of the primary experiment, some being of a more subtle character, suitable for the requirements of ophthalmic practice; but the above-described test is sufficient for the everyday needs of the medico-legal expert, because it is impossible for any malingerer to successfully evade a thorough application of it.

EXAMINATION OF THE EYE
113

If a patient is suspected of suppressing his ability to read test-types, the following experiment is helpful :

Place him 20 feet away from a pier-glass, upon which is fastened a card of Snellen's test-types, and induce him to indicate the line beyond which he can no longer read the letters. Then stand him 10 feet nearer the mirror, place a test-type card with similar letters of the same size, but printed backwards, in his hand to be held facing the pier-glass in front of his chest, and tell him to read the letters which he sees reflected on the mirror, as he is now standing at half the distance from the mirror that he was in the first place, should he be ignorant of the laws of reflection, he will usually, if a malingerer, boldly read double the number of lines he read in the first instance.

Defective sight following an accident calls for heavy damages, and great care and much patience must be exercised in all such cases. For a lad of tender years to deliberately and intentionally exaggerate slight loss of visual acuity must be somewhat unusual. The following case, occurring in the practice of the author, is of interest :

B. Y., aged thirteen, had his right eye injured, the result of lime accidentally entering it. There was some disfigurement, but it did not amount to much, and was obviously, from the point of view of damages, insignificant. The lad complained, however, of loss of sight.

He was tested with different-sized letters. His left eye was covered, and he was asked to read with the right eye type of a certain size at a measured distance. Intuitively it was felt that he was pretending not to be able to read what he really could. At first he said he could only read at 20 feet what he should have been able to read at 80 feet—that is to say, he only read one-quarter of the normal range. After repeated examinations, which consisted in covering the right eye and getting him to read with the left, and then quickly covering the left and getting him to read with the right, at the same time constantly changing the test-cards, he became confused, and, forgetting his part, he read letters which showed his vision had improved to one-third the normal range. It was now suggested that he could read even better still with a glass in front of his eye, to which he readily assented. With this he read half the normal range, but—the glass used was a *plain* one !

This was now pointed out to the lad himself, and to his father, and they were told that it was obvious he was trying to deceive. He then read letters indicating that, in a single hour, the vision of the right eye had so improved that he could now read two-thirds of the normal range. No amount of coaxing could make him read better than this, nor could he. But this amount of vision (two-thirds the normal range) with one

MALINGERING

eye, and perfect vision in the other, is practically normal vision ; indeed, the author frequently passes for service electric-car drivers who have no better vision than this. No doubt the accident had produced a mistiness of the fluid inside the eye, which had gradually cleared up. The lad had had at one time some defect of vision, but at the time of my examination it had practically disappeared. At the trial an ophthalmic surgeon gave evidence in his favour, and the jury awarded £25, which was fair, for there was some disfigurement, and he had suffered pain.

For the detection of pretended monocular vision a prism of either 10 or 12 degrees is very useful. There are various ways of using it. Let us assume that it is fraudulently contended that the right eye is blind. A pair of ordinary spectacle trial frames, which have circular flat pieces of metal hinged at the sides of the frame, is placed on the patient's nose. The right eye is covered by closing the hinged shutter over the right side. He is asked to read small print with the left eye through the edge of a prism. The effect is to cause some divergence of the left eye. Now the right or alleged blind eye is suddenly uncovered, and he is asked to continue reading. He is bound to see double for a moment. In order to see with both eyes he *must* overcome this divergence. If, therefore, at the moment of withdrawal of the shutter he suddenly hesitates, it shows that for the moment he had double vision, and is accommodating so that he may see with both eyes, whereas if the one eye is blind he goes on quietly reading with the other as before.

If the patient does, in fact, only see with one eye, he will fail, except after much practice, to put a pin into a small hole pierced in a piece of cardboard. He may be able to do this quite easily when using both eyes, but with monocular vision it is very difficult. The value of this test is easily proved by shutting one eye and trying the experiment.

With monocular vision stereoscopic vision is lost. By means of an ordinary stereoscope, it may be demonstrated with great certainty whether a patient is using one or both eyes. Most of the ordinary double photographs prepared for the stereoscope have a description of the subject printed at the bottom of one photo only—generally that opposite the right eye. This printed matter, when looked at through the stereoscope, is seen with the right eye only, and if, therefore, it is read, it proves that the right eye is not blind.

EXAMINATION OF THE EYE

Now, if the printed matter is covered over by means of a strip of paper, and the same or other words are written at the bottom of the photograph which is opposite the left eye, and the patient again reads the description, he sees also with his left eye.

A special stereoscopic picture has been prepared. Opposite the right eye there is a picture of a boy, and opposite the left that of a man. These viewed through the stereoscope are seen separately if the eyes are closed alternately, but if looked at with both eyes, the boy is seen on the man's back. The opportunity of catching out a malingerer with this device is obvious.

The following test is based on the fact that a sheet of glass of any particular colour allows rays of the same colour to pass through it, and therefore anything of the same colour cannot be seen. If, for instance, one wore green glasses, one would not see that grass was green.

Print on a piece of ordinary note-paper the letters THEORY. The alternate letters are to be made with a very soft red, and the others with a soft black pencil. Let us suppose the person to be examined says he cannot read with his right eye ; put a piece of ruby red glass (a piece of the red chimney of a photographic lantern suits admirably) in front of the left eye, and the patient is asked to *spell* the letters in front of him. If he spells THEORY, then he sees with the right or alleged blind eye. The ruby glass absolutely prevents the red letters being seen with the left eye, and as he *has* read the red letters, he must have done so with the right eye. It is very important not to mark the letters heavily, or the impression of the letters, apart from colour, will be left on the paper, and can easily be read ; hence the recommendation to use a soft red pencil ; red ink is not suitable.

Restriction of Field of Vision.—The perimeter is the usual instrument used for testing this condition, but its value is doubtful in cases of simulation, for the malingerer can often regulate his statements by noting certain parts of the instrument, such as a rivet or screw. The best method, therefore, is as follows :

Each eye must, of course, be examined separately. After eliminating the possibility of binocular vision, a slate or large

MALINGERING

sheet of paper is taken, and the field of vision is recorded first at 1 foot, then at 2, 3, 4, and 5 feet. Diminution of the field of vision will, of course, decrease normally with the distance, but the malingerer not infrequently repeats them as similar, and the well-known " tubular " field is sometimes elicited. This, of course, betrays him. It is well, however, to remember that the tubular field of vision is often found in true hysterics. This, however, can be negatived if the absence of the usual stigmata of this neurosis is proved.

Another method of testing the field of vision is to stand about 1 yard in front of the patient and direct him to keep his eyes steadily fixed on your own. He should then close his right eye while the observer closes his own left, and the patient should be asked to indicate when he catches sight of a small white object, such as a small square of cardboard inserted into the end of a penholder, which should be moved in a circular fashion and kept equidistant from the patient and observer, and should be gradually brought into the field of vision. If there is marked contraction of the field of vision, it should be accurately noted.

Fraudulent Use of Atropine or Eserine.—Beware of pupils which have been surreptitiously dilated by atropine or cocaine. Such a thing is not unknown in compensation cases. Atropine may be used to dilate the pupil in simulated epilepsy, but the duration of the paralysis of accommodation and dilatation of the pupil would, if the patient be kept under observation, clear away any doubt.

Conceivably eserine, or pilocarpine, might, with a similarly fraudulent object, be instilled into the eye prior to medical examination for the purpose of contracting the pupil. It must never be forgotten that, although comparatively rare, in a small number of cases the examinee may have the morphia habit.

Simulated Ptosis may be exposed by suddenly, and without hesitation or warning, asking the examinee to look at the ceiling. Involuntarily the lid rises.

The impossibility of feigning insensitiveness of the cornea is also to be remembered. In an assumed fit the eyes are kept closed, or are blinked at intervals, but the pupils react to light and accommodation.

EXAMINATION OF THE EYE

Defective vision is complained of as the result of accident in a very large number of cases. Most litigants, when enumerating the list of symptoms and inconveniences which they allege to be the result of their accident, complain that they do not see so well as they did before the accident. Now, diminished vision as the result of an accident may, of course, occur; but it must be clearly understood that no claim of this sort can be admitted unless it is set up and substantiated upon pathological grounds —viz., actual fundus, or other changes which can be definitely seen and sworn to. It is necessary in all these cases to test very carefully for myopia and hypermetropia, and, above all, to remember presbyopia.

In a remarkable number of cases middle-aged persons who allege failing sight as an additional ground of claim have been proved, with very little trouble, to be merely in need of plus lenses; it is only the enforced rest of convalescence and the general search round for symptoms, that have led them to observe a defect which, although previously existing, was unnoticed.

The most trying period through which a claimant has to pass is when the amount of damages is being arranged with the defendant or his insurance company. Many who, until the time of enforced idleness after, it may be, some trifling accident, have not noticed that their near point has been gradually receding for years, suddenly discover it then, and not unnaturally apply the *post hoc ergo propter hoc* argument with some persistence. One or two plus lenses produced at the psychological moment cause this item to disappear from the statement of claim.

It is well to bear in mind that total blindness in one eye may happen after head injuries, and very few symptoms be apparent. Two such cases have recently come under my observation. In both the patient was ill for but a few weeks, as the result of a fall on the head. Few marks of violence were visible, yet in each case the orbital plate of the frontal bone had been broken in the neighbourhood of the optic nerve, which was thereby either wholly or partially severed, with the result of complete and permanent loss of function—*i.e.*, total blindness of one eye.

CHAPTER VII

EXAMINATION OF THE EAR

PRETENDED deafness is somewhat difficult to detect, and its discovery depends on the amount of expert knowledge which can be applied, and much also depends upon the method and skill with which the examination is conducted.

An old-standing deafness can be diagnosed from the voice. The characteristic monotone of the deaf is only found in pronounced and genuine cases. A man who is deaf in one ear and who wishes to hear, naturally and involuntarily turns his head towards the speaker. Vowel sounds are better heard than consonants. Deep notes carry better than high, and a clearly articulated whisper carries better than words pronounced loudly. No man who can hear ordinary conversation at 19 or 20 feet can justly say he is deaf.

I once heard a Judge very neatly catch out a reluctant juryman, who complained that he was too deaf to serve. " I regret," said the Judge in kindly, sympathetic, and subdued tones, " to hear of your affliction. How long have you suffered ?" The innocent ruse was quite apparent to everyone but the unhappy juror, who promptly replied that he had been deaf for a long time. " But," said the Judge, " you heard me just now ; you will do nicely. I cannot excuse you."

Before proceeding to the examination of the hearing power in a case of suspected feigned deafness, the meatus should be examined by reflected light. It is well to assume the deafness, and to let the patient understand, both by manner and pitch of voice, that it is taken for granted. If wax is present, this should be removed forthwith. The claimant's doctor, if present, should be asked to do this. It is *never* wise to perform

118

EXAMINATION OF THE EAR 119

even so simple and necessary an act without first obtaining (preferably in writing) the claimant's consent to do so.

Cerumen which has long been present is often difficult to remove, and may even necessitate a delay of twenty-four hours, during which a weak solution of bicarbonate of soda should be frequently instilled into the ear, to facilitate the removal of the wax. This is, of course, an inconvenience, but thoroughness is the keynote of all medico-legal examinations which are of any value.

> B. Z.—On one occasion, when I was examining a claimant at the office of a solicitor who did a large business in Workmen's Compensation cases, it was stated by the doctor retained by the solicitor that the claimant was deaf and had diminished vision. He had had a head injury, and the inference was apparent. The difficulty with his sight was obviously presbyopia, and this, when it was put to him, the doctor admitted. The otoscope revealed the presence of cerumen, which, when it was discovered, the doctor also admitted, and so the case gradually crumbled away.

It is a matter of much importance for the examining medical man to take with him to all examinations the necessary instruments which he may require for a thorough examination (see p. 60).

Cerumen which has been long embedded in a meatus is often associated with a temporary blocking of the Eustachian tube, and Politzer's bag often instantly removes persisting deafness of this nature.

There are two varieties of deafness one may have to deal with. First, the result of injury to the sound-conducting apparatus—*i.e.*, the tympanum and ossicles ; second, the result of the derangement of the internal ear, known as nerve deafness.

Normally, when a tuning-fork is made to vibrate and is held opposite the outer canal of the ear, it is heard for a longer period than if the base is applied to the bone behind the ear. If the sound-conducting apparatus is *damaged*, the tuning-fork, when placed against the skull, will be heard for a longer time than when it is placed opposite the external ear. Should the tympanum and ossicles be wholly *destroyed*, the tuning-fork, when placed on the skull, will be heard, for sound will still reach the brain through the bones of the skull.

The appearance of the tympanum is important : a ground-

120 MALINGERING

glass appearance is often associated with a gradual, slow sclerosis of the connective tissue in the middle ear, with gradual and increasing deafness. It is, of course, well known that rupture of the tympanum does not necessarily carry with it appreciably diminished hearing. The examiner's capacity to estimate the effect, from a hearing-point of view, of abnormalities in the tympanum depends upon his knowledge of ear disease.

Riveters, boiler-makers, and artillerymen, from the nature of their occupation, are often partially deaf.

Rupture of the Tympanum.—There are several causes of a solution of continuity of the drum of the ear, but the two which interest us most are, first, rupture caused by air pressure —*i.e.*, by a severe blow over the outside ear—and, second, rupture as the result of fracture of the base of the skull. If the tympanum has been ruptured it is of much importance to discover which of these causes has produced the condition. This is not really a question of malingering, but the claimant is sure to assume the worst, and, if wrong in his assumption, the consequences to the defendant are the same as if he were intentionally malingering. A blow over the ear which ruptures the drum must, of course, be a severe one, but the amount of resulting hæmorrhage is never great, often amounting only to a few drops of blood. If the wound is kept aseptic, it rapidly heals and does not produce deafness. If, on the other hand, it suppurates, very serious immediate and remote consequences may follow. The amount of hæmorrhage accompanying rupture of the tympanum which is the result of fracture of the base is always great. The important diagnostic point between rupture of the tympanum caused by a blow on the ear, and rupture produced by the much more serious condition of fractured base is, that in the latter condition the hæmorrhage is accompanied by a discharge of cerebro-spinal fluid. The usual symptoms of fractured base are hæmorrhage from nose, mouth, ear, and sometimes bruising behind the ear, which appears a few days after the accident.

Perforation or rupture of the drum is much more common as a result of disease than of accident. It is a matter of the utmost importance to tell whether a rupture is recent or of old standing, and this can only be done if an opportunity is afforded

EXAMINATION OF THE EAR 121

of examining the ear immediately after an accident. Rupture which is recent is fairly apparent, but a rupture that is a week old is frequently indistinguishable from an old perforation due to disease.

TABLE SHOWING THE DIFFERENCE IN SIGNS OF A RECENT RUPTURE AS COMPARED WITH OLD-STANDING DISEASE.

Recent.	Old-Standing Disease.
Edges, clear linear cut radiating from centre to edge.	Edges thickened by scar tissue.
Not adherent to inner wall of ear.	Often adherent to inner wall of ear.
Edges bruised and covered with dried crusts of blood. No pus.	Much pus everywhere.
No inflammation except at rupture.	Whole of the drum inflamed, and whole of tympanum, middle ear, and meatus may be inflamed.
Slight deafness, which passes off when tympanum heals.	Varies from slight deafness to complete.
Middle ear escapes.	Middle ear infected.
Rupture does not take place without an accident.	A hole in the tympanum, common in childhood from disease.

Result of Fracture of Petrous-Temporal.—Fracture of the petrous-temporal bone passing through the internal auditory meatus would almost certainly involve both the seventh (facial) and eighth (auditory) cranial nerves, seeing that they run together at this point for about $\frac{1}{2}$ inch ; therefore deafness from this cause is generally accompanied by some facial paralysis.*

Nerve Deafness.—In nerve deafness caused by the derangement of the internal ear, if a tuning-fork is applied to the bone behind the ear, the time during which the vibrations can be

* It will be remembered that the seventh and eighth cranial nerves enter the internal auditory meatus, and run together as far as the bottom of that meatus. At this point the eighth (auditory) pierces foramina which conduct it into the internal ear. The seventh (facial) continues its course alone in the canal, and emerges from the base of the skull through the stylomastoid foramen.

122 MALINGERING

heard is less than the period for which they can be heard when it is applied outside the meatus. Rinne's test is therefore positive. The fork is heard for a relatively less time in the case of a person with normal hearing. If the tuning-fork is placed in the middle of the forehead (Weber's test), the sound is heard more loudly on the normal side. This is the converse of the result in middle and external ear deafness, in which, of course, the vibrations are heard more loudly on the affected side. In a case of nerve deafness the use of Galton's whistle will demonstrate considerable loss of high tones, and the patient often complains of distressing noises in the head. If the usual signs of nerve deafness, such as bone conduction being the less effective, are present, and yet the patient admits that he hears the highest notes of the scale as plainly as he hears the lowest, further tests should be studiously applied.

There are many causes of nerve deafness ; probably the most common are extension of mischief from the middle ear and otosclerosis. Other frequent causes are traumatism (where fracture of the skull has involved the auditory nerve), syphilis, rheumatism, and gout. Nerve deafness may also come on suddenly after such infectious diseases as enteric, influenza, and diphtheria ; and it may occur transitorily from the use of drugs such as quinine, salicylates, and so on.

Complete Deafness in One Ear.—This is very common after accidents. Assuming that deafness is alleged in the left ear, a tuning-fork is placed behind the left ear, and the right ear is closed. Even though the left ear is completely deaf, the vibrations will be conducted by bone to the sound ear and be heard, yet a malingerer will frequently deny all knowledge of the sound.

Deafness in One Ear only.—If, when the sound ear is apparently closed by placing the whole hand over it, but leaving a chink between the fingers, the examinee states that he hears nothing, there is sufficient evidence of malingering.

Total Deafness.—It must be seldom, indeed, that anyone would have the temerity to allege complete deafness when he did, in fact, hear well with both ears. If any such case arose, it would be very easy of detection, for obviously no sane man could successfully keep up for any length of time such an abnormal and repulsive existence.

EXAMINATION OF THE EAR 123

Method of Testing Hearing.—This must be done with much accuracy. One ear should be closed either by means of Hawkesley's clay (often used by officers in target practice) or by insisting upon the palm of the hand accurately covering the meatus of the ear and being firmly pressed against it. The patient is then blindfolded, and he is tested at varying distances by means of a watch, tuning-fork, or whispering. The results must be definitely recorded. If malingering is being attempted, it is impossible for accuracy to be maintained, and the recorded results will vary in an amusing way. The hearing distances will be found to gradually increase as the testing continues. For instance, the patient is asked whether he hears the watch at, say, 12 feet. If he answers in the negative, the examiner noiselessly approaches the patient, until, perhaps, at 2 feet he admits that he hears it. This is noted, and the experiment repeated several times. The bandage covering his eyes is removed, and the whole experiment is fully explained. The eyes are again blindfolded, and the experiment repeated. At every stage a careful record should be made in writing. In time the examinee becomes very uncertain of his ground, and his answers become so inaccurate as to prove he is not speaking the truth.

The Stethoscope Test.—I am satisfied that what has been described as the stethoscope test is wholly unreliable. The method suggested is to place the earpieces of a binaural stethoscope into the ears of the examinee, and to speak to him from the chest-piece ; the tube leading to the sound or hearing ear is pressed between the finger and thumb, so that no sound is transmitted to the hearing ear. Questions are now put, and if they are answered the allegation is that they *must* have been heard by the alleged deaf ear through the indiarubber tube leading to that ear ; and as an aurist writes : " The malingerer will soon be caught out." Unfortunately, it is not the malingerer who is " caught out," but the examiner, as anyone can easily prove to himself by trying the experiment. As a matter of fact, it is impossible with an ordinary stethoscope to prevent sound being transmitted, however tightly the earpieces fit the ear. The examinee, in fact, hears quite easily if both indiarubber tubes are blocked, and the test, though pretty theoretically, is useless.

The idea, however, is a good one, and I have had prepared for me by the Holborn Surgical Instrument Company an instrument (Fig. 9) which, though somewhat clumsy, is perfectly satisfactory. Instead of the ordinary small bone end-pieces of the binaural stethoscope, there are two glass bell-shaped receivers which are made large enough to contain the whole auricle. The free edge is fitted with an indiarubber cushion, which is capable of being inflated, thus permitting accurate adjustment, and effectually preventing sound being transmitted

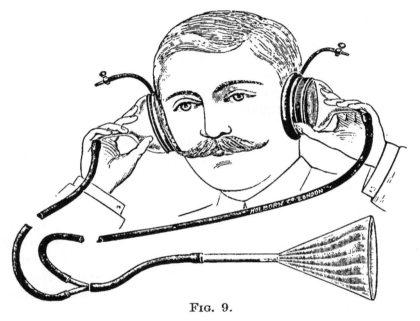

Fig. 9.

between the instrument and the side of the head. This latter arrangement is exactly similar to that which is found in all mouth-pieces of nitrous oxide gas apparatus. The summit of each bell-shaped receiver tapers off into a short glass tube, which may be seen in the diagram supporting the ring and little fingers of both the right and the left hand. To these tubes are attached two pieces of indiarubber tubing, each 9½ feet long. The other ends of the rubber tubing are joined to a Y-shaped metal connection, the tail of which is attached to an ordinary glass funnel by a piece of rubber some 6 inches long.

As in Blackwell's binaural stethoscope, all constrictions are

EXAMINATION OF THE EAR

avoided where the rubber joins both the glass bell-shaped receivers, the Y-shaped connection, and the glass funnel.

The three orifices of the Y-tube connection and the glass funnel have knife edges, so that there is no lessening of the calibre anywhere. The sectional area of the indiarubber tubing between the glass funnel and the Y connection is equal to the sectional area of *one* of the longer tubes. There is thus no narrowing of the lumen of the tube from the ear of the patient to the mouth of the examiner when one of the long tubes is compressed in the experiment about to be described.

The long tube leading to the right ear is of red rubber ; the left is of black. Now, if the examinee holds the glass receivers close against his ears, and the examiner, standing apart the full length of the tube, speaks into the glass funnel in a low voice, it is obvious that sound can only be transmitted to either ear *through* the instrument. Let us suppose that the patient who is being examined claims to be deaf in the right ear. The black tube is pinched, and he is asked in a low tone whether the instrument fits comfortably. If he answers the question, it is obvious that he does, in fact, hear with the right—that is, the alleged deaf ear.

Should he be so wary as to avoid this trap, a constant succession of questions passed down either of the tubes, not necessarily in accurate rotation, will certainly lead to his downfall if the deafness is non-existent. If a list is previously prepared showing the sequence of the tests to be made, when replies are received and are noted, they are conclusive proof of the truth or otherwise of the allegation of infirmity.

From actual experiment I find that if the indiarubber tubing is too short, sound is, in spite of the arrangement of the apparatus, transmitted by aerial conduction, presumably through the skull ; therefore, the tubes should be of the length above described. Practically one avoids all possibility of transmission except through the tubes by speaking from another room, the door of which is left just sufficiently ajar to avoid kinking the tubes.

This also facilitates the manipulation of the tubes so that the examinee cannot frame his answers according to the tube he sees pinched.

CHAPTER VIII

EXAMINATION OF THE BACK

Pain in the Back.—This is perhaps the most common affection for which compensation is claimed in the Law Courts. Lumbago is a popular description of pain in the muscles, joints, and fascial sheaths of the back. It is common, has often a very acute onset, and frequently shows itself first when an attempt is made to rise from a stooping position. We can therefore easily understand that even an honest man engaged in some hard manual toil, when suddenly affected with an acute, sharp pain in the back, readily assumes that it must be due to some effort he has made. A dishonest man, with the Workmen's Compensation Act before his eyes, can without much difficulty remember a history of some effort, strain, or sudden slip, which will account for his pain. A great difficulty in dealing with these cases is that in a large, fleshy individual, as these people often are, it is far from easy to make a satisfactory examination of this part of the body, and practically all we have to go upon is the man's own statement, which is of little value, that he experiences pain at some particular spot. Broadly speaking, we have to make up our minds on two points : the first is whether the pain is real or assumed, and the second whether it is due to disease or accident.

To take the second point first, the most frequent affection of the back is lumbago. The distinguishing features of this are that it is bilateral, widespread, relieved by pressure, and mostly experienced when making certain movements ; that it usually yields to treatment, rest in bed, salicylates, massage, and·so forth ; and that there is generally a history of the patient's having worked in a damp and unhealthy place.

126

EXAMINATION OF THE BACK 127

C. A., aged thirty-five, was sent to me for examination in respect of an alleged accident on duty, for which he had been on the sick-list twenty-eight days. He said that whilst at work he felt something " give way " in his back. Admittedly he had had no medical attendance during the past sixteen days. He reported himself unfit to visit me, and was examined at his own house. Later, although reported as fit to do so, he again refused to visit me when ordered, and declined to furnish a medical certificate from his doctor unless his employer paid for it. Finally, he was brought to my house in a cab.

Examination.—He was a healthy, powerful man, who showed no signs of disease. There was on his back the remains of a plaster. On the pretext of removing this, his back was vigorously scrubbed, and he made no remarks as to tenderness. Later, although he said he could not stoop,· I caused him to touch his toes on two occasions. He complained of pain when touched anywhere. Whilst his attention was taken up with the question as to whether the electric current was or was not flowing, he made no complaint of firm pressure with the metal electrodes along the spine.

He was obviously deliberately malingering, and I certified him as fit to resume duty at once. He returned to work a few days later, did light duty for two days, and then stopped. After a few days he resumed work at window-cleaning, but continued to attend the electrical department of a hospital. He was submitted to me for re-examination. I arranged for the presence at the consultation of the surgeon in charge of the electrical department of the hospital he was attending. The man now complained of pain in his loins. As the result of careful physical examination, we satisfied ourselves that there was nothing the matter with him. When told that he would therefore have to go back to full duty, he at once agreed, saying he was " happy to do so." He evidently felt the game was up. This employee had deliberately malingered ; his defiance of authority, and his readiness to take full duty when detected, proved him to be a most undesirable servant. He was therefore dismissed.

Result.—He commenced arbitration proceedings against his employers, and the case was heard at the County Court four and a half months later, resulting in a decision in favour of the employers.

A few weeks subsequently I was examining one of this man's fellow-workmen, who volunteered the following interesting piece of information : that C. A. informed him, *three days prior to the alleged straining of his back,* that he was suffering from lumbago !

Other less common conditions are affections of the kidney and spinal cord, internal growths, and, in women, diseases of the generative organs, all of which should be kept in mind and, if necessary, examined for.

Movable Kidney.—It is impossible that any exertion, however violent, could displace a normally fixed kidney. Judging from a considerable number of cases in which I have known

128   MALINGERING

this condition alleged as a result of traumatism it may be stated with some assurance that clinically the condition must be accompanied by other and grave signs of injury.

Displacement of a kidney is attended by severe pain over the renal area, not infrequently by bruising, and hæmorrhage into the bladder, and, as a rule, a very considerable amount of shock.

It will be remembered that normally the kidney cannot be felt by palpation, but that if it is displaced it can be felt between the palpating hands during the act of expiration following a deep inspiration.

Some men, and a great many women, have a displaced kidney without knowing it, and in a large number of cases it produces no symptoms. Not infrequently, however, the condition is accidentally brought to light in the course of a thorough examination after an accident. The discovery of pain in the renal area is followed by a careful examination; a displaced kidney is found, pain is admitted, there may be some external bruising, and the hasty and serious diagnosis is at once made that the patient is suffering from a traumatic displacement of the kidney, and large damages are of course claimed. Such cases ought not to be considered fraudulent. The mistake is not that of the patient.

The More Usual Back Injuries.—With regard to accident, the most usual injury is a tearing of the fibres of some of the lumbo-sacral muscles, or a sprain of one of the numerous vertebral joints, or of the sacro-lumbar joint itself. In such cases there is a history of an unusual strain or a slip whilst carrying some heavy burden, a sense as of something having given way, and acute pain at a definite spot.

The affection is therefore almost invariably unilateral. Such a pain is likely to last, if at all severe, several weeks.

A fall or a blow on the back, producing the physical conditions which I have just referred to, runs a very definite course, and the symptoms and their duration correspond to those of similar injuries produced in other parts of the body. Not so, however, when an injury—say, to the head, shoulder, or knee—is accompanied by backache, for the pain is then but the expression of a mental state, and has no organic basis in the spine, but is merely referred to it.

EXAMINATION OF THE BACK 129

The treatment for this latter condition is psycho-therapeutic, and this particular department of medicine is not only difficult from the point of view of the medical man, but is one which demands the active co-operation of the patient, a co-operation which many of us in our particular class of work find too often conspicuous by its absence.

The diagnosis may sometimes be made easier by the help of a skiagram, which may reveal the presence of periosteal elevations where muscular attachments have been torn from the bone. It is, however, when we come to determine whether the pain complained of is real or assumed that our worst difficulties commence. The first thing to do is to get the applicant to point out with one finger the exact spot where he feels the pain. This is marked with a blue pencil, and after a little interval he is again asked to indicate the spot. He should not see where he is pointing, and, if the pain is an assumed one, he may point out a spot several inches away from the first one. He will probably complain of the lightest touch, and his attention must be distracted by various means. One way is to ask him whether the other side hurts him, at the same time applying firm pressure to it. His attention being diverted to the sound side, it may be possible to put considerable pressure on the affected side without eliciting evidence of pain. Another method is to leave the back altogether and go over his chest with the stethoscope, commencing in front. On auscultating the back, it will quite likely be found that the claimant will bear firm pressure with the stethoscope on a spot previously declared painful to the lightest touch. A third and most valuable method is the use of the battery, as described in Chapter XII.

If a man really has pain in the upper part of his back, this can generally be elicited by bending the head forward, while the trunk is held rigid, thus stretching the vertebral muscles, and if it can be produced without pain the probabilities are that the pain alleged is imaginary.

With regard to movements of the spine, a claimant will probably declare that anything but the slightest movement is painful to him. He should be asked to bend forward as far as he can without causing pain, and the amount of flexion should be noted. He should subsequently be asked several times to bend his spine while he is engaged in conversation and his

9

MALINGERING

attention distracted, when it will generally be found that the amount of movement made varies widely. Other useful points are to watch the claimant as he unfastens and fastens his boots or gets into his clothes, and casually to drop something on the floor on the chance that he may pick it up. Simple ruses like these will often succeed, though their chances are becoming more and more remote, as applicants are now more thoroughly coached in the parts they have to play. It is well to try to get a man to bend his back by one of these means directly he enters the room and before the *formal* examination begins.

C. B.—On one occasion, when examining a back which was said to be stiff, I dropped my pencil intentionally, early in the interview, and the claimant nimbly picked it up. Later on, when examining his back, he alleged that all stooping was impossible, and would not even attempt to bend his back. I said nothing, but had him cross-examined at the trial on the incident. He then swore that no such incident occurred. I believe he had never noticed, or had no recollection of, the little courtesy he unwittingly paid me.

In a report of a case by Dr. Handson, which was subsequently submitted to me for an opinion, I find the following astute observation, which I quote literally :

" The situation of the pain varies on the two sides. On the right side it is extremely localized, and is brought on either by movement of the joint or by pressure. From his exclamations and facial contortions, the pain amounts to agony, but it had one very peculiar feature.

" To test him, I suggested that if the pressure was localized to the tender spot, the pain was very intense ; but if by putting all my fingers of both hands together I made a long line of pressure, the centre of which line of pressure was over the tender spot, then, no matter how hard I pressed, though, of course, the tender spot was pressed on, there was no pain. It was interesting to find, as I suggested, that the latter experiment was painless.

" Later, again with my fingers in line, I pressed very lightly with all my fingers but one. With this one I pressed hard on the tender spot, but again he agreed that there was no pain. I then lifted all the fingers but the heavily pressing one, when, as before, only one finger being in place, the agonized contortions recommenced.

" The test discredits there being any pain on pressure worth considering."

Sometimes, as the result of a blow on the sacrum or coccyx, organic nerve disease is alleged. Now, the cord ends at the lower border of the first or second lumbar vertebra, and it is im-

EXAMINATION OF THE BACK 131

possible to have any pyramidal trouble as the direct result of a lesion of the sacrum. The only possible way in which anything serious can be brought about would be an injury to the cauda equina, and, following this, an inflammatory lesion travelling upwards towards the cord; but it must be remembered that before a condition of this sort could be brought about one must of necessity have a considerable amount of meningitis and neuritis, with consequent wasting of the muscles.

The above possibility, even in the absence of any symptoms, is by no means too far-fetched for suggestion in the witness-box with a certain class of witnesses, and it is well, therefore, to remember that in a case of this sort the presence or absence of degeneration of muscular tissues is of very great moment.

History.—C. C., a ground-workman in the employ of one of the Metropolitan Borough Councils, stated that a tar-tank collided with the barrow he was wheeling, knocking him over, and injuring his back and abdomen. I was asked by the Borough Council, nineteen months after the occurrence, to examine him, as he had not even then resumed work. The examination took place in the presence of a medical man, who is also a lawyer.

Examination.—C. C. told me he had difficulty in passing water, and had pain in the back and hip. I asked him to pass water in my presence, and from the smallness of the stream suspected stricture. He admitted having had gonorrhœa a long time ago, and the appearance of the urine, which I took home and examined, was clearly indicative of an old-standing condition consistent with gonorrhœa and stricture ; it was also consistent with enlarged prostate gland, but wholly inconsistent with any condition which might arise from traumatism.

There was no physical sign of injury to the hip ; he allowed, without protest, free flexion of the thigh upon the abdomen, and rotation outwards of the hip to a degree incompatible with the presence of any disease in the joint.

There was no evidence of any sort to support the allegation of pain in the back. Pain is a subjective symptom, and when complained of for a long period in a medico-legal case of this sort, with nothing objective to account for it, may not unreasonably be viewed with grave suspicion. Here was a man who complained of pain in his back whose muscles were not wasted, who early in the examination bent his back freely, touched his toes, and took off his boots with perfect freedom ; but who, when his attention was drawn to his back, stated that he could not bend it at all, and when pressed to do so bent a little way, and then said it was impossible to bend farther. It was particularly interesting to note that when the whole examination was over, upon my suddenly re-entering the room I found him with his back freely bent in the act of lacing his boot whilst the foot rested on the floor.

132　MALINGERING

He complained of pain in his back on the slightest pressure, but when his attention was centred upon the question as to whether the faradic current of my battery was or was not flowing, he allowed firm pressure with the handle of the electrode upon the same area without protest. Again, whilst the battery was buzzing loudly, unknown to him the current was turned off by a switch in the handle of the electrode, and he still complained bitterly of the current, thinking, no doubt, that he ought to make a complaint if the current was being applied to the spot which he had alleged to be tender. I reported that he was neither accurate nor truthful, but a malingerer.

Result.—Arrangements were made for an examination by a medical referee of great experience, who agreed with me, and supported my evidence at the hearing of the arbitration proceedings.

At the hearing the medical assessor, who sat with the Judge, said he agreed with our evidence, and judgment was given for the Borough Council.

History.—C. D., a labourer, aged thirty-four, was said to have strained himself whilst assisting to lift a pail over a wall. He was taken to hospital, but not detained. This occurred six and a half months previous to the date on which he was sent to me by an insurance company for examination on behalf of the employers.

Examination.—When he entered the consulting-room, and during the first part of the examination, he held himself stiffly, but gradually assumed an easy posture as the examination proceeded.

He told me that on bending or twisting the body he had a pain in his back, and that he was unable to lift weights.

He complained when his back was touched even lightly. No anatomical change was found in the muscles of the back. With some difficulty he was induced to lift a heavy gipsy coal-scuttle, weighing 28 lbs., and it was perfectly obvious from his manner of doing so that the alleged difficulty was a mere pretence. When asked to move, bend from side to side, and stoop freely, he gave no sign of muscular restraint or painful action. It was noticeable that when he thought he was unobserved the movements were much more free than they had been in the first instance. As an evidence of his want of veracity, it may be mentioned that when the battery was applied, he repeatedly said he felt pain from the current when, in fact, it was not running.

Every organ of this man's body was healthy. There was no evidence forthcoming that he was suffering ; on the other hand, there was the strongest presumption, not only from the facts disclosed by my examination but on theoretical grounds also, that any strain (or even tear) of tendon or muscle which this man might at one time have sustained must have wholly recovered many weeks previously.

Here was a strong man, with well-developed muscles ready and waiting to be used, who had made up his mind he would not use them so long as he could obtain 16s. 9d. a week without exerting himself.

EXAMINATION OF THE BACK 133

Result.—In this case the employers entered into an agreement with the claimant to pay him a sum of £18, which agreement, when filed with the Court, was objected to on the grounds that it had been obtained by undue influence, and that the amount was inadequate. As it turned out, the man ultimately accepted a lesser amount—£15 —than that mentioned in the agreement.

It cannot be denied that grave organic disease may follow a jar to the spinal cord, but it is Ferrier's experience that the pre-existence of syphilis in all such cases is a *sine qua non*. This authority states that in his experience locomotor ataxia, disseminated sclerosis, paralysis agitans, or progressive muscular atrophy, may follow a jar to the cord, provided a syphilitic taint is present.

Railway Spine.—What in the days of Erichsen used to be called " railway spine " or " concussion of the spine," and was supposed to be based on organic changes in the spinal cord, is now known as " hysterical spine," in which there is alleged hypersensitiveness over various areas, generally the sacro-lumbar region. It is, in truth, merely a psychical condition, which is particularly intractable to treatment. There can be no doubt that in former days railway companies were mulcted in large sums, and that introspection and gross exaggeration brought heavy damages in their train. Modern methods of psycho-therapeutics would have led to different results.

In the ordinary so-called " railway spine " there is no proof that the spinal cord has been jarred ; indeed, the analogy between concussion of the brain and alleged concussion of the spinal cord is far too readily accepted. It is true that the brain fully fills the brain-case, and that a jar upon the skull directly jars the brain ; accordingly this organ at post-mortem examinations is often found to be lacerated. The anatomical relations of the spinal cord are, however, entirely different. The cord does not nearly fill the spinal canal, but is surrounded by a large quantity of cerebro-spinal fluid, and is suspended in the fluid by lateral ligaments at intervals throughout its whole length. The cord is thus particularly well protected, and it is extremely doubtful whether concussion of the spinal cord can ever occur.

" **Workmen's Compensation** " **Back.**—A working-man told a friend of mine that, prior to his visit for the purpose of examination, he got the following sage advice : " ' When yer get 'urt,' 'e

134 MALINGERING

says, ' say it's yer back ; the doctors can't never get round yer back.' "

However true this statement may have been formerly, the mere allegation of pain in the back is not such a bogey to some of us *now* as it was in the past, but experience teaches that this is still the mental attitude of a large number of those who are prone to malinger.

Rheumatism and Rheumatoid Diseases.—A careful study of the possibilities of deception in this particular region will well repay the student. Rheumatoid arthritis, osteo-arthritis, and spondylitis deformans are coming to the front as conditions which are said to be caused or increased by traumatism. We are all familiar with the bent spine and characteristic gait of the elderly workman who is the subject of the deforming effects of what, for want of a better name, must be called " rheumatism."

Rigidity of the spine occurs mostly in men, and they are nearly always employed in manual labour. It has been variously attributed to rheumatism, gonorrhœa, syphilis, hereditary tendencies, and to injury ; but a very large number of cases are found in which the disease cannot be traced to any of these causes, and where hard laborious work itself seems to determine the onset. When the work involves keeping the back bent for considerable periods on end, rigidity is very prone to come on, as in gardeners and agricultural labourers. Most of us have seen in country lanes this spinal rigidity in old, infirm labourers, where no question of injury or of the Workmen's Compensation Act ever arises. Pathologically, the condition seems to consist of osteophytic outgrowths from the free margins of the vertebræ and from the intervertebral articulations. If these bony outgrowths are extensive, they sometimes meet, producing ankylosis of neighbouring vertebræ.

There may be, in addition, ossification of the ligamenta subflava, and, indeed, of any of the ligaments of the spinal cord. Ossification not infrequently penetrates the capsules of the intervertebral joints, and of the joints between the ribs and the vertebræ.

These ossifications are well shown by X-rays, which in these cases are invaluable. This condition, although usually confined to the spine, may affect other joints. There is no mistaking the symptoms : the spine is rigid either as a whole or in part, and

EXAMINATION OF THE BACK

may be straight as in the well-known poker-back, or bent (as is sometimes seen) to a painful curve. The disease, as already indicated, sometimes extends to the hips and shoulders, and abnormal sensations, such as numbness, pins-and-needles, formication, etc., are no doubt due to pressure on the nerves as they leave the foramina.

Rarely indeed do we have to deal with a condition of this sort as the result of accident. The symptoms of spondylitis deformans have been set out in some detail for the purpose of indicating the type of the disease which in a milder degree is often met with on thorough examination of any patient, be he the subject of an accident or not. The occupation, for instance, of a carman predisposes to stiffness of the spine, possibly by inevitable exposure, or it may be by the incessant jolting of the springless vans that are driven.

Spondylitis deformans may, and apparently often does, exist for many years without any symptoms other than the moderate amount of backache, which is so often attributable merely to work. This condition is, of course, liable to exacerbation from even a slight accident, or it may be from prolonged exposure alone. There is no doubt that in anyone whose back is becoming stiff a jar, fall, or blow is liable to produce a certain amount of temporary disability, which is commonly attributed to lumbago, sciatica, etc.

What frequently happens is that a healthy man of forty or forty-five with commencing rheumatism of his spine gets just such a knock or a blow as any member of a football team may meet with during a match ; but, remembering the Workmen's Compensation Act, the workman puts himself on the sick-list, keeps his back stiff, becomes introspective and self-centred, and then draws from clubs and insurance companies sick-pay which, in the aggregate, may amount to as much as, if not more than, the wages he earns whilst at work. It is estimated that probably five millions of people will, under the National Health Insurance Act, be insured in more than one society. It is illegal to insure in two *approved* friendly societies, but there are, of course, many others.

When such a case enters into the purview of contending lawyers, the back is X-rayed, small osteophytic outgrowths may here and there be found in his spine, and much is, of course,

MALINGERING

made of them. The Judge and jury, not appreciating the significance of these slight changes as shown in the X-ray photograph, are unwittingly misled, and damages follow.

The same condition occurs not infrequently without any accident whatever. If in middle life a man who feels his back beginning to get stiff gives up every form of exercise and all free movement, the back will in many cases become gradually more and more fixed, until free movement without pain becomes impossible. There can be little doubt that the pain or inconvenience from a slight jar will pass off under proper treatment—*i.e.*, rest. Most cases of this sort can be cut short within a few days, or at most a few weeks, if the medical man in charge has the courage to speak frankly, and the claimant has sufficient incentive to return to work before he becomes obsessed with the idea of an injured back.

If a working man finds his back stiff, and he believes that it is stiff as the result of an accident whilst at work, he will as a rule systematically not bend his back if by any chance it hurts him to do so. A workman ought to understand that it is his duty, not only to himself, but also to his employer, to put up with some slight inconvenience, and return to work for the sake of maintaining his efficiency.

As a rule, at this stage his apathy has no relationship to the question of malingering. It is difficult for a half-educated man to understand that even painful exercises may be remedial. Moreover, it must be remembered that he probably knows of a certain number of serious back injuries which fellow-workmen have met with, and not unnaturally he is apprehensive.

C. E. stated that, as the result of an accident three years and eight months previously, he had been unable to work at his occupation of a scaffolder's labourer.

This man had been subjected to many examinations by various medical men, and was said to be suffering from traumatic neurasthenia.

I was asked to examine him in conjunction with a surgeon of eminence.

At the time of our examination, he complained of pain between his shoulders and on each side of his neck ; of stiffness in his neck and the upper part of the back ; of giddiness on walking or sitting still ; that his head would swim when he lay down ; that he felt fidgety and irritable ; that he was " nervous as a kitten," and constantly apprehensive of something behind him. Later in the course of the interview, and obviously as an afterthought, he added that he vomited every

EXAMINATION OF THE BACK

morning, that his appetite was bad, that he had sleepless nights, and that he passed " matter " from his bowels.

He gave his age as forty-seven, but looked older, and apparently had a large family, ranging in age from twenty-six to three and a half years.

Examination.—He was well nourished, his eye was bright, his skin clear, and circulation good. He held his back stiffly. In the course of the examination he allowed considerable movement of the lumbar spine; but when picking up his boots at the close of the examination, he did so by kneeling on the ground and going through contortions which were quite unnecessary, considering his own statements with regard to his back. The stiffness in the cervical region was, however, a definite symptom, and an X-ray photograph of that region of the spine, taken at my instigation, showed definite ankylosis between the fourth and fifth cervical vertebræ. This was due to a definite organic lesion known as " spondylitis deformans "—a disease of slow progress, which chiefly affects manual labourers past middle age. It is generally associated with similar changes in other joints. In this case there was a certain amount of osteo-arthritis, a similar condition, in one of the claimant's shoulders. The relationship of this condition to injury is always an extremely difficult one to determine ; it often occurs in patients in whom there is no suggestion of injury, but occasionally it appears to follow a definite injury. In this particular instance it appeared to have reached its highest development in an area of the spine (cervical) remote from the part injured, which, according to the history of the case, was the lower part of the spine.

The claimant's account of himself and his condition was full of inconsistencies, and we believed his account of many of his symptoms to be distinctly exaggerated. Whether he suffered from traumatic neurasthenia, as alleged, immediately after the accident, three years and eight months previously, it was difficult to say, having regard to the lapse of time ; but it appeared extremely improbable that any patient, after suffering so long from severe traumatic neurasthenia, should look so well as this man did at his examination.

It appeared to be a case where spondylitis deformans had gradually developed during a long period of rest, and commenced about the same time as the injury occurred. There was no real evidence to connect the condition of the back with the injury, beyond the fact that the one was observed after the beginning of the other ; but it would be almost impossible to say that the injury had no influence whatever upon the condition of the back. It would also be impossible to say whether, had he resumed work when he was first asked to undertake light work, the oncoming of the present condition of the back might not have been very considerably delayed.

He was not now capable of doing a good day's work at his former occupation, partly on account of his back, and also because of the irregular and loafing habits acquired during the last three years. He probably realized this, and, in order to retain his compensation, exaggerated such symptoms as did exist, and introduced others for which no physical foundation could be discovered.

MALINGERING

I therefore hesitated to advise strong measures, not because I thought him incapacitated, but because I feared we might not be successful in Court.

A few weeks later, I was informed that this man had been caught stealing *from his master* (who had been paying him compensation for nearly four years), and taking away *on the back alleged to be injured* a bag of lead weighing some 49 pounds. He was convicted, and sentenced to six weeks' imprisonment. I visited him in prison, and had a consultation with the senior physician there. The doctor stated that he had not chosen the particular work the prisoner was engaged in on account of any alleged disability connected with his back.

Here was a man who for just on four years had received half-wages from his employer ; who declared himself unfit for even light work ; who had recently been caught carrying nearly 50 pounds of lead on a back alleged to be injured ; who, on being sent to prison, performed the ordinary prison tasks, which included cleaning his cell, without grumbling or protest.

Result.—On his leaving prison the case was set down for arbitration, and was settled for a small sum.

A septic condition of the mouth is a very common contributory cause, if not the origin, of many of the conditions which are classed under the term " rheumatism."

The condition into which the working classes allow their teeth to degenerate is deplorable. Pyorrhœa and gingivitis seem to be almost more the rule than the exception, and front teeth which must have been loose from the presence of tartar are not infrequently said to be in this condition as the result of an accident.

The appearance of the whole mouth and of other teeth which are more or less loose, and of which the patient is heedless, will assist in the diagnosis.

Those familiar with actions for damages are frequently confronted with cases of which the following is a hypothetical example :

The recipient has a compound fracture of the tibia and fibula, and, after say three months, fairly good union has been obtained. By means of a couple of crutches, he moves himself with much care and deliberation. The ankle-joint has become stiff. So-called massage is imperfectly performed by an unskilled attendant or by a relative. Time passes, and perhaps about the seventh or eighth month the employer becomes impatient, and sends his medical man to examine and report on the claimant. The suggestion is then made that he ought to be fit for work in a few weeks. The bare audacity of such an unsympathetic attitude is bitterly resented, and further medical evidence is sought to controvert, in Court if necessary, the evidence of the employer's doctor.

EXAMINATION OF THE BACK

Some stiffness or rigidity of the back is discovered by the plaintiff's doctor. The back is X-rayed, and a few osteophytic outgrowths are discovered in the neighbourhood of the sacral or lumbar region. Hey presto ! From that day the case takes on a totally different aspect. The statement of claim is amended to include injury to the spine. Not unnaturally, under the influence of suggestion, the back becomes stiffer, and the crutches which had been discarded before the employer's doctor saw the claimant are uncarthed and again brought into use. At the trial an X-ray photograph is produced. No X-ray expert is called, who would, if asked, inform the Court that these osteophytic outgrowths are not indicative of any disease due to traumatism, but are frequently met with when X-ray photographs are being taken for other purposes, such as the examination of the kidney. The Judge and jury see the osteophytes. The plaintiff is asked if he ever felt anything the matter with his back before the accident. The jury cannot get away from the idea of the crutches, the pitiful tale and counsel's eloquence, and heavy damages follow. If our legal friends and sympathetic jurymen knew more of the sticks, crutches, and elaborate dressings that are sometimes left behind in medical consulting-rooms, they would be less sympathetic with doubtful cases. The law is that the defendant should have the benefit of any doubt, but what the defendant objects to is that the plaintiff so often gets the benefit even when there is not any reasonable doubt.

When disease exists in the spine, Nature's warning is pain. When pain exists, stiffness and rigidity naturally follow. It is reasonable, therefore, to believe that if there is no pain, no stiffness, and no rigidity, there is no actual disease.

When the back is bent, each separate vertebra moves a little upon its fellow, and each spinous process is separated a little from those of the neighbouring vertebræ. If, therefore, when a patient stoops, the fingers of the examiner's two hands are pressed first between the spinous processes of the cervical and upper dorsal regions, and the patient is asked to slowly raise himself to the erect position, and the spinous processes are found to separate upon flexion of the spine and approach each other as the spine is straightened, and this without pain, it goes a long way towards proving that there is no disease at the particular spot examined. By asking the patient to stoop two or three times, the whole spine can be examined in this way.

Recently, in dealing with a most determined malingerer who for months kept his back so bent that his face always looked to the ground, I was able to induce him, when stripped, to lie absolutely flat on a sofa without complaint. Subsequently most of the man's clothes were placed under his back, thus

140 MALINGERING

arching it in exactly the opposite direction to that in which he held it before, and this without any complaint.

Alleged pain in the back, in the vast majority of cases, is mental, not physical. The idea of a tender spot, or of pain, takes possession of the patient. As will be seen from a report already quoted, an examinee who was complaining of pain and tenderness in a particular spot was told that very firm pressure with the palm of the hand made over the alleged painful area in this neighbourhood would not produce pain, and, although very firm pressure was applied, no complaint *was* made; yet, when pressure with a single digit was applied, bitter complaint followed.

Sometimes patients can be induced to stand on their tip-toes, and then come heavily down on their heels. No question should be asked as to whether pain has been produced along the spine. If it has, there is no doubt it will be mentioned; but if it has not, there can be no very tender area.

Another and a good plan in examining a spine is to fix the pelvis with both hands, and ask the patient to rotate the body by inducing him to look over his right shoulder and then over his left. Patients, as a rule, do not appreciate the importance of movement in this position.

Sciatica.—It is well to remember that when sciatica is assumed, it is generally by people who have had previous attacks and therefore know the symptoms. My experience of feigned sciatica is the same as that of malingering in general—namely, that the disease is seldom, if ever, assumed without the suggestion of an old slight attack, the recovery from which is not admitted.

This disease, even when of long duration, does not produce very obvious atrophy, although, as a rule, there is *some* generalized wasting. In true sciatica the space between the trochanter major and the tuberosity of the ischium, where the nerve finds its exit from the pelvis, is, as a rule, exquisitely tender. The popliteal space, also, is not infrequently tender, but it is well to remember that hypersensitiveness is limited to the exit of the nerve from bony foramina, the other parts being, in a genuine case, only slightly or not at all hypersensitive.

A genuine sufferer from sciatica stands with his hip and his knee flexed, the result being that the pelvis on that side is lowered. In walking the limb is spared as much as possible,

EXAMINATION OF THE BACK 141

and the hip is still kept flexed. If asked to sit on the floor, he will let himself down very carefully on the sound buttock. On the floor he supports himself with his arm, or sits only on the sound half of his body. In slight cases these postural peculiarities may not be obvious at first sight, but some of them will be found on careful observation.

If an inflamed sciatic nerve is put on the stretch, the pain is increased. When, therefore, the patient is put in a sitting position, the sciatic nerve is already at its full normal stretch at the hip-joint; and if the knee is then extended and the ankle flexed, it is made sufficiently taut to produce pain if sciatica is present, although, of course, this movement can be made normally without pain.

If the whole leg is now flexed upon the body, the sciatic nerve is so stretched as to be distinctly painful if sciatica is present. If sciatica is being feigned, these movements at once arouse the suspicion of the patient, and even at the preliminary stages of the test exclamations of pain are elicited long before any tension is made on the nerve.

I have been able to satisfy myself of the absence of any real sciatica by the very simple process of asking the patient to straighten his knee, and raise the sole of his foot to the level of my hand, whilst inquiring sympathetically as to whether the sole of the foot was sensitive to pin-pricks. If no pain is complained of in this position (that is, with the knee extended and the ankle and hip flexed), then one may say that no sciatica is present.

C. F. was sent to me complaining of a " terrible pain " in his coccyx, which extended all round to the front of the abdomen, and up his spine to the back of his head ; he declared that he could not walk on account of a " dead " feeling, that he had no appetite, and had lost weight.

It was alleged that two years previously he fell over the step of a door on board ship. The accident was not reported for five days, and five weeks later a medical man stated that he was unable to work owing to an injury to the coccyx. Ever since he had been comfortably off—in receipt of nearly a pound a week in half-wages under the Act, and also a considerable amount of club money. The shipping company's doctor examined him several times, and said there was no means of ascertaining whether the alleged pain was genuine or not. Various attempts were made to settle the case for a small sum, without success. Four months before I saw him, he was found in bed suffering from what he described as an " attack of paralysis," which had lasted a fortnight, and gave a history of similar attacks previously, but the

MALINGERING

company's officer who visited him remarked that C. F. "looked remarkably well, considering he is said to suffer from occasional delirium, partial paralysis, loss of sleep, loss of appetite, and loss of flesh."

Examination.—This claimant was a typical traumatic neurasthenic, with a very considerable spice of wickedness thrown in. There was not the slightest doubt that he had made no attempt to ignore the many morbid sensations which were the outcome of his own brooding, for he was fully aware that as long as these allegations were sustained the Workmen's Compensation Act might be construed in his favour.

During the examination, when firm pressure was applied in the region of the coccyx, he turned round, glared at me, spoke rudely, saying gruffly that he "would not be pulled about." He was told with the utmost deliberation and calmness that in that case I should not proceed with the examination, and that, in accordance with the provisions of the Workmen's Compensation Act, his pay would be stopped if he did not submit to examination—that it really did not matter to me whether I examined him or not. The effect was magical; not only did he allow equal pressure without even wincing, but he became perfectly amenable to a thorough examination.

There was not the slightest organic basis for any of his symptoms; indeed, it was impossible that the pain which he described could arise from the coccyx, for the alleged pain did not follow the line of the nerves therefrom.

As far back as a year previously this man had been X-rayed, and a very definite statement was then obtained from his medical attendant that he had no organic disease at that time. It was incredible that he should have remained ill, and that no physical signs should have developed during a whole year.

My opinion was that C. F. was suffering from a functional neurosis —that is, a neurasthenic condition, the proper treatment for which would be return to work. Neurasthenia following an accident varies very much in degree, and I satisfied myself that the present condition of the claimant did not preclude his undertaking light work. Under these circumstances, I thought it my duty to tell him very frankly my opinion, and when he saw that I was assured of this, he eventually agreed that he *was* fit for light work, and would do it if any could be found for him.

Three months later he was sent to me again for examination. It appeared that he had been induced to start work several times, but would not settle down, and finally stated that his health would not permit him to do any more.

In addition to the pain in the coccyx, he now complained of blood-spitting and frequency of micturition.

Having been idle for two years, he had now become obsessed with the idea that he was wholly incapable of working; unfortunately also his wife was a genuine believer in his disabilities.

His doctor informed me that he saw the bleeding, but in spite of repeatedly examining him when the hæmorrhages took place, he was unable to discover any cause for them. In my opinion, the hæmorrhage was unconnected with the accident, and I believed that ulti-

EXAMINATION OF THE BACK

mately it would be found to come from the throat or upper air-passages.

I was of opinion this was not a case to fight for the following reasons :

1. C. F. was somewhat pale, and would have the sympathy of the arbitrator.

2. His own doctor was prepared to swear that he was ill, and fit for nothing but light work, and did not disassociate the hæmorrhage from the accident.

3. It would be impossible to deny that the man was still neurasthenic, and, rightly or wrongly, the Court would hardly listen to the suggestion that he had contributed to his own incapacity, still less to the suggestion that the best treatment for it was diversion of the mind by resumption of (light) work.

4. The applicant would probably call the surgeon at the hospital, with whom his own medical attendant had been in communication, and one had to bear in mind that the surgeon hinted at chronic arthritis of the spine, which is the latest refuge of those who are destitute of a diagnosis.

5. He would bring his wife, who would " prove " his utter incapacity to do anything.

With regard to the future, I believed there was ground for hoping either that his courage would be re-established, or, more likely, that his doctor would get tired of him.

Fifteen months later I re-examined him. C. F. did not in any way appear to be an ailing man ; he was ruddy, healthy-looking, and had his moustache waxed ; wore a gold ring on his finger ; his manner was aggressive, and on more than one occasion he spoke in a loud blustering tone of voice. He insisted on his wife being present during the examination.

He declined to give any information as to what medical attendance he had recently had.

He complained bitterly of being subjected to so many medical examinations ; but when it was pointed out to him he had not been medically examined for over a year, and that his employers were legally entitled to an examination every two months, he shifted his ground, and complained of having been induced to attempt light work.

With regard to the alleged pain in the back, on thorough examination nothing could be found to indicate disease of any sort, and it was interesting to note that he did not now complain of pain in his coccyx as he had formerly done.

He now complained of pain over the bladder and incontinence of urine, and seemed to rely strongly on this as an evidence of continuing disability. He had in readiness for me one or two pairs of pants, which he stated showed evidence of this, and was genuinely distressed when I refused to examine those which he had in readiness, but insisted upon examining those which he was then wearing, which disclosed *no* signs of urine-stains. Although he stated this symptom had lasted for two years, I noted that he had not mentioned it at my first examination.

MALINGERING

Incontinence of urine is not infrequently complained of by men of this type, who know that this symptom is one often associated with serious disease, and it is a common practice to feign it. What this man did not know was that it is a *late* symptom following on serious nerve disease, the presence of which could be detected by the ordinary physical examination of the nervous system. He was subjected to the usual tests for disease of the nervous system, with negative results, except that his knee-jerks were exaggerated. It transpired that his doctor had sent him to hospital on account of the hæmorrhage, and the claimant thought it unfair that I should have any information with regard to this, for he felt sure I should write to the hospital doctor for his views. It appeared that he took his own discharge after four weeks, and that his exit synchronized with some inquiries which the authorities of this institution made with regard to his alleged continuing disability from his accident.

When he entered the hospital, he gave a history of many hæmorrhages, one being as much as a whole pint of blood, but during his stay no tubercle bacilli were found, no hæmorrhage occurred, and no disease of coccyx, testicle, bladder, or rectum was found. In consequence of his complaining of incontinence of urine, the surgeon at the hospital ordered that a steel bougie should be passed each night, and one of his reasons for leaving was his objection to this. This treatment was, no doubt, ordered under the belief that the alleged incontinence was of the nature of a mental condition, and was intended merely to have a moral effect.

It appeared that he then went to several hospitals trying to get an opinion that he had phthisis, though it is hardly conceivable that even the wide meshes of the Workmen's Compensation Act would include traumatic tuberculosis in a case of this sort.

I ascertained that soon after obliging me to visit him he resumed work, possibly with a view to stating in Court that he had once more tried work and been unable to do it. He refused to give me the name of his employers, stating that he did not want the firm to know that he was receiving compensation, and admitted that he had made a misstatement to this effect when filling up one of their forms.

A month later I saw him in consultation with a surgeon, who entirely agreed that there was nothing the matter, and was prepared to substantiate the view I had already expressed.

It appeared that his present doctor had been attending him for some time *without knowing of any supposed accident*. This was either artfulness on C. F.'s part, or might be construed into a tacit admission that the present condition was not caused by accident.

His present doctor then admitted that C. F. had brought himself into a weak state by not resuming work six months after the accident.

In short, here was a man who more than three and a half years after the accident still declared himself wholly unfit for work on account of it, but did not present any physical signs, and now made no mention of his original complaints. The previous symptoms of neurasthenia having now wholly disappeared, he had in my opinion degener-

EXAMINATION OF THE BACK

ated into an artful malingerer; his doctor, as I had anticipated, had got tired of him, and I believed the time had come when further payment should be resisted.

Result.—The case was taken to Court, and resulted in judgment for the employers.

Frequency of micturition is very often complained of, but is of itself of little significance. Difficulty, incontinence, or retention occur often in association with definite disease of the nervous system, when the obvious results of injuries can easily be recognised. Yet time after time robust, healthy men complain of either frequency or incontinence of urine, thinking in their ignorance that it might fairly be attributable to some alleged disease of the spine.

CHAPTER IX

EXAMINATION OF THE UPPER AND LOWER EXTREMITIES

Muscular Atrophy.—Paralysis of various parts of the body is a symptom often complained of by malingerers. As a rule, such paralysis is a limited one, limited to one limb or portion of a limb, and it is rare to find an extensive lesion, such as a hemiplegia or a paraplegia, simulated. A recent writer tells an amusing story of a suspected malingerer, who said he had lost the use of his limbs.

> "It was in the days before electrical apparatus was up to its present efficiency, and electrical testing of muscles was in its infancy. The man alleged loss of power of both legs, the condition having lasted for about two years. He was brought to the infirmary in an ambulance, and was detained in one of the medical wards for diagnosis and treatment. He was suspected of malingering by the physician in charge, and was sent on a trolley to the Electrical Department to have his muscles tested and treated if necessary.
>
> "By accident, and on account of the less efficient apparatus available at that time, a huge electric spark passed between the man and an electrical machine which he was lying near. He jumped off the trolley, and his heels were last seen in the vicinity of the infirmary gate."

The usual history given is that, after an injury to the shoulder or any other joint, the patient is paralyzed in the limb affected. He uses the word " paralysis " in a very loose sense, for it is very rarely indeed that he alleges total inability to move the limb. What he really means is that he has not the full power that he should have. On examining him, signs of organic disease should be carefully sought for. These are, of course, the wel -known cardinal symptoms : wasting and flabbiness of muscles, blueness, decreased temperature, vasomotor changes, reaction of degeneration, and secondary contractions.

146

EXAMINATION OF THE EXTREMITIES   147

Pretended muscular weakness of an indefinite character, with loss of sensation and the presence of pain, is a very common combination of symptoms complained of by a malingerer. Fortunately, not even the most artful can seriously interfere with the normal reflexes. The muscles complained of may waste from disease or disuse, but no one has control over the electric stimulation of muscle tissue.

Hemiplegia is seldom feigned. The following table may be of some assistance in differentiating the organic from malingering or functional hemiplegia.

	Organic Hemiplegia.	Functional Hemiplegia.
Distribution of paralysis	Usually face, arm, and leg.	Face very rarely affected.
Knee-jerks	Increased.	Normal or increased.
Superficial abdominal reflexes	Frequently lost on paralyzed side.	Present.
Plantar reflexes	Extensor response (Babinski sign).	Flexor response or absence of reflex.
Ankle clonus	Present.	Absent or a pseudo-clonus.
Rigidity	Present in later stages.	May be present or absent.
Contractures	Present in later stages: obey anatomical laws, in which flexors and adductors overcome extensors and abductors.	Irregular spasmodic contractures may occur— e.g., inversion of foot.
Gait	Leg swung round from hip.	Leg dragged behind as if it were a log.
Anæsthesia	Severe cases may be accompanied by hemianæsthesia.	Hemianæsthesia common, taking whole of one-half of the body: at other times it may be the typical glove or stocking anæsthesia of an arm or leg.
Visual fields	Hemianopia may occur when there is hemianæsthesia.	Crossed amblyopia with more contraction of field of vision on anæsthetic side.

148　　　　　　　MALINGERING

With regard to wasting, care must be taken that this is not too readily assumed because of difference in measurements between opposite limbs. It is fairly common to find cases of marked congenital asymmetry, for a description of which see pp. 167-174. Moreover, a certain amount of wasting and flabbiness will follow if a limb is deliberately unused for any length of time. In the absence of these symptoms, we should next endeavour to find out whether or not there is genuine lack of power, and one of the first things to do is to try and determine whether the limb is being used or not. In the case of the upper extremity, the hands should be carefully examined and compared, to see whether the skin of one is markedly cleaner and softer than that of the other. If they are stained with tobacco-juice or are both equally dirty, and if callosities are equally well marked, the inference is obvious. Similarly, the man who complains that one leg is powerless, but whose boots are equally worn down, presuming they are not a new pair, is certainly not telling the truth.

With regard to the lower limbs, the difficulties of exposing the simulated lack of power are much greater, and it is fortunate that they are, on the whole, less often complained of. The claimant's gait should be carefully watched ; he should first be induced to balance himself on his toes only, in the fashion of a ballet-dancer. A large number of persons suffering from alleged disabilities of their lower extremities can assume a tiptoe position when their boots and stockings are removed, and maintain it for a very considerable time ; and this may be prolonged if they are allowed to steady themselves by placing the tips of the middle fingers of each hand on those of the examiner. Not infrequently I have induced an impostor, when in this attitude, to steady himself on the terminal phalanges of the injured extremity.

The patient should be placed on a couch, and movements against resistance carefully tested, as will be described when dealing with the arms.

The next thing to do is to find out in what movement the alleged lack of power is evidenced, and to get him to exert or make use of the weak muscles to the limit of his capacity.

Immobility of a joint is always followed by change in the corresponding muscles. In slight cases this may amount only

EXAMINATION OF THE EXTREMITIES

to flabbiness, but in prolonged cases there will be more or less actual wasting of the muscles.

A shoulder-joint, for instance, which is the subject of a severe and chronic arthritis, invariably shows first a flabbiness, and then an atrophy of the deltoid and other muscles.

Speaking generally, the nerve filaments distributed to articulations come from the larger nerve trunks in the neighbourhood, which supply the muscles clothing the joint; and the trophic changes which take place in the muscles have a direct ratio to the changes going on in the joint.

When a claimant alleges that, as the result of injury, he has loss of power in his shoulder, arm, or hand, disproportionate to the physical signs present, the following experiment is useful in determining his *bona fides*, and the extent of the incapacity.

Fig. 10.

Fig. 11.

The patient is induced to hang by both arms on to a small trapeze attached to the ceiling of the examiner's consulting-room. He is then gently raised off his feet by means of a small block and tackle attached to the trapeze, and encouraged to suspend himself for as long a period as he will, holding on by both hands (see Fig. 10).

In case it should be contended that he really hangs to the trapeze chiefly by the strength of the uninjured limb, a cross-bar is placed loosely through the triangle of the trapeze (Fig. 11), and he is then instructed to hold on to the cross-bar, and is once more lifted off his feet by the block and tackle. If care has been taken that the hands are equidistant from the trapeze bar, it is obvious that he must be using equal strength with both hands, for were he not doing so the cross-bar would at once slip sideways through the triangle as soon as he is raised off the ground, instead of which, in the majority of cases, it retains its position.

The patient is then weighed, and a note taken of the fact

150 MALINGERING

that he is able to _suspend_ half his weight with the injured limb.

Many patients, when suspended by the trapeze, may in addition be induced to raise themselves by their arms so that their chins are brought to a level with the bar of the trapeze.

Another useful method is to lift the arms at right angles to the body in a horizontal position, and then suddenly to withdraw all support. If one arm were really incapable of being raised, as is so often alleged, it would drop limply to the side when the support is removed. Often, however, what happens is that it remains in position for a second or two, and then, as the patient becomes aware of the trick that is being played on him, it is gradually allowed to fall to the side. The movements of the two arms under these conditions should, of course, be carefully compared.

Sometimes, when an examinee says that he cannot raise his arms because of alleged paralysis of the deltoid and other shoulder muscles, if the upper extremity is placed by the examiner in a horizontal position, and the patient be sympathetically exhorted to be very careful how the arm is allowed to fall to the side, not infrequently he will slowly and gradually let the limb down, showing that the muscles are still capable of exercising their functions.

Patients sometimes allege that they cannot raise the arm above a certain height. This height should be carefully noted, and the patient repeatedly asked at intervals during the examination to show again and again to what height he can raise it. If he is a malingerer, not infrequently it will be found to vary. Sometimes, when the attention is diverted, the patient allows free manipulation of the arm. My favourite device is to ask whether proper notice of the accident was given, a point on which patients lay enormous stress, though its value is by no means obvious.

Meantime, it is a good plan to watch the facial expression when a joint which is alleged to be painful is being moved, and this can be done quite unobtrusively by placing the patient in front of a mirror and examining the joint from behind.

The following experiment also is useful in the case of a patient who alleges that he cannot raise his arm above his head on account of injury. He is asked to stand with his hands resting

EXAMINATION OF THE EXTREMITIES   151

lightly on the back of a chair, and his attention is diverted from the injury. On the pretext of examining his back, the medical examiner induces him gradually to step backwards away from the chair, thus lowering his shoulders and extending his arms until, from the hips upwards, he is practically in a horizontal position. It will be seen that his hands are now actually high above his head, although he does not recognize this, because he is in a horizontal instead of a vertical position. Allowance must be made for the support afforded by the chair in considering the question of *weakness* of the shoulder muscles.

An alien who met with an injury to his shoulder stated that he could not raise his arm from his body more than a certain height, and this he demonstrated by raising it to no more than a right angle. It seems almost incredible that, upon my suddenly asking him how high he could raise it before the accident, he shot it high above his head !

> C. G. complained of one thing only, and that was inability to raise his arm above a right angle. He had fractured his clavicle some four months previously. When asked to take off his vest, which was, very tight, in his struggles he raised both arms high above his head without noticing that he was doing so, and without complaint. The attention of his medical attendant, who was present, was drawn to this. The doctor seemed much impressed by this silent confirmation of my contention that no real disability existed.

An accident which is comparatively rare in general practice is not infrequently met with by those who are called upon to examine accidents for insurance companies. The condition referred to is a dislocation from its groove of the long head of the biceps. The symptoms are at first somewhat puzzling. Certain movements of the arm forwards and backwards, combined with flexion of the elbow by the biceps, cause a loud creaking sound to be heard in the neighbourhood of the shoulder-joint, which is very apt to be mistaken for disease of that joint. Careful examination with the stethoscope during movement locates the sound near the bicipital groove.

In my experience it is generally caused by a weight falling on the arm or shoulder when the former is in an extended position. My experience, also, which is limited to a few cases only, is that the injury is neither so intractable nor so serious as might be imagined.

It should be remembered that bones are kept in their position

152   MALINGERING

at the joints not only by ligaments, but by the normal tension, even at rest, of the muscles which surround them. In the later stages of drunkenness these muscles become relaxed, and thus the normal muscular protection of the joint is weakened. Instinctively, when in the act of falling, one puts out his hand to protect the head and face, and the muscles of the whole upper extremity from the shoulder to the wrist tighten, and come into action. The wrist may be broken, but a dislocation is rare. A tipsy man, however, falls in a lump, probably directly on his shoulder, his muscles being in a state of relaxation, and a dislocation occurs.

Not infrequently patients complain that they have lost all power of bending the elbow. To test the truth of this, slowly flex the patient's elbow-joint, and then with a great exhibition of force suddenly attempt to straighten the forearm ; when the power is *not* lost there will be more or less resistance to extension, due to the sudden involuntary contraction of the biceps, which the malingerer, taken unawares, cannot control.

Weakness and inefficiency of grip in the hands is often complained of, and the following means may be taken to test its reality. The patient should be asked to clasp his hands as firmly as possible, and the position of the thumb should be noted, for a much firmer grip is obtained if the thumb is opposed to the other digits. If, therefore, the patient makes the movement with his thumb abducted, he is certainly not trying his best. Another method is to get him to grip the observer's hands with his own hands crossed ; he will often get confused, in this position, as to which is the " paralyzed " and which the sound hand, and will so give himself away. If this fails, success may be obtained by getting him to do the gripping movement behind his back, when he is still more likely to get confused.

Another method suggested by Leon Gallez is to ask the patient to press an ordinary dynamometer (see Fig. 12) with the sound hand. The reading is shown to the patient, and he is now given another dynamometer in the other (injured) hand, and quickly and abruptly instructed to press both as hard as possible. Gallez states that, if the patient is simulating, he will be unable to control the sound hand, and the reading will be much less than it should be.

EXAMINATION OF THE EXTREMITIES

In testing the power of closing the fingers on the palm, a useful plan is what is called the "bilateral method," in which the patient is first asked to squeeze the examiner's hand with the hand which he alleges is defective in grasping-power. He is then asked to squeeze both one's hands simultaneously. Involuntarily, he will then contract more powerfully with the "weak" hand, if simulating, than at first. Do not forget that the hand can be much more firmly clenched when the wrist is extended than when it is flexed.

A good test for estimating alleged inability to close the fist is to ask the patient to bare his forearm, and partially flex the fingers on the palm. The examiner then interlocks them with the fingers of his own hand, asking the examinee to close

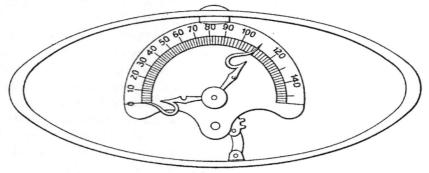

Fig. 12.

his fist, thereby squeezing the examiner's fingers. It is now explained to him that an attempt is to be made to forcibly straighten his fingers, and that he is to resist the attempt. Not infrequently no attempt is made, and the fingers are straightened without any force whatever.

If during the experiment the surgeon palpates the anterior surface of the forearm, he may find that the flexor muscles are not being put into action, and that they remain, in fact, soft and flabby. Anyone who is only pretending to perform a certain muscular movement—say, of the hand or arm—and who, in fact, is really suppressing the movement, involuntarily throws into action the antagonistic set of muscles, and these can be felt to harden during the process.

It is a good plan at this stage to describe to the examinee in very simple language the anatomical arrangements, and to

MALINGERING

point out that one knows when he is not even attempting to close his fist from what one sees and feels taking place in the forearm. When the experiment is repeated, the lesson has had its effect. In nine cases out of ten, the malingerer resists, and after repeated experiments, accompanied by firm exhortation and a display of omniscience, the grasping-power of the hand, as a rule, improves marvellously.

History.—C. H. stated that, after being at work heaving up ashes on board ship, he found a blister on the palm of his left hand, was taken to hospital at a foreign port, was operated on, and remained there two and a half months.

Twenty-five months after the accident, he was sent to me complaining that he had no strength in his hand, that he could not do any hard work on account of it, and had " slight pain from contraction of the thumb."

The case originally was one of septic poison in the palm of the left hand, which apparently healed up with some degree of stiffness, and impaired movement of the thumb. The company's medical examiner reported that the man was malingering, and when the company's application came before the Judge for review, he referred the dispute to the medical referee, who, sixteen and a half months after the accident, reported that the present condition was " feebleness of grasp, with slight swelling, tenderness of the palm, especially of scar-tissue, the result of suppurative processes and of operations following a septic inflammation of the hands, and wasting of the muscles controlling movement of the thumb." The medical referee stated as his opinion " that by gradual and progressive exercise C. H. could be enabled to do his ordinary work as fireman on board ship, and that probably such treatment ought to be extended over a period of four to six months from the present time."

Eight months later, the company's doctor reported that he found some of the muscles of the thumb wasted, due in his opinion to want of use, and that he considered him quite capable of doing his ordinary work if he wished to do so.

Examination.—From inspection of this man's hand, I formed the opinion that there was really nothing the matter with it. The following experiments were made :

1. He was induced to hang by both hands on to a trapeze, and was suspended with both his feet off the ground by means of a block and tackle, and so continued to hang for some time holding on by both hands.

2. In case it might be contended that he was really hanging to the trapeze by the strength of the right, uninjured hand alone, a cross-bar was placed loosely through the triangle of the trapeze itself, and he was instructed to hold on to each end of the cross-bar. He did so, and was again lifted off his feet by the block and tackle ; it was obvious that he was using equal strength with both hands, for had he not done

EXAMINATION OF THE EXTREMITIES 155

so the loose bar would have at once slipped sideways through the triangle, instead of which he maintained it equably.

3. He was then weighed, and found to weigh 10 stone 11 pounds, so that with the left, the injured, hand he suspended a weight of 5 stone 5½ pounds.

4. He was then asked to lift a gipsy coal-scuttle full of coal. This he did, and the weight of it was 30 pounds.

5. He was asked to grasp the fingers of the examiner's hand tightly with his left hand, and to resist his fingers being straightened. At first he obviously let go voluntarily, allowing the fingers to be straightened with ease; but when it was pointed out to him that it was apparent he was letting go, he tightened his fingers so that they could scarcely be straightened.

6. When asked to bend his left elbow and resist extension of his arm; he did so with such strength that it could not be straightened.

7. He was asked to close his fist tightly, the examiner meanwhile directing his attention to the swelling of the muscles of the forearm which close the fist. At first he did it in such a half-hearted manner that the muscles did not swell up, but upon insistence he closed both fists tightly, and one could feel that the muscles of both arms were equally firm.

The only sequela of this claimant's accident was a linear scar in front of his hand. This was not tender, and the skilful surgical treatment employed had prevented the Dupuytren's contraction which so frequently follows injury to the palm.

There was slight want of use of the muscles which draw the thumb towards the palm of the hand. This claimant was proved to be a powerful, able-bodied malingerer, and probably had been fit for work for many months.

It was pointed out to him that he was able to suspend a weight of 5½ stone with his injured hand alone, that he could lift 30 pounds, and that it was preposterous for him to say he could not work. He was exhorted to take his courage in both hands and start work. His reply was: "I do not suppose they would take me now at my age [forty-two]; they do not take men over forty."

A month later, at the application for review of the case, at the County Court, an award was given for the employers.

Not infrequently very simple tests are of the utmost use, but it is important to recognize that usually the method of applying the test determines its success or failure. Very often, for instance, when a patient comes into the room, he will reciprocate a hearty grasp of the hand, but will absolutely refuse to grasp one's hand firmly during the ensuing examination.

C. I., whilst in the act of scrubbing a floor, had the misfortune to run a needle deeply into the palm of her right hand. An insurance company, for whom I act, paid half-wages for two years, and then

MALINGERING

sent her to me for examination. Immediately upon entering the room, and before the examination had commenced, the woman was asked to close the fingers of the injured hand, and to resist my forcibly opening her fist, and this she did without complaint, demonstrating that she had no pain or loss of power. But later on in the examination, and upon a subsequent examination two months later, she complained bitterly of the most intense pain when the hand was touched, however lightly. An X-ray photograph proved that the needle was still in the hand, but lying parallel to, and snugly embedded between, the bones of the palm of the hand, in which position it was hardly possible for it to cause pain. An unsuccessful attempt had been made by a surgeon to remove it.

C. I. was obviously in a very highly strung, nervous, and excitable condition, and the opinion I formed was that she had got the *idea* of the presence of the needle in her hand on her mind, and that this was making her ill. As work was the only cure for this condition, I recommended that her weekly allowance should be stopped, as she would then be compelled to take up her old employment again. This was, of course, contested, and at the trial much medical evidence was given. It was noticeable that, although two doctors were called to support her contention that the presence of the needle accounted for her nervous condition, her own family doctor was not put in the witness-box. The Judge, after considering the matter for two months, decided in favour of the insurance company, and stopped payment. A month after his decision, one of the medical men who had given evidence in opposition to my view, kindly informed me that to his surprise he had learned that the applicant had just had a serious operation for a large cancer in another part of her body, from which she was undoubtedly suffering at the time of the trial. Six weeks later I learned that she had recovered from the operation for cancer, had returned to work with the needle still in the same part of her hand, proving, as I had contended at the trial, that its mere presence was not the obstacle to work.

It will be noticed that, whilst the applicant in this case resisted my forcibly opening her fist *early* in the examination, at subsequent examinations she complained bitterly when the hand was even touched.

As it subsequently turned out, this was a procedure of the utmost importance in the case, and, in fact, the judgment which the insurance company ultimately obtained in their favour hinged upon this one incident. For the Judge, in adjourning the case for his consideration, remarked that if he decided to accept this part of the evidence he must find for the company.

A useful method of testing whether a patient is really using the flexors of his fingers is to ask him to grasp firmly

EXAMINATION OF THE EXTREMITIES   157

a small round vial, the outside surface of which has been oiled. If this is suddenly pulled sideways from his grasp, the fingers will, if he is malingering, remain open.

Some cases present extreme difficulty, not so much on account of the precise knowledge required in determining the question to be solved, but on account of the fraud which so often complicates cases of genuine accident. Cases are constantly cropping up in the Courts, of which I may cite the following as illustrations :

> C. J. met with an accident to the back of her hand, and was away from work for three or four days. On examination four weeks afterwards, there was loss of power of flexion of the terminal joint of the middle finger of the same hand, and it was evident that the leader which bends the joint had been torn, a somewhat serious injury from the employer's point of view, inasmuch as nothing but an immediate operation could cure it. She was very emphatic that this injury had happened at the same time as the trifling injury which she undoubtedly did sustain to the back of her hand. Upon very careful inquiry, it transpired that she had not noticed anything amiss with the middle finger at the time of the accident to the back of her hand, nor had she mentioned the former to her doctor within the first forty-eight hours. If the finger had been injured at the time, it meant that the leader had been forcibly torn across. I refused to believe that this happened at the time of the accident for which she was claiming compensation, for it could not have happened without causing immediate and severe pain. I believed it was an old-standing injury, which she wished to make her employers pay for. At my suggestion careful inquiries were made, and independent evidence was forthcoming that the facts were as I thought. The woman still protested, and upon my informing her that no further payment would be made in connection with this injury, she said she thought it was " very unjust." Finally, she said she would not trouble about it, and as her own doctor had advised her to go back to work that day, she proposed to do so.

The following case illustrates the value of adopting a firm attitude where one is satisfied that the time has passed for leniency and consideration :

> *History.*—C. K., a painter, fell off a ladder whilst at work. He attended for seven weeks as an out-patient at a large general hospital for treatment of dislocation of shoulder-joint, simple fracture of radius and ulna at right wrist, and abrasions.
>
> The alleged disability still continuing nineteen weeks after the accident, he was examined on behalf of his employers by a doctor who reported that C. K. had recovered sufficiently to return to work without further delay, and that his wage-earning capacity should not be less than before the accident.

MALINGERING

Compensation was stopped, and work offered him by his employers. He replied that he would " think it over," and nothing was heard of him until three weeks had elapsed, when an application for arbitration was issued. In an interview a few days later C. K.'s solicitors admitted to the employer's representative that the applicant was not then under medical treatment. A small sum was offered in settlement of the claim, but C. K. persisted in his demand for £80.

Examination.—Six and a half months after the accident, when I was asked to examine C. K. on behalf of his employers, he told me that his shoulder had now wholly recovered, but that he was still unfit for work on account of the condition of his right wrist. The wrist was slightly twisted (the result of the fracture of ulna and radius), but this slight lateral displacement was insufficient to interfere with his working capacity. Although a certain amount of muscular wasting, due to disuse, was present in the right forearm, it was evident that he had been using his hands for ordinary work, because they were both equally dirty.

He was asked to turn the hand palm up, and then palm down, whilst at the same time I opposed movement, and in several other ways satisfied myself that the hand had wholly recovered. He complained that it got tired when he worked, but I pointed out to him that at first this must needs happen after a long period of idleness. To carry out his line of argument to its logical conclusion would involve never working again, if he had not sufficient pluck to endure a little inconvenience for the first few days. Finally, he told me that he had used his hand to paint two doors, but that it took him four hours, whereas in the ordinary way he would have finished in an hour. Upon pressing him, however, he admitted that he had not used the right hand at all whilst painting the doors.

In my report to the insurance company representing his employers, I stated that the claimant was a lazy fellow, who had been taking advantage of his employers, that he was fit for work, and must certainly have been so for some months. This statement I was prepared to uphold in the witness-box at the arbitration proceedings.

Result.—A few days subsequent to my examination, I was informed that the applicant, who had originally claimed £80, now indicated his willingness to accept about £2, and in these circumstances the legal advisers, on behalf of his employer, decided to pay this small sum rather than go to the expense of taking the case to Court.

Wounds.—Wounds may be self-inflicted, or genuine wounds, following an accident, may be intentionally kept open.

C. L. tried unsuccessfully on several occasions, by means of alleged trifling injuries, to obtain his discharge from a service in which he is entitled to a handsome pension if found permanently unfit for work as the result of an accident in the execution of his duty. Irritated by my persistent refusal to recommend a pension, he produced a pustular eruption and an inflamed condition of the adjacent tissues of the

EXAMINATION OF THE EXTREMITIES 159

long extensor of the great toe. A medical friend enveloped the whole foot in a firm case of plaster of Paris. The wound healed, and he returned to work within three weeks, and has given no trouble since.

Mr. Percy Botterell, at a meeting of the Medico-Legal Society, related an interesting case of a man who had part of one finger amputated as the result of an accident, for which he was paid compensation for several months. Later on he returned to work as an able-bodied seaman, but in a different ship.

He now made further claim on the ground that the stump of the amputated finger had become tender. His claim was admitted, and compensation was paid for a few weeks. He ceased attending for his weekly allowance, and it was then discovered that he had entered a hospital, the complaint now being a swelling of the hand and forearm, which he alleged was the result of the original accident.

The swelling and œdema having no obvious origin, suspicions were aroused at the hospital, and the whole arm was put in plaster of Paris, when the whole of the swelling and œdema rapidly disappeared, only to recur a few days after the plaster was removed. A second time the arm was encased in plaster of Paris, and again the swelling disappeared. A few days after the removal of the second plaster of Paris case, the arm was found to be again swollen and œdematous. This time circular marks were noticed upon his forearm, which corresponded to two thick elastic bands which were found in the man's possession. He was expelled from the hospital, and forthwith commenced proceedings for the recovery of his compensation, but upon the above history being proved by the surgeons and a nurse from the hospital his claim was dismissed. Criminal proceedings were set on foot, but the Judge held that, as the man was a foreigner, he may not have understood the nature of his acts !

Many medico-legal examinations degenerate into a matter of the workman pitting his wits against those of the medical examiner. In the case about to be related, for example, the manœuvre of pretending to assist in lifting a gipsy coal-scuttle conclusively settled a case which would otherwise have been somewhat difficult to expose.

C. M., aged twenty-two, whilst working as a trimmer on board ship, was struck by an iron splinter on the little finger of the right hand. Three weeks later the finger had to be amputated at the second joint. After ten weeks, the wound having healed, he was certified by the shipping company's doctor as fit for work. He then complained that the stump of the little finger became black and painful, that he could not straighten it or the ring-finger, and that the pain ran right up his arm. An independent medical man examined the hand, and reported that he was quite able to work, that he made no complaint of firm pressure on the alleged painful stump when his attention was held in another direction, and that although he said he could not grasp a ruler, he was ultimately induced to do so quite firmly. The employers stopped compensation. At the subsequent arbitration proceedings the medical referee, who sat with the Judge, expressed the opinion that the man was wholly disabled. Compensation was continued, with the result that the successful applicant became so much worse that he could not even sign his name!

Examination.—Eight months after the amputation he was sent to me for examination, with a view to an application being made for the termination of the award. At this period he appeared to have dropped his contention with regard to the amputated finger, resting his complaint chiefly on the ring-finger. While engaged in conversation, he allowed firm pressure on the stump without complaint. There was a slight tendency to Dupuytren's contraction of the ring-finger, the result of a previous accident; this had left a scar in the palm of the hand. He admitted that the scar was present prior to the accident to the little finger, and was in no way connected with it. He tried to make one believe that when the fist was closed, the ring-finger could not be closed as tightly as the other fingers, and that there was no power of grasp in that finger. He appeared to be a curious mixture of simplicity and artfulness, and it was some time before I was able to prove that he was affecting a disability which did not exist. As an evidence of his astuteness, I may mention that he informed me that his solicitor had told him he had better attend alone at my house, but he had explained that it would be wiser for him to come with his employer's officer in order that he might "get some information out of him." This seemed suspicious of a desire for a lump sum.

FIG. 13.

On applying a current of electricity to the forearm, stimulating the exact muscles which pull the ring-finger down on to the palm of the hand, they acted at once, irrespective of his volition, showing that the nervous and muscular tissues were intact and in order. He was induced to close his fist and resist it being opened; it was only after repeated trials that he forgot himself, and grasped tightly with the alleged powerless ring-finger as well as the others.

On being requested to lift by the semicircular handle a gipsy coal-scuttle, weighing 28 pounds, he at first refused even to try, but after considerable insistence was persuaded to make a serious effort. He complained that the brass handle hurt the front of the ring-finger. After the handle had been covered with cotton-wool, he was induced to hook it up with the ring-finger alone, but even then declined to try to lift the scuttle off the ground. I said we would try it together, and applying both my hands to his forearm, whilst he kept the ring-finger acting as a hook, we pulled together, lifting the scuttle off

EXAMINATION OF THE EXTREMITIES   161

the ground. It is obvious that my assistance was merely a pretence, inasmuch as, although I did help to pull, I could not possibly help him in keeping bent the ring-finger, upon which the whole weight was suspended. His remark after this performance, " But you helped me," showed that he had been deliberately pretending incapacity.

Result.—Six weeks later, as the applicant did not appear at the hearing, the Judge terminated the compensation, but it was arranged that the case might come on again for trial a fortnight later. Meanwhile the applicant was said to have heard of a job, which he decided to take, and abandoned his claim three days before the date appointed for the further hearing.

Knee.—Injury to a working man's knee-joint always gives rise to anxiety, and, if permanent, it is a very serious matter for him. Fraudulent attempts to claim compensation for permanent incapacity on account of injury in this region are common.

C. N. struck his right knee-joint whilst at work, injuring it; two weeks later he was declared by his employer's doctor to be fit for work. At the end of a subsequent five weeks he was sent by his employers to another doctor, who declared him fit for light work, which he was offered, but declined. A fortnight later he was sent to a third medical man, who declared him fit for work on the level. He was supplied with an elastic knee-cap, but declined to do any work, and stated that he was permanently disabled, and would never work again. He was, after ten months, sent to me for examination and report. There were no signs of disease of any kind in his right knee-joint, and as there was no muscular wasting, it was evident that he had not been trying to save his knee-joint. When he was undressed I was able, without causing pain, to bend his knee so that his calf touched the back of his thigh. When asked to stand upon his toes, he did so on the extreme joint of each great toe after the fashion affected by professional dancers, and this he did without complaining of any pain.

He had the knack of making the muscles of the right knee-joint quiver when he walked, but when it was pointed out to him that this was obviously intentional, and wholly unnecessary, it ceased; indeed, he subsequently walked up and down my consulting-room, quite naturally, without any lameness. He complained that he could not work because his knee " gave way "; when asked voluntarily to make his knee give way, in order that I might observe actually what happened, to my surprise he jerked back his knee-joint, making the whole knee stiff. I had expected him to bend his knee and fall on the floor. Now, it is quite obvious that if the movement he described to me did occur while he was at work—which, by the way, from a surgical point of view, is impossible—then it could not possibly do any harm, even if he were on the rigging of a ship. This man was a sailor. I gave as my opinion that he was perfectly well, and was fit for any work that a sailor should be asked to do. His weekly payments were

11

MALINGERING

stopped; his solicitor withdrew proceedings, and nothing more was heard of the case. This man was off work for ten months for a trifling injury; he had been shamming most of the time, and I think firmer treatment at the initial stages would have been the truest kindness.

It will be noted that this man saw three medical examiners separately. No. 1 said he was fit for work. No. 2 said that he was fit for "light work." No. 3 hedged, saying he was fit for "work on the level." Finally, the employer or his representative supplied an elastic stocking. Now, the knee-joint was injured or it was not; either the man was fit to work or he was not. A considerable experience of this class of cases has taught me that they require firm treatment : a strong line is best for all concerned.

The result of the following case gave me a special pleasure, for the man who was an employee endeavoured to influence me by referring to his acquaintance or intimacy with a public man, of whom he supposed I should stand in proper awe. The statement *did* influence me, but not in the way intended.

C. O., after being for four weeks on the sick-list, complained of being still unable to work, owing to an injury to his knee. No abnormality being found, he was told to resume duty at once. As he did not do so, he was again sent to me a few days later. Still nothing could be found; he stated, however, that his knee swelled when he walked. Having measured his knee, I sent him out to walk for two hours. On his return no swelling was discovered by measurement. He was told to resume work forthwith, which he did.

Alleged pain in the knee-joint, especially when attributed to acute synovitis or a slipped semilunar cartilage, may be proved to be false or exaggerated, as follows : the knee-joint is semiflexed, and the patient's attention drawn away from it to the ankle-joint; then the foot is freely abducted and adducted, and if the patient complains of no pain at the knee, it is obvious that the rotation of the head of the tibia produced by the ankle movement has not strained the knee-joint, as it would if the knee were the seat of any inflammation or dislocation.

C. P. was condemned by a house-surgeon to wear for many weeks a back splint for an alleged stiff right knee. I removed the splint, and directed her to sit down and take off her right boot, meanwhile I eagerly plied her with questions as to exactly what happened at the moment of the accident—whether the company's servants had been becomingly polite, what she said, what they said, and so forth—all of which was no business of mine. It was intensely interesting to her, however. She forgot the present and lived in the past, removing her boot in the usual way as she spoke—*i.e.*, she crossed her legs and bent her knee !

EXAMINATION OF THE EXTREMITIES 163

C. Q. sustained a fracture at the junction of the middle and lower thirds of the left leg, owing to the end of a sling of railway metals suddenly swinging round and striking him.

Seven and a half months later he was sent to me for an opinion as to his fitness to resume his ordinary work. His employers had had frequent opportunities of seeing this man personally when he called for his compensation (13s. 6d. a week), and it appeared to them that he was fit for work ; they also had a confirmatory report from one of their medical officers.

Examination.—He complained that he was unfit for anything but light work, because, although admittedly the bone had firmly united, he was still " too weak." He looked a strong, able-bodied man, the picture of health and strength. On examination, I found that the leg had been very well set, union was perfect ; there were the remains of some thickening, but the circumference of both legs at knee and ankle was the same. It seemed preposterous for this man to suggest that he was in any way affected as the result of the accident. That he was in possession of full use of his limbs was evidenced by the fact that I caused him to stand on the tips of the toes of both feet (after the style of ballet-dancers), which he did for a considerable period, even turning right round whilst thus balancing himself. I then steadied him slightly with my hands, and he stood for some time on the fore part of his left foot alone, and yet he told me he was too weak to work.

He informed me that he had seen another doctor only the day before, who had told him it would be a year before he could do full work. It transpired that C. Q. was then doing light work for his cousin, a barge-owner, the duties consisting of " cleaning the shores," for which he received 15s. a week.

Result.—Here was a man who was manifestly abusing his privileges under the Workmen's Compensation Act. As the result of my medical examination C. Q. returned to his work.

A slightly flexed position is the most comfortable one for the knee-joint, and this position is, as a rule, assumed when either sitting or lying. More especially is this the case if the knee-joint is the subject of pain or swelling. Occasionally a malingerer keeps his knee rigid, as if in a vice. The idea seems to be to impress the examiner that there is an entire absence of all movement, and that the condition is correspondingly serious.

C. R. stated that whilst unloading a ship he injured his left knee. There were no physical signs as the result of his alleged accident. He had suffered from varicose veins for many years ; this he admitted. He refused to bend his joint except to a very slight degree, asserting that even this caused him intense pain. I therefore had both knees X-rayed, with negative results. Later, he was induced to consent to being put under an anæsthetic. When he had been suitably prepared by fasting and was in sight of the couch and apparatus, it was explained to him that if he could now bend his knee the anæsthetic

MALINGERING

would be unnecessary. This he did at once voluntarily, flexing the knee so that the calf pressed on his hamstrings !

He was then asked to stand upon a chair, and to get on to it by putting his left (injured) leg first on the chair. He did so, and thus raised his whole body (more than 11 stone) on his injured knee without complaint !

Ulceration of the Leg.—A large number of working men suffer from chronic ulceration of the leg, and, provided it is not the result of an accident, continue to work for months, and sometimes years.

In the event of a subsequent accident to the adjacent parts, it is always a somewhat difficult matter if the plaintiff attempts to associate the old-standing complaint with the accident. This is especially the case where, as sometimes happens, an opportunity of examining the case is not afforded for some considerable time after the receipt of the injury ; for, as is well known, wounds following an accident sometimes rapidly develop an ulcer-like appearance.

C. S.—I was asked by a firm of solicitors to examine, on behalf of the defendant, an actor, aged forty-one, who alleged that he had injured his leg in a street accident. His statement was that he finished his business that day, but on undressing in the evening found his pants sticking to his leg, and treated the wound himself. The allegation was that he had lost some fifty engagements at music halls ; yet, although he was losing so much money, he did not try to hasten his recovery by seeking medical aid until *seven months* after the accident.

Examination.—On examining the whole of the leg, I found a large varicose vein running up to the groin, and the remains of an old-standing varicose ulcer at the lower part of the shin, which had the appearance of having been recently healed. The appearance of a recently healed varicose ulcer is characteristic ; there is usually a thin, glistening, bluish piece of skin wholly or partially surrounded by a dappled area.

C. S. contended that the blow on his leg was the sole cause of the condition. He had effectually evaded any dogmatic medical statement by preventing the defendant having a medical examination until the wound had healed. It was impossible for anyone to say with certainty, from mere inspection, when the ulcer had first occurred, though from its appearance I felt prepared to say with some confidence that it must have been a somewhat serious one. My view was that at the time of the accident he had an ulcer, probably of very old standing, and that he made up his mind he would have it healed at the expense of the defendant.

I felt sure I was dealing with a fraudulent claim, and that his story was so unsound that he would have difficulty under cross-examination in convincing a jury of his *bona fides.*

EXAMINATION OF THE EXTREMITIES   165

Result.—About two months afterwards, at a County Court, the case was heard by the Judge sitting with a jury, and a verdict was given for the defendant.

It is not unusual for a malingerer to conceal the early stages of his disease, and thus make additional difficulties for those who have to report on him. Sometimes these cases are exceedingly difficult, and much firmness is necessary. The following case might, under other circumstances, have ended disastrously :

History. — C. T. complained that whilst engaged as an electrical engineer in a night shift, he suddenly fell across an iron bar, injuring his left groin.

Examination.—He had a bubo on the left groin, and a healing soft chancre beneath the prepuce. Being suddenly taxed with the origin of his complaint, he admitted it, and as he was attempting to obtain money under false pretences he was discharged from his employment.

A few days afterwards he furnished a certificate to his employers from his own doctor, stating that he had been in attendance on him for some time and that he was not suffering from venereal disease, and that his injury was the result of an accident.

I was asked under the circumstances what should be done, and I advised that no notice should be taken.

Shortly afterwards, however, another certificate to the same effect came from a surgeon at a well-known hospital.

It would appear that the man had been artful enough to wait until the soft chancre healed before he consulted the surgeon, who believed his statements, and indeed lectured upon the case to a number of medical men who happened to be present, as one of traumatism, and therefore non-venereal.

I subsequently saw both surgeons and explained the circumstances. The man's own doctor admitted that he had subsequently discovered the soft chancre, though he had not done so at the time he wrote the certificate.

Artificial or Self-induced Dermatitis.—This form of dermatitis is usually found on the extensor surfaces of the left forearm, on the fronts of the thighs, and of the shins. As a rule, the knees are exempt. It is produced in various ways. Simple rubbing with a wet finger will in many people cause ulceration of the skin. Another very frequent method is using a match, preferably one of those which strike on any box, the head of which is dipped in water and rubbed up and down on the skin. Strong mineral acids, again, are frequently used.

The characteristics of the eruption are as follows : There are

MALINGERING

usually a number of long, narrow ulcers running in a longitudinal direction; on the shin, for example, they run up and down. They are sharply circumscribed, and the skin around is healthy. They are often very deep.

This vertical arrangement of a series of linear ulcers is very characteristic. The original character of the lesions is in some cases masked by secondary infections, which may set up a considerable amount of cellulitis in the neighbourhood of the lesions; this must be reduced before the true nature of the disease is manifest. After the subsidence of the secondary inflammation, a rapid cure can be effected in all cases by an occlusive dressing under plaster of Paris.

CHAPTER X

ASYMMETRY

The study of asymmetry is a very important one in medico-legal work.

It will often account for what is apparently the wasting of a limb. Such symptoms as backache, sciatica, and general weakness, are sometimes due to a shortening of one side of the body, which causes an undue strain on certain joints and ligaments. This strain has passed unnoticed while the patient was in good health prior to his accident, and his attention is first called to it when the debilitated condition which ensues from an accident occurs. He naturally attributes it to his accident, and may continue to be disabled by it for a long time, whereas the use of proper remedies to overcome deformities—such as a cork sole to his boot—would speedily result in relief of his pain.

Asymmetry is very much more common than is generally supposed. One authority found, as the result of an examination of a large number of limbs, that only some 12 per cent. were of the same length, the differences varying from $\frac{1}{8}$ to 1 inch. Young, who measured a large number of boys, found 70 per cent. of unequal limbs, the great majority being shorter on the right side. These cases were exclusive of those having any disease which might account for the shortening, such as infantile paralysis, flat-foot, genu valgum, coxa vara and valga, and congenital dislocation of the hip.

How this asymmetry arises is difficult to explain. It is, apparently, a congenital defect, and it has been noted that where the father and mother have· both been shorter on one side—say the right—the child has the same defect even more marked. It is, therefore, probably hereditary in most cases. It may possibly be due to the artery of the smaller limb being not so large as its fellow. Another explanation is that it is set

167

168 MALINGERING

up by a faulty habit. A child who persistently stands at ease on one leg will be apt to have that leg compressed, shortened, and smaller than the limb on the other side.

Tubby, who has gone into this matter very thoroughly in his work on " Deformities, including Diseases of the Bones and Joints," has generously put at my disposal the figures

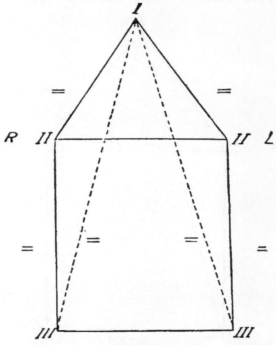

Fig. 14.—To demonstrate Measurements for Symmetry and Asymmetry.

R., Right; *L.*, left; *I.*, centre of sternal notch; *II.*, anterior superior spines; *III.*, internal malleoli; = represents equality of measurements.

which demonstrate his method of measurement. To his chapter on Asymmetry I am indebted for much of what appears in the following few pages.

He points out that the figures are highly diagrammatic, and that they do not pretend to any accuracy in the proportional measurement of the trunk, pelvis, etc. When viewing the patient from behind, which, of course, is necessary in examining for asymmetry, the figures must be reversed.

ASYMMETRY 169

The method of measurement about to be described is the best for discovering in which part of the body shortening has really taken place.

On each side of the body three measurements are taken: The first from the sternal notch to each internal malleolus (see Fig. 14, dotted lines *I.* to *III.*, and *I.* to *III.*); the second from the sternal notch to each anterior superior spine (see

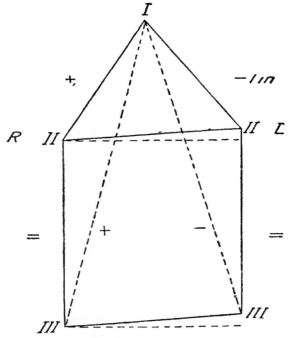

FIG. 15.—SIMPLE ASYMMETRY.

The left half of the trunk is smaller than the right, but the legs are equal.

Fig. 14, *I.* to *II. L.*, and *I.* to *R. II.*); and the third from the anterior superior spines to each internal malleolus (see Fig. 14, *II. L.* to *III.*, and *R. II.* to *III.*). This method of measurement is recommended for all examinations where legal questions are involved.

Often the question of fitness or otherwise for work turns upon the alleged shortness of one limb compared with the corresponding limb. The legs may, as is shown in the above diagram (Fig. 15), be of equal length when measured accurately from each anterior superior spinous process to the corre-

MALINGERING

sponding malleolus, yet, owing to one side of the trunk being smaller than the other, there is considerable deformity, which is probably congenital.

A very common condition, as illustrated in Fig. 16, met with as the result of fracture of the thigh or leg bones, is one where the halves of the trunk are equal, but one leg is shorter than the other.

The condition just described in Fig. 16—namely, that of simple shortening of one limb, is not infrequently com-

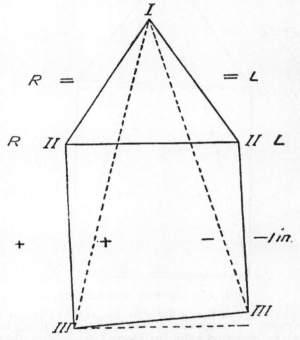

FIG. 16.—SIMPLE ASYMMETRY.

The halves of the trunk are equal, but the left leg is shorter than the right.

plicated by the trunk on the same side also being smaller than the trunk on the opposite side (see Fig. 17), thus producing a condition of asymmetry of the whole of one side of the body. It is not difficult to see that in a case of this sort a comparatively slight shortening, as the result of an accident to one limb, might readily *appear*, on account to the trunk deformity, to be much more than it really is.

ASYMMETRY

If the defect in the body was always on one side only, the difficulty in detection would not be great. Sometimes the right side of the trunk may be larger than the left, but the leg of that side may be shorter. If the shortness of the right leg exactly compensates for the lengthening of the trunk on the right side, the asymmetry will not be apparent. In the

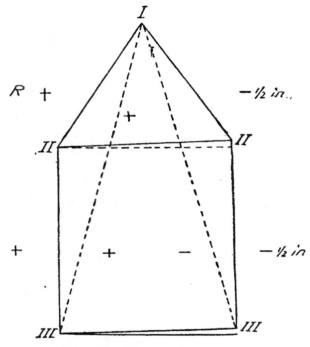

Fig. 17.—Simple Asymmetry.

The left side of the trunk is smaller than the right; the left leg is shorter than the right. Though the shortening of the left leg is only ½ inch, if the limb is measured from the sternal notch it would appear to be 1 inch.

diagram on p. 172 the trunk on the right side is 1 inch too long, and the right leg ½ inch too short, the combination resulting in the whole of the right side being ½ inch too long.

It occasionally happens, however, that the difference in measurement from the sternal notch to the right and to the left anterior superior spinous process is entirely nullified by a difference in the length of the legs, so that as the net result, when measurements are taken from the sternal notch to the right and left internal malleolus, it is found that one whole side is *not* shorter than the other. This is called " compensated crossed asymmetry " (see Fig. 19).

When supporting deductions as to the amount of actual shortening arrived at by this method, it should be remembered that the measurement from the sternal notch to the internal

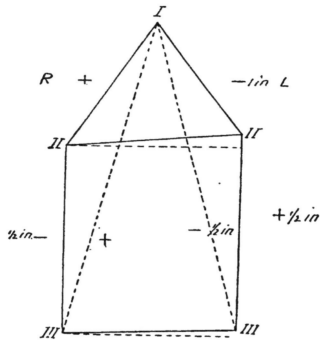

Fig. 18.—Crossed Asymmetry, Non-compensated.

The right side of the trunk is larger than the left, but the right leg is shorter than the left, and the compensation is not complete—*i.e.*, *R. I.* to *III.* is greater than *L. I.* to *III.*

malleolus is one side of a triangle, and the others are two sides of the same triangle; therefore, the two together must be greater than the one. This is not dealt with by Tubby, but geometrically, of course, it is a fact. Questions based upon this might conceivably be put in cross-examination with a view to making the deduction appear to be inaccurate, but as the allowance to be made for this factor is only about 9 per cent., the effect, when dealing with a half, or even a whole inch, is of very little moment.

ASYMMETRY

Besides differences in length, it is quite common to find very considerable difference in the circumferential measurements of the limbs, this being much more the case in the arms than the legs. Rawitsch, who took measurements of 500 soldiers in all classes of society, found that in only 25 per cent. were the arms equal in measurement. He took three measurements:

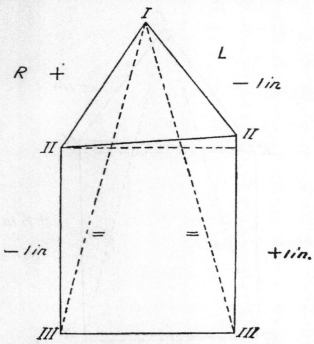

FIG. 19.—CROSSED ASYMMETRY, COMPENSATED.

R. I. to *III.* = *L. I.* to *III.*, but *R. I.* to *II.* > *L. I.* to *II.*, and *R. II.* to *III.* < *L. II.* to *III.*

1. The shoulder, which was taken by getting the patient to put his arms out horizontally, and then carrying the tape vertically round the shoulder under the axilla.
2. The arm, at the middle point.
3. The forearm, at its point of greatest circumference.

He found that—

In the arms:
In 27·6 per cent. they were the same in measurement.
In 3 per cent. the left arm was bigger than the right.

MALINGERING

In 13·8 per cent. a difference of ½ to ¾ inch in favour of the right.

In 26 per cent. a difference of ⅜ inch.

In 29·6 per cent. a difference of less than ⅜ inch.

Of the forearm :

In 22·4 per cent. the measurements were identical.

In 1·4 per cent. the left was greater than the right.

In 10 per cent. a difference of ½ to ¾ inch in favour of the right.

In 25·4 per cent. a difference of ⅜ inch. .

In 40·8 per cent. a difference of less than ⅜ inch.

Rawitsch concludes from his measurements that a difference of ⅜ to ¾ inch round the arm and forearm are not indicative of any anomaly or disease.

In the author's opinion measurements, however carefully taken, at the shoulder-joint are useless. So much depends upon the prominence of the great pectoral muscle in front and the latissimus dorsi behind.

These asymmetrical conditions are very important to remember; and when a man complains, for example, that one arm is wasted after an accident, more especially if it is found that there is a general diminution of all the muscles, that there is no sensory or trophic disturbance, and that the one limb is not markedly colder or bluer than the other, careful measurement *should be taken of the whole body,* when it may be found that this asymmetry of the arm has its parallel in a diminution of length of one leg or of one side of the trunk.

CHAPTER XI

EXAMINATION BY X-RAY PHOTOGRAPHY

Radiographic Examination.—In investigating suspected injury or disease of the bones, X-rays are becoming more and more used. By their application we have at our disposal a more or less certain means of proving or disproving the existence of an organic basis for the symptoms complained of. It is advisable that there should be such an examination in all cases where there is the slightest prospect of its affording any assistance.

It should be an invariable rule to have all bone or joint injuries photographed by X-rays before going into Court. It is well to remember that, whether the defendant takes this precaution or not, the plaintiff probably will. In view of the fact that radiograms are useless, and are in fact very apt to mislead unless very carefully taken, it is obviously prudent always to employ a competent radiographer.

C. U. had her thigh broken as the result of gross carelessness. Ten months later I was asked by the defendant's solicitor to examine the case in consultation with their medical man, and to report whether I could support him in the suggestion that the incapacity was being unnecessarily prolonged. In my report I was able, however, to point out, without the help of the X-rays, that there was an ununited fracture, and furthermore that the plaintiff's solicitor had very wisely obtained an X-ray photograph of it a few days before ! It amused me to discover that, by the instructions of the plaintiff's solicitor, a portable apparatus had been taken to a house some distance from London, and the photograph taken with the utmost secrecy. As my report advised that from a medical point of view we had no case, the defendants, under the circumstances, were naturally glad to settle ; and the rod in pickle (over which, no doubt, there had been much gloating) was never presented to me in the witness-box.

176 MALINGERING

X-ray examinations should always be thoroughly conducted. For example, the use of the fluorescent screen alone may lead to most inaccurate conclusions ; and it is possible for even a skilled observer to overlook such an obvious injury as a transverse fracture of the shaft of the tibia. The screen examination should, therefore, never be solely relied upon alone, but in all cases the radiographic method should be employed. By this means accurate recognition of injury or disease of bone is assured ; moreover—and this is very important in medico-legal cases—a permanent record is obtained.

C. V., a dock labourer, sustained an accident owing to a large piece of chalk (weighing over one hundredweight) falling on his *legs*. He had no bones broken, but sustained injuries from which the first medical man who examined him reported he might be expected to recover within a few months. He continued to complain of pain and inability to use his left leg, and was examined at intervals of every few months by numerous surgeons, who found wasting and shortening of the left thigh. Sixteen months after the accident payment was stopped on the advice of a medical man who saw him on behalf of a company. Arbitration proceedings were commenced. It was claimed for the plaintiff that the condition of his leg was due either to a local neuritis or to injury of the head or spine as a result of the accident. The defence, I believe, relied on the contention that the condition was congenital. The County Court Judge decided in the man's favour, and ordered the weekly allowance to continue.

Some months later he was sent to me for examination. There was considerable wasting and some shortening of the left thigh bone. A radiogram, taken at the suggestion of an eminent surgeon who saw the case with me, showed clearly that the whole condition was due to arthritis deformans of the hip-joint, probably of some years' duration. X-ray examinations showed the presence of the same conditions, but to a less degree, in the other hip and in both knee-joints. He was, in fact, the subject of constitutional articular disease, as shown by radiograms of four different joints of his body. The appearance in each case pointed to the conclusion that the disease could not have existed for less than two years ; but the pain at the left hip-joint, the shortening of the left leg, and the wasting of the muscles of the left thigh, all of which were proved to be present as early as the first arbitration proceedings, indicated the commencement of arthritic hip-joint disease long prior to the date of the accident. There was no evidence that the accident even aggravated this condition ; therefore, so far as the accident was concerned, no incapacity for work remained.

Payment was by my advice stopped, and I suggested that if arbitration procedings were again taken, a totally different defence should be set up from that presented at the first trial. A Medical Assessor sat with the Judge, and I produced the X-ray photographs, and proved that the man's disabilities resulted from old-standing hip-joint disease, which had neither been produced nor accelerated by his accident. The County Court Judge decided in the company's favour, and discontinued the man's allowance.

Radiograms are often found to be valueless for diagnostic purposes owing to the fact that sufficient attention has not been paid to the relation between the source of the X-ray and the part which is to be examined. Striking distortions may be the result of such an omission. In dealing with bone injuries, it is advisable, when possible, to have *two* views of the same limb, one secured in a direction at right angles to the other; for when radiographed in one direction only, a frac-

Fig. 20.   Fig. 21.
(From Ironside Bruce's " X-Ray Examination " in Choyce's "System of Surgery.")

ture may be invisible; further, an accurate estimation of the amount of displacement of the fragments in a case of fracture can be obtained only by this means. The illustrations (Figs. 20 and 21) represent the same injury—namely, fracture of the left fibula. In Fig. 20, which is a postero-anterior view, there is no evidence of fracture, the broken ends of the fibula being in perfect apposition. In Fig. 21, the lateral view, an undoubted fracture, with a certain amount of displacement of the fragments, is plainly seen in the position marked ⇛——➤

Until recently the only guide to the best position for the X-ray tube has been the observer's experience, and the method

178 MALINGERING

usually followed has been to place the tube in some indeterminate relation to the part. Now, however, there is a disposition to adjust the tube definitely and accurately. When this is done, the advantage gained is obvious. Dr. Ironside Bruce has produced a work in the form of an atlas, which presents many advantages, for it contains radiograms of the normal at different ages (five, fifteen, and twenty-five), each secured with the tube in a definite anatomical relationship. Thus a certain knowledge of normal radiographic appearances is afforded, and enables the radiologist to secure a radiogram of any part of the body in a given case identical with that to be found in the atlas.* The position in which the subject should be placed has been made clear by photographs, and the relation of the tube to some familiar and accessible anatomical point has been defined in each instance. A prudent man will always see that, in addition to the radiogram of the affected part, a comparable radiogram of the normal part of the same subject is produced. For example, if a patient complains that his knee-joint has been injured, and on X-ray examination the presence of osteo-arthritis in the alleged injured knee is revealed, it is obviously of the utmost importance that the *un*injured knee should *also* be examined, for not infrequently it will show equal, or it may be still more marked, evidence of the same disease.

If the normal is to be used for the purpose of comparison with the abnormal, it is absolutely necessary that both the normal and the abnormal views should be secured with the tube in exactly the same relation to the part examined. There often appears in a radiogram some peculiarity which can only be explained by comparison with the normal—for example, when dealing with a case of injury to bones in which the epiphyses are still separate, and in which one cannot be certain whether there is displacement or not.

It should be remembered that it is one thing to look at a radiogram, and quite another thing to be able to interpret it correctly, and it is amusing to see skiagrams solemnly handed round to a jury, who examine them with much anxiety and apparent intelligence. Radiograms should always be inter-

* " A System of Radiography," Ironside Bruce. London : H. K. Lewis, 1907.

EXAMINATION BY X-RAY PHOTOGRAPHY   179

preted to the Judge and jury by those accustomed to dealing with them.

Radiograms are specially useful in cases of fracture, for they show whether or not good union has taken place, and how far the bones have returned to their proper position. In cases of osteo-arthritis the radiogram often shows the presence of bony abnormalities.

Radiograms cannot, of course, demonstrate muscular injuries, but when the attachment of a muscle to the bone has been torn away and it carries with it some portions of periosteum or bone, the outline of the bone is irregular and wavy.

It is an advantage to be present when the radiogram is being developed, for an opportunity is thus afforded of viewing the plate whilst it is still wet, it being then at its best for this purpose, as the subsequent drying process causes some loss of detail. Prints often fail to reveal changes which are manifest in the plate, and their use for demonstrating purposes is to be deprecated. Yet how often are they produced for the Judge and jury to inspect, and erroneous statements made, and damaging opinions formed, which too frequently end in a miscarriage of justice ?

I always make it a rule to be present when the radiograph is taken, to follow the plate into the dark-room, initial it, and be at hand when it is developed. Under these circumstances, no mistake can be made, such as the wrong plate being produced, and one is able in the witness-box to identify the skiagram. There is also the additional advantage that during the time the plate is wet, after it has been removed from the fixing-bath and washed, infinitesimal changes can there and then be discussed with the radiographer.

I have, by modifying an existing apparatus, produced what I hope may prove a useful instrument for the purpose of the inspection of radiograms in Court (Figs. 22 and 23). It consists of a small triangular-shaped metal box, the base of which is some 10 by 9 inches, with two sloping opal glass sides. On one side, in front of the opal glass, the negative of the radiogram of the part in question is fixed, and on the other the negative of the corresponding part of the same person, or, if this happens to be abnormal, a skiagram of the same part of a normal subject.

Inside the box are placed four small incandescent electric lamps of eight candle-power each, the current being supplied by a 60-ampère H.R. 4-volt accumulator, which is carried separately from the instrument. This affords a brilliant light, and shows up every detail in a very clear way. The apparatus is a little heavy, but portable, and is handed by the usher to the Judge and jury. Small slips of paper, with arrows and a word or two of description, can be pasted on the plate, and certainly help to elucidate any point which is being made.

FIG. 22.   FIG. 23.

It is a good plan to offer to personally explain to the tribunal these details, and actually point out any abnormalities that may exist.

No radiogram should be produced in Court unless it is the work of a competent medical radiologist; yet hundreds of pounds are often obtained from defendants by means of untrustworthy radiograms taken by amateurs or unqualified persons. It is a good plan, when an opponent intends to make use of a radiogram taken, let us say, by a local chemist, to subpœna that gentleman, and to prompt counsel with a few conundrums to be solved by the witness when in the box.

Radiograms are as easily faked as are the trick representations of a cinematograph show. A skiagram is not a photograph in the ordinary sense; it is really a reproduction of a series of shadows of tissues which have different opacities to the X-rays. Obviously these shadows, by crossing or over-

EXAMINATION BY X-RAY PHOTOGRAPHY 181

lapping one another, may destroy the characteristics of each. The view presented is the same as if the whole subject were on one plane ; therefore form, size, distance, and position, have all to be reasoned out. It is scarcely fair to exhibit a picture in Court which will delude innocent people. These shadows must be photographed *secundum artem.*

CHAPTER XII

THE USE OF ELECTRICITY IN ALLEGED MALINGERING

THE utility of the electric battery in assisting to unmask the malingerer will have been noticed in many of the illustrations which have been given. A battery producing the faradic current only is required, and this may be obtained at very little cost. It should have a break key in one electrode; thus it will be possible to cut off completely the current from the patient unknown to him (whilst the coil is buzzing loudly), by simply depressing a small knob with the thumb (see Fig. 24).

Method of Using.—The indifferent electrode—that is, the one which is simply used to complete the circuit—may be of any shape or size.

Before actually proceeding to use the test, the battery should first be tried on oneself to ascertain what is the exact strength of the current about to be used. Moisten the skin of the patient over the area to be tested ; the water should be warm and freely used, both on electrodes and skin. It will need frequent renewal during the examination. No salt need be added ; a weak current is all that is necessary.

When a patient is malingering he may simulate either increased sensibility or loss of power.

Alleged Increased Sensibility.—If a man under examination complains of pronounced tenderness at a particular spot, it is well known how difficult it is to deny or affirm such a purely subjective symptom.

A weak current of electricity would increase pain or sensitiveness if genuine. The malingerer often complains that his alleged hypersensitive area is rendered more painful by the

182

THE USE OF ELECTRICITY 183

electric current. The truth or otherwise of this may be demonstrated by the following manœuvre :

A noisy faradic battery is set in motion, and the indifferent electrode applied to the body at some distance from the alleged painful spot ; the other handle, in which is the break key, is gradually, from some distance, approached to the painful spot. The break key is depressed and the current entirely cut off, although the battery is still left in noisy action. The patient

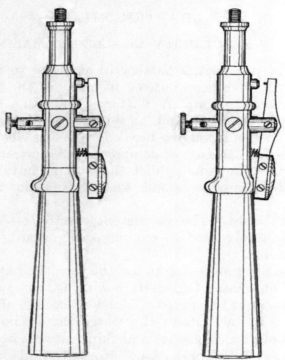

Fig. 24.—Testing Electrode Handle with Break Key.

is asked to state very definitely whether the current is felt to a greater or less degree as the handle approaches the painful area.

In a surprising number of cases ignorant but determined malingerers, hearing the battery still in action, and assuming that the current *must* therefore reach them, have told me that the pain produced over the alleged painful spot was so intense that it amounted to " agony." The pain is sometimes

184 MALINGERING

described as being similar to that produced by the " stab of a knife," and so forth ; indeed, on several occasions yells and howls have been produced which have been heard through closed doors in different parts of my house.

History.—C. W., a carman, aged thirty-two, stated that whilst lifting a bookcase he suddenly strained his back. Two years previously he had had a similar accident, for which he received sick pay for twenty-three weeks. He belonged to several sick clubs.

Examination.—I saw him three weeks after the accident in consultation with another medical man. On entering the room he walked lamely with a stick, and stood with his back bent. Both the degree of lameness and the angle at which he held his back varied considerably as time went on.

When asked to strip and indicate the spot where the pain was situated, he stooped in the process of undressing without much complaint, and as he was obviously acting I tested him with the electric current. The two poles of a faradic battery giving a weak electric current were applied to his shoulders, one pole was left stationary and the other was gradually approached to the alleged painful area ; at the same time the current was switched off, the coil still buzzing loudly. On three separate occasions he complained bitterly that the effect of the current was *more severe* over the area of the alleged strain than elsewhere.

After a thorough and complete examination, he was advised to return to work. At first he was defiant, and remarked, " I suppose there are other doctors I can go to." I told him that of course there were many, but that the number he might consult would not make the slightest difference to my opinion or my report. At this stage he forgot himself and stood upright ! Both the result of the battery test and his sudden alteration of position were pointed out to him, and the suggestion made that possibly the electric current had cured him. He saw that the game was up, and promised to return forthwith to " light work " if it were procured for him.

The electric test should always be repeated two or three times to prevent a mistake being made, for it is obvious that the conviction of a flagrant fraud of this sort should be put beyond the possibility of error. Moreover, it is almost sure to be suggested later that a mistake was made, and if the examiner can say that the experiment was repeated on three separate occasions, it is all to the good.

I would, however, warn those who apply this test to apply it exactly as above described ; otherwise an unfair conclusion might possibly be come to in the case of a nervous or hysterical person. If, for instance, the current is, on the first application, applied over the painful area, and on the second and subsequent

THE USE OF ELECTRICITY 185

occasions the current is cut off prior to reaching this spot, it may be (or at any rate it will be suggested) that the first application of the current acted as a mental suggestion, and the subsequent complaints were the result of the powerful stimulus given to the mind by the initial application of the current to the alleged painful area. When no current reaches the spot prior to the complaints of knife-like sensations, etc., this suggestion cannot be made, especially if, as indicated above, the experiment is repeated several times.

I have found this test very valuable in demonstrating a malingerer to his own doctor—a procedure, however, which is not always wise. It should never be given away in the case of a doctor attached to a running-down solicitor.

Occasionally—very occasionally, when by intuition I feel that the circumstances are exceptional, and that I can effect a *coup d'état*—I tell the patient. I do not, however, recommend this, for it tells with more effect in the witness-box—preferably in the course of cross-examination.

History.—C. X., as the result of a collision at sea some eight months previously, fell on an iron railing, injuring his back. At the time of my examination he complained of pain in his back and chest.

Examination.—Whilst waiting his turn for examination he pretended he was so feeble that he could not stand even for a few minutes. During the examination, except when called to order, he puffed and blew as if he were short of breath.

With regard to his chest he indicated no special area as being painful, but complained of the whole of the front of his chest. The result of the examination, however, revealed nothing abnormal as the result of the accident.

With regard to his back, he complained of pain at the fourth lumbar spinous process. Suspecting him, and in order to test him, I applied the faradic current from an electric battery to his back, and, whilst the coil was still buzzing loudly, switched off the current as the pole of the battery reached the alleged painful area. On two separate occasions as the electrode approached its vicinity he complained bitterly. He yelled so loudly, and spoke so boisterously, that I had to insist upon his controlling himself ; indeed a patient who was waiting in a room some distance from my consulting-room heard him yelling. After repeating the experiment, I explained to him what had actually taken place. He evidently appreciated the mistake he had made, for upon applying the current for the third time, he made no complaint !

In order to satisfy myself with regard to the alleged tenderness in the chest I used a stethoscope over the whole of the front of his chest. Believing that I was merely examining his chest in the ordinary

MALINGERING

way, he made no complaint, though I took occasion to press with very great firmness on the alleged painful area.

It was, therefore, perfectly obvious that C. X. was a very bad actor, that he was not suffering as the result of his accident, and I advised his employers accordingly.

On receipt of my certificate his weekly allowance was stopped, and he made no protest.

The experiment sometimes fails. It seems almost incredible, but recently, on two separate occasions, I satisfied myself that claimants had actually been coached in the details above described so as to thwart the discovery of an imposture. But even so, it affords a convenient way of solving the very difficult question as to whether a patient really suffers the pain he alleges when pressure is applied on a particular spot.

Assuming the patient has been coached in the test above described and it does not have the desired result, the following procedure should be adopted : His eyes are covered, or he is asked to look well to one side ; he is then directed to say definitely and at once when he feels the electric current, which, it is explained, is to be switched on and off at intervals as the electrode is moved over and in the neighbourhood of the painful area. It is surprising how often very firm pressure by the electrode will be borne without the slightest complaint, while the patient's attention is taken up in attempting to decide whether a weak current of electricity is or is not flowing on a certain area which he has, either consciously or unconsciously, taught himself to believe is sensitive to the slightest touch.

Alleged Loss of Power.—If complaint be made of loss of power, the test should be carried out as follows : Start the current. Place the testing electrode (in which there is the break key) upon the muscles in question with the thumb depressed (for motor points see Chapter XXVI.). The patient is, of course, receiving no current. Now sharply raise the thumb ; if the muscles are normal, a contraction will immediately result. The patient, of course, does not at the precise moment expect the sudden stimulus, and has no time to voluntarily inhibit it. Moreover, if the current is fairly strong, he cannot prevent the muscle contracting ; besides, if he attempts to do so, the *opposing* muscles will be seen to enlarge. Assuming there has been a normal response to the electrical stimulation, *any loss of power cannot be due to a local lesion*, for any

THE USE OF ELECTRICITY

physiological interruption would (assuming the injury were not less than two days old) have resulted in diminution, if not in entire absence, of response to the faradic current.

History—C. Y.—I was asked by an insurance company to examine, in consultation with a doctor who was familiar with the case, a man who was said to have been suffering from lead poisoning for fourteen months. An opinion as to his fitness for work was required.

Examination.—He complained of weakness, inability to do anything, accompanied by complete loss of power in the whole of the upper right arm.

When asked to move the arm, elbow, and hand, he declined even to try, and when the arm was taken up it flopped down as if it did not belong to him. Giving him to understand that I was satisfied with regard to the paralyzed condition of his arm, I proceeded to examine his lungs, and lifted up his arm at right angles to his chest, to examine the side of his chest. He continued to hold it up himself ! He was next asked to bend both elbows, and upon my attempting to straighten the arm alleged to be paralyzed, he prevented my doing so —presumably because he thought he must oppose everything.

Absence of muscular wasting negatived the presence of local disease. In testing his sensation he was directed to look to one side, was lightly pricked alternately on the right and left arms, and asked to say " No " when he did not feel it and " Yes " when he did. When the right side was touched he said " Yes," and when the left side was touched he said " No," thus giving himself entirely away.

I now resumed the examination of the right arm. As is well known, in genuine lead poisoning the nerves which supply certain muscles become so diseased that nervous impulses cannot be sent to them from the brain, and, similarly, nervous impulses cannot be made to travel along the nerves even by means of a faradic current. The current was therefore applied, and the freest contraction of the muscles was obtained under the stimulus of the faradic current, showing that if lead palsy had ever been present, he had now wholly recovered from it ; indeed, when the current was applied with some strength, he drew his arm away so violently that a strong steel rod belonging to the instrument was bent.

The date of the onset of his alleged paralysis was inconsistent with the development of true lead palsy. Notwithstanding the fact that a few days before he had complained of paralysis of the right leg, when he was instructed to strip and walk round the room, feeling no doubt that he would have an inappreciative audience, he did so without lameness. There was no doubt he was clumsily acting.

He was living in a small room, the temperature of which could not have been less than seventy when we called ; it contained seven people, including a sympathetic wife who obviously believed in him. There was nothing amiss with him except the mental deterioration of prolonged idleness and introspection, and the physical disabilities produced by an environment in which it was impossible to maintain health.

MALINGERING

Result.—Compensation was stopped, and he took proceedings under the Workmen's Compensation Act. At the hearing I gave evidence as above, and judgment was given for the defendants.

If the response to electric stimulation is doubtful, compare the effect of the same strength of current on the muscles of the opposite side of the body—that is, convert them into a standard. It should be remembered that a response does not preclude injury to the central nervous system, nor does it exclude functional disease—*e.g.*, hysteria.

If no reaction can be obtained with the faradic current, a further examination should be made with the galvanic current, and the muscles thoroughly and carefully tested for the reaction of degeneration.

The condition of a patient who emerges from this test successfully requires further investigation. If he has a definite nervous lesion, the diagnosis and prognosis may be matters of some considerable difficulty, and it has not been found possible within the limits of this book to discuss them fully. A short account of electric testing will also be found in Chapter XXVI.

CHAPTER XIII

HERNIA AND MALINGERING

ACTUAL malingering in cases of hernia is comparatively rare, although occasionally patients present themselves with swelling in the groin, usually glands or cysts, and claim that these are herniæ resulting from traumatism. Even a cursory examination, of course, reveals the true nature of the case. It is, however, very common indeed for a workman to state that he is suffering from hernia as the result of a strain occurring in his work. Such cases are not only common, but very difficult to deal with, for, of course, it is open to any workman who has a hernia to try to make capital out of it. It is very easy to make up a history, and, in most cases, where time has elapsed, we have only the man's statement to depend upon.

The average layman has very little knowledge of how common rupture is, and how much hard laborious work is done day by day by men suffering from this complaint ; and very few are aware how much fraud is attempted in connection with claims for rupture. Barnard states : " There is probably more fraud connected with claims for rupture produced by accident than can be found in all the other cases of fraud for the rest of the body. Of the cases that claim compensation for damages for hernia as being caused by a sudden strain, probably not one in ten is genuine."

In view of the frequency of this disability among workpeople, all employers of labour would be wise to have a medical examination made before employing a man, and insurance companies might well suggest this as a general principle, so that employers may know whether an employee is, or is not, free from rupture when he is engaged.

189

190   MALINGERING

I propose to deal with this matter under three heads :

    1. Cases in which the hernia may fairly be attributed to traumatism.

    2. Those which may be definitely stated to be not attributable to strain or accident.

    3. Those in which the cause is uncertain.

1. When the Hernia may fairly be Attributed to Traumatism. —The patient will give a history like the following : that, while undergoing a strain, such as lifting a heavy weight in the course of his employment, he suddenly felt something wrong in the groin ; or it may be that he slipped whilst carrying a weight ; or was following his usual work under strained conditions, as, for example, if he had his legs widely separated ; or if, being an old man, he was put to work too heavy for his years. He will complain of pain of such severity that he had to cease work. On examination, the hernia will first of all be found to be a small one, not larger than a small lemon. It will be more or less painful on handling, the abdominal walls may be good, the other possible hernial openings will be closed, and there will be no marks of a truss having been worn. The hernia may at the outset be strangulated, in which case there is marked pain and vomiting, collapse, etc., and an operation may have to be performed forthwith ; if so, tears in the abdominal wall may be found, with extravasation of blood.

The following is a typical case of rupture produced whilst at work :

    C. Z., an employee, whilst in a sitting position, reached up to pull down a board, when his left foot, which was stretched out against an iron bar, slipped, and he at once felt a sudden strain and an acute pain in the left groin. His story is that he worked for the remainder of the day, being in pain all the time, and had to relieve himself by sitting down occasionally when he could. On returning home, at the earliest possible moment, he laid down on his bed, and next day, being unable to go to work, he consulted a doctor, who did not examine him, but gave him a lotion, and told him to rest in bed. This somewhat unusual method of treatment was continued for four days. It would appear that during this period he was actually sick, and had abdominal pain, which he described as " dull, deadly, and dismal." His statement was that there was no swelling, but that he noticed a hardness in the neighbourhood of the groin, and not un-naturally being dissatisfied with what may be euphemistically de-scribed as the expectant treatment he was receiving, he changed his doctor, and applied to a hospital, where, later on, he was operated upon.

HERNIA AND MALINGERING

There is no doubt that this man narrowly escaped with his life, for, certainly, the symptoms pointed to a partially strangulated hernia.

The interesting point is that there is no doubt about the exact time when the rupture did, in fact, take place. The symptoms were, from the very first, of an urgent character ; a less plucky man would soon have demanded more efficacious treatment.

The peritoneum *cannot* suddenly stretch so as to produce a sac which would allow a hernia to appear suddenly at the external ring or in the scrotum. If a rupture really came down suddenly, as is so often described, the man would be so ill from the bowel or omentum being nipped that he would then and there be in imminent danger of his life, and would probably require operation straight away.

The Departmental Committee on Compensation for Industrial Diseases which sat to inquire what diseases should be scheduled as arising out of and in the course of employment, reported as follows :

" The evidence which we have received from authorities of eminence is definitely to the effect that hernia may, though very rarely, be due to a sudden strain, in which case it would be the subject of compensation, if caused by the employment, as an accident. But what usually happens is that some cough or particular strain brings down a little farther a hernia, which has been slowly developing, so as first to make it prominent and attract attention."

2. **Cases which may definitely be said to be not Attributable to Strain or Accident.**—On examination, the following points will be noticed : First, the hernia is a large one. It descends into, or partially into, the scrotum ; it is painless to handle ; it either slips back easily into the abdominal cavity, or it is wholly or partly irreducible. In the former case the ring will be found to be large, and the inguinal canal straight ; in the latter case the hernia will probably contain omentum, and is irreducible, owing to the presence of old-standing adhesions. The abdominal walls will be weak, overladen with fat, and the other hernial openings will show evidence of laxity. Such a series of points marks a hernia of long standing, which has come on gradually, and become more and more marked in the

MALINGERING

course of time, and can under no circumstances be fairly described as due to an accident. Marks of a truss will be found if looked for ; the truss will have been left off—for the day ! ·

The following is a typical case wherein hernia, alleged to have been *due* to accident, was shown, on examination, to be of old standing :

> D. A., an employee of a large public body, put himself on the sick-list, and obtained a medical certificate to the effect that he was suffering from an inguinal hernia *produced in the ordinary course of his work.* It was stated to have occurred on a certain date at a specified hour. Now, what were the facts ? The man worked for a fortnight after the injury ; he did not complain at the time—indeed, he only mentioned it casually to his doctor, who was called in to attend to his wife a few days before he was examined. The appearance of the hernia, which was large, the history of no pain, sickness, vomiting, or inability to work at the time of the alleged seizure, made it impossible to believe that this was, in fact, a hernia of recent origin—indeed, it was evident he had had it for years, and the fact that some few months before he was sent back to work at the point of the bayonet for deliberate malingering added considerable weight to the opinion formed.

This second group is by far the most frequent in claims for compensation, but between these two classes there exists another :

3. **Cases in which the Cause is Uncertain.**—This is an intermediate, debatable class, in which there is a marked predisposition to hernia, with a history of a slight strain which can only be considered as a *contributory* factor in the production of the hernia.

A keen controversy has raged between those who assert that, since practically no hernia can occur without the pre-existence of a hernial sac, *all* ruptures should be classed as diseases and *none* as traumatism, and their opponents, who, whilst generally acknowledging the necessity for the pre-existence of a hernial sac, nevertheless hold that, without strain, the patient might quite well have gone through life without ever developing any hernia at all, and that, therefore, the hernia should be classed among those things due to accident.

In these debatable cases patients generally give the following history : that, as the result of some unusual strain in the course of their work, they felt something give way in the groin. They complain of very little or no pain, and do not cease work.

HERNIA AND MALINGERING 193

Another equally common history is that the workman accidentally finds a swelling which is painless, and does not necessitate absence from work, and that he remembers quite clearly having, a few hours or days before the occurrence of the tumour, undergone some special strain or accident, and he is firmly of opinion that the one is the result of the other.

On examination, a small rupture is found, easily reducible, as a rule, not painful to handle, with a small ring, and no sign of the use of a truss.

From an anatomical standpoint these cases present no difficulty ; the real difficulty is that, unless an operation for a radical cure is performed, the tissue changes cannot be sworn to,

A recent rupture has a thin, transparent sac which has been compared to tissue-paper. There is no mistaking an old rupture as seen when the radical cure is being performed. The sac, instead of being like tissue-paper, is thick ; the omentum, from its presence in the sac, has changed from a delicate thin membrane into a thick, brawny mass containing swollen veins. This is often adherent to the sac. The opening through which the rupture passes becomes circular, its edge is thick and rounded, and the pressure from above displaces it somewhat downwards. Not infrequently large masses of fat are found in the sac, which, judging from their relative size to the neck of the sac, must have grown there. An old sac is always thick and adherent to the surrounding tissues.

Now, what has happened has been as follows :

There has been a natural predisposition to a hernia, a pre-existing sac, reaching, it may be, as far down as the bottom of the scrotum, like the finger of a *new* glove, closed in the sense that a finger of a *new* glove is closed (Fig. 25, left side), and into the opening of which a knuckle of bowel has been slowly insinuating itself for some time (Fig. 26, right side). A series of strains occur, and gradually, by each succeeding strain, the glove-finger becomes opened up, and the rupture, from being unsuspected, at last, most likely during some exertion, more or less suddenly becomes fairly noticeable.

The question, therefore, how far such a rupture can be called " accidental " is a thorny one ; for all grades of cases occur, from those where there has been a considerable strain, and in which, therefore, the accident factor predominates, to those where the strain has been very slight, and in which, therefore, the congenital factor is by far the more important.

The diagnosis in these cases turns very largely upon the history, and history in a case of this sort must always be an unsatisfactory thing on which to decide so important a point; but where there has been a definite strain or accident likely to cause such a condition as rupture, if the man complained of it either at the time or very shortly after, and at once reported the

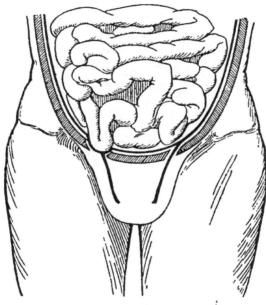

Fig. 25.

alleged strain or accident, and can call witnesses as to the fact, then, in spite of his predisposition, it could be successfully argued that, had it not been for the strain, he would have escaped rupture, and that, therefore, the rupture was due to accident, and not to disease.

Too often herniæ from which men have suffered since birth, and which have been restrained by efficient trusses, are held to have been suddenly aggravated during work at a particular hour on a particular day. Even an efficient truss in time wears out. Few working-men so afflicted quite appreciate the dangers

HERNIA AND MALINGERING

of going without a truss temporarily, and it may very well be that trusses are often laid aside. Frequently in the course of a large number of physical examinations of the working-classes I come across men who have ceased to wear their truss for no better reason than that it became worn out ; and a large number of those which are in use are valueless, either from loss of elasticity or because they obviously never fitted properly.

It must be remembered that members of the working class are most unobservant of their persons ; for instance, men go

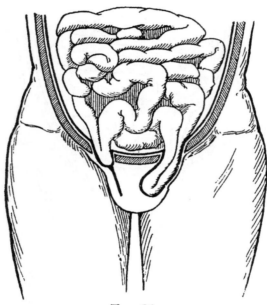

FIG. 26.

about totally blind of one eye without the least suspicion of it, until, for some reason or other, the eyesight is tested ; others are quite unmindful of tumours or swellings.

This can be the only explanation of such a case as the following :

D. B.—A boy employed by a large public body was sent to me for examination. His story was that a month previously, whilst lifting a large drum of oil from the floor on to a bench, he fell and strained his left side. He consulted a doctor the next day for a large swelling in the left groin, which he stated had never pained him. He did not go off duty. He was obviously straightforward.

MALINGERING

On examination, I found two large, abnormally patent, internal abdominal rings, which admitted the tip of the forefinger easily on both sides. It was arranged that he should obtain a double truss, and continue at work pending admission to hospital. There was some considerable delay in obtaining admission, but four months after the accident he was operated upon by a hospital surgeon. My deputy, who was present at the operation, informed me that it revealed an old sac of at least three years' standing, containing an adherent strip of omentum 3 or 4 inches long. The sac did not quite reach the testicle. There was congenital thickening round the neck of the sac.

Is a Man wearing an Efficient Truss fit for Work?—The following reports may be of interest, as they deal with cases in which an attempt was unsuccessfully made to prove in Court that, because men with ruptures had to wear trusses, they were consequently unfit for work.

As will be seen from the reports, it was not denied that the trusses were efficient, but the contention was that the mere fact that a truss had to be worn was in itself evidence of incapacity for work.

History.—D. C., whilst lifting a bunker on board ship, stated that he felt a rick in his right side. It appeared that he did not complain at the time, but went on working for two days, suffering, it was alleged, pain in his right side meanwhile. His statement was that he consulted the ship's doctor two days later, was put on the sick-list, was laid up for a fortnight, and then resumed work for nine days. When the ship arrived in port he saw the company's doctor, who advised operation. He was then wearing a truss. He then consulted a doctor privately, who at first advised operation, but upon D. C. obtaining a more satisfactory truss, stated that it was not necessary.

Examination.—The truss he was wearing when he presented himself for my examination was rather large and clumsy, but for a man of his class, engaged in the rough-and-tumble of work, the use of a truss of that kind, if a mistake at all, is one on the right side.

It was evident that if D. C. continued to wear the truss, and kept it properly applied, the rupture could not come down. Indeed, it was a mechanical impossibility for it to be brought down whilst he wore the truss, even if he tried. He was made to kneel and jump on to his feet, and to come down suddenly on his heels, and the effect was watched. The truss remained perfectly effectual. In fact, this man's disability amounted to nothing more than the inconvenience which everyone must feel when first wearing an appliance of this sort. He stated that he had had the truss he was then wearing for two and a half months, but judging from its very cleanly appearance and the absence of perspiration stains upon the leather lining of the pad, I was of opinion that, if he did wear the truss at all, he did so at very rare intervals.

With regard to the question of operation, it is open to anyone with

HERNIA AND MALINGERING

a rupture to be operated upon. The risk nowadays is comparatively small, but where, as in this case, an efficient truss was worn, there could not be the slightest occasion to urge an operation, especially as the certifying surgeon of the company was prepared to certify him fit to go to sea. His lungs, heart, and kidneys were all healthy, and there was no physical reason why he should not undergo the operation. He stated that one of his relatives died under an operation, but as the operation in question was performed in consequence of a perforated enteric ulcer it was difficult to see why a fatal result in such a case should deter him from undergoing a simple operation for hernia. After a patient hearing the Judge, who had with him a medical assessor, decided that there was nothing to prevent the claimant returning to work as an able-bodied seaman.

One should remember that a large number of the labouring classes now at work are in this man's condition.

D. D., who was sent to me for examination, told me that whilst at work at the docks a handspike he was using struck him on the thigh and abdomen. He stated that he fell on his head, cutting his lip and face—these soon healed—and that the only other injury he received was bruising of the thigh, with pain in the upper part of his stomach. Subsequently he consulted a medical man, who bandaged his injuries, and continued to see him every three weeks for a period of eleven months. The allegation was that he had a hernia which was caused by this accident, and that prior to the occurrence he had no hernia, and that in consequence of the hernia he was unfit for work.

Examination.—In this case the question as to when the claimant first complained of the hernia was of paramount importance from a medical point of view. He made distinctly contradictory statements to me. First, that he did not complain of the rupture until four days had elapsed ; but when I was about to take this down in writing, he said it was on the second day he complained to his doctor ; subsequently he said it was a week after the accident that he obtained a truss from his doctor.

On physical examination a right-sided hernia was found, which from its appearance had probably been present for some time prior to the date of the accident. D. D. appeared quite to understand his position with regard to operation, which he firmly, almost aggressively, declined. As he was wearing an efficient truss, he was fit for any kind of laborious work that could possibly be demanded of him. A man with a rupture, provided he can be, and is, fitted with an efficient retaining apparatus which is maintained in a state of efficiency, is practically as good a workman as a man who has no rupture.

This man's case was complicated by the fact that one doctor was reported to have told him that, whilst he was fit for ordinary work, he must take care, especially when using a heavy hammer, etc. This same medical man had, a short time before, given evidence in a County Court that he had passed for ordinary work on board ship a

MALINGERING

very large number of men who had ruptures, but were wearing efficient trusses.

As the result of a long conversation with this man, it became evident that he had made up his mind not to go to sea if he could help it. He based his objection on the grounds that he might require medical attention at sea, and be unable to get it ; that he had an opinion from a medical man that he was not wholly fit for laborious work ; and that at sea, if wanted in a hurry, he might not have time to put the truss on.

Thirteen months before the accident he had been examined by a Shipping Federation doctor, who certified that there was a slight tendency to hernia. It was impossible to dogmatically deny or affirm the presence of a rupture before the alleged accident, but I was prepared to give evidence to the effect that the condition was quite compatible with pre-existing rupture.

Result.—Ten weeks later, at the County Court, the Judge terminated the compensation, providing for the award to be kept open by the payment of a penny a week.

The Frequency of Hernia.—In one section of my work, of 9,456 consecutive candidates for entrance examination that have passed through my hands, 163 have had hernia—*i.e.*, 1·7 per cent.

Of the number of candidates who had hernia, 94—*i.e.*, 58 per cent.—were passed after obtaining suitable trusses or undergoing operation, and 69—*i.e.*, 42 per cent.—were rejected.

Complaints after Radical Cure.—Apart from temporary inconvenience, such as delayed closure of the wound, the subsequent working out of stitches, and so on, patients sometimes complain of persistent pain and discomfort in the neighbourhood of the wound when this is soundly healed. In all such cases two conditions should be remembered : First, the pain may be due to the presence of a coexistent varicocele, which has escaped notice at the operation, the removal of which will put an end to the discomfort complained of ; the other condition is that of constriction of the cord, as the result of the too complete closure of the inguinal canal by the operation. If this has occurred, the testicle of that side will atrophy, so that this organ should be carefully examined. If neither of these conditions is present, and no abnormality can be found to account for the pain, it is probably a neurosis ; for it must be remembered that scars in this neighbourhood are exceedingly likely to become the objects of too close attention on the part of the patient, and he will readily become the victim of painful

HERNIA AND MALINGERING 199

sensations which are mainly psychical, and can only be removed by appropriate mental treatment. ·

If convalescence is allowed to continue beyond the necessary period of rest required after an operation for hernia, a feeling of incapacity becomes a fixed idea amounting in some cases almost to a delusion.

I am confident that we should hear much less of hernia in the Law Courts if working-men who have been operated upon would, six weeks from the date of the operation, consult the surgeon who operated as to their fitness or otherwise for work, instead of going to lawyers and the " expert witnesses " who are associated with some of those gentlemen.

One difficulty in these cases arises from the suggestion, which is sometimes made, that, notwithstanding a successful operation, a truss is necessary, the allegation being that the necessity for a truss makes it impossible for a seaman to return to his ship.

Now, it is well to have clear views with regard to the position of working-men after the radical cure of hernia. Everyone knows that tens of thousands of working-men are doing their ordinary work after the radical cure for rupture, and that no truss or other restraining apparatus is necessary. Some surgeons advocate that in certain strenuous occupations, such as that of gas stoker, a truss should be worn as a precautionary measure, as a larger number of cases in which the operation has been performed seem to relapse in this particular vocation than in any other.

Relapses after the radical cure for hernia are by no means very infrequent, and depend, it is well known, upon three things—the dexterity with which the operation was performed, the condition of the abdominal wall in the neighbourhood of the inguinal canal, and the nature of the work in which the man has engaged subsequent to the operation.

Assuming a hard, firm cicatrix, and absence of bulging at the seat of the operation, it is unfair to say that a man is, because of the possibility of a relapse, unfit for work ; and, even assuming that a truss has to be worn as a precautionary measure, my opinion is that a working-man may do *any* work whilst still wearing a truss, provided he takes the ordinary precaution that a prudent man would do—viz., take care that the truss continues to fit, and does not become loose.

MALINGERING

Although it is difficult to credit, the author has actually had to give evidence in Court as to whether a workman, who had had an excellent result from the radical cure for hernia, had, in fact, really recovered.

D. E., a seaman, aged twenty-eight, whilst moving a ventilator on board ship, strained himself, causing rupture on the left side. The ship's doctor applied a truss. D. E. did light work till his arrival at the London Docks, when an operation was performed for radical cure of the rupture. In due time he was discharged with a certificate of fitness for light work. As his employers could not obtain light work for him, compensation was continued for five months. A medical man certified that there was no foundation for his continued complaint of pain, and payment was stopped. The case went to arbitration. The claimant's doctors stated that he was only fit for very light work ; that further operation, though necessary, would be dangerous ; and the Judge ordered the compensation to be continued.

Eight months after this award he was sent to me for examination, with a view to an application for termination of the compensation.

He told me that his condition was worse than before the award, that he had pain on every movement, and that the surgeon at the hospital had confirmed the opinion which appears to have been expressed by his doctors at the arbitration—namely, that a nerve or other structure was implicated in the scar-tissue.

When requested to strip, D. E. asked for the assistance of a seat, but when this was refused undressed nimbly without any help. I found a perfectly healed scar of an old operation for hernia, the best result I had ever seen. The moment my hand was laid gently on the neighbourhood of the scar, he winced visibly ; but when his attention was directed to pressure on the *other* groin, and he was asked if he felt any pain, he replied more than once that he did not, taking no notice of continuous pressure meantime upon the left, which was the side said to be painful.

He was wearing a suspensory bandage for alleged pain in the left testicle ; when he replaced this after examination, he applied the buckle and strap over the area in the groin which was said to be tender, twisting the spare end two or three times around the bandage at the exact spot where it passed over the alleged painful area !

Whilst dressing he pretended he was unable to lace his boots without placing his foot on one of my chairs, evidently unaware that he had previously been observed putting on his socks and boots by lifting his feet from the ground only so far as was necessary to allow these articles to be slipped over each foot. Obviously, if pain had really been present at the groin, the line of least resistance would have been to sit down, crossing each leg alternately on the other ; whereas placing the foot on a chair entailed bending the body at an acute angle at the hip, and thus causing pressure upon the groin, the position he pretended he wished to avoid.

He had carefully tutored himself to believe that a few unimportant

HERNIA AND MALINGERING 201

swollen glands at the groin were sensitive, and gave me no hope that he would ever work again. The opinion I formed was that he was deliberately malingering, and that there had been nothing the matter with him for some time.

Steps were taken upon my advice for an immediate application for a review.

Result.—The hearing of the case in the County Court resulted in an award terminating payment of compensation as from the date of my first examination, with a declaration of liability in the event of recurrence of incapacity. The man, therefore, had received four months' compensation to which he was not entitled, and which it was impossible to recover. The employer made an unsuccessful attempt to recover costs. The last hearing alone cost the employer £30.

Surgical operations, with their gruesome details, the chances of failure, and the possibility of death under an anæsthetic, are dreaded, and I think rightly so, by most normally constituted people. Yet it is my experience that workmen seeking to postpone the date of return to work have actually welcomed the thing which, above others, most of us wish to avoid. Those whose nervous organization is less active, whose mental processes are less alive, who mentally feel less acutely, do, I suppose, object less to surgical operations, perhaps because of the mystery which surrounds them ; or it may be they are to a large extent ignorant of the possibilities, or have much faith. Making all allowances, however, for the factors, known and unknown, which determine the modern craze for surgery, the following case is, I think, unique—at least, it certainly is in my experience :

History.—D. F., aged eighteen, alleged that whilst aloft washing the mainmast he was jammed between the stays, and as a result sustained a rupture at the seat of an operation for traumatic rupture performed four years previously. He stated that he was in hospital under the care of a consulting surgeon for nearly six months, undergoing two operations under chloroform, and having " gas nearly every day." He was no better, and afterwards was again operated on at the same hospital. Subsequently he was declined, on medical grounds, for service at sea. D. F. was discovered to be a pronounced " sea-lawyer." He constantly talked of the result of his case, although there had been no suggestion of taking the matter to Court ; indeed, his compensation had been paid continuously. except for a short period when he refused to attend for medical examination. As he was evidently of an abnormally litigious disposition, and the matter was likely to be taken into Court eventually, I was requested to medically examine him with a view to giving evidence, if necessary.

Examination.—The left groin evidenced a good deal of operative interference ; there was a bulging of the abdominal wall on the left

MALINGERING

side, which was stated to be painful, but when engaged in conversation D. F. allowed firm pressure, and did not wince until I was certainly hurting him. The hospital surgeon who saw the case with me agreed that it was obvious he had no pain there, and that all that was required to prevent future trouble was a properly fitting truss.

I made every endeavour to understand this lad's mental attitude. He said he suffered great pain, which always came on at 9 p.m., and he retired to bed two hours earlier in order to avert it. He said he was indoors most of the day, but his looks belied him, for he had the ruddy appearance of one who spent much time out of doors. He made no complaint of the hardship of undergoing so many operations. Why was he so willing to undergo operations if he were not genuinely ill ? Perhaps the keynote of the whole situation lay in his statement that he was looking forward to the decision of the Court in his case, as he wished to go back to America ! I concluded that he was lazy ; he disliked the life at sea, and his half-wages under the Workmen's Compensation Act enabled him to walk about the streets of London with what to him was a comfortable allowance.

When he was sent to me, he was waiting admission to another hospital for further operation, which apparently was that the abdo minal wall should be strengthened by inserting a silver filigree plate. I saw the surgeon who was to perform the proposed operation, and pointed out to him that the mere presence of the plate (whether surgically useful or not) would easily convince a jury that the lad was hopelessly disabled, if they were invited so to find.

I proposed as an alternative that D. F. should enter a hospital, be fitted with a truss, and kept under observation during the period of temporary inconvenience which all patients experience when first wearing a truss.

When admitted to the hospital, it was arranged that he should at first wear a spica bandage in order to get used to the truss. After a few days he told me he was quite willing to go to sea, but the doctor would not pass him if he had to wear a truss. He was informed that this was not so. I paid him several visits at this critical period. One day I was sent for urgently, as he had packed up his things and announced his intention of taking a week's holiday with a friend ! It was pointed out to him that he had received sick-pay for two years, and that the treatment (for which the shipping company was paying) was on the point of being completely successful. Finally, he agreed to remain. He then told me that he had long ago made up his mind not to return to sea, but proposed to endeavour to enter the London Fire Brigade, possibly because he knew that I (as examining medical officer of the London Fire Brigade), owing to the specially strenuous nature of the work, never pass candidates who have been operated on for hernia or who wear trusses. The house-surgeon showed me the lad's truss ; it had obviously never been worn. I made it fit, and he wore it. He afterwards left the hospital wearing the truss, and said he was perfectly comfortable. Shortly afterwards he joined a ship.

A few weeks later he was sent to me by the shipping company, the

HERNIA AND MALINGERING

allegation being that the use of the truss caused pain, and that he had an internal gathering, which had given rise to six epileptic seizures abroad !

A careful consideration of his detailed description of each attack showed several inconsistencies. No sort of evidence, except his word, that he ever had had the fits alleged was forthcoming, for the witnesses were either summoned *when the fit was over*, or were such as would not be able to decide between a genuine and a simulated fit. I had no doubt that the attacks were either of a purely hysterical nature, or feigned for medico-legal purposes—in fact, nothing but a dodge to keep himself on the sick-list. I learned at the hospital that, prior to leaving it, he had witnessed more than one severe epileptic seizure.

I advised the company to cease payments and repudiate the claim. His sick-pay, which had been recommenced, was therefore stopped.

Result.—He went to an Institution for Working Boys, and endeavoured to bring Clerical influence to bear on his employer ; but the latter interviewed the secretary, and satisfied him that the less done for D. F. the better, and soon after D. F. vanished from the arena of distressed mariners, at least so far as the Port of London was concerned.

CHAPTER XIV

EPILEPSY, APOPLEXY, HEAT-STROKE AND MALINGERING

Two problems face us where epilepsy is alleged as the result of an accident :

1. Whether the epilepsy is real or feigned.

2. Whether it can be legitimately attributed to the accident or not.

The differences between real and simulated epilepsy are many and striking, and a man has to be a very clever actor, and to have had many opportunities of studying his part, if he is to deceive a competent observer.

The table on p. 205 shows the chief differences.

The well-known devices of producing froth by chewing soap, and blood by pricking the gums well, of course must not be forgotten.

It is seldom that one gets an opportunity of observing a case of simulated epilepsy, for very obvious reasons. A lay person may very readily be deceived, but not so a medical man ; hence these attacks are arranged for in the absence of medical men. As a rule, the question of true or feigned epilepsy has to be very largely decided upon the evidence of eye-witnesses—a very unsatisfactory method, but often the only one possible. I once gave evidence in a case where it was suspected, with good reason, that a large number of witnesses were in league with the claimant. Unfortunately, this was not found to be the fact until some time after the action had been tried and substantial damages awarded and dispersed. It is of the utmost importance in examining witnesses to abstain from putting leading questions, and to encourage a spontaneous statement of what was actually observed. Each witness should

EPILEPSY AND MALINGERING 205

be examined separately, and their statements compared. Only when a full description has been given, and the witness has, as it were, exhausted his recollections, should questions be asked.

Symptoms.	Real Epilepsy.	Simulated Epilepsy.
Aura	Present.	Absent.
Fit : time and place	Fit takes place at any time by day or night, whether onlookers present or absent.	Shammer makes sure of the presence of spectators before having a fit.
Onset	Patient turns pale, cries out, and falls anywhere, regardless of circumstances—*i.e.*, as readily into a fire as on to a sofa, often injuring himself severely.	Fall not so abrupt, and in such a way as to avoid injury.
Colour	Marked pallor of face just at first.	Pallor absent.
Course	Patient becomes stiff all over, and more or less livid.	These symptoms, especially the lividity, nothing like so well marked.
Pupils	As a rule, dilated, staring, insensitive to light.	Normal size, react to light by contracting.
Passing of urine	Frequent.	Never.
Passing of fæces	Occasional.	Never.
After the fit	Patient often stupid, dull, sleepy for a time. He answers in a confused, dreamy sort of way, but is sometimes very irritable.	These symptoms absent.

I have a vivid recollection of a case which gave serious trouble from the fact that the workman had been previously examined by many medical men ; and critical examination of a very voluminous dossier, consisting of the medical reports of many doctors, showed in the clearest way possible that suggestion after suggestion had been made, negative answers being

MALINGERING

given to the first examiner and affirmative ones to the second. For instance, the first examiner inquired whether, during the alleged fit, the patient had frothed at the mouth, to which the witness quite truthfully replied in the negative; but to the second examiner, when the same question was asked, an affirmative answer was given. The second examiner asked the witness if the patient had bitten his tongue, and, as nothing of the sort had taken place, this fact was frankly stated; but, on the question being put by a third medical examiner, the witness stated that the tongue had not only been bitten but bled profusely, and, later on, told me that the tongue was so badly bitten that the patient had to live on slop-food for a week or ten days. This was proved to be untrue by adopting the precaution of getting the details in the absence of the members of the family, and subsequently by finding from the man's wife (who cooked his food) that, in point of fact, at no time had he had different food from the rest of the family. It transpired that she knew nothing about the alleged swollen tongue.

Many years ago I was waiting for a train at a large Metropolitan station, when piteous sounds from an adjoining platform attracted my attention. On going over, I found a man being held down on an ordinary luggage-trolley by many bystanders, and surrounded by a sympathetic crowd. The picture was one which no medical man could mistake, and those who were holding the writhing figure were told with some assurance to desist; this they at once did. To the astonishment of everyone, the sick man stopped his convulsions, and deliberately rolled himself over and over across the platform in the direction of the permanent way. The crowd naturally expected an explanation. A significant smile sufficed for a reply. The impostor, for such he was, now turned and reproached me for my interference, evidently preferring to be left to the tender mercies of his sympathizing friends.

On passing through the station some months afterwards, inquiry revealed that the bystanders had changed their line of treatment very quickly, and suggested that the sick man should be treated by means of the engine-hose: he then suddenly recovered. He was a loafer who was being transferred from one workhouse to another; he was in the habit of having

APOPLEXY AND MALINGERING   207

" fits " at the various stations, and as soon as these were over monetary contributions were always forthcoming from sympathetic but deluded bystanders.

The following case illustrates the difficulties which sometimes arise when the defendant has had no opportunity, until long after the accident, of examining the injured man :

Statement of Claimant.—D. G., a painter, aged thirty-nine, stated that whilst stirring up colour, between nine and ten in the morning, he suddenly became sick and felt faint. He fell, but felt no pain anywhere. He had his cap on at the time. He then went home in a tramcar, and next day his wife sent for the doctor who had seen him the day before. The parish doctor was then called in, who attended him once, and ordered him into an infirmary, where he remained two months, and subsequently he attended a hospital for diseases of the nervous system as an out-patient.

Present Complaint.—Pain in his right knee, and some loss of all kinds of sensation in his toes ; weakness in the right arm.

Preliminary Statement.—The suggestion is that this man's illness is the result of a sunstroke, that the sunstroke occurred whilst he was at work, and that therefore his employer is liable under the Workmen's Compensation Act.

The point is a very important one, and as everything depends upon the history and the physical examination of the patient, I have taken care to go thoroughly and carefully into the matter.

History.—The history of this case is important.

1. It is to be noted that the alleged sunstroke occurred early in the morning.

2. I asked him to detail his symptoms, and he did not mention pain in his head, which is an invariable accompaniment of sunstroke.

3. He evidently became unconscious suddenly, his own statement being that he felt faint and fell.

These symptoms are characteristic of what is called apoplexy, or " a stroke," and are not the symptoms of sunstroke.

Physical Examination.—There is no wasting of the muscles of his right arm. His power of grip is normal. I asked him to close his fingers upon mine, and to forcibly resist my attempting to open his, and this he did satisfactorily. It is evident, therefore, that he had not at the time of examination lost the power of grip in his right hand.

To test the power of his right hand I asked him to suspend himself on a trapeze in my consulting-room. In case, however, he was putting most of his weight on the left hand, I took the precaution of putting a loose bar over the trapeze, and he suspended himself from the loose bar. As the bar was loose, had he been using his left hand more than the right it must inevitably have slipped, which however it did not do, thus showing that he was able to suspend at least half his weight by means of his right hand.

MALINGERING

Vision.—His sight is somewhat defective, being with Snellen's test-types with the right eye nil, and with the left one-third. This was improved by plus lenses.

General Condition.—His tongue is normal, and he speaks with an exceedingly bad stutter, which, he says, has become much worse since his illness. His heart and urine are normal. The left leg is normal in every way, including knee-jerks. With regard to the right leg, the knee-jerk in this leg is exaggerated ; Babinski sign is absent, but ankle clonus is present. There is no Rombergism, and no Argyll Robertson pupil. Both pupils are normal. When measured, the right thigh at its middle is found to be $\frac{1}{2}$ inch less in circumference than the corresponding part of the left one. The thigh is consequently somewhat wasted.

On asking him to bend his knees in a sitting posture, and to resist my forcibly straightening them, it is quite evident there is some loss of power in the muscles of the right leg. The sensation is normal, and he can stand for some time on the toes of both feet together.

Opinion.—When blood coagulates in one of the vessels of the brain, the result is called " thrombosis "; when blood coagulates elsewhere, and the clot is washed up to a small bloodvessel in the brain and there blocks the vessel, it forms what is called an " embolus." The result of either is much the same—viz., an apoplexy, or stroke. This, and not a sunstroke, has happened to the claimant, and it took place on the date of the alleged sunstroke. In this case the plugging was probably due to an embolus.

An apoplexy may also be produced by rise of blood-pressure in the brain and consequent rupture of a bloodvessel.

It will be remembered that this man is a painter ; that he was in a stooping position at the time of the seizure ; and that he had his cap on at the time. The attack was in the early morning, between nine and ten o'clock, and the heat was unlikely to be excessive at that time. The exact temperature of the atmosphere on the day and hour of the attack is important, and can be obtained from the Meteorological Office. Sunstroke attacks those who are exhausted ; X had barely begun his day's work. I have already referred to the admission that he had no headache, which is an invariable accompaniment of sunstroke.

It is quite evident from the physical signs that the attack was followed by a one-sided paralysis, which is characteristic of apoplectic stroke, and is very rarely if ever seen in sunstroke.

From this he has to a very large extent recovered, wholly in respect of his right hand, but not completely as regards his right leg.

Although he is undoubtedly recovering, and the weakness of the right leg is his sole disability, yet, from his manner, I am satisfied that he certainly does not mean to do any work if he can help it. In his present condition it would be impossible to say that he would be safe on a ladder, and he is, therefore, wholly unfit for this particular part of his work, although he could do almost anything else.

I held a consultation with the medical superintendent of the

APOPLEXY AND HEATSTROKE

	Cerebral Apoplexy.	Heatstroke.
Frequency ..	Common.	Rare except in tropics, and not common there.
Conditions under which it occurs	Anything causing a rise of blood-pressure in the brain, as in straining, especially in a stooping position; also disease of blood with increased tendency to clot and disease of vessels.	Excessive heat, more especially if the air is moist and still; a temperature of 95° under these conditions is more likely to cause it than one of 115° if air is dry and moving.
Predisposing conditions	High arterial tension, such as occurs in full-blooded people and those who suffer from kidney and heart disease. (N.B.—Painters are specially subject to these diseases.)	Prolonged and exhausting work. Soldiers after a long march, stokers, etc. Very unlikely to occur early in the morning.
Facial aspect ..	Face flushed and dark.	Face pale.
Period of insensibility	May be prolonged into days.	Usually a few minutes only.
After-effects ..	Usually paralysis down one side of the body, which takes some considerable time to clear up, and often fails to clear up completely. Paralysis may take a good many hours to develop (24 to 48 hours).	Usually none. Occasionally headache and so forth; paralysis very rare, and then not definite hemiplegia, but of a few groups of muscles only.
Headache ..	Not a marked symptom.	Very marked symptom.

MALINGERING

infirmary where the claimant had been an inmate, who agreed with me in my conclusions.

Result.—County Court proceedings followed. The medical aspect of the case was not tried, for the Judge decided that, assuming heat-stroke, D. G. was at the time of the attack running no more risk than anyone else who happened to be at work on the particular day and hour of the alleged accident, and that the attack, whatever it was, although it arose " in the course of," did not " arise out of " the man's work. Judgment for defendants.

I give a table on p. 209 which may be useful to others who have to give opinions in similar cases.

CHAPTER XV

INSANITY AND MALINGERING

THE simulation of insanity is more usually found among criminals who attempt to use it as a means of escaping the penalties of their misdeeds. It is, however, occasionally made use of by malingerers, and is then, as a rule, fairly easy to unmask, for the insane state is peculiarly difficult for the layman to imitate successfully. He generally starts with the ideas obtained by the study of melodrama or sensational novels, and, as a rule, he selects mania as the particular form of insanity to simulate. It is fortunate this is so, for it is about the most difficult form to feign successfully, whereas melancholia might, one would imagine, be very easily assumed ; with this form, however, as a rule he has very little to do.

In considering any case of alleged insanity, great care must be taken to eliminate general paralysis of the insane, inasmuch as this disease often manifests itself in its early stages by slight alterations in the mental, moral, and social characteristics and conduct of the patient.

Generally speaking, it may be said that every type of insanity has its own *facies*, its own characteristics, its special mental picture, and to anyone who has had experience in a lunatic asylum it is often easy to decide, almost at once, the class in which a veritable lunatic should be placed. This particular atmosphere is very difficult for the layman to catch. The malingerer is very anxious to catch your attention, and to press the symptoms upon you, whereas the real madman cares but little what you think of him. The malingerer asserts vigorously that he is mad. Now, it is a well-known fact that the insane person will not admit that he is mad ; on the contrary, he may assert that there was never a more sane person than

MALINGERING

himself to be found, and it is only when he begins to realize that he has been mad that recovery may be expected. Moreover, the continuous simulation of such a disease as mania entails upon the simulator a physical strain which he cannot long support ; accordingly, whereas the true maniac will continue his ravings, his excitement, his delirium, whether under observation or not, until he is exhausted, the simulator, directly he believes himself unobserved, will promptly take a much-needed rest.

The letters which insane people write are very characteristic, and can hardly be imitated ; moreover, each particular type of insanity produces its peculiar variety of letter, so that, having perused the letter, one can almost always give a diagnosis. So characteristic are these letters, and so important are they in the diagnosis of insanity, that in many cases they are the best evidence obtainable, and a man who in ordinary conversation appears perfectly sane, and in whom it is very difficult to find any evidence of the insanity which you know exists, will give himself completely away in his letters. In any case where the simulation of insanity is suspected, one should be exceedingly careful to be quite sure of one's ground before coming to a diagnosis of malingering. As I have said before, it is a rare form of malingering ; it is so readily discoverable that if one is in any doubt the probabilities are that the insanity is real. The family history should be gone into carefully, evidence of alcohol and of syphilis searched for, and, if necessary, the patient should be kept under observation for a time.

These cases are rare. The following case, which I saw for a firm of solicitors, is interesting :

History—D. H.—Not long ago a firm of solicitors, acting on behalf of a Metropolitan Borough Council, asked me to investigate the medical aspect of an extremely interesting case.

The facts related to me were, briefly, as follows : Four months previously a board fell on the head of a man who was at work in a shaft. The man brought an action against his employers under the Employers' Liability Act. Two medical men gave evidence at the trial that the man had not quite recovered from the injury to his head, but would be well in a month. Prior to cross-examination of the plaintiff, owing to want of time, the case was adjourned.

A few days after the case was adjourned, the plaintiff was alleged to have gone out of his mind, and to have jumped out of the window whilst labouring under the delusion that he was at the bottom of a

INSANITY AND MALINGERING

shaft, and it was stated that his insane idea was that he had to get to the top to save people's lives by means of pumps. The police obtained a three days' detention order, and took him to a Metropolitan infirmary. The medical man who gave evidence for him at the trial examined the man again, and reported *that he had delusions, and that they were due to the knock on the head*, and that it would be many years before he recovered, if, indeed, he ever did so. Upon this report being filed, the case was adjourned *sine die*.

An examining magistrate subsequently ordered the man's discharge from the insane ward of the infirmary.

The point I was specially asked to investigate being the question of insanity, in order to arrive at a just conclusion I interviewed separately the persons who had had most to do with the plaintiff during the attack.

1. The medical superintendent of the infirmary to which the claimant had been taken, informed me that he was not in any way responsible for the man's detention, and that he had only cursorily examined him.

2. The chief attendant told me D. H. admitted he had been drinking, and that his wife had become alarmed. He did not see the man till eight hours after his admission, when he " appeared to be sobered." For the first day he was sullen, spoke of fancying he heard pumps, and gave the attendant the impression that he was " not a lunatic."

3. The plaintiff himself I saw in the presence of his medical man, who had given the report to the Court that he was insane. As to the attack, the man told me he had been out with a friend for some hours, during which time he had three glasses of " four ale." At this point the doctor interrupted my examination by remarking that the man would not be able to tell me about anything further until the time when he left the infirmary some days later. I pointed out that this was an unfair remark to make in the presence of the patient. When I asked the patient what happened next, he stated he remembered nothing of what happened in the infirmary. I persisted, however, and further questioning elicited the fact that the day after his admission he knew perfectly well he was in an infirmary, that on two separate occasions he had been seen by a magistrate and a doctor, that on one occasion he had been asked to scrub floors, that he was apprehensive of being kept longer in the infirmary, that he feigned sleep, and got his discharge the second time he saw the magistrate and the doctor. More than once he told me I should not catch him !

4. I saw also the plaintiff's wife, who told me that when her husband came home at the time of the attack he talked nonsense, did not recognize the children, had an idea that he was to save men from drowning by the use of pumps, and finally attempted to jump out of the window. She said he got on to the leads of the roof, which on examination proved to be a protected flat roof-garden.

5. I also interviewed the medical man who had been asked to certify the plaintiff to be a lunatic ; he narrated in detail the particulars of his first interview with the man, and stated that he was abso-

MALINGERING

lutely sane and quiet, showing no signs of drink, or anything else to account for the alleged temporary insanity. The plaintiff's wife told him that her husband persisted in talking of pumps, so she went for a policeman. This appeared to the doctor an unsatisfactory reason for such a step, but as he was not required to inquire into motives he had not pressed this point with the woman. Had the question of motive been raised at the time, the idea of simulation would have occurred to him. He refused to certify the man insane ; the magistrate adjourned the case, and a week later, as the plaintiff appeared quite sane, he was discharged. The man had had very little food during the day upon which the attack was alleged, so that the quantity of very inferior ale he had taken on a practically empty stomach might easily have affected him.

From these particulars it will be seen that, admitting strange conduct, I now had to decide : Was it due to the effect of the head injury ? was it assumed insanity ? or was the man merely tipsy ? The first proposition was untenable, for it was preposterous to suppose that a comparatively slight injury to the head four months before was the sole or main cause of an attack of acute mania—considering the known indulgence in alcohol on what was practically an empty stomach ; an attack, moreover, which passed off in a few hours when the patient was prevented from obtaining further supplies of drink.

My view was that the attack was partly simulated, and partly the result of alcohol, for the following reasons :

1. He deliberately tried to deceive me, stating he remembered nothing of what happened in the infirmary, but upon careful examination I found he remembered the events of each day.

2. He was so mentally alert that he actually stated that whilst in the infirmary (as a lunatic) he pretended to be asleep, fearing if he admitted sleeplessness it would mean prolonged detention.

3. He admitted to the attendant that he had been drinking.

4. A magistrate and an independent medical man, after two careful examinations, declined to authorize his further detention.

5. Three days before the attack he had had the unusual experience of appearing as plaintiff in a lawsuit, and must have been aware that his cross-examination was yet to follow.

6. He was unusually alert during my examination, stating that he knew me well by name, having been at one time an employee of the London County Council, and he was particularly careful in parrying any inquiry which might involve him in difficulty or discredit.

Result.—After hearing my evidence, the Judge decided that the plaintiff had not made out his case so far as the insanity was concerned, but awarded him £30 on another issue.

Melancholia.—Simulation of melancholia is comparatively rare, and fortunately so, inasmuch as no form of insanity can be feigned so easily. What, however, cannot be simulated are the concomitant symptoms, such as wasting, sleeplessness, low blood-pressure, and so forth.

INSANITY AND MALINGERING 215

Delusional Insanity.—This would at first sight seem a form of insanity easy to imitate, but where the malingerer fails is that he is unable to keep up the part he is playing. The victim of delusional insanity generally has one fixed idea, such as, for example, a woman believes she is the real wife of a person of position ; the idea being real to her, the rest follows quite logically. She demands to be clothed in a manner worthy of her supposed position ; she demands sufficient respect to be shown to her, and so forth. The malingerer is much more apt to pretend a number of silly fancies ; he shifts from one to another, and is not logical in his arguments.

Dementia.—This is a frequent form of pretended insanity, but should never deceive anyone ; for dementia never comes on suddenly, but is always preceded by a more or less prolonged period of some other form of insanity, usually mania or melancholia. The statement, therefore, that a man, as the result of an accident, is forthwith plunged into the vegetative life of a dement would immediately arouse suspicion.

Mental Symptoms which may follow Traumatism.—It will be interesting to describe the sort of mental condition which may ensue upon, and be legitimately connected with, an accident affecting the head.

Most head injuries escape after effects, but they may be followed within a short period (a few weeks) by such symptoms as—

1. Great irritability : a man previously of a placid, equable temper, will become morose, subject to fits of temper, and irritable even from very slight causes.

2. Headaches of a congestive type.

3. Inability to stand any excesses ; a man whose head could formerly stand an ordinary amount of alcoholic drink may now show signs of great excitement after drinking a single glass of beer.

4. More marked mental symptoms : delusions of persecution, auditory and visual hallucinations, or melancholia.

5. Fits ; post-traumatic epilepsy.

Between the onset of these symptoms and the accident there will usually be some prodromal symptoms. The patient is not quite himself, and there is more or less headache, giddiness, and similar symptoms present.

CHAPTER XVI

HÆMORRHAGE AND MALINGERING

ONE of the most frequent allegations made by imaginative malingerers is that they have either passed blood by the bowel, or have brought blood up.

The difficulty of disproof in either case is, of course, quite apparent, and no one knows it better than he who is alleging the hæmorrhage.

Hæmorrhage from the Mouth.—The public is obsessed with the fixed idea that blood coming from the mouth, be it hæmoptysis or hæmatemesis, or merely the result of gingivitis, is an indication of a very serious condition, and, should bleeding follow an accident, that it must necessarily be the result of the accident. There are few medical practitioners who cannot recall cases of blood appearing in the mouth, in which the most careful and prolonged examination of every possible source, sometimes over a considerable period, has proved that no accurate idea could be formed as to where it came from, and the sequence of events has also proved that the bleeding, wherever it came from, has been of no importance. It would be overstating the case to say that hæmorrhage caused by tubercular ulceration of a small bloodvessel in the lung would necessarily be accompanied by recognizable physical signs in the chest, but it should not be forgotten that hæmoptysis is as a rule associated with, or soon followed by, *some* other signs of pulmonary tuberculosis.

Much is often gained by the microscopical examination of the blood, and sputum, if any. The presence, for instance, of alveolar epithelium would be very significant.

It is always unwise to form decided opinions upon limited data ; but where the data are, as in cases of this sort, necessarily

216

HÆMORRHAGE AND MALINGERING   217

few, one is compelled to form an opinion upon actual experience, and, judging from the examination of a considerable number of medico-legal cases—amounting in one year alone to 844—I have formed the opinion that the bare statement of coloured expectoration following an accident may be pretty safely ignored unless there is corroborative evidence accompanied by physical signs.

Fortunately, in most cases, before the trial of an action, time will settle the point. It is difficult to believe, as is so often alleged, that a strain or blow or fall on some part of the body remote from the lung can, at an indefinite period, varying from weeks to months, be the direct cause of blood being expectorated.

Hæmorrhage from the Bowel.—The difficulties in a case of this sort are obvious. Hæmorrhoids and malignant disease should in all cases be carefully excluded. It is a common experience that a hæmorrhoid which has existed for years, and bled occasionally, is set down as the direct result of an accident. Bleeding from the bowel is one of the favourite pretences of the out-and-out malingerer.

The following is an illustrative case :

D. I. injured his ankle, and was on the sick-list for no less than eleven months, during the last four of which he was certainly capable of doing his work. His employer showed him every possible consideration, not only paid half-wages (as compelled to do by law), but voluntarily arranged for efficient massage, offered light work, and in every way tried to encourage D. I. to return to work. At last the weekly payments were stopped, and arbitration proceedings followed, with the result that the County Court Judge made an award of a penny a week. His employer generously offered to give him not only work, but light work. This he did for three weeks, but work of any kind did not suit D. I. He had done no work for nearly a year, so he entered an infirmary, his alleged complaint being " hæmorrhage from the bowel." Soon after his admission blood was, in fact, found the first time he went to the water-closet ; but the medical superintendent of the infirmary, evidently suspecting, ordered him white mixture, and gave instructions that he was to be kept absolutely in bed, and the bedpan to be used. No more hæmorrhage occurred, and upon his being suddenly confronted with me (I had seen him at intervals for a year, and given evidence against him at the trial some few weeks before) he at once left the infirmary. His employers again gave him work, and I am informed that he is at the present time doing satisfactorily the laborious work of drilling

MALINGERING

holes in iron girders, upon which he was engaged prior to the accident, and that he has been continuously at work, and has made no complaint of his foot or any other portion of his anatomy since his return.

The following letters, in large type, were found on the infirmary-card which was placed at the head of his bed: F.I.V.C.P. Upon inquiry being made as to what these letters signified, it was explained by the medical officials of the institution that they had a special significance, and indicated a malingerer, in that they were the first letters of " Finds Infirmary Very Comfortable Place " !

CHAPTER XVII

ACCIDENTS WHERE PRE-EXISTING DISEASE IS PRESENT

ONE of the anomalies of the law as it at present stands is that no account is taken of the influence of pre-existing disease in determining the results of an accident; and yet this is very important, as the same accident will in a healthy man have no serious effects, but may, for instance, in a syphilitic unmask a grave disease like tabes, or rupture an aneurism; in the tuberculous it may set up joint or lung disease, or in the neuropathic may determine a bad attack of neurasthenia.

In considering this question, it is important to discriminate between those symptoms which would, in the very nature of things, have occurred whether there had been an accident or not, and those which have been determined or precipitated by it. As an example of the former, take the case of the rupture of an aneurism. It was held by the House of Lords that the widow of a man who had an aneurism which ruptured whilst he was doing his *ordinary* work was entitled to recover under the Workmen's Compensation Act, death being held to be the result of an accident. As an example of the latter, take the man who has had a tuberculous hip which has completely recovered, and who subsequently sustains a severe accident to the joint with a recurrence of the disease. It is obvious that in the first case the decision is inequitable, whereas the second is in a totally different category.

It will be interesting to consider a few of the diseases which lie latent in the body, and which may, on the occurrence of an accident, spring into life and have very serious consequences. Amongst these I would place first of all syphilis, more especially in the later stages of the disease.

I often have sent to me, on account of trivial accidents, cases

MALINGERING

which show the early signs of tabes or general paralysis of the insane. With diseases like these common in a large population, it follows that a certain number will meet with accidents, and their subsequent troubles are invariably attributed to the accident. It is a complication in these cases that the symptoms of the disease are often unmasked and precipitated by the occurrence of traumatism. The injured man may have been genuinely ignorant that there was anything the matter with him, and after an accident truthfully believe that his troubles are entirely due to it ; and yet, when we come to examine him, from the condition of his pupils, knee-jerks, etc., we know the disease must have been on him some time prior to the accident.

In syphilis there may be, and often is, extensive damage to the bloodvessels. Anyone suffering from syphilitic endarteritis obliterans must sooner or later have a deficient circulation. This may be in a limb which is the subject of an injury, and gangrene may follow, whereas the same degree of traumatism in a healthy person would have had no serious effect.

Aneurism, again, is practically confined to syphilitics, and is as regularly attributed by its victims to overstrain.

Syphilis concerns us again in yet another of its manifestations, for it is an undoubted fact that in syphilitics even a slight traumatism may set up a gummatous ulceration.

Alcoholism is a potent factor in influencing effects of accidents. An accident may precipitate an attack of delirium tremens which may end fatally. The degenerative changes which take place in practically every organ of the body in alcoholism are likely to render more severe and perpetuate what should have been slight and transient results of traumatism.

The importance of a neuropathic inheritance in determining the occurrence of post-traumatic neuroses is considered in the chapter devoted to those diseases, but it may here be said that it is doubtful if these diseases ever occur in people of absolutely sound stock and constitution. In the degenerate children of degenerate parents the slightest of shocks may cause the most severe nervous disorders, which have very important and far-reaching results in traumatic cases. How often, for instance, has a comparatively slight traumatism been the forerunner of true epilepsy ?

ACCIDENTS WHERE DISEASE IS PRESENT   221

The secondary effects of gonorrhœa, again, such as gonorrhœal arthritis, are likely to be attributed to traumatism alone.

It has already been pointed out that in osteo-arthritis exacerbations of the disease occur if the affected joint or joints suffer injury.

Tubercle is one of the commonest diseases; post-mortem examinations of persons dying from diseases other than tuberculosis show that there are very few of us who have not at one time or another been affected by it. Any individual may therefore have a tuberculous focus lying latent and unknown to him. Interference with such a focus is liable to set up a generalized form of the disease. Take the case of a man who has, for example, a tuberculous testicle, and who has the misfortune to receive a blow on it; such a blow under ordinary circumstances, if he were healthy, would probably have no ill effect, but in him it may set up a general tuberculosis. Such a case has recently been recorded.

In practically almost every case of tuberculous bone and joint disease there is a history of an accident, usually of a trivial nature, and in a certain proportion of these cases the traumatism has been sufficient in predisposed persons to set up a severe form of the disease.

Cases have been recorded even of pulmonary tuberculosis following directly upon an accident involving the chest.

CHAPTER XVIII

REPORTS ON PROBABLE CAUSES OF DEATH AFTER THE EVENT

ONE may be called upon to advise either an insurance company or a firm of solicitors without having an opportunity of examining the case ; indeed, it not infrequently happens that the action has arisen after the death of the bread-winner. No question of deliberate fraud arises in these cases ; but in attempting to hold the balance evenly, there is the danger of being misled by written statements of witnesses who, are naturally very sympathetic with the widow of their late comrade, and whose powers of observation are much below the normal, especially in what they may have considered, at the time, trifling circumstances.

The following cases, although they do not perhaps in one sense rightly find a place in a work devoted to malingering, and raise questions rather of medical jurisprudence than fraud, are, however, quoted at some length, for they illustrate interesting points which may be useful to the reader.

The first case is that of a metal-worker, who was burned on the head and neck by an alloy of tin, lead, antimony, and copper. The injury was produced in the usual way, the spoon which was being used having been allowed to become moist with water. The molten metal was said to have fallen over the man's head, burning his neck and shoulders. He died six months later of acute septicæmia, following a carbuncle.

I was asked to advise upon this question. Was there a reasonable presumption of cause and effect between the burn and subsequent carbuncle ? It appeared that the man did not stop working until forty-three days after the burn, and there was some loose sort of evidence to the effect that

REPORTS ON PROBABLE CAUSES OF DEATH   223

the wound healed up about four or five days after the accident. It also appeared that the deceased was suffering from Bright's disease in a fairly advanced stage at the time of his death. The plaintiff's case was that the carbuncle which produced the septicæmia arose from the penetration of a germ into the wound caused by the molten metal. On the other hand, the defence suggested that an advanced stage of Bright's disease, and the concomitant deterioration of the deceased's health, especially predisposed him, apart altogether from the burn, to the infection of carbuncle.

In other words, the plaintiff's alleged direct causation was, in the defendant's view, a matter of coincidence.

In reviewing the case, the following statement was made :

D. J.—A carbuncle is produced by a small micro-organism (*Staphylococcus pyogenes aureus*). This germ is found naturally on the skin, even in health, but sometimes penetrates the skin at the seat of a hair-follicle, inflames the tissues beneath the skin, and in any condition where the health is lowered may end in a carbuncle.

It is very well known in the practice of medicine that the two conditions known as diabetes and Bright's disease especially predispose to carbuncles. The deceased D. J. was admittedly, by the post-mortem report of the superintendent of —— Infirmary, suffering from Bright's disease. He was therefore predisposed to carbuncle.

It appears that D. J. sustained certain burns produced by molten metal. It does not appear that there was in any way a serious accident, for I cannot find that he even stopped work. The only remedial treatment he had seems to have been first-aid from his fellow-workmen. He did, however, put himself on the sick-list forty-three days after the accident above referred to.

I understand that it may be alleged that the germ producing the carbuncle found entrance into this man's body in consequence of :

(1) A weakened condition of the skin, the result of the burn, or
(2) The fact that the skin never had healed.

With regard to (1), I am prepared to state that it is impossible that the germ could be facilitated in its entry into the body by the mere fact that there had been a burn which had healed weeks previously. The presence of scar-tissue, which is really tougher than the skin, and free from the presence of hair-follicles (down which, as already explained, the germ penetrates), would *in itself* hinder rather than facilitate the entrance of the germ into the body.

(2) On the other hand, if I believed that the original burn had *not* healed prior to the commencement of the first symptoms of the carbuncle, it would be impossible to deny that an open wound, if it existed, would form a ready entrance for the specific organism producing carbuncle.

224 MALINGERING

The case, therefore, turns almost wholly upon the question as to whether or not this man did, in fact, wholly recover from the burn.

Assuming that the burn had healed, the fact that the carbuncle itself was found in the neighbourhood is not such a strange coincidence as would at first appear, for the back of the neck is by far the commonest site on which carbuncle appears.

The following report, to a large extent, speaks for itself:

D. K., a vanman, was slowly driving up a hill, when he was seen to suddenly fall forwards from his seat in the van, striking the ground first with his head. A passer-by went at once to his aid, and although there was blood in the neighbourhood of the wound, the deceased admittedly never moved after reaching the ground. He was known to be suffering from marked heart disease, and the question which I was asked to decide was whether his death was entirely due to heart disease. It was stated in the evidence given by the doctor who attended him that the fact that there was some bleeding from the wound proved conclusively that the man was alive after the fall.

My opinion was based upon the report of the coroner's inquest.

I am of opinion that this man died as the result of heart disease, that he died suddenly whilst sitting in the cart, and that his fall occurred, and his subsequent injuries were received, after death.

The Statement as to Bleeding.—It is important that the anatomical facts with regard to hæmorrhage should be clearly understood, otherwise the erroneous medical assumptions which have already been made in this case may be repeated.

The blood is contained in the arteries under pressure. This is proved by the fact that when an artery is cut the blood spurts, and may do so several feet. It will be noted that no witness speaks of actual spurting of blood, as occurs in life, and the impression formed by reading the depositions is that blood *oozed*, and did not spurt out, after death.

When, therefore, a scalp-wound some 3 inches long — as was found on this man's head—is inflicted on the body of a man who has died only a few seconds previously, a considerable amount of blood would certainly ooze from the wound—*i.e.*, he would certainly bleed.

It is a fact that as much as 2 or 3 ounces have escaped from the arteries of dead persons, and it can also be proved that an even larger quantity escapes from veins. Bleeding after an accident is no physiological proof that life is not extinct; of this there is no doubt.

The wound was on *the back of this man's head*, and was therefore in the most dependent position, and the blood would naturally drain from the open wound, more especially when he was being carried, as he would be, face upwards.

A wound of this sort, occurring immediately *after* death, would stop bleeding (that is, draining from the wound), when, and only when, the blood in the artery coagulated—*i.e.*, clotted—which would not take place under a few minutes.

REPORTS ON PROBABLE CAUSES OF DEATH 225

The vessels of the scalp are particularly prone to bleed ; this is a well-known fact with regard to ordinary surgical wounds in that region, and the reason for this is that they are not (as in the limbs and the rest of the body) lying in large masses of flesh, muscle, etc., but upon the bone of the skull, and are embedded in the tough, firm tissues of the scalp. Their position, therefore, keeps them from contracting and collapsing as other vessels in other parts of the body do when cut or injured. Contraction, collapse and coagulation are Nature's methods of stopping hæmorrhage.

It must not be forgotten that the witness who saw the accident would be shocked at the whole of the circumstances. He would, consequently, not be able to testify accurately as to details. The appearance of even a small quantity of bright red blood, which would smear the scalp and head generally, would give an *impression of quantity* out of all proportion to that actually present.

I can find no mention of any attempt being made to treat this wound even by first-aid measures ; no one seems to have even *thought* of applying a handkerchief to the open wound, which they might have been expected to do, if they thought D. K. was alive.

It is very noticeable that no single witness suggests that he saw any evidence of life ; indeed, the carman who saw the deceased fall distinctly states, "I saw no sign of life at all"; and his significant statement, "I can't say if he was alive," is followed by the further statement that "the road was in a good state," and gives the impression that at the moment he was carrying his mind back to the *time* of the actual occurrence of the fall. Indeed, this witness seems only to have been clear about two things—that he saw blood, and that there never was any sign of life.

His statement that the nurse at the hospital "saw the bleeding " means, of course, that she saw the blood, for had D. K. actually been bleeding on his arrival at the hospital, he must have been alive for some time after the accident.

Post-Mortem Condition of Heart.—The medical witness who made the examination admits that the heart "was diseased pretty extensively, of some years standing." His statement that D. K., had " valvular disease and heart-muscle disease " is of considerable moment, for disease of the muscle of the heart is particularly prone to be followed by sudden, fatal syncope.

Disease of certain of the valves of the heart is more likely than that of some others to end in sudden death, and it is important to ascertain *which* valves were actually involved. This is not stated in the post-mortem report.

The Medical Witness's Theory as to the Cause of Death.—The medical witness has taken up a position which at first sight is difficult to controvert. What he says, in effect, is : " This man had a serious fainting attack, fell, and severely injured himself. I do not know that either the attack of syncope or the fall separately would have killed him, but I believe the fall was the last straw, as it were, and that he might have lived had he not had the fall."

15

226 MALINGERING

It will be noticed that the value of his evidence depends entirely upon whether this man was alive when he reached the ground, and his sole reason for stating that the man was alive was that blood was found on his scalp at the post-mortem.

I have already dealt with this subject, but I would here add that so far from the blood which was found in the neighbourhood of the wound being an evidence of life, I can confidently affirm that, *assuming as a fact that this man died before he fell*, the accident could not have occurred as it did without blood being found in the neighbourhood of the wound.

The possibility of a man having a fainting attack, falling, and so injuring himself as to make the fainting attack a fatal one, cannot, of course, be denied. In this particular case—apart from the hæmorrhage, the presence of which I think I have explained—the statement of the alleged sequence of events cannot be anything but a theory. Against this theory there are the following points worthy of consideration :

1. The heart was doubly diseased—*i.e.*, both in muscle and valve.

2. Fatal syncope is extremely common in this condition.

3. No witness attempted to say that he ever saw the man give any sign of life after his fall. Even the carman who was passing at the time could not give any evidence of life to support the doctor's theory that the man was alive after the fall.

4. It is not suggested that the deceased was jolted off his cart, for the horse was proved to be quiet.

5. Had this man been killed by the fall, one would have expected a few involuntary movements, such as sighing, or deep respirations, to have been observed prior to his actual decease.

In this connection it is interesting to note that a case, identical in details, has recently been decided — Thackray *v.* Connelly, 1909, 3 B.W.C.C., 37, as reported in Knocker's " Accidents in their Medico-legal Aspect," p. 958. In this case the point at issue was heart disease or concussion, and the Judge decided in favour of heart disease. In D. K.'s case we have the ingenious theory advanced that he died, not of heart disease, nor of concussion, but from the two taken together.

If it can be proved that the concussion was post-mortem, which I certainly think it can be, the verdict should go in favour of the company.

Conclusion.—I am of opinion that the evidence given at the inquest points to death from a sudden fatal attack of syncope—*i.e.*, stoppage of the heart's action as the direct result of previously existing serious heart disease, and that the accidental fall which followed upon his dying while sitting on the cart neither caused nor accelerated his death.

The case came to Court, and the plantiffs failed to establish their case.

The possibility of tuberculosis being caused by an injury opens a wide field for the speculative lawyer. It cannot be denied that, assuming the presence of tubercle bacillus, traumatism

REPORTS ON PROBABLE CAUSES OF DEATH 227

may, under exceptional circumstances, be the determining or predisposing cause of its renewed activity. Dr. Theodore Williams, at a recent meeting of the Insurance Medical Officers' Society, stated that he had seen symptoms gradually develop after traumatism where there had been an injury of some sort, such as a fall from a horse, or a blow; and said that when a patient had had well-marked tubercular disease in the right lung, even though there were but few signs remaining, he would warn such a patient of the danger of a kick from a gun or a blow in boxing, in case the slight traumatism might provoke to fresh activity the old focus of infection.

The following opinion was based upon medical certificates and statements in the case of a man who, whilst at work on board ship, suffered from an immediate hæmoptysis, as the alleged result of a strain. He never worked again, and died some nine and a half months after the bleeding. The widow claimed that the accident caused the hæmorrhage, and was accountable for her late husband's death. As acceleration was likely to be raised as an alternative plea, occasion was taken to deal also with that point.

The report—as all reports written to laymen should be—is expressed in popular language :

Opinion—D. L.—I have taken occasion to read over the whole of the papers submitted to me in this case, have consulted with Dr. X, who examined the deceased, and have searched the recent literature on the subject.

In this case two important questions at once present themselves :

1. Was the phthisis of which D. L. undoubtedly died caused by the accident ?
2. Alternatively, did the accident *accelerate* the disease, if pre-existing ?

1. Did the accident cause the phthisis ?

There is but one answer to this, and that is, that it is impossible for the accident to have *caused* the disease.

Phthisis is an infectious disease produced by the tubercle bacillus, and it cannot be produced in any other way.

D. L. was first examined by Dr. X some six weeks after the accident. It is reported that this examination showed well-marked physical signs of what might be described as old-standing phthisis. Indeed, Dr. X on that occasion discovered the tubercle bacillus present.

Further, the post-mortem examination some eight and a half months after Dr. X's first examination showed unmistakable evidence, in one lung at least, of the disease having existed for many years. I refer to

MALINGERING

the fibroid condition—a condition which is well known to take years in its formation.

2. Did the accident *accelerate* the pre-existing disease ?

Assuming, then, pre-existing disease, the following points require consideration :

(1) *Nature of the Accident.*—The allegation seems to be that D. L. was lifting a heavy weight from the side of the ship with another man, or men, when the others suddenly let the weight go, and consequently the whole strain was put upon the deceased. Now, it must be admitted that, if this be true, a very severe sudden strain must have been put upon D. L. He was suffering at the time from phthisis, and the hæmorrhage which is alleged to have immediately taken place is not at all an unlikely event.

(2) *Cause of Hæmorrhage in Phthisis.*—The tubercle bacillus forms a hardening and a new growth in the lung. This, as the disease advances, breaks down and ulcerates. If it happens to be in the neighbourhood of a bloodvessel, the ulceration eats into the wall of the bloodvessel and causes hæmorrhage. In the case of D. L. this must have taken place ; the sudden strain precipitated the ultimate and inevitable rupture of the bloodvessel. Some blood was, of course, thrown up, but much must have remained loose in the lung-tissue in the form of a large blood-clot.

One could not deny that as the result of the strain an encysted tubercular mass (not necessarily at the site of an alleged injury), might be ruptured, and the tubercular process, which was undoubtedly going on in this man's case, would thus receive, as it were, an impetus.

If such a theory were put to one in the witness-box, one would be unable to deny its *possibility*, and the inevitable inference would be drawn.

According to Dr. X's notes, the deceased stated to him at an examination some five months after the accident that he had had other small hæmorrhages frequently for many days after the occurrence of the first hæmorrhage.

(3) *Result of Hæmorrhage in the Lung.*—The next process in the pathology of a hæmorrhage is that the blood-clot is attacked by pathogenic germs which are everywhere present, but only capable of multiplying when one is in an unhealthy condition. These are technically known as streptococci and staphylococci. They reach the blood-clot, break it down, and form what are well known in phthisical cases as " cavities "—*i.e.*, holes in the lung.

It will be seen from Dr. X's report of the post-mortem examination that cavities were, in fact, present.

It is true that the original blood-clot is not likely to have produced *many* such cavities, but a clot with a large number of these microscopic germs rapidly produces others, and so the tubercle bacilli are enabled to multiply by millions in these cavities.

When considering the question whether this attack of hæmorrhage did or did not accelerate this man's disease, it must be remembered that we have here a man who had been medically passed as fit for

REPORTS ON PROBABLE CAUSES OF DEATH   229

sea ; who was, in fact, working up to the moment the accident occurred ; who has never worked since ; and who actually died of acute phthisis within ten months after the accident.

(4) *Dr. X's Conclusion.*—Amongst the papers submitted to me I find notes written in Dr. X's handwriting ; these are evidently notes of a report, and state that at the examination he conducted six weeks after the accident the condition of the lung (though far advanced in phthisis) was quiescent.   Dr. X bases his opinion that it was " a very doubtful question whether the accident accelerated the disease " (phthisis) on two grounds : (*a*) On account of the lack of sputum (expectoration), and (*b*) on account of the small number of tubercle bacilli which were found.

I do not agree with Dr. X's conclusion, because the process which has been described must at first be necessarily a somewhat slow one ; the blood which did not come up, and which clotted in the lung, would not break down and cause a cavity for several weeks, and the germs referred to would take a few weeks to multiply and invade the other tissues.   This apparently they did, for D. L. (considering the report of the post-mortem examination) must have gone rapidly downhill during the eight and a half months he lived after Dr. X's first examination.

General Conclusions.—1. D. L. had phthisis before his accident.

2. The accident accelerated the disease, but it is impossible to say to what extent.

This report was, of course, not satisfactory to the employer, who sent it, with all the documents, to another medical man. Quite a different report, expressing a totally opposite opinion, was given.   This was supported in Court in the witness-box, and the widow was deprived of any compensation under the Workmen's Compensation Act.   After the case was over, the employer sent me all the papers, including the second medical opinion he had obtained, and asked me what I thought *now*. I said I was more convinced than ever my view was correct, *with which he agreed !*

A very common error made by those who are not frequently called upon to write reports in medico-legal cases is to give an opinion, but to give no reasons for the opinion.   Not unnaturally many medical men argue that a layman, having referred a difficult case to medical authority, should accept that authority without question.   I am confident, however, as the result of experience, that this is a mistake.   It is always difficult for those who have for many years habitually expressed themselves in technical language to make medical matters clear to laymen ; nevertheless, it is worth while doing

230   MALINGERING

so, because the fact must not be overlooked that in many
instances reports are for the information of persons who have
to decide whether or not claims shall be resisted. It is, therefore, of the utmost importance that a medical report should be
in logical form, and clearly indicate the grounds upon which
the ultimate conclusion has been arrived at by the medical
examiner.

Further, there is nothing undignified in giving the reasons
for one's judgments. The decisions given by the Judges in
all the Courts are always accompanied by their reasons, and
the fear of explaining why one has come to a certain decision
reminds one of the advice given by a Scotch attorney to a
friend who had recently been elevated to the Bench, and about
whose decisions he was somewhat anxious : " Never add any
reasons in your judgments, Donald ; for, whilst they will
probably be right, your reasons may be wrong !"

The following case was submitted to a competent medical
man, and a very definite, sound opinion was given by him
upon the facts ; but his certificate merely stated the opinion,
giving no grounds for the decision, and failed in that it did
not discuss the facts as they were stated in the depositions of
the various witnesses. Consequently, it did not satisfy the
employers, who referred the case to me ; indeed, it was only
subsequently to their receiving my report that I learned that
they had had a previous opinion which had not inspired them
with sufficient confidence to take action.

Opinion—D. M.—I have carefully perused the papers submitted to
me in the case of the death of D. M.

It appears that on January —, 19—, the master of the ship is said
to have received a superficial graze on the back of his hand. This
apparently is sworn to by two witnesses, one of whom, F., was at
the opposite side of the ship at the time of the alleged accident.
Both witnesses speak of the abrasion having rapidly healed ; there is
not the slightest evidence to connect this abrasion with the master's
subsequent death nine weeks and three days later.

It is quite apparent, in view of the symptoms described—persistent
pain in side, difficulty in breathing, disregard of food, increasing
pallor and emaciation, and the subsequent removal at hospital of a
large quantity of pus—that the deceased died from empyema.

Empyema consists of a collection of matter (pus) in the chest,
between the outer surface of the lung and the inner wall of the chest.

Now, whilst I have no doubt that the first alleged accident to the
hand on January —, 19—, cannot be connected in any way with the

REPORTS ON PROBABLE CAUSES OF DEATH   231

death, there is just the *possibility* that the second accident—the blow on the side three days later—might, by breaking a rib or ribs, have caused traumatic pleurisy, with effusion, for effusion not infrequently results in empyema.

In this connection, however, the important points to my mind are the history of the alleged injury to his side, and the conduct of the injured man immediately afterwards.   What do we find ?

F. states : " The sheet struck him [the master] on the right side. He did not seem to be much hurt, and he then went to his cabin, and *had his dinner.*   This would be about 12 o'clock.   The master came up on deck again at about 6 p.m., and I did not hear him make any complaint of feeling any effect of the blow he had received."

L. states: " . . . Caught the master a sharp blow on the right side. . . .   He stopped working for a few minutes, after which he did not appear to be in any pain, and made no complaint of feeling any effects of this blow during the remainder of that day."

It is true that he complained of pain the *next morning ;* but if he had had a traumatic pleurisy, the result of a fractured rib, he must have had severe pain at the time of the blow, disabling him forthwith from further work.

After due consideration, therefore, I have come to the conclusion that one cannot fairly say that this man's death was in any way attributable to any accident.

Pleurisy, with effusion, is most frequently of tubercular origin.   I think this poor fellow was probably ill at the time, and that, as his symptoms appeared to develop coincidentally with his comparatively trifling bruise, the men working with him not unnaturally, after thinking the matter over, put the two together, and came to the erroneous *post hoc ergo propter hoc* conclusion.   The entries in the log give sufficient evidence that *at the time* the writer considered the matter of no importance.

I have no doubt that want of early proper medical attention, and the delayed removal of the pus, and so forth, were material factors in bringing about the fatal issue.

The deceased's doctor suggests that the empyema was an evidence of blood-poisoning produced by the graze on the back of the hand. Empyema is sometimes the result of blood-poisoning, but it is the *last* stage of a terribly serious general disease—*i.e.,* general blood-poisoning—which would have attacked the whole system, and shown itself by numerous abscesses in different parts of the body.

If the empyema had been the result of the hand injury, the glands of the arm-pit would have become inflamed ; it would, indeed, have been the *last* symptom of a general blood-poisoning, which the master certainly did not have.

I am satisfied the case *does not* come within the four corners of the Workmen's Compensation Act, 1906.

The case was compromised by the payment of £100.

The following case illustrates two points : (1) The importance, as already emphasized, of setting out in detail reasons for

232 MALINGERING

arriving at a conclusion which a layman could not be expected to accept without explanation ; (2) the importance of recognizing the legal liability of employers where disease, which is not necessarily the cause of death, has accelerated it.

D. N., the deceased, aged forty-seven, teacher at a technical school, was showing a pupil·how to file piping when the file slipped, and he fell with his legs crossed, fracturing his thigh. He died twenty-six days later, and I was subsequently asked to consider the depositions taken at the inquest, and to give an opinion as to whether the circumstances attending the deceased's death were such as to indicate that the death resulted from or was accelerated by the accident.

Opinion.—The deceased was evidently a heavy and plethoric man. The post-mortem examination showed that he had a fatty heart— that is to say, not fat *round* the heart (as is popularly supposed), but the muscle fibre of the heart was replaced by fatty deposit, thus weakening the contracting power of the heart.

I see that the witness S. states that during life he examined the heart once or twice, and that the sounds were " rather faint." This medical witness states that there were no signs of shock for some time prior to death. Were it contended that this man died of shock in the ordinary sense I should not agree, for it is quite apparent from the evidence that there were no symptoms of shock.

But there are other considerations.

Here is a man, unhealthy, flabby, well advanced in middle-life, who is suddenly, as the result of a serious accident, laid on his back. His whole environment is changed. His secretions and normal tissue changes are thrown out of gear. His heart is already fatty. The amount of normal muscular tissue has therefore been diminished. The enforced rest in bed, the sudden change, and the pain he must have endured, cannot but have tended to slow down, and therefore to enfeeble, what healthy muscular tissue remained in his heart. People with fatty hearts always have faint heart-sounds—that is, the impulse is not powerful, because the heart has not the driving force. Such persons not infrequently die from any cause which disturbs the balance of vital energy which is necessary for the innervation of the heart.

In this case I think the question is : Did the circumstances of his accident so disturb the balance between the natural nervous force which regulates the heart's action, and the processes which tended towards syncope ? I think it is impossible to deny that the fracture had just that influence which produced the syncope which ended in death.

I am of opinion, therefore, that this accident undoubtedly accelerated this man's death, and that from the post-mortem picture, as I see it in the report, there was, apart from the intervening accident, no reason to anticipate a fatal issue for some considerable time at any rate.

REPORTS ON PROBABLE CAUSES OF DEATH   233

The sum of £300 was paid to the widow under the Workmen's Compensation Act.

The following case illustrates the uncertainty of the result when a medical question has, of necessity, to be decided by a layman. I think my professional brothers will agree with me that there was very little doubt, from a medical point of view, as to the cause of the death of the deceased ; but the evidence of a fellow-seaman, whom the Judge specially called in the case, seems to have influenced His Honour in favour of the deceased's dependants.

It was Savage who said that our judgments are arrived at by one of two methods—either by reason or sentiment. These two parallel methods of arriving at a conclusion, he points out, cannot possibly converge. Defendants are heavily weighted when the Workmen's Compensation Act is invoked in the interests of a widow and dependants.

History—D. O.—The deceased seaman, aged twenty-eight, was ordered to repair the topsail after a gale whilst at sea. He went aloft with the usual foot-ropes, his chest and stomach rested on the iron, and he had to lean over the yard in different positions to mend the sail. He was aloft some five hours, considerable seas rolling meantime, so that he required to keep a tight hold. Thirty-six days later he first complained, saying he had pain in his chest, and a cough. In a few days he seemed all right, and made no further complaint to the captain. Forty days later—*i.e.*, seventy-six days after repairing the sail—he was found looking very ill, suffering from acute pains in the stomach. He was taken to the water-closet, and then to his berth, and given a dose of castor-oil. The evening of the same day he died. He had always been a strong, healthy man. The day before his death he ate cold meat and potatoes.

The case set up for the applicant was that in consequence of the deceased's work in repairing the sail an aneurism was produced, which caused his death.

Opinion.—I have carefully perused the papers submitted to me, and am requested to give my view as to whether the statements contained in these papers show that the deceased died from an accident or from natural causes.

I have come to the definite conclusion that there is no evidence whatever that this man died as the result of an accident. It will be noticed that the deceased boatswain went aloft to repair a sail (E.'s statement) ; this, I take it, would be in the ordinary course of a sailor's duties. It will be noticed that he complained vaguely of pains in his chest, and *that*, apparently, not until two days later (M.'s statement). From that time until eleven weeks later he appears to have been pretty well, and kept at his work. Indeed, he was at work right up till five hours before his death.

MALINGERING

The sudden onset of the illness, the severe abdominal pain (entry in official log), the faintness, the collapse, the desire to go to the lavatory, the sudden termination of the disease, ending fatally—all point to an internal rupture, rapidly supervening peritonitis, accompanied (as it always is) with collapse, and finally cardiac failure.

The exact nature of the rupture it is impossible now to state. The likelihood is that it was one of three things :

1. Ruptured abdominal aneurism.

2. Gastric ulcer, which perforated ; this would be consistent with the alleged indefinite pains in the chest.

3. Abscess of the appendix suddenly bursting into the abdominal cavities ; this in all probability was the real cause.

To my mind there is not a vestige of real evidence upon which the deceased's dependants can in any way substantiate a claim for compensation in respect of accident.

Had the condition been produced by pressure on his chest whilst in the rigging, severe pain would inevitably have been felt *at the time.* It will be noted that though two witnesses (G. and M.) mentioned that the deceased did, within a few days of the date he went aloft to repair the sail, refer to some indefinite pains in his chest, yet he was not incapacitated. Moreover, even whilst in port on two occasions the deceased did not avail himself of the opportunity of seeking medical advice ashore. Indeed, no treatment of any sort appears to have been applied or desired, except the homely remedy of alcohol at night, and so forth.

I am of opinion that a claim for compensation cannot be seriously maintained in this case.

The County Court Judge held that death arose out of and in the course of employment, and awarded the widow the sum of £213.

The following case shows the importance, in circumstances of this kind, of disregarding the finding of a Coroner's jury :

History—D. P.—On a certain date (a year before I was asked to report) the deceased woman fell and hurt her ankle. She never walked again after the accident, and died some three and a half months later.

At the inquest the family doctor stated that the deceased D. P. was a healthy woman, but admitted that he had not attended her prior to the accident.

Opinion.—I was asked, after perusal of the depositions in the case, to state whether, in my opinion, the death was due to traumatism.

Now, assuming the facts to be correctly stated, it cannot be denied that the accident did contribute to, and in some measure accelerate, the fatal issue ; but, on the other hand, the result of the post-mortem examination left very little doubt that the woman had been a hard drinker, so that the accident could not be regarded as more than a small contributory factor in the causation of death.

The family doctor appeared to be of opinion that this woman

REPORTS ON PROBABLE CAUSES OF DEATH   235

became insane and had delusions as a direct consequence of the accident, and that her death was, in point of fact, attributable to her accident and ensuing insanity.

Now, the post-mortem revealed that the " heart-muscle "—by which is meant practically the whole heart, for, with the exception of the valves, it is all muscle — was almost entirely replaced by fat; and that the cause of death was " cardiac fatty degeneration of heart, failure of circulation, congestion, and coma." Presumably (according to the family doctor) this followed the onset of insanity. I think this is an entirely mistaken view of the case.

It is well known that a fatty heart in a woman of fifty-one might at any moment prove fatal in one of two ways : (1) by sudden failure to overcome the resistance of the arteries ; (2) by gradual failure to distend the arteries through a more or less prolonged illness, ending finally in syncope.

In the latter case it is a very usual condition for patients, as a consequence of failing circulation through the brain, to ramble, to become confused, and mistake their surroundings ; and by those not accustomed to deal with mental disease this degree of dementia might quite honestly, but erroneously, be termed " delusions."

This point is more important than at first appears, for this reason : Delusions are universally accepted as being evidence of insanity. Now, if this woman's insanity was attributable to the accident, it would entail much greater legal liability on the employers than it would if the heart disease took its natural course and ended fatally, with the usual symptoms of weakness, mental confusion, etc. It must be admitted that the shock of the accident hastened the fatal issue ; but the findings of the family doctor's post-mortem examination afford evidence that the woman could not in any case have lived much longer than she did, for the doctor had found fatty heart and atheroma of the aorta. On the other hand, were the jury persuaded that death resulted from insanity brought on by the accident, the liability would obviously be considerably enhanced.

There are certain points that have a bearing on the question of causation of death, and which, I think, should be put to the doctor at the trial. For instance, had the patient a temperature ? If she had a temperature, this would strongly support the theory that she died of heart disease, and not of insanity, for delusional insanity *per se* is not accompanied by a rise of temperature.

It would be interesting to know whether the doctor would seriously maintain in cross-examination that a woman with a heart which was " almost entirely replaced by fat," with " atheromatous patches in the aorta," was, as he seems to have stated at the inquest, a " healthy woman," and whether the atheroma could have developed in three months !

Result.—High Court action. The doctor repeated the evidence he gave at the inquest as above. The jury awarded £128.

CHAPTER XIX

THE MEDICAL MAN'S POSITION AS REGARDS LIBEL AND SLANDER

THE position of the medical practitioner when reporting upon a patient's condition is to a large number of practitioners a matter of obscurity. Many doctors refrain from frankly expressing their opinion about a workman's condition, as regards recovery from the effects of accident, or about the reasonableness of the steps he may have taken, or failed to take, to hasten his recovery therefrom, when such expression of opinion is likely to prove detrimental to the workman, for fear of being presently worried by actions for libel or slander.

A few remarks upon this subject, and upon the law of libel and slander, may not be out of place here.

Of course, no man may disparage another without taking the consequences, and in certain circumstances and under certain conditions the disparagement may be actionable ; but when a medical man is asked to report, either verbally or in writing, upon a case in which there is a dispute, he is at liberty—indeed, it is his duty—to express quite freely, and, if he chooses, in forcible language, his honest opinion.

It is important to note that the opinion, either verbal or written, must be given exclusively to those who call for the examination and report, or to their proper advisers.

Although in law there are technical distinctions between " defamation," " libel," and " slander," there is no practical difference between them. W. Blake Odgers, K.C., Recorder of Bristol, in his well-known work on these subjects, states : " Words which produce any perceptible injury to the reputation of another are called defamatory. False defamatory words, if written and published, constitute a ' libel '; if spoken, a ' slander.' "

236

LIBEL AND SLANDER 237

The learned author before mentioned states that a person has the right, *in certain circumstances,* to state plainly what he honestly believes to be true of another, and to speak his mind fully and freely concerning his character. In such circumstances the occasion is said to be privileged.

Privilege is of two kinds—qualified and absolute.

Qualified Privilege.—A person is protected by qualified privilege if he is speaking or writing of another honestly and *bona fide* for the public good, but we are here more particularly interested in the other and larger aspect of the matter, viz., absolute privilege.

Absolute Privilege.—This covers cases where the public service or the due administration of justice necessitate a complete immunity—*e.g.,* anything said by a Judge on the Bench, or by a witness in the box, or written by a medical man in his report or statement of evidence. In such cases the privilege afforded by the occasion is an absolute bar to any action.

Blake Odgers says that, where there exists between the parties such a confidential relationship as to throw on one person the duty of protecting the interests of the other, it is not only excusable but imperative that he be privileged in expressing his *bona fide* and honest opinion, although the other may not have asked him directly for it. Absolute privilege, he points out, extends to such a confidential relationship as exists between a solicitor and his client, between a principal and his agent, and, indeed, wherever any trust or confidence is reposed by one in the other, where it would be the duty of the one to volunteer information to the other, and where one of the parties could be justly reproached for silence.

Hardly a stronger case could be shown to come within this rule than that of a doctor and an employer, or his representative, who asks for advice upon the condition of a man making a claim for compensation. Medical certificates or reports furnished by medical men *bona fide* and without malice, being of a confidential nature, are therefore privileged.

Statements made to a solicitor by a medical witness for the purposes of his proof are therefore absolutely privileged, as will be seen from the following case which was decided in the Scotch Court :

MALINGERING

Mrs. McEwan consulted a medical man, Sir Patrick Watson, of Edinburgh, with a view to obtaining evidence to obtain a judicial separation from her husband. Sir Patrick seems to have been consulted at a later period by the lady's husband with a view to giving medical evidence on his behalf, and against Mrs. McEwan. In due course a report was made to Mr. McEwan's solicitor. This Mrs. McEwan alleged was libellous, and a breach of professional secrecy under Scottish law, as it was partly based on Sir Patrick's former examination when acting on her behalf. The Court held " the communication is absolutely privileged."

This case was taken to the House of Lords where the question of privilege was dealt with, and the following is an extract from the judgment of the Lord Chancellor on the point :

Lord Halsbury : " By complete authority, including the authority of this House, it has been decided that the privilege of a witness, the immunity from responsibility in an action when evidence has been given by him in a court of justice, is too well established now to be shaken. Practically, I may say that in my view it is absolutely unarguable ; it is settled by law, and cannot be doubted. . . .

" It appears to me that there is but one point in this case— namely, whether the preliminary examination of a witness by a solicitor is within the same privilege as that which he would have if he had said the same thing in his sworn testimony in court. I think the privilege is the same, and for that reason I think these judgments ought to be reversed " (Watson *v.* McEwan, H.L., 1905, A.C. 480).

In the case of Kennedy *v.* Hilliard (10 Ir.C.L.R. 209) Chief Baron Pigott said : " I take it to be a rule of law . . . a witness, in giving evidence, oral or written, in a court of justice shall do so with his mind uninfluenced by the fear of an action for defamation or a prosecution for libel " (see also Munster *v.* Lamb, C.A., 11 Q.B.D. 604).

It is obvious, therefore, that a medical man may express his opinion quite freely, either in his report or in the witness-box, upon any case submitted to him, provided the opinion is honest and *bona fide*.

If it can be proved that a medical man has acted maliciously, the statements complained of would not, of course, be *bona fide*, and it would, indeed, be difficult to see how privilege, qualified or absolute, could be pleaded.

CHAPTER XX

CONDUCT OF THE MEDICAL WITNESS IN COURT

IT is the duty of a medical expert to give opinions on medical subjects, and to draw deductions from facts which he has observed himself, or as to which documentary or other evidence has been placed before him. The medical witness should bear in mind that he must be able in every case to give reasons for his deductions ; these are frequently asked for, not only in examination in chief but in cross-examination.

When giving evidence on behalf of patients, medical witnesses are almost always faced with the unpleasant fact that, presuming on the friendly relationship which usually exists, they are expected to be partisan, and make the most of such injuries as their patients have suffered.

A medical expert in large practice—one whose evidence is, I notice, received with much respect by the Courts, told me that the usual terms upon which he and several of his friends contracted with running-down solicitors were : " No damages, no fee ; but the lost fee to be tacked on to the next case."

Now, what are the chances of a witness of this sort speaking the truth ? It may be assumed that he who tenders such evidence as this is impecunious, or he would not sell himself to work of this kind. All chance of future employment by his patron, the solicitor (and even his fee), depend upon his grossly exaggerating when giving evidence on oath.

Surely it is worse than a farce gravely to ask a witness of this description for his opinion as to how long the claimant will be incapacitated from work.

The best preparation for the witness-box is a thorough and complete examination, which should be directed to discovering not only what is present but observing what is absent. For

239

240 MALINGERING

instance, the presence of the results of a former accident, or of congenital defects, often influences the result of a case.

> D. Q. complained of inability to walk on account of alleged pain of many months' standing, the result of an accident to his right ankle. Very little evidence of traumatism being forthcoming, he was induced to strip, and a large suppurating gumma involving a fourth of the tibia of the left leg was discovered.

Absolute accuracy being essential, measurements should be made with a tape, not with the eye. Before entering the witness-box the witness should refresh his memory from standard works of authorities in order that his evidence should be accurate, and because excerpts from these books may be quoted. Clever counsel will often take isolated sentences and endeavour to use them to their own advantage, and familiarity with the context is the only means of reply. If a passage is quoted with which the witness is not familiar, he should ask to have the book handed to him, and he may be able to show either that the author is not a recognized one or that the work is out of date.

Those unaccustomed to giving medical evidence would be well advised to discuss the whole bearings of the case with a medical friend, preferably one of an argumentative disposition. In this way he may discover many of the points which will be raised against him.

Much experience in the witness-box suggests the following rules to be observed in giving evidence :

1. Speak slowly and distinctly.

2. Watch the Judge's pen. When he stops writing resume your evidence.

3. Look at Counsel as he propounds his question, but direct your reply to the Judge and jury.

4. Answer the exact question put. If any explanation or amplification is necessary, the witness has a right to give it after having given a direct answer.

5. Seldom, if ever, use technical language ; if it is imperative to do so, explain it.

6. Put aside all bias, and be absolutely candid. Remember that you have sworn not only to tell " the truth " but " the whole truth." This, I take it, refers to *suppressio veri*.

7. A medical witness should be scientifically exact, lucid, and succinct.

CONDUCT OF MEDICAL WITNESS 241

8. Remember that, in medicine at any rate, anything is possible, therefore get the credit of willingly admitting it.

9. Never give evasive answers.

10. Never guess.

Counsel sometimes attempt to force an answer in the direct affirmative or negative. Medical questions can be easily framed which, if answered by " Yes " or " No," would lend themselves to unfair inferences. A well-known illustration of that type of question is : " Have you given up beating your wife ?" The correct reply should be : " No, the reason being that I have not commenced to do so."

If asked whether a malignant disease, which has been discovered after an accident, is the result of that accident, the only answer which an honest witness can give is that as science has not yet discovered the cause of cancer, he is not prepared either to deny or affirm that a malignant growth may be caused by an accident, provided, of course, that its appearance and other circumstances do not point to its dating from before the accident.

It is a habit with some counsel to frame a question purporting to be based upon an answer which has been elicited, but with just that slight alteration in the adjective used which may subsequently make all the difference at the crucial stage of a case which is hanging in the balance. This must never be allowed to pass—the correction should be made at once.

Above all, never lose your temper, however irritated. Remember that the object of cross-examination is to test your knowledge or your candour.

CHAPTER XXI

MEDICAL ASPECT OF THE WORKMEN'S COMPENSATION ACT, 1906

I PROPOSE to deal with the provisions of the Act as regards (1) the employer's right to medical examination of a workman ; (2) the workman's liability to submit to medical examination ; (3) the refusal of a workman to undergo an operation ; and (4) cases decided upon application to revise or terminate weekly payments.

I. **The Employer's Right to Medical Examination of a Workman.**—It may not be altogether unprofitable to consider in connection with this question of malingering what rights are conferred upon employers by the Workmen's Compensation Act, 1906.

The Act provides as follows :

> *Schedule I.* (4). Where a workman has given notice of an accident, he shall, if so required by the employer, submit himself for examination by a duly qualified medical practitioner provided and paid by the employer, and, if he refuses to submit himself to such examination, or in any way obstructs the same, his right to compensation, and to take or prosecute any proceeding under this Act in relation to compensation, shall be suspended until such examination has taken place.

It should be observed that this provision applies only where a claim is made, and where no weekly payment is being made.

The following provisions apply to cases of weekly payments :

> *Schedule I.* (14). Any workman receiving weekly payments under this Act shall, if so required by the employer, from time to time submit himself for examination by a duly qualified medical practitioner provided and paid by the employer. If the workman refuses to submit himself to such examination, or in any way obstructs the same, his right to such weekly payments shall be suspended until such examination has taken place.
>
> (15) A workman shall not be required to submit himself for examination by a medical practitioner under Paragraph 4 or Paragraph 14 of this Schedule otherwise than in accordance with regulations made by the Secretary of State, or at more frequent intervals than may be prescribed by those regulations.

WORKMEN'S COMPENSATION ACT, 1906   243

There are other requirements in the Act with regard to a workman submitting himself for medical examination to a medical referee, but we are not concerned with this point at the moment.

The Regulations made under the Act by the Secretary of State with respect to medical examinations provide that —

1. Where a workman has given notice of an accident or is in receipt of weekly payments, the medical examination shall be made at reasonable hours.

2. Where he is in receipt of weekly payments he is not required, after one month from the date of the first payment of compensation, or, if the first payment is made under an award, from the date of the award, to submit himself for examination, except at the following intervals : Once a week during the second, and once a month during the third, fourth, fifth, and sixth months, and thereafter once every two months. If an application is made after the second month to review the weekly payment, then he may be required to submit himself to one additional examination.

No. 55 of the original Regulations made under the Act deals with the procedure to be adopted where the workman refuses to submit to a medical examination, and, shortly stated, it entitles the employer to apply to the Court for a suspension of the workman's right to compensation, or his right to take proceedings under the Act, until he submits to an examination. Where the right to compensation is suspended, no compensation is payable in respect of the period of suspension. This is provided by Schedule I. (20), which is as follows :

Where, under this Schedule, a right to compensation is suspended, no compensation shall be payable in respect of the period of suspension.

It is important to note that the Regulations made under the Act have the same force and effect as though they were actually embodied in the Act itself.

In considering the question of malingering, an important provision is contained in the Act of 1906, which gives the right to either party to apply to the Court for a revision of the weekly payments. This provision is contained in Schedule I. (16), and is as follows :

Any weekly payment may be reviewed at the request either of the employer or of the workman, and, on such review, may be ended, diminished, or increased, subject to the maximum above provided, and the amount of payment shall, in default of agreement, be settled by arbitration under this Act.

MALINGERING

Provided that, where the workman was, at the date of the accident, under twenty-one years of age, and the review takes place more than twelve months after the accident, the amount of the weekly payment, may be increased to any amount not exceeding fifty per cent. of the weekly sum which the workman would probably have been earning at the date of the review if he had remained uninjured, but not in any case exceeding £1.

Thus the employer, where malingering is suspected, can apply to the Court to review the weekly payment.

It would seem that the following deductions may be drawn from the decisions in the cases hereinafter detailed :

1. The employer cannot be required to pay a fee for the attendance of the workman's doctor if he attends the examination.

2. The workman has no absolute right to have his doctor present at an examination, although in many, if not in most, instances it is not unreasonable that he should be present, and in some cases it is even desirable.

3. The County Court Judge or Arbitrator is to decide whether it is reasonable for the workman to require his doctor to be present.

4. A solicitor's office, or other place of business, is not a proper place for medical examination, and the workman's solicitor is not entitled to be present.

5. It is not unreasonable for the workman to require the examination at his own place of abode or at the residence of his own doctor ; that is, he is not bound to attend at the residence of the employer's doctor.

Cases decided by County Court Judges or Arbitrators can be carried to the Court of Appeal only on questions of law, or mixed questions of law and fact.

What a County Court Judge or Arbitrator finds as a fact will not be interfered with if there is evidence upon which he can reasonably so find. If, for instance, a County Court Judge finds as a fact that a man who was known to be suffering from aortic regurgitation died whilst at his work, and that his death arose out of, and in the course of, his employment, provided there is evidence to support the finding, neither the Court of Appeal nor the House of Lords can override the decision, inasmuch as the law is that the County Court Judge who investigates the facts is the sole judge of what the facts are.

WORKMEN'S COMPENSATION ACT, 1906

The Court of Appeal and the House of Lords can, and do, reverse decisions on points of law, but with these this work does not concern itself.

The actual practice of the Workmen's Compensation Act is laid down in the Schedules of the Act, and the Regulations made by the Secretary of State, and where these require elucidation, the law, on particular points, is made, or more correctly speaking explained, by actual cases which come before the Courts.

It is my intention, therefore, to quote a few leading cases (several of which I was personally interested in) that have decided important questions with regard to the time, place, circumstances, etc., under which medical examinations under the Workmen's Compensation Act should be conducted.

Until quite recently some solicitors demanded that their clients should be examined at their offices, where, in many cases, there was not even the semblance of accommodation for a proper medical examination. To this objection was added the inconvenience, and what to many medical men would be the embarrassment, of the presence of a solicitor or his clerk, who was apparently instructed to assert his authority by interrupting the examination by such exclamations as " Don't answer that question," when the legal gentleman in question, or his representative, considered that his client was likely to make some admission adverse to his case.

It is perfectly obvious that there are often circumstances connected with the occurrence of an accident which the medical examiner ought to be made fully aware of before he proceeds with the examination, and whilst it is clearly not his duty to get or use any information of a legal nature, it is unfair and indeed improper that a medical examination should be hampered by restrictions of this sort.

It was, therefore, to bring to a head a state of affairs which was both embarrassing and humiliating that I took a stand in one or two of the cases about to be recorded, the result of which was of the greatest possible benefit to the profession, for several of these cases were taken to the Court of Appeal, and the decisions thus obtained have swept away all those petty hindrances and humiliations which most of us felt to be intolerable.

246 MALINGERING

II. **The Workman's Liability to submit to Medical Examination.**—No fee is payable by the employer for the attendance of the workman's doctor at an examination. The following case, which went to the Court of Appeal, is my authority for the foregoing statement :

A workman who met with an accident was required by his employers to submit himself for medical examination. The Arbitrator, before whom proceedings were pending, made an order for the examination, but on condition that the employers bore the expense of the attendance of the workman's medical man at the examination. The employers appealed against the decision of the Arbitrator, and the Court of Appeal held that he had no power to impose such a condition, and allowed the appeal (Osborn *v.* Vickers, Sons & Maxim, 1900, 2 Q.B., 91).

It occasionally happens that when malingering is suspected it may be best to make a surprise visit.

In 1908 a case came before His Honour Judge Mulligan, at the Swaffham County Court, in regard to a dispute which had arisen under the Act of 1906, in which it transpired that a medical man had made an examination of the workman without giving him notice of his intended visit, so that he could notify his medical attendant. Upon this point the learned Judge made the following statement :

" Another question of general interest to litigants on this circuit arose, and in this way : Dr. Watson, being aware that Purse [the workman] was a patient of Dr. Alexander's, thought it right to make a surprise visit at 2 p.m. on December 17, when he found Purse alone and in bed. Mr. Keefe says that this was contrary to a rule of etiquette prevailing in the medical profession ; that Dr. Watson should have informed Dr. Alexander, so that the latter might accompany him, and that Dr. Alexander should be compensated by an increased or qualifying fee. Now, when a second doctor is called in by a patient, or his friends, to advise or to treat that patient, I can well understand that the first doctor should be informed and meet the second (except in urgent cases). Such a rule would, if I may say so with respect, seem just in principle and beneficial in practice. But I do not see how that principle can apply when a strange doctor is going, not for the purpose of advising or treating the injured, but to

WORKMEN'S COMPENSATION ACT, 1906   247

make an examination on behalf of a third person.   On the
contrary, if a doctor be requested by a master to ascertain the
condition of an injured workman with a view to resisting a claim
for compensation, it may be the duty of that doctor to make
a surprise visit at a reasonable time.   A doctor so requested must
exercise his discretion, with which this Court is loath to interfere.
I find no ground for any complaint against Dr. Watson " (Purse *v.*
Hayward, 125 L.T., 11, and 1 B.W.C.C., 216).

It is not an unreasonable request on the part of a workman
that his medical man should be present at the examination if
the County Court Judge or Arbitrator does not, upon the evidence
before him, decide otherwise.

It is open, however, to a County Court Judge or Arbitrator to
decide, upon evidence, whether under the circumstances of any
given case a workman is reasonable in requiring his doctor to
be present.   Obviously, in most cases, such a request would
be eminently reasonable, but there might, of course, be occasions upon which the County Court Judge or Arbitrator would
hold it to be unreasonable.

In 1909 a case came before the Judge of the Durham County
Court in which a workman, who had met with an accident arising
out of, and in the course of, his employment was required to
submit himself for examination by a medical practitioner in
accordance with the provisions of the Act.   The workman expressed his willingness to submit to an examination, but only upon
condition that his own medical adviser was present at the time,
and the County Court Judge held that this was not a refusal to
submit to the examination.   The employers appealed against
this decision, and in the course of the argument in the Court of
Appeal Lord Justice Farwell stated that reasonableness was a
factor in these cases, and it was a matter for the County
Court Judge ; and Lord Justice Kennedy observed that at the
most this would be only delay, and not refusal.

The Master of the Rolls held that the conduct of the workman
did not amount to a refusal, the other Lords Justices concurred,
and the appeal was dismissed (Devitt *v.* Owners of s.s. *Bain-
bridge,* 1909, 2 K.B., 802, and 2 B.W.C.C., 383).

It would appear that, in the opinion of the Court of Appeal, it
is not unreasonable for a workman to demand that a medical
examination at the instance of his employer shall take place

248 MALINGERING

at his own doctor's residence, but that it is unreasonable to demand that the examination shall take place at the solicitor's office.

Under the award of His Honour Judge Bacon, sitting at the Whitechapel County Court in 1910, the employers of a workman who was injured whilst engaged at his work were ordered to pay a weekly sum of fifteen shillings. After a time the employers required the man to submit to a medical examination, and he was requested to attend at the employers' doctor's residence in London. The workman, through his solicitor, declined to attend at the doctor's residence, on the ground that it was a matter of physical impossibility for him to do so ; but his solicitor stated that the man would only submit himself for examination at his (the solicitor's) office.

It was pointed out by the employers' solicitors that the workman had been able to attend at their offices regularly to receive his weekly payments, but the workman's solicitor insisted upon the examination taking place at his office. The employers' solicitors again required the man to attend at their doctor's residence, and sent ten shillings to cover his cab fare. This was, however, returned by the workman's solicitor, who then offered to allow the examination to take place either at his office or at the surgery of the workman's doctor. The employers refused to agree to either of these proposals, and stopped the weekly payments, so the matter came before the County Court Judge, who held that no refusal to submit to medical examination within the meaning of the Act had taken place. The employers, however, appealed against this decision, and, in the course of the proceedings in the Court of Appeal, Lord Justice Fletcher Moulton said : " It seems to come to this : he [the workman] insisted that you [the employers] should come to him, and you that he should come to you. I don't see there is a pin to choose between you on the merits." Lord Justice Farwell remarked : " The solicitor's letter claiming the right to have the man examined at his office is simply preposterous " ; and the Master of the Rolls said : " Speaking generally, I do not think that a medical examination ought to be conducted at a solicitor's office, nor at any other business place, because, necessarily, there are no such medical appliances at a business office as there would be at a surgery, nor the same conveniences in an

WORKMEN'S COMPENSATION ACT, 1906

office for stripping and examining a sick man, but to some extent, no doubt, the question would be affected by the nature of the workman's incapacity."

In the result the appeal was dismissed on the ground that the workman had not refused to submit himself for examination or obstructed it; that both parties had taken a wrong view; there was no law prescribing where the examination should take place, and, as long as the man offers to submit to examination, and is not unreasonable in saying where it shall take place, he cannot be punished in the manner in which he might be if he acted otherwise (Harding v. Royal Mail Steam Packet Company, 4 B.W.C.C., 59).

The following case I record with some hesitancy, as it refers to myself, but it so strongly emphasizes the right of the medical examiner to refuse to examine at a solicitor's office that I feel I am not justified in omitting it.

A case came before His Honour Judge Woodfall at Westminster County Court in 1910, on an application by the employers for a stay of proceedings against them, and the suspension of the workman's right to compensation until he should submit himself for examination by the respondents' doctor. The workman refused to submit himself for examination by the medical practitioner provided by the employers, except upon condition that the workman's solicitor should be present at the medical examination. It was alleged on behalf of the workman that this condition was necessary because of the behaviour of the medical man, selected by the employers, to workmen examined by him.

His Honour, after hearing the evidence, stated that he must accede to the application, and proceeded as follows* : " I really have no evidence on which I can say that the workman here has any reason, apart from his personal dislike, to refuse to be examined by Dr. Collie. I have seen a good deal of this doctor here. He has given evidence in a great many cases, and I am bound to say there have been a great many cases where his evidence has been very damaging indeed to the workman. It does not always carry the day. He has only given his medical opinion, and I can understand workmen do not like to be exam-

---

* This report is given in full because otherwise it might be suspected that the lacunæ concealed unpalatable truths.

MALINGERING

ined by him. But what I have to consider is : does he act fairly as a medical man ? And I cannot say he does not. It is said that he asks questions as to what compensation they will take. I have no hesitation in saying that, if a doctor does that, he is going beyond his duty, but he has never done it before me. I have no evidence of it. There has never been a case in which such a thing has been suggested. I have nothing to do with what has taken place elsewhere. All I can say is as to what has taken place before me in this case, and I do not think one can decide it on the hypothesis, the general effect of which is : whether you would allow a layman to be present when it was a case of a woman. What I have to consider is whether this workman is unreasonably obstructing.

" What is the man's own evidence ? He does nothing more than say he spoke sharply to him. I think that is perhaps very likely. Dr. Collie is a man who is, perhaps, peremptory in his manner. All the other things he complains of are : that he told him not to use a stick. That is Dr. Collie's opinion. It may be it is wrong. It may be the man felt, and honestly felt, that he could not get along without the stick ; but that is the doctor's opinion. I have no ground for saying it was not an honest opinion. He told him to leave his bandage off. The same thing applies there. The man says : ' I do not care if any other doctor told me to leave my bandage off ; I should not do so.' That may be very likely. Again, it is a matter of medical opinion. The doctor advised him to leave the bandage off, as he thought he did not want it. The workman feels he does, and continues to wear it. That is no ground for saying the doctor is so unfair in examination that a workman refuses to be examined by him. It seems to me to be going a very long way to say that the defendants are not to have the services of their own medical officer, who is a man of great skill, and of obvious ability. The defendants are entitled to his services. I see no ground for saying the workman has any just cause or reason for refusing to be examined by Dr. Collie in the presence of another medical man. The question is whether the examination is to take place in the presence of laymen. I can only say, speaking as a layman, that it is a preposterous thing to say that a layman is to be introduced to a medical examination. Dr. Collie is the only medical gentleman who has given evidence, but he confirms that view, speaking for

WORKMEN'S COMPENSATION ACT, 1906   251

the medical profession. It seems to me open to every objection to have a layman present, and entirely contrary to our own experience, when we consult our medical man. He will not allow a layman to be present.

" It is said that the workman must be protected. He is protected. The Act protects him. It says : You may if you like have your own medical man present, and it shall not be held to be an obstruction if you insist on having your own medical man. It is said that the doctor may be young and will be overwhelmed. I do not know who the doctor may be ; I do not know whether he is a man of such inexperience that he would be overwhelmed, or, indeed, that Dr. Collie would overwhelm him. But I must say that such a consideration as that appears to be one I cannot entertain. I must assume there will be a properly qualified medical man present on behalf of the applicant. That being so, if the workman refuses to be examined, I must accede to this motion and stay the procedings " (Perry v. The London County Council, 129 L.T., 360).

An order was made by His Honour staying the proceedings, and also suspending the right of the workman to compensation.

About two months after this case was decided the workman's solicitors wrote stating that he was prepared to submit himself for examination by the employers' doctor, and asked to be informed when and where the examination was to take place. He was asked to attend at my residence at a certain time, and a small sum for travelling expenses was forwarded to him. He attended the appointment, and as a result of my report, my opinion being confirmed by another medical man, no further payment was made to the workman.

Another case raising practically the same question (in which the solicitors engaged in the previous case also acted for the workman) came before His Honour Judge Bray at the Clerkenwell County Court in 1910. In this case the workman, upon being required to submit to an examination either at the residence of the employers' doctor, at the man's own house, or at the residence of his own doctor, refused to see the particular doctor selected by the employers, except on condition that the examination took place at his solicitor's office, or, if at the doctor's residence, then only in the presence of his, the work-

MALINGERING

man's, solicitor, the reason for this condition being that the particular doctor (myself) selected by the employers was alleged to have treated other workmen brutally, and as shammers and malingerers.

The objection of the workman's solicitor to the employers' doctor was, as regards the allegation of brutality, based upon information said to have been given by several workmen during a period of four or five years, the brutality being that he called the men shammers and malingerers, and one man said he " treated them like dogs." The use of the electric battery, it was said, sometimes caused unnecessary pain, and it was further alleged that his opinions were prejudiced and therefore untrustworthy, and his statements inaccurate and unreliable ; also that he had examined a workman without proper notice to the solicitors, and on another occasion endeavoured to induce the workman to agree to terms without consulting his solicitor.

His Honour found that the allegations against the doctor were not proved, and that the workman's conditions were so unreasonable as to amount to a refusal to submit himself for examination, and therefore made his award in favour of the employers.

In giving his reasons for the award, His Honour said, even if he assumed that the particular complaints and allegations were well founded, he was unable to see how the presence of the workman's solicitor would be a more efficient protection to him than that of his medical man, who, in fact, could observe far more intelligently than a solicitor what was being done. His Honour also pointed out that the doctor who was called for the workman had said that there was no necessity for a lawyer's presence if a doctor were present, and that the workman's doctor should always be there. His Honour also stated that he had assumed the charge of brutality and other allegations were well founded, but he was satisfied they were not ; that there was, in his opinion, no real foundation for the charge of brutality, and, although the doctor might have expressed strong opinions upon the prevalence of malingering, and sometimes have mistakenly charged a man with shamming or malingering who, in fact, was not so doing, and although a man might well resent the suggestion, it was unfair and unreasonable to base upon this a serious charge of brutality. There was no objection, in his opinion,

WORKMEN'S COMPENSATION ACT, 1906

to the use of the battery on the ground that it caused unnecessary pain.

With respect to the other allegations, the doctor's opinions might often be mistaken, and his recollection of what passed at the interviews might be defective, but that he improperly examined a workman behind the solicitor's back, or improperly tried to induce a workman to settle without consulting his solicitor, was, he was satisfied, untrue. The offer by the employers to have the examination in the presence of the workman's doctor was a reasonable one, and the solicitor's presence was quite unnecessary for the workman's protection.

In considering what is a refusal to submit to examination under the Act, His Honour stated that, in his view, so long as a workman was willing to submit himself under reasonable and unobjectionable conditions, there was not a refusal ; but he found that the conditions required by the workman were objectionable and unreasonable, and that there was a refusal to submit to medical examination within the meaning of the Act.

The workman appealed against this decision, and in the course of the proceedings the Master of the Rolls said : " I think, speaking for myself, that a solicitor's office would be the worst possible place for the workman to be examined at. The Judge has found that the presence of the solicitor was not necessary for the protection of the workman. How can we say he was wrong ?" He expressed the opinion that the facts did not justify the contention that the solicitor should be present at the examination.

Counsel for the employers were not called upon to argue the case, and, in giving judgment, the Master of the Rolls said :

" It is rather curious that in the case we have just decided "— i.e., Harding v. Royal Mail Steam Packet Company, 4 B.W.C.C., 59—"·I should have expressed the opinion that it cannot be too well known that a solicitor's office is not, in ordinary circumstances, a proper place at which to hold a medical examination of a workman. And I can only emphasize what I there said on that point.

" This is an attempt by the workman's solicitors to dictate to the employers where the man shall be examined by their doctor. By Paragraph 14 of Schedule I. of the Act, it is clear that if the workman is required by his employer, during the period in which he is receiving compensation, to undergo a medical examination,

254 MALINGERING

the workman must, from time to time, as required, submit himself
for such examination by the duly qualified medical practitioner
who is to be provided and paid by the employer. The Act gives
the employer, therefore, the sole right to select the medical man
who shall examine the workman ; it does not give the workman
any right to impose conditions such as are claimed here. I agree
with the County Court Judge's admirable judgment. The appeal
fails."

The other two Lords Justices expressed their concurrence in
the views expressed by the Master of the Rolls (Warby *v.* Plaistowe
and Co., 4 B.W.C.C., 67).

The effect of this case clearly confirms the previous decision—
that a solicitor's office is not a proper place in which to require
the medical examination to take place, and that the presence of
the workman's solicitor thereat is not necessary, nor a reasonable
requirement on the part of the workman.

The *Lancet* (March 25, 1911), in commenting on these cases,
remarked :

> " Apart from the interest of these cases to medical men who
> may be called upon to make such examinations as Dr. Collie was
> asked to make, it is satisfactory to note that that gentleman's
> conduct has been completely vindicated by both Judge Woodfall
> and Judge Bray, in whose courts discussion took place with regard
> to it, and before whom the serious allegations referred to with regard
> to it were made."

And the *British Medical Journal* (April 29, 1911) made the
following statement :

> " To sum up the result of these cases, the employer's doctor
> cannot always insist on conducting an examination at his own
> surgery, but he is justified in refusing to examine a workman in a
> solicitor's office or in the presence of a solicitor. For the part which
> he has taken in obtaining definite pronouncements on these points,
> the profession would appear to be under considerable obligation
> to Dr. Collie."

Another case upon this point came before the Scotch Courts
in 1910. In this instance a workman, having made a claim under
the Act of 1906, was required to submit to a medical examination,
which the workman refused to do except upon condition that his
own doctor was present at the examination. The Sheriff (the
arbitrator) before whom the matter came, and before whom it
was conceded that there were no special circumstances in the

WORKMEN'S COMPENSATION ACT, 1906   255

case which called for the presence of the workman's medical attendant, held that the workman, by insisting upon the condition referred to, had refused to submit to examination ; and the workman appealed against this decision.

The Lord Justice Clerk, in the course of his judgment, said he took it that the workman came to the Court as the representative of the whole class of workmen to have it decided whether a workman was entitled *as matter of right* to refuse to submit himself for examination unless his own medical man were present, and, that being the question, he had no hesitation or difficulty in deciding that the workman was not so entitled, and, in his opinion, the medical man making the examination ought to be allowed to make it—except in special circumstances—without being interfered with by anybody, or watched by anybody, provided the employer employed a proper medical practitioner well qualified to make the examination and to supply a report. His Lordship pointed out that where it might be dangerous to the workman to undergo the examination without tbe doctor being present who knew him and knew the state of his health and constitution, and who, if anything was being done in the course of the examination, could suggest that something ought to be done, or ought not to be done, such circumstances as these might justify the condition being imposed that the workman's medical man should be present, but those special circumstances did not arise in the case before him, and the appeal was dismissed.

From this decision the workman appealed to the House of Lords, but the appeal was dismissed, the decision of the arbitrator and the Court of Session being upheld by three of their Lordships, Lord Shaw dissenting.

Earl Loreburn, the Lord Chancellor, stated that the question seemed to him to be whether or not one side or the other had acted reasonably in a particular case, which was a question of fact for the arbitrator ; but his Lordship inclined to the view that in most cases, perhaps in nearly every case, it was quite reasonable on the part of the workman to desire the presence of his own doctor, although sometimes it might be unreasonable because of inconvenience or expense, or for other reasons ; but there was no absolute right in the workman to have his doctor present at the examination.

256 MALINGERING

Lord Atkinson concurred in the Lord Chancellor's view, but considered that the burden of proving that the workman's request was unreasonable was not thrown upon the employer, but that the workman had to prove that his request was reasonable.

Lord Gorell concurred in the previous judgments, and pointed out that under the statute the employer had the right to have the examination in order to see what his position was, and the workman had to submit to it, and if he raised any objection by reason of his desire to have his doctor present he raised a condition, and it was for him to justify it.

Lord Shaw, however, dissented from the judgments of the other Law Lords, and considered it was reasonable for the workman to require the presence of his own doctor, and that it was for the employer, denying the right of the workman, to establish that his denial was a reasonable one (Morgan v. William Dixon, Ltd., 1912, A.C. 74, and 5 B.W.C.C., 184).

This is the latest case that has come before the highest tribunal upon this point, and the effect of it appears shortly to be that the workman has no absolute right to have his doctor present at the examination, but that, generally speaking, it is not an unreasonable requirement, although in some cases it may be, and that the reasonableness is a question of fact for the County Court Judge or arbitrator to decide.

III. **The Refusal of a Workman to undergo an Operation.** —Broadly speaking, the following rules may be laid down as warranted by judicial decisions in the cases hereafter quoted. These cases are of much interest and of considerable difficulty ; they not infrequently occur in practice, and deserve notice :

1. A workman may forfeit his right to compensation if he refuses to undergo an operation which is necessary to restore his condition, provided it does not involve any great risk.

2. The workman must act reasonably in the circumstances of the case, or forfeit his right to compensation.

3. If the workman is *bona fide* advised not to undergo an operation, generally speaking, it would not be unreasonable for him to refuse.

4. The question whether the workman's conduct is or is not reasonable in the circumstances is a question of fact for the County Court Judge to determine upon the evidence before

WORKMEN'S COMPENSATION ACT, 1906   257

him : he has not merely to decide whether the operation is one which the workman should have undergone.

5. The onus of satisfying the County Court Judge is upon the employers if they contend the operation is necessary, unattended by serious risk, and likely to be successful.

In the year 1908 a question was raised before His Honour Judge Mulligan, sitting at the North Walsham County Court, as arbitrator in a case under the Act of 1906, whether a workman who was in receipt of weekly compensation had, by his conduct, disentitled himself to a continuance of the compensation in consequence of his refusal to submit to an operation, the employers contending that, by refusing to undergo the operation, he had forfeited his right to the weekly payments. The employer's doctor and the workman's doctor were both of opinion that the workman's eye, which had been injured by the accident, should be removed in order to prevent possible affection of the uninjured eye. The workman, who stated he was adverse to anæsthetics, declined to undergo the operation. His Honour, in giving judgment, said : " I do not see anything in the statutes requiring a workman to submit to such an operation. I cannot add a new ordeal, trial by ' Lancet,' to the words of the Act, and therefore hold that his refusal affords no ground of defence " (Nudd v. Riches, 125 L.T., 90).

This case does not appear to have been carried farther.

The following case seems only to have decided that a workman cannot be required to undergo an operation where serious risk is involved :

A question relating to the obligation (or otherwise) of a workman, who had sustained injury arising out of, and in course of, his employment, to undergo an operation, came before the Judge of a County Court, and subsequently before the Court of Appeal. The evidence of the doctors showed that there was a serious element of risk attending the operation, and the County Court Judge held that the workman was not bound to submit to it. When the matter came before the Court of Appeal at the instance of the employers, after hearing arguments by counsel for both parties the Master of the Rolls expressed the opinion that there was nothing in the Act which cast an obligation upon the workman to undergo an operation, and

17

MALINGERING

pointed out that the risk likely to attend the particular operation was serious, and the appeal was dismissed (Rothwell v. Davies, 19 T.L.R., 423, and 5 B.W.C.C., 141).

The decision in the following case seems to confirm the view that the real question to be considered is whether the workman's conduct was, or was not, unreasonable, and that in the circumstances of this case it was not.

A workman had his little finger crushed in an accident whilst at work. Part of the finger was amputated, but slight adhesions remained after the wound had healed. The employers contended that the man was fit for work, and that work would be beneficial to him, inasmuch as, by working, the adhesions would be broken down; also that the condition of the man's finger was due entirely to his refusal to use it. A few days before the case came before the County Court Judge, the man underwent another operation, and a further part of his finger was taken off. The County Court Judge held that the man was fit for work, and that his refusal to work was the cause of the condition of the finger, and unreasonable, and reduced the weekly payment to one penny. The workman appealed to the Court of Appeal, who reversed the decision of the County Court Judge. The Master of the Rolls, in delivering judgment, said if the man had been told that he must either go back to his old work, and at the cost of great pain and suffering for a considerable time break down the adhesions, or that he must submit to a second operation, and he had said he would do neither, it would have been quite proper for the County Court Judge to say he had acted unreasonably, and that his continued incapacity was due not to the accident but to his refusal; but such was not the case. His Lordship also stated that there was no evidence that the workman had acted unreasonably, and he declined to accept the view that a man who had not had medical advice on this point ought to, of his own knowledge and his own will, have undergone great pain by resuming his old work, when he could not possibly foresee that the great pain which would be produced might be beneficial instead of most injurious to the finger (Burgess v. Jewell, 4 B.W.C.C., 145).

The following case very clearly endorses the view that, if the operation necessary to restore the man's condition is one

WORKMEN'S COMPENSATION ACT, 1906   259

that does not involve any great risk, the workman must undergo it or forfeit his right to compensation.

A workman employed by an engineering firm injured his right foot in February, 1907. He was treated in hospital, and, after two or three small operations, the big toe and part of the second toe were removed. An X-ray photograph disclosed that a piece of bone had been detached from the big toe, and was then loose in the stump. He was offered light work in January, 1908, which he refused, and compensation, which had previously been paid, was stopped. A temporary arrangement was made for the continuance of the weekly payment until May, when he was again examined by the doctors for both parties, and they both advised him to submit to an operation for removing the detached piece of bone ; but this he refused to do. The matter came before the County Court Judge, when all the medical witnesses were of opinion that the man ought, in his own interest, to undergo the operation. The Judge held that the operation was of a simple character, involving practically no risk, the man being thirty-five years of age, and apparently in good health. He also found that it was doubtful if the man's toe would ever get right without an operation, and, after stating that he felt bound by the decision in the case of Rothwell v. Davies (p. 257), made an award in favour of the man for a continuance of the weekly payments. His Honour, however, stated that but for this decision he should have followed his own view of the law, which was supported by a Scotch case, and found for the employers.

When the case came before the Court of Appeal upon the appeal of the employers, the Master of the Rolls stated that the case gave the Court an opportunity of setting right a certain misapprehension as to what was decided in the case of Rothwell v. Davies (p. 257). His Lordship pointed out that in that case the County Court Judge had found the workman had acted reasonably in refusing to undergo the operation, and he could not take that case as lending any support whatever to the suggestion that a man may decline to submit to a trivial operation not involving any serious risk, but of such a nature that any reasonable man, in his own interest, would undergo it. His Lordship also stated that a continuance of the man's disability would be due not to the original accident, but to his unreasonable conduct

260 MALINGERING

in refusing to undergo the operation, and that the employers were entitled to succeed, and reversed the decision of the County Court Judge.

Lord Justice Fletcher Moulton said : " In my view, a workman must behave reasonably, and if the incapacity or the continuance of the incapacity after a certain time is due to the fact that he has not behaved reasonably, then the continuance of the incapacity is not a consequence of the accident, but a consequence of his own unreasonableness. To hold the contrary would lead to this result : that a workman who had an injury, however small, might refuse to allow it to be dressed, and let a trivial wound become a sloughing sore, and lead to partial or total incapacity, for which the employer must compensate him. That is not the meaning of the Act. You cannot draw a line between ' dressing ' and ' operation ' . . . . The distinction is between being reasonable and not being reasonable."

Lord Justice Farwell agreed with the views expressed by the other Lords Justices, and quoted part of the judgment of Lord McLaren in a case before the Scotch Courts (Dennelly v. William Baird and Co., Ltd.), in which his Lordship, in dealing with a case where the operation was not attended with risk to health or unusual suffering, said : " If the sufferer, either from defect of moral courage or because he might be content with his defect, refuses to be operated upon, I should have no difficulty in holding that his continued disability to work at his trade was the result of his refusal to submit to remedial treatment, and, therefore, he is not entitled to further compensation." Lord Justice Farwell said this expressed his own view so entirely that he desired to adopt it (Warncken v. Richard Moreland and Son, Ltd., 1909, 1 K.B., 184).

The deduction to be drawn from the next case seems to be that if the workman has acted reasonably in the steps taken in consequence of the accident, and those steps result in death, the employers are liable.

In October, 1908, a workman employed in a calico-printing works received injury to his hand whilst attending to a machine in the course of his employment. He received medical attention at an infirmary, and it was stated that in the usual course the hand would have to be amputated ; but the infirmary surgeon proposed to perform the operation of grafting skin

WORKMEN'S COMPENSATION ACT, 1906   261

upon the hand so as to preserve the hand intact. The first stage of the operation was performed under chloroform, and was successful. In the December following the accident, the workman was placed under chloroform with a view to completing the operation, but died while under the anæsthetic. The effect of the medical evidence was that the second stage of the operation was not dangerous, though painful; that the administration of an anæsthetic for the purpose was reasonable; and that there was no ground for apprehending death as a result. The County Court Judge found that the operation was not a usual one, but was a bold experiment; that the cause of death was not the accident, but the effect of the anæsthetic, and held that the employers were not liable. The dependants of the workman appealed, and the Master of the Rolls, in delivering judgment reversing the decision of the County Court Judge, said that the true test was whether the step taken to obviate the consequences of the accident, and to make the man a sound, able-bodied man, was a reasonable step to take, and in his opinion the course pursued by the workman was not only courageous but reasonable in the interest of the employers (Shirt v. Calico Printers' Association, Ltd., 1909, 2 K.B., 51).

The following case makes it clear that in law the question to be determined is whether the workman has acted reasonably in the circumstances in refusing to undergo an operation, having regard to the advice given to him, and not merely whether the operation is one that he should have undergone.

In November, 1908, a seaman, who was fifty-one years of age, whilst at sea was injured in a gale of wind and sustained a double rupture. About three weeks later, on arrival in England, he was advised by one of the visiting surgeons of the hospital to undergo an operation. Soon after this the employers suggested that he should submit to an operation; the seaman's medical attendant advised him not to submit to the operation, and he therefore declined. The seaman applied to the County Court Judge for an award of compensation, but the employers denied liability beyond the period when the seaman would have recovered if he had undergone the operation.

Evidence was given before the County Court Judge by an anæsthetist, who advised the man not to undergo the operation. One of the doctors said the man was suffering from

262 MALINGERING

Bright's disease, and thought it would be dangerous for him to undergo an operation without an anæsthetic, and that with kidney disease the administration of a general anæsthetic would entail a risk to his life; and, moreover, there was a slight enlargement of the heart. The visiting surgeon of the hospital stated that, in his opinion, it would not have been unwise for the man to have been operated upon; that the use of a general anæsthetic would have been a risk, but not a great one; and, if local anæsthetics were used, there would be no appreciable pain and no appreciable risk to life, and another doctor supported this view. The County Court Judge considered the case fell within the decision of Warncken v. R. Moreland and Son, Ltd. (p. 259), and that the workman had acted unreasonably in not undergoing the operation, and declined to allow compensation after February 25, 1909. The workman appealed against this decision, and on the case coming before the Court of Appeal the Master of the Rolls said that the test was clearly laid down in the case of Warncken v. R. Moreland and Son, Ltd. (p. 259), and, he thought, indicated, although not quite so clearly,-in Rothwell v. Davies (p. 257); namely, that there was no power to compel a man to undergo an operation; on the other hand, he must act reasonably. His Lordship drew a distinction between this and Warncken's case, inasmuch as in the present instance there was evidence that the man had not acted unreasonably, having regard to the advice he had received; whilst in Warncken's case it was otherwise, his own doctor having advised him to undergo the operation. Lord Justice Fletcher Moulton and Lord Justice Farwell concurred in the views expressed by the Master of the Rolls, Lord Justice Farwell being of opinion that the real question underlying these cases is whether the continuance of the incapacity is due to the original accident, or due to the workman's unreasonable refusal to take a step which any reasonable man would take. The appeal was therefore allowed (Tutton v. Owners of s.s. *Majestic*, 1909, 2 K.B., 54).

The next case is important from the fact that the Court of Appeal reaffirmed their previous decisions to the effect that it is unreasonable, in certain circumstances, for a man to refuse to undergo an operation which does not involve much risk.

In 1909 a workman who had met with an accident in the

WORKMEN'S COMPENSATION ACT, 1906 263

course of his employment refused to undergo an operation, which the employers considered essential, and the County Court Judge held that as the operation was not a dangerous or difficult one, and as the workman's own doctor had advised him to undergo it, in his own interest, it was unreasonable for the man to refuse. The workman appealed to the Court of Appeal, and, in the course of the proceedings, the Master of the Rolls referred to the decisions in Tutton *v.* Owners of s.s. *Majestic* (p. 261), and Warncken *v.* R. Moreland and Co., Ltd. (p. 259), and stated that the law applicable to cases of this kind was settled by those two decisions, and, having regard to the facts and circumstances in this instance, if ever there was a case in which a man acted unreasonably, it was this case. The other Lords Justices concurred, and the appeal was dismissed (Paddington Borough Council *v.* Stack, 2 B.W.C.C., 402).

Finally, the following case appears to establish the law that a workman must submit to a reasonable operation if the employers can satisfy the Court that the operation is *likely* to be successful, as it would be impossible in some instances to produce evidence to the effect that the operation *must* (in point of fact) prove successful ; but that the onus is upon the employers to satisfy the Court that the operation is advisable in the interests of the workman, and also that the workman's incapacity is due, not to the accident, but to refusal to undergo a reasonable operation.

A ship's fireman burnt some of the fingers of his right hand. A few days after the injury one of the blisters burst, and septic matter entered. The wound was dressed and probed several times by the ship's doctor, but the man refused to undergo any more incisions. The doctor suggested an anæsthetic, and warned him that, if he did not submit to the operation, he might lose his finger and perhaps his arm.

When the ship reached port, the man went into a hospital and had his finger amputated. The ship's doctor, in giving evidence, stated that the man could have resumed work in ten days if he had submitted to the operation, and that his cure would have been permanent ; but the workman's doctor stated that, in his opinion, further lancing or cutting at the time it was suggested would not have saved the finger. The County Court

264 MALINGERING

Judge held that the workman had acted unreasonably in not submitting to the small operation, but he was not able, on the evidence, to determine whether the suggested operation would have saved the finger, and he therefore found in favour of the workman.

The employers appealed to the Court of Appeal, who held that the onus was upon the employers to show that incapacity was not due to the injury, but due to the workman's unreasonable refusal to submit to the operation ; further, they held that the employers had failed to show that the suggested operation would have resulted in a permanent cure, and therefore they upheld the decision of the County Court Judge.

The cases of Warncken v. Richard Moreland and Son, Ltd. (p. 259) and Tutton v. Owners of s.s. *Majestic* (p. 261) were referred to by their Lordships in giving judgment, and they said that they were not departing from the principles laid down in those cases, nor from anything they had there said ; but in this case it was impossible for the Court to say that the County Court Judge was wrong in holding that the onus of proof of the employers' contention was upon them, and that they had not discharged it ; but if the employers could have shown that the man's condition was not due to the loss of his finger, but was due to the unreasonableness of the workman in refusing to undergo the operation, it having been found that the refusal was unreasonable, then the employers would have succeeded (Marshall v. Orient Steam Navigation Company, Ltd., 1910, 1 K.B., 79, and 3 B.W.C.C., 15).

CHAPTER XXII

MEDICAL ASPECT OF THE WORKMEN'S COMPENSATION
ACT, 1906 (*Continued*).

IV. Cases decided upon Application to Revise or Terminate Weekly Payments.—Numerous cases have come before the Courts in respect of the employer's right to have the weekly payment ended or diminished, and by workmen to have the weekly payments increased, and it may be useful to consider some of those falling in the first category, so far as they have reference to malingering or suspected malingering.

As. the question whether the circumstances are such as to justify a review of the weekly payment is one of fact for the County Court Judge to decide, most of the cases upon this point are disposed of without reaching the Court of Appeal, and are rarely reported. I purpose setting out in some detail a few of the cases upon this subject which have come before the Court of Appeal.

Every form of injury is liable to be followed by secondary effects upon the nervous system. By many it is thought that the nervous effects of injury show themselves mostly in the more cultured classes, and that the stolid, less receptive nervous system of manual labourers is not so likely to be affected by the after-effects of injury. My experience is that such is not the case, and that labourers do, as a matter of fact, suffer, and often suffer severely, mentally from the after-effects of injuries. Again and again instances have come under my notice where injuries have been received in some catastrophe which has received much publicity, and those injured seem to have been profoundly influenced on the sensitive and emotional side of their characters. The condition is an unmistakable

265

266   MALINGERING

and definite entity, and one feels that it is dependent to a very
large extent, if not entirely, upon introspection and love of
sympathy, combined with loss of courage.

The law of this country is that, although a workman
may have recovered from the physical injury caused by the
accident, the after-effects of it must not be disregarded in
considering the man's capacity for work.

A collier, who had sustained an injury to his leg, had been paid a
weekly sum for a considerable time after the accident, and the
employers, considering the time had arrived for a review of the
weekly payment, applied to the County Court Judge.

Evidence was given before the Judge that the muscular injury to
the man's leg caused by the accident had come to an end, and
that he was restored to his condition before the accident so far as
muscular power was concerned, but that he was suffering from
traumatic neurasthenia, the result of the accident. The Judge
thought the workman was able to work, as, according to the medical
evidence, the loss of sensation from which he was suffering did not
affect his capacity for work ; and, although the workman thought he
was incapacitated because he mistakenly and unreasonably believed
that he could not work, the Judge found that he was not totally
incapacitated for work, and reduced the weekly payment to a penny a
week. The workman appealed to the Court of Appeal.

The Master of the Rolls, after referring to the evidence, said he
accepted the County Court Judge's findings of fact, and stated that His
Honour had found that the workman was not malingering, and that he
was not shirking the work with any desire or intention of avoiding it,
but that it was sufficient for the employers to show that the muscular
mischief was at an end. His Lordship was, however, entirely unable
to assent to that view, and it seemed to him an entire fallacy to say
that a man's right to compensation ceases when the muscular mischief
is ended, but the nervous or hysterical effects still remain. His Lordship referred to certain specific findings of the County Court Judge,
and stated that the result of those findings was that the workman
was still suffering from the accident, in that he had not wholly recovered from the nervous effects, which were just as real and just as
important, and made him unable to work ; but he hoped that nothing
he said would ever be supposed to give any countenance to malingering.
If the County Court Judge had found that the man was malingering,
the position would, of course, have been entirely the other way, and
that would have been a question of fact for him, and the Court would
not have interfered with the finding. In the circumstances, the decision of the County Court Judge was reversed, and the appeal allowed.

Lord Justice Fletcher Moulton said that, so long as the nervous
consequences remained, the man was entitled to compensation just
as much as if his muscular power had not recovered.

Lord Justice Farwell remarked that the fallacy which appeared to

WORKMEN'S COMPENSATION ACT, 1906 267

underlie the County Court Judge's decision was that he had disregarded the nervous affection (Eaves *v.* Blaenclydach Colliery Company, Ltd., 1909, 2 K.B., 73, and 1 B.W.C.C., 329).

The question whether a man is or is not malingering is one which is practically always finally decided by the arbitrator or County Court Judge, the only possible variation of this being that, if the Court of Appeal consider that the evidence upon which the County Court Judge formed his opinion did not justify his finding, the Court of Appeal may reverse it. But the higher Courts, not unnaturally, decline to interfere with decisions upon questions of fact which have been investigated by a Judge who has seen the witnesses, observed their demeanour, and formed a deliberate opinion upon the facts as stated before him at the trial.

A workman, who was injured in a colliery in 1903, was paid £1 a week for some four years, when light work was given to him, but he stated he could not perform the work, and that he suffered pain. The matter came before the County Court Judge on an application to review the weekly payment. Evidence was given on behalf of the employers that the man could follow light employment, but the workman's doctor said the man was still suffering from the effects of the accident; the man might suffer from hysteria, but if so, and if there were imaginary pains, those pains would be felt as acutely as if they were real. His Honour held that the hysteria was exaggerated intentionally, that the man could follow light work, and had never made a genuine attempt to do such work. He decided in favour of the employers, but expressed the hope that there would be an appeal in order that there might be some guidance in such cases, which were becoming frequent. The workman appealed to the Court of Appeal, and the Master of the Rolls made reference to part of the evidence which went to show that if the man had been compelled to work he would have recovered.

Lord Justice Farwell pointed out that the evidence showed that if the man had stuck to his work he would have recovered, but he gave up as soon as his heart failed him, and it was held by all three Lords Justices that there was ample evidence to justify the County Court Judge in his ruling (Price *v.* Burnyeat, Brown and Co., 2 B.W.C.C., 337).

Although a workman may have recovered from the physical effects of his accident, nervous affections, naturally and directly arising from the accident itself, must not be disregarded in deciding whether or not the workman is incapacitated : on the other hand, employers are not liable to pay compensation for nerve trouble brought on by worrying or brooding over the

MALINGERING

accident, or fear of returning to work because of possible consequences, if, in the case of a reasonable person, such worry or fear would be unjustifiable.

It seems almost unnecessary to say that it is the duty of a workman who has received an injury, and has recovered from its physical effects, to use his best endeavours to make himself fit for work. In actual experience it is found that in many of the cases which come before medical men who are asked to report as to fitness or otherwise for work, the crucial point to be considered is not whether, for instance, certain fractures have united or certain wounds have healed, but, is the workman fit for duty ? Too often the original injury has been wholly recovered from for weeks, months, or even years, but the injured man has allowed the idea of his injury to obsess him, and has given way to a nervousness which a reasonable man would overcome, and so has indefinitely postponed that return to work which would have enabled him to forget the accident.

In November, 1907, a female relief-stamper met with an accident in the course of, and arising out of, her employment, whereby she lost the terminal phalanx of the middle finger and half the terminal phalanx of the ring finger of the right hand. She had been paid half-wages for many months, when her employers applied to the Judge at the City of London Court to terminate the weekly payments on the ground that she was quite fit physically to resume her former work. They were willing, in the event of her returning to work, to pay her the full wages she had been receiving, or as much more as she could earn at her work. Two doctors gave evidence that the injured woman could do her work quite well. Judge Rentoul said it was of the very greatest importance that it should be decided, once and for all, whether a workman or workwoman physically fit, but feeling nervous at working the same class of machine, and therefore refusing to try it, should be considered unfit within the scope of the Act, and whether such a person could be compelled to go back to work or the compensation cease. He said he must hold that the compensation must cease, as the whole of the medical evidence showed the girl to be fit for her work in all respects, except in regard to timidity produced by the accident. It was possible that all her life she would shy at using the machine. Was she, then, to go on receiving compensation for ever ? The longer she kept off trying, the worse it would be. A doctor, called for the workwoman, thought she might try to work; and the Judge directed that the payments be reduced to 1d. a week. He thought it was strong conduct on the girl's part that she had not tried to work. He gave the employers the costs of the application (Pearson v. Pimms and Sons, Ltd., 126 L.T., 301).

WORKMEN'S COMPENSATION ACT, 1906   269

In the following important case the County Court Judge stated quite clearly that, in his opinion, the workman was " a typical neurasthenic case from a legal point of view," and hinted that he would be very glad if the case were taken to the Court of Appeal, so that it could be finally decided whether an employer must continue to pay weekly wages to a man who only *thinks* himself unfit for work.   As will be seen, the Master of the Rolls, in the Court of Appeal, upheld the decision of the County Court Judge.

A workman met with an accident under circumstances which brought it within the terms of the Act of 1906.   The accident was not of a very serious character, and after a while the man went back to work for a short time, but appeared to be unable to do full work. After a stay at a convalescent home, he again returned to his employment, and continued at it for eighteen months, earning full wages.   He left work again, and applied for weekly compensation. At this period work was slack, and the man would have earned no more by following his employment than he would get from the weekly payments under the Act.   The County Court Judge expressed the opinion that the workman was practically playing at work, that it was no use to him, and he was no use at the works ; also that his action was influenced by the slackness of work, and that the effect on the funds of the man's trade union was also a factor in the case, the idea being to relieve the union by claiming under the Act ; and he found that the refusal to continue work was due to nervousness, which an average reasonable man could overcome.   His Honour was of opinion that, if the man had been a wealthy man, and desired to get back to hunt or shoot, he would have done it.   He said : " This is a typical neurasthenic case from a legal point of view, and I have to give my decision upon it.   If the law be that the average reasonable man is allowed to stay away from work on account of nervousness, this case will be upset, and this very person, who fancies himself unable to work, will continue to draw a pension from the rest of the community, who will have to pay.   I do not think this is the meaning of the Workmen's Compensation Act."   His Honour declined to allow compensation, and the workman appealed against this decision.

The Master of the Rolls, having referred to the findings of the County Court Judge, said he did not wish to use the word " malingering " if he could find another word to express what he meant, but he thought the County Court Judge meant that the workman had left his work under circumstances which threw suspicion on his conduct, and it was impossible, upon those findings, to interfere with his decision, and there was no doubt that the result of payment of compensation took away all stimulus for work.   Both the other Lords Justices concurred, and the appeal was dismissed (Turner *v.* Brooks and Doxey, Ltd., 3 B.W.C.C., 22).

270 MALINGERING

As has already been stated, it is not unusual for the memory of an accident so to linger as to alter the mental outlook of a man who at one time has been genuinely injured. In the following case the County Court Judge held that physically the workman had recovered from the accident, but he had fostered a mental condition, the effect of which was that he would not work, and that consequently the mental condition could not reasonably be held to be the result of the accident itself.

An application was made by the employers to the deputy County Court Judge for a review of the weekly payment to a workman, aged thirty-nine, who had received injury in the course of his employment in May, 1905. The original injuries had been to the back, several ribs, and the right kidney. In December, 1908, the parties consented to the case being referred to one of the medical referees, who certified that at the time of the examination the workman was only suffering from stiffness of the muscles of his back, due to long disuse, which made him afraid to use them, and that he was fit for his ordinary work, especially if he resumed it in a gradual and easy manner. Upon this report the County Court Judge reduced the weekly payment to 1d. The man returned to work for short spells, but finally gave up in February, 1909, owing, as he stated, to the pains in his back.

The matter again came before the deputy Judge for a review on an application by the workman in June, 1909, and, after hearing the medical evidence on both sides, the deputy County Court Judge thought the case should be reported upon by both medical referees of the Court. These gentlemen were supplied with copies of the medical evidence, and the workman was examined by them. The one who had examined the man before reported that he saw no reason to alter the opinion he had formed in December, 1908, and that the man had worried and brooded so much over his accident that he had worked himself up to such a state that he anticipated failure. The other medical referee reported that he was of the most definite opinion that the man had thoroughly recovered from the effects of the accident, and that physically he was quite able to follow his usual work if he chose to do so, and he could only surmise that his mind would not allow him to summon up courage to persevere with his work.

His Honour, after referring to the reports of the medical referees, stated that it was perfectly plain that physically the man had quite recovered from the accident, and *that he could not hold that his mental condition was the result of the accident*, and he considered that his refusal to interfere with the order reducing the weekly payment to 1d. would be a greater incentive to the man to get himself fit for work than a sea voyage or the advice of a brain specialist, as was suggested by his counsel. The workman appealed against this decision, and the Master of the Rolls stated that he agreed with the very full and

WORKMEN'S COMPENSATION ACT, 1906   271

adequate judgment of the County Court Judge, and the other Lords Justices having agreed the appeal was dismissed (Holt *v.* Yates and Thom, 3 B.W.C.C., 75).

The possibility of an injured workman having, in addition to his accident, serious internal disease is one which a medical examiner should always keep before him. It will be noted that in the following case the Judge remarked that he was satisfied the woman was not malingering, and that her apparent incapacity was due, as I had ventured to suggest when giving evidence, to her nervous mental condition. He stated that he believed the accident was not *per se* the cause of her disability, but that some other nervous influences were at work.

This was wholly justified by the subsequent history, for, long after the trial was over, I obtained definite information from the doctor on the other side that the applicant was at the time of the trial, unknown to everyone, suffering from advanced malignant disease of the breast, and that soon after the trial she underwent a serious operation, from which she speedily recovered, and at once resumed her old work—that of a charwoman.

Towards the end of 1909 a question came before the Judge of the Southend County Court for decision in regard to the conduct of a person who had received an injury which brought the case within the Act. The injured person was a charwoman, and the injury, which was sustained in 1907, was caused by a needle penetrating the palm of her hand. It became embedded between the shafts of the third and fourth metacarpal bones of the right hand. She was advised by a doctor on the day of the accident that it would be dangerous to attempt to remove the needle, as it would involve opening the palm of the hand, and there was a possibility of inflammation being set up, but that the needle would cause her no trouble—indeed, it might work itself out or get near to the surface, so that it could be easily extracted. She became so nervous and worried in consequence of having the needle in her hand that she was advised to have an operation performed, which was done in November, 1908, but without success, and the needle remained in her hand. All the medical witnesses called at the hearing were agreed, in view of an X-ray photograph which had been taken, that the condition of the woman's hand could not be attributed to the original penetration of the needle into the hand or its presence there since, and if no operation had been performed she would have been fit to work shortly after the happening of the accident. The question to be decided, therefore, was whether the operation had produced the woman's present condition. After reviewing the medical evidence, His Honour stated that he was satisfied the woman was not

272   MALINGERING

malingering, and that her apparent incapacity to use the hand arose from *her nervous mental condition,* which induced in her a firm belief that she could not use her hand owing to the continued presence of the needle. She was suffering from what His Honour described as " false neurasthenia," and he said if the woman had acted reasonably her hand would have been available for work soon after the accident, and therefore the absence of reasonable conduct and care had broken the chain of causation, and that the principles laid down by the Court of Appeal in the cases of Warncken *v.* R. Moreland and Son, Ltd. (p. 259), Tutton *v.*Owners of s.s.*Majestic* (p. 261), and Marshall *v.*Orient Steam Navigation Company (p. 263), applied to the case. His Honour also said : " I think that in judging what is reasonable conduct I must apply the ordinary test—namely, in this particular case, what would an ordinarily prudent and reasonably minded person have done ? The applicant omits to do what a reasonably minded and prudent person would have done. I think she was unreasonable in her conduct in not having exercised or worked her hand in a reasonable manner, which would have prevented the condition of things which now exist." The Judge's award was therefore in favour of the employer (Steele *v.* Bilham, 128 L.T., 416).

How long a workman who has undoubtedly been injured may postpone his return to work after he has recovered from his original injury is always an interesting question. Muscles accustomed to regular, steady exercise soon get out of condition, and this loss of condition frequently conduces to a postponement of the return to work. It was pointed out by the Judge in the case about to be quoted that the Workmen's Compensation Act is intended to compensate for loss of wages, so far as that loss is *due to accident.* It is obviously not fair to compel an employer to pay weekly allowances after a workman has recovered from his original injury merely because his muscles have been allowed to become what a member of a football team would describe as being " not in good training." The question whether, in such circumstances, a workman is entitled to any payment, and, if so, how much, is discussed in an interesting case which came before the Judge of the Colne and Nelson County Court.

In August, 1911, a workman had been injured ; the medical men on both sides admitted it. The effect of their evidence was that the only thing which substantially affected his wage-earning capacity was his want of muscular power, and that this was due, as is usually the case, to his not having, for a considerable time, made use of his muscles as he had done before the accident. His Honour, after referring to the medical evidence, stated that he could not look upon the man's

WORKMEN'S COMPENSATION ACT, 1906   273

capacity to do his old work, or his opportunities for getting his old work, as having been substantially diminished by the accident, and awarded him 4s. a week only. His Honour went on to state as follows : " I have often pointed out in previous cases that the sole object of the Act is to compensate workmen for the loss of wages so far as that loss is due to the accident. If a workman who has been injured has so far recovered that he is able to earn some wages, but makes no effort to earn those wages, his loss of those wages cannot be said to be due to the accident, but is simply due to the workman having made no effort to earn them. If, therefore, as in this case, the workman has chosen not to work, when the evidence shows that, so far as the accident is concerned, he is nearly as fit to work as he was before the accident, I cannot find that the loss of wages is entirely or even mainly due to the accident. A workman can, according to the Act, be compensated for what he is unable to earn, but cannot be compensated for what he declines to earn " (Lidderdale *v.* Robinson, 132 L.T. 12).

The following illustrates a class of case which is very familiar to those who see many cases in which claims are made under the Workmen's Compensation Act :

In December, 1909, a milkman and cowman injured his left wrist and cut the forefinger of his right hand as the result of a fall in the course of his employment. He attended a hospital at once, was X-rayed, and continued as an out-patient for six weeks. At the end of this time his wrist was examined under an anæsthetic, and moved freely. He admitted that this had improved the condition of the wrist, but attended as an out-patient until April, 1910. He was paid weekly compensation for a month. He claimed that he could not milk with the right hand alone, and applied to the County Court Judge for an award for half-wages. Two of his doctors admitted what was obvious, that since January he could have worked with his right hand only, but the man said he could not work at all, and had no power of grip. One of the doctors called on the workman's behalf, who saw him three months after the accident, said he then found the wrist enlarged, and, on the man's statement and his own examination, he gave a certificate that he was suffering from fracture of the wrist, and was unable to work, and at the time of the hearing—viz., April— he considered he was unable to work, but that he would be able to work at a future date. He admitted that the symptoms were consistent with sprain.

The employers tendered evidence that the X-ray photos showed that there never had been a fracture, and a doctor deposed that under an anæsthetic in January, 1910, the wrist was freely movable, but after the effect of the anæsthetic had passed away the milkman resisted all movement, and that in his opinion the man could work if he liked.

The County Court Judge stated that he thought the workman was shamming, and was then, and had been for a long time, at all events ever since Christmas, fully able to work and earn full wages, and that the sums already paid by the employers were sufficient to satisfy

274 MALINGERING

all claims under the Act. The workman appealed against this decision. His counsel, having read the evidence given before the County Court Judge, submitted that there was no evidence upon which the Judge could have found as he did. Counsel for the employers were not called upon, the Master of the Rolls stating that the appeal was hopeless, and, the other Lords Justices agreeing, the appeal was dismissed (Roberts v. Benham, 3 B.W.C.C., 430).

If a workman is fit to undertake work of any description, it is his duty to endeavour to obtain it, and the employer is not liable to pay full compensation when a workman is able to work and earn *something*. The following decided case illustrates this point :

A workman in 1907 had his right femur fractured by an accident ; his right leg was in consequence 1½ inches shorter than the left, and he was permanently lame. In 1908 he was awarded 15s. a week compensation, and in 1911 the employers applied to the County Court Judge to have the weekly payment reduced on the ground that the man was able to do light work. The employers called evidence to support their contention that the workman was able to undertake light work not involving much getting about ; they tendered no evidence that the man had been offered light work, or that it was obtainable, but the man admitted that he had never tried to get light work. The Judge reduced the weekly payment to 10s., against which award the workman appealed.

Counsel for the workman argued that there was no evidence of a change of circumstances to justify the County Court Judge in reducing the weekly payment. The employers' counsel was not called upon. Lord Justice Fletcher Moulton pointed out in the course of the proceedings that the medical evidence was to the effect that the man had so far recovered as to be fit for light work, and in giving judgment the Master of the Rolls said : "I think this is a perfectly clear case. A man meets with an accident, and gets compensation paid him for a time. The employers apply for a review to terminate or diminish the award. Medical evidence is called, including the evidence of the man's own doctor. Shortly, their evidence is that the man has so far recovered that he is now fit to do light work which does not require much getting about. The man says in reply, ' I have never tried to get light work,' and he seems to have taken up the position that he is entitled for the rest of his life to do no work. In these circumstances the Judge has reduced the payments from 15s. to 10s. a week. The ground of the appeal is that there is no evidence on which he could reduce the award to that sum. I think there is evidence on which he could do so." The appeal was therefore dismissed (Anglo-Austrian Steam Navigation Company, Ltd., v. Richards, 4 B.W.C.C., 247).

The question whether a workman who has received injury arising out of, and in the course of, his employment has or has not recovered from the effects of the accident is also one of

WORKMEN'S COMPENSATION ACT, 1906   275

fact for the arbitrator or County Court Judge to determine upon the evidence given before him, and, as before stated, findings of *fact* by the Arbitrator or County Court Judge will not be interfered with by the Court of Appeal if there is evidence to support them.

The following case is confirmatory of the above statement. It is one in which there was some slight physical defect still remaining as the result of an accident. The County Court Judge, acting as Arbitrator, found *as a fact* that the defect existed, *but no longer incapacitated* the workman from working. The case was taken to the Court of Appeal by the workman, and the appeal was dismissed.

> In December, 1910, a bricklayer's labourer met with an accident by which his finger was injured, under circumstances which entitled him to the benefits of the Act. The workman received compensation up to April, 1911, when the weekly payment was terminated by the County Court Judge upon the application of the employers, on the ground that his incapacity had ceased. The Judge found that, although the finger was still slightly stiff and bent, there was no likelihood of recurrence of incapacity. The workman appealed against this decision, and his counsel argued that the Judge should have made a suspensory award, and should also have considered the question whether the man was hampered in the labour market. Counsel for the employers were not called upon. All the members of the Court of Appeal agreed that the appeal should be dismissed (Edmondsons, Ltd., v. Parker, 5 B.W.C.C., 70).

If the workman's incapacity is due to his unreasonable failure or refusal to undertake work which would be beneficial to his recovery, he is not entitled to compensation, the employer being only liable to pay compensation in respect of wages which the workman is *unable* to earn, and not of wages which he *refuses* to earn.

The following case is condensed from over twenty pages of the law reports. It confirms the view that it is not necessary for an employer to prove, in order to enable him to stop payment, that a workman who has been injured in his service, and has partially recovered, is able to obtain suitable employment. The employer is not bound to provide him with such work, nor to prove that he can actually obtain it. If the workman has so far recovered as to enable him to undertake work of a suitable kind, it is his business to get it.

MALINGERING

In 1904, a workman, who was employed on the tramways of a Corporation, fell from the top of a car and injured his right arm, and compensation was paid to him by the Corporation. He was subsequently employed by them to drive a horse and trap, and in July, 1908, met with a second accident, and received half-wages from the date of that accident until September 24 following; payment was then stopped. In May, 1909, he applied to the County Court Judge for an award, claiming half-wages from September 24, 1908. At the hearing before the County Court Judge, medical evidence, which was very conflicting, was tendered, and the learned Judge called in the medical referee, who reported that there was considerable loss of power in the man's upper extremities, and many other evidences of serious disease of the nervous system, and it was quite uncertain that those conditions would after a while improve ; that the man was then absolutely unfit to follow his occupation of driving a horse, and all he was fit to do was such work as a watchman's, which would require no muscular power in his arms. An award was made by the Judge in favour of the workman for half - wages from September, 1908. In September, 1910, the employers applied to the County Court Judge to review the award, and by arrangement only one medical witness was called on each side. The doctor who was called for the employers said there was nothing the matter with the man but a slight swelling in the left wrist, which was not sufficient to prevent him doing his work, and the general effect of his evidence was that the workman was a malingerer. On the other hand, the workman's doctor said that the effect of the accident was such that the man was not able to do the work that he had been doing before the accident, and that he was suffering from traumatic neurasthenia. The man himself stated that he could not do his former work, and that he had, without success, made nine applications for work at delivering bills, three or four for employment as a watchman, and one for employment as a postman. The County Court Judge, having regard to the conflicting evidence, again called in the medical referee, and he reported that the man was suffering from impacted dislocation of the bones of the left carpus as a result of the injuries received by him in July, 1908 ; that this condition greatly weakened the grasp of the left hand, and quite incapacitated him from driving a horse and trap in the usual manner ; but the man was then quite able to do any form of light work, more particularly such as would require principally the use of the right hand. The County Court Judge reduced the weekly payments from 9s. 2d. to 8s., stating that he was of opinion that the man had greatly improved since the making of the award, and, taking all the circumstances into consideration, he came to the conclusion that 8s. a week was a proper and sufficient weekly payment to be made to the man in respect of the incapacity from which he was suffering.

The workman appealed. The consideration of the case occupied the Court of Appeal a considerable time, all the Lords Justices delivering judgments. Lords Justices Fletcher Moulton and Buckley

WORKMEN'S COMPENSATION ACT, 1906   277

agreed in dismissing the appeal, but the Master of the Rolls dissented from the view taken by them.

A few extracts from their Lordships' judgment may be given :

The Master of the Rolls said : "This state of facts raises the question whether an employer, admittedly liable to pay compensation for an accident which disables.the man from following his former occupation, can obtain an order for the termination or reduction of the compensation by merely proving physical ability to do light work without either offering to provide such work or adducing some evidence that light work can be obtained in the neighbourhood where the man resides, and of a suitable character."

"In my opinion, apart from authority, this question should be answered in the negative. The effects of the accident have not been removed, and I cannot think that the workman ought to have his compensation reduced merely on the ground that he is physically able to do a different kind of work, which, in truth, cannot be procured. It is not a case in which the effects of the original injury have completely disappeared so that the man is as capable as ever he was. In that case the employer, who does not guarantee the labour market, is free from all further liability."

Lord Justice Fletcher Moulton said : "The appellant (the workman) put forward an alleged principle of law to the effect that where partial incapacity has been caused by an accident, the employers are bound to show not only that the workman is capable of doing other work, but that he is able to obtain it, and that otherwise he is entitled to an award as for total incapacity. If any such principle of law exists or is deducible from the decisions of this Court, it must have a most important effect on the rights of parties under the Act, and I therefore propose to examine the question from the point of view of principle first, and then to examine the decisions that have been cited in support of it, to determine whether this contention of the appellant can be sustained. . . .

"When the incapacity ceases, the employer is entitled to be relieved of the obligation to make the payment. The diminution of earning-power has ceased, and with it has ceased the right to compensation. In the case of continuing incapacity, it is equally clear that the payments depend on the diminution of earning-power" (Cardiff Corporation v. Hall, 1911, 1 K.B., 1009, and 130 L.T., 505).

The pension which certain workmen become entitled to for injury under the terms of their service has often been disregarded when the amount of compensation under the Workmen's Compensation Act is being assessed, and this practice has caused much dissatisfaction among employers.*

When considering this matter, it is necessary to remember

* This has a very direct bearing upon malingering and exaggerated sick claims, and I propose to discuss the question very briefly.

MALINGERING

the provisions of the Act in relation to compensation payable in case of injury. Schedule I. (3) provides as follows :

> " In fixing the amount of the weekly payment, regard shall be had to any payment allowance or benefit which the workman may receive from the employer during the period of his incapacity. . . ."

The method prescribed by the Act for ascertaining the amount of compensation or varying a weekly payment in case of disagreement is by arbitration ; but if the amount is agreed between the parties—when the workman has not returned to work, or is not earning the same wages as he did before the accident—a memorandum thereof has to be sent to the Registrar of the County Court to be recorded in accordance with rules made under the Act. Where it appears to the Registrar that an agreement for redemption of a weekly payment, and in certain cases fixing the weekly payment, ought not to be recorded or registered because of the inadequacy of the amount, he may refuse to record it, and the matter is then referred to the Judge of the County Court, who may make such order as in the circumstances he thinks just. It frequently happens that a workman is entitled, after a certain number of years' service, to a pension, the sum, as a rule, being larger as the years of service increase. In some instances a pension is not payable until the person entitled to it reaches a certain age, but in others it becomes payable when disability from accident sustained in the course of duty ensues.

It appears to be the general practice—at any rate, it certainly has been so in the numerous cases which have come under my notice—for the Registrars and Judges of County Courts *not* to allow *any* deduction in the amount of compensation (payable for such disability) on account of any pension to which an injured workman is or may become entitled. It will be observed that the Act says, " *Regard* shall be had to any benefit, etc., which the workman may receive," not that it *must be actually taken into account when fixing the amount* the injured workman is to receive under the Workmen's Compensation Act ; and it would seem, from the practice to which I have referred, that the provisions of the Act are in form satisfied if the fact of the workman being entitled to a pension is formally stated and not overlooked, although not actually taken into account by way of deduction. There does not appear to be

WORKMEN'S COMPENSATION ACT, 1906   279

any reported judicial decision upon the point, although it is one of considerable importance.

From the employer's point of view it is urged that it is unfair that an injured workman who becomes entitled to a pension should also receive full compensation under the Act, especially in those cases where the pension becomes payable *simply in consequence of the accident* as distinct from length of service.   It would seem to be reasonable for the employer to contend that the object of his giving a pension (especially when it is paid as the *result* of an accident) is to compensate the man in the event of inability to work or sustaining injury, and that therefore he should not be called upon in addition to pay compensation under the Act to the full extent.

There is, however, something to be said from the workman's point of view.   He would, no doubt, contend that a pension is practically deferred pay, as he would probably be receiving higher wages if he had no right to a pension, and that but for the accident he would in all probability be able to serve his employer longer, and thereby in time become entitled to a larger pension.   He would in some cases, no doubt, be able to urge that the accident had put an end to his opportunity for improving his position, and therefore it was fair not to take into account, by way of deduction, any sum he received as pension.

A fair way to deal with the difficulty would be to take all the circumstances of the particular case into consideration, and then decide whether the whole, or any part, of the sum payable as pension should be deducted from the amount payable under the Act.   This does not appear to be the general practice of the Registrars of the County Courts.   They " have regard " to the fact that the workman is receiving a pension, but they do not take it into account by way of deduction.

We often " have regard to " the condition of our impecunious acquaintances, but we do not always take their condition into account.   I think there is little doubt that had the law enacted that we shall " have regard " *to them*, we should also have had to give practical *proof* of our regard !

CHAPTER XXIII

THE NATIONAL INSURANCE ACT, 1911.

THE interesting question arises as to how far the incidence of malingering will be affected by the passing of the recent National Insurance Act. Under this Act some twelve millions of workpeople will be compulsorily insured, and it is to be feared that malingering must necessarily become much more frequent.

If we turn to the experience of foreign countries, more especially of Germany, we find that this has indeed been the case, for since the passing of their Insurance Acts the amount of malingering has gone up by leaps and bounds.

It must be remembered that heretofore people who have been insured against sickness have insured themselves. They have been the best of the working-classes. In very many cases such workmen have taken a personal pride in the club to which they have belonged. This is more especially true in the rural districts, where it often happens that men who are seriously ill will not claim from the club, so that its funds shall not be depleted, and they pride themselves on never having taken sick-pay. It may be that a proportion of these, resenting the compulsory deduction from their wages, will make up their minds to get their contributions back again by claiming sick allowances.

The operation of the Workmen's Compensation Act has demonstrated that the incentive to gain has too often caused exaggeration of slight injuries and prolongation of disabilities resulting from accident. Now, under the National Insurance Act not only accidents but illnesses are included, and it is obvious that disabilities arising from illness are far more easily

280

THE NATIONAL INSURANCE ACT, 1911   281

simulated, and will I fear cause more difficulty, than those resulting from accidents.

As sickness benefit is only payable from the fourth day of the illness, there will probably be a strong temptation to prolong slight ailments.

The French Republic, as is well known, owns the railways. When the lines were taken over by the State, it was announced that every day of illness would be paid for. The influence of State ownership on what our neighbours call the " right to illness " is somewhat remarkable. Prior to this change, in the year 1909, there were 474,000 days of sickness, which, after the transference, in the year 1911, rose to 656,000 days. In 1911, 54 per cent. of the railway employees were " ill " at one time or another.

It may be contended that the amount which is received under the Act—viz., ten shillings a week—is a small one, and not likely to tempt men in good employment to claim sick-pay unnecessarily ; but it must be remembered that there are amongst the insured a certain number of men who are getting beyond middle life, and who for many reasons may be tempted to prolong any illness that may befall them. A man who has been engaged in laborious and monotonous toil for fifty years or more finds it increasingly irksome, and naturally the desire to escape grows strong as time goes on. His physical powers are beginning to deteriorate ; he is more easily tired, is often beginning to have rheumatic changes in his joints ; and, as is well known, lumbago, sciatica, spondylitis deformans, and varicose ulcers occur more frequently to people of the working-classes as age advances. Although none of the conditions are in themselves absolutely crippling, all tend to render work more laborious, and in these days, when the tendency is to speed up the rate of work, it is small wonder that a man so afflicted begins to turn his thoughts to how he can escape from his daily toil.

One has reason to be somewhat apprehensive about the working of the National Insurance Act, seeing that even the Old Age Pension Act has in some cases had an injurious effect, as the following case illustrates :

History—D. R.—I was asked by an insurance company to investigate the case of a horsekeeper, aged seventy, who alleged that fourteen months previously he fell whilst ascending a ladder, that he had

282   MALINGERING

suffered with his back ever since, and was unfit for work as a result of this mishap.

It appeared that after being laid up for seven weeks D. R. resumed work for six months, when he gave up work on his own account, and became entitled to an old age pension. He was allowed to live on in his rooms for three months, and then was sent to an infirmary, where he remained nearly three weeks.

I had an interview with the medical superintendent of the infirmary, who told me that no mention had been made by any relative of any accident.

Examination.—I examined him in the presence of his doctor, who, having attended him for years gratuitously, evidently looked sympathetically upon the case. D. R. complained to me of pain in his back. When asked to indicate the exact spot, he pointed to a place which I marked with coloured pencil on the flesh, and subsequently he indicated five different places ranging over an area 5 inches square. In fact, his back appeared to be tender almost anywhere when it was suggested to him. It was pointed out to his doctor that when one asked D. R. to bend, and pressed one's fingers deeply between each pair of spinous processes, the vertebræ moved freely upon each other, which they certainly could not have done had there been any spinal disease. The back was not only not diseased, but was unusually supple for a man of his years.

The old man's claim was a preposterous one, which in the interests of justice had to be resisted. There was not the slightest foundation for the allegation that the accident caused his incapacity for work. True, it would be impossible to assert in a court of law that there could be no connection between the alleged fall and any abnormal sensations he may have felt in the region complained of ; but these sensations were in my opinion mental, not physical, born not of the disease, but of cupidity. He had made no complaint to anyone until he was asked to vacate his house. His doctor, however, held that if he had had no injury he would not have had backache, and that therefore the insurance company was responsible ! It was apparent that the cause of his inability to work was not pain, but age, and this he himself had tacitly admitted by claiming an old age pension.

Result.—The solicitors acting on behalf of the insurance company denied liability, and no further action was taken by the plaintiff or his solicitors.

A working-man will under the Act receive ten shillings a week, and he may possibly have other sources of income. His grown-up children will very probably contribute to the expenses of the household, or his wife may make a little money by nursing, charing, etc. In short, to men between sixty and seventy years of age there will be a strong temptation to defer the return to work. There is the danger, too, of attempts being made to tide over periods of unemployment by going

THE NATIONAL INSURANCE ACT, 1911   283

on the sick-list. A number of men who are past middle age will be insured ; their employment will in many cases be of an irregular and precarious nature, and the temptation to go on the sick-list for lumbago, sciatica, rheumatism, or similar complaints will be great. The symptoms of these complaints are almost entirely subjective, and there is difficulty in refuting allegations with regard to them.

The danger of old age and intercurrent disease complicating a claim for a comparatively slight accident is well illustrated by the following case :

D. S.—I was asked to examine a man, aged sixty, who was said to have fallen with a truck and two sacks of flour into a barge six weeks previously, and sustained a contusion of his right *elbow*.

Examination.—D. S. complained of pain in his right hand, inability to close it firmly, and some pain at the right elbow-joint.

There was a soundly healed scar on the arm, but the muscles of the forearm were slightly wasted, and the hand somewhat puffy. He was of poor physique, evidently in an impoverished condition ; he had received a genuine, though not serious, injury, and was likely to recover in about a fortnight.

He volunteered the statement that he had no intention of remaining on the sick-list too long, but, on the other hand, refused to come to my house on the plea that he was too ill, although he was quite able to do so. I advised the case should be watched, for, admittedly unconnected with the accident, he had a huge hydrocele, which alone would interfere with his work, and might cause a desire to prolong his convalescence unnecessarily.

My prognostication was confirmed, for he had not resumed work seven weeks later, and was sent to me, still complaining of inability to use his right hand, which presented no abnormal sign except the clean, pale appearance due to want of use.

To test the power of the right upper arm, he was asked to bend the arm at the elbow, and resist my straightening it, which he did successfully. When the hand was alternately pronated and supinated, he—thinking he ought to oppose everything done to him—exerted considerable muscular power to prevent the manipulation ! When asked to close his fist and prevent my opening it, he did so with considerable success.

This man, old for his years, had evidently made up his mind he would never work again, the real cause of his unwillingness being, in my opinion, the hydrocele (about three times the size of one's fist), which he owned was a great inconvenience to him. He was certainly not now justly entitled to further compensation on the score of the accident, and I had good reason to fear his case would be a difficult one to deal with.

Three weeks later, when he was examined by a surgeon in consultation with me in the presence of his doctor, D. S. alleged that the hydrocele had *become larger since the accident.* This new allegation recalled to my mind a conversation I had had with him on the *first* occasion I saw him, when he had suggested (somewhat tentatively) that the hydrocele was *caused by* the accident.

Owing to prolonged disuse, the grip of the right hand was not now equal to that of the left, nor could he be persuaded to completely flex the first two fingers ; but it was obvious that if he returned to work at once he would recover the full use of the hand.

Three and a half months later, on examination, D. S. looked pinched and ill. Albumen was present in the urine in considerable quantity; there was no other evidence of active disease, but he had the appearance of a man who had recently come through some acute illness— probably influenza—without receiving proper care and attention. The hydrocele was even larger than before. When asked why he had not been to hospital to have it attended to, he said he had not sufficient money, at the same time admitting that it troubled him so much he was " afraid to do anything with it." He appeared to be obsessed with the idea that the hydrocele was made worse by the accident.

There was a tendency to commencing Dupuytren's contraction in the fingers of *both* hands, quite unconnected with the accident. There was also some difficulty in closing the first and second fingers on to the palm, due to old-standing rheumatoid arthritis.

As an old soldier he had probably lived hard, and, until his accident, worked hard in the docks ; his working days were over, and he knew it.

Result.—His employers felt sympathy for him in his troubles, but were of opinion that he would have been better advised if, instead of starting arbitration proceedings against them, he had asked their assistance. They felt reluctantly obliged to contest such an obviously unjust claim. He was, in fact, in no worse a position than thousands of other working-men who happen to be past their work.

The case was heard in the County Court, and the Judge (who was assisted by a medical referee), after hearing the evidence, stopped the case, deciding in favour of the employers.

As to the precautions to be adopted to prevent any great increase of malingering being due to the existence of this new source of income, the first thing I would suggest is that the medical man should be placed in a position of absolute independence. One welcomes, therefore, the provisions of the Act whereby, in the case of a man who belongs to a club instead of being attended by a " club doctor," he will have the choice of being attended by any one of the doctors on the panel for the district.

In addition to the payment under the National Insurance Act, many men will be in receipt of weekly allowances for accidents from one or more clubs, and the total amount

THE NATIONAL INSURANCE ACT, 1911   285

of their incomes when ill will be actually more than when working.

Against the advantage of free choice of doctor must be set the danger that one member of the medical panel may be induced to give certificates too easily, and to put men on sick-pay too readily, in the hope of thereby winning popularity and increasing his clientèle.

It is therefore advisable that medical men should be appointed to whom doubtful cases could be referred. Such men should have a special training in dealing with doubtful cases of malingering ; they should have no local associations, and each one should have a circuit which he would traverse at stated periods. If such appointments were made, a local medical man who is in doubt as to whether a certain individual is abusing the National Insurance funds would have the opportunity of advising a consultation with the medical referee of the district.

The odium of sending back to work a man reluctant to resume would thus be removed from the shoulders of the doctor who was actually attending him, who would naturally be averse to performing such an unpleasant duty. The mere fact that such inspectors were appointed would tend to counteract the laxity and favouritism which might otherwise be shown.

In Germany it has been found that it pays the administrators or managers of Pension Funds (which are equivalent to our Approved Societies) to appoint special doctors to examine persons in receipt of sickness benefit. Experience shows that they have saved the funds more than the amount of their salaries. Approved Societies in this country will probably be forced, within a short time, to appoint special medical men to examine members in receipt of sickness benefit in order to prevent abuse of their funds.

CHAPTER XXIV

LEGAL AID SOCIETIES

WITH the great change which has taken place in vehicular traffic during the past few years, by the arrival of mechanically propelled vehicles, there has come also an immense increase in the number of street accidents. In the year ending December 31, 1911, over 15,000 people were injured and 410 killed in the streets of London. During the ten months ending October 31, 1912, 428 persons were killed by vehicular traffic in London, 304 of these deaths being due to mechanically propelled vehicles and 124 to horse-drawn vehicles. During the last ten years the annual death-roll from traffic accidents in London has become four times greater than it was. To that fact, and the Workmen's Compensation Act, may be attributed the rapid growth of what is a serious evil. There are now, principally in London, but also throughout the provinces, a number of societies, many of which call themselves legal aid societies, or by some other name signifying that their business is to help people in need of legal advice and assistance. The sole business of some of these societies appears to be that of inducing injured employees to make speculative claims for damages, too often of an exaggerated, and sometimes even approaching a fraudulent, character. It is immaterial how trivial a claim may be, it is equally immaterial whether the claimant has the means to support the claim : the case is taken up on sheer speculation.

The affairs of some of these " societies " for the so-called assistance and benefit of the poor should be thoroughly investigated. In certain cases the title of " society ' is simply used as a cloak for advertising or touting for cases by speculative firms of solicitors. The procedure is simple, and is as impudent as it is ingenious. An office is taken, sometimes only a poky

286

LEGAL AID SOCIETIES

room, and from this address large numbers of plausible pamphlets and circulars are issued broadcast, the purport of them being that when legal advice or assistance is required it can be procured free, at such-and-such an address, by joining such-and-such a society, and paying the very modest sum of one penny. The handbills referred to are circulated freely, and their inviting proposals appeal to the cupidity of the ignorant and credulous.

Cases in which flagrant touting has taken place are occasionally reported in the public press, and quite recently an account appeared of how a man was arrested for hawking at one penny each coupons of a society which carried with them a promise that legal assistance would be obtained provided that 10 per cent. of the damages recovered should be deducted by the society. It appeared that the Magistrate had previously adjourned the case for the attendance of the secretary of the society, who, however, merely sent a representative, with whom the following conversation took place :

> The MAGISTRATE : Are these coupon books sold to men to hawk about the streets ?
>
> The REPRESENTATIVE : No price is charged for the books. They are given, the object being to circulate the tickets for the benefit of poor persons.
>
> The MAGISTRATE : In one word, for advertisement ?
>
> The REPRESENTATIVE : Possibly.
>
> The MAGISTRATE : Your society, with the object of picking up chance litigants, subsidizes street beggars all over London. A nice state of things !
>
> The REPRESENTATIVE : I don't agree. If the men choose to beg, we can't help it.
>
> In sentencing the prisoner to five days' imprisonment the Magistrate said he was sorry to find that there was a society like this to help beggars.
>
> The prisoner asked, " What have I got five days for ?", and the Magistrate referred him to the secretary.

It is well known from what class of persons the ordinary tout is recruited. He is frequently an unemployed clerk of a solicitor, or a broken-down member of one of the two branches of the legal profession.

Cases are brought into the net by the e persons haunting the side-doors of our large Metropolitan hospitals, and button-holing the distressed relatives of those who have met with accidents, or by a ghoulish alertness in studying the newspapers for announcements of accidents in factories and streets, and in sending circulars to injured persons or their friends, and in following up the circulars with a personal call upon them.

At a recent inquest there was a striking instance of the procedure followed in such cases. A solicitor said he appeared on behalf of the relatives of the deceased man, but according to a newspaper report it transpired that a clerk had called upon the dead man's brother and induced him to " knock off " work and go to the solicitor's office. When it was stated that the relatives did not desire to be represented by the solicitor he withdrew, stating that he absolutely discountenanced the conduct of the clerk, of which he was in ignorance.

For their pains so-called Legal Aid Society touts receive a proportion of the commission deducted by the " society " from " damages " obtained, and the effect of these activities is to set employees against employers, and to accentuate the unfortunate antagonism that exists in some quarters between one class and another.

The following is an example of their tactics, which came under my personal notice some little time ago :

D. T.—I was asked, on behalf of an insurance company, to examine a workman who had fallen several feet from a dock, sustaining slight injuries to his arm, foot, and back He told me that he was nervous about beginning work again. On examination I found D. T. had wholly recovered. The workman, who impressed me as being perfectly straightforward, informed me that a stranger called at his house the day following the accident, saying he was the representative of a certain legal aid society. The visitor did not ask the injured man whether he was a member of the society, but when asked how he (the visitor) knew of the accident he gave a non-committal reply, and proceeded to fill up a membership ticket for the injured man. The society, he urged, would assist him in his case, adding that he " ought to get a decent sum." The workman protested, stating he had no desire for the society's help, and that he certainly did not wish any proceedings taken, for he had been three years with his employers, and had a " good job." The stranger promised to take no action, but urged the workman to write to the legal aid society, which he represented, to tell the officials how the firm behaved in the matter, and left a penny to defray the cost of postage.

A week later a well-known firm of solicitors wrote to the workman to the effect that his society had placed the matter in their hands, that they would be glad if he would give them a call, and that in the meantime he should not " negotiate with the other side."

LEGAL AID SOCIETIES

Although he had on no occasion paid anything to the funds of the society, a membership card, which was presented to him, stated that he was a member of the society for one year from the day following the accident, by virtue of his having paid one penny. Shortly afterwards the society, in defiance of the workman's repeated instructions to the contrary, actually sent one of their representatives to call upon his employers, ostensibly on the workman's behalf!

In a recent accident which occurred in London, in which a considerable number of persons were more or less seriously injured, the majority of the injured had received on the morning following the accident as many as four letters from different legal aid societies, offering to take up their cases free of charge, and recommending them to have nothing to do with those responsible for the accident.

The condition imposed on claimants, when this angling has been successful, is usually the deduction of 5 per cent. to 10 per cent. of the damages recovered ; but nothing is said about the costs, which presumably also find their way into the coffers of the society or its legal satellites. In cases other than actions for personal injuries, advice can usually be obtained " on terms." The reason for this distinction is subtle. Actions for personal injuries can be instituted at little cost—*i.e.*, Court fees only. They are often tried before sympathetic juries ; they can be conducted by counsel who may not have been paid the fees marked on their briefs ; and the plaintiff has everything in his favour. It is the unfortunate defendants who have to find the money, for if they should win the case they have no prospect of securing payment of their costs.

No pretence whatever is made of keeping any record of the members of these legal aid societies, nor is it a condition precedent to a claim being taken up that even the penny should have been paid for nominal membership. In many instances it may be that injured persons are quite legitimately assisted, and I do not suggest that claims made through the instrumentality of such societies are necessarily fraudulent, but it is obvious that the system is open to the gravest abuse. I believe in the majority of cases no balance-sheet is published, and the question naturally arises, " What is done with the percentage ?" Of course, there can be no doubt that at least

MALINGERING

some of this is diverted into the pockets of the solicitors and their touts. I have before me the prospectus of one of these societies, for circulation amongst workmen, setting out at length a list of cases, with the nature of the injuries said to have been sustained, and the amounts received from the employers. That it is a very profitable business, and keenly sought after, may be gathered from the fact (already stated) that very many members of the working classes, on meeting with accidents, received by the first post next morning letters from some one or more of these legal aid societies offering assistance ; and it is quite a common thing for a man who has been injured to be pestered by the representatives of these societies.

In this connection I remember a case in which both employer and employed were subjected to much annoyance by the importunities of a solicitor's tout trading under cover of a legal aid society.

Although employers of labour know how to treat these parasites, the ignorant working-man does not. He is insidiously taught to set a commercial value upon his misfortune, and to think more of what the unearned increment may be than of how soon he will return to duty.

D. U.—A rough, ignorant navvy, who could neither read nor write, was sent to me for examination. He told me that he was selling his furniture, for he had had no food at home, and though absolutely starving had walked a considerable distance to my house. Owing to the slipping of a tool, he had sustained an accident to his hand, from which he had recovered ; indeed, he had probably been fit for work for some time.

From the papers submitted to me by an insurance company concerned, it appeared that his employers had had considerable correspondence with a solicitor acting for a legal aid society with reference to the case.

The accident happened on a Friday, and on the following Monday he was asked by the society to call at their office. He did so, and was asked by the society's representative " if he would take a lump sum, or what he would do." He said he did not want a lump sum, but would see his employer on the matter, whom he subsequently found had already been approached by a solicitor acting for the legal aid society. He was then informed by the legal aid society's official that " they could not help him so long as he continued to receive half-wages from his employers "!

I arranged light work for D. U., and enabled him to escape from the toils into which he might have fallen.

LEGAL AID SOCIETIES

One sometimes hears of claimants who, some time after their cases have been settled, call on the defendant and ask what amount had actually been handed over to their solicitors.

The methods of some of these legal aid societies have at various times been commented upon from the Bench, but as yet nothing has been done. I sometimes wonder if organizations of this kind are, strictly speaking, legal, for their sole object appears to be the promotion of litigation, and this upon the terms of " no damages, no pay." One cannot help being surprised that this condition of affairs has not yet received the attention of the Law Society. The promotion of claims of a speculative character by solicitors must bring discredit to the legal profession. My chief concern, however, is that the system is productive of cases in which there is gross exaggeration, and a direct incentive to malingering and fraud. A perusal of the High Court jury lists from time to time will afford an instructive lesson on the question of actions for personal injuries which are set down for trial, and these lists, of course, take no account of the immense number of similar actions brought in the County Court. How instructive it might be if reliable figures could be obtained showing how many cases have been settled out of Court by defendants rather than risk the expense of defending actions, more especially cases settled for small sums and small costs which are nearly blackmail!

The truth is that the vast majority of successful defendants have no prospect whatsoever of securing their costs.

The appointment of a poor man's lawyer has now become absolutely necessary. If the present state of affairs, with its attendant evils, is to be remedied, the duties of the office of poor man's lawyer must be entrusted to some person of unquestioned integrity, who might, I suggest, be appointed under the supervision of the Government. Excellent work in this direction is, I believe, done by the committees of certain religious bodies in the Metropolis, but, unfortunately, these committees are not nearly numerous or strong enough to deal adequately with the cases which arise.

CHAPTER XXV

EPONYMIC SIGNS

IT sometimes happens that counsel, in order to confuse the medical witness, suddenly asks, in cross-examination, whether So-and-so's sign is present. If the witness is not familiar with the particular word, as, of course, so often happens with these eponymic signs; the only safe course is to say that one is probably familiar with the sign, but cannot for the moment connect it with the inventor's name, and, if counsel will indicate the nature of the test, the witness will give the Court the necessary assistance.

I have seen a medical man nonplussed and laughed out of Court because he could not for the moment connect the well-known name of Romberg with the test he first described. Counsel asked, " What is Romberg's test ?" The witness could not for the moment associate the great German's name with any particular test, and simply said he did not know. Much was made of the admission, and the doctor was worried as to whether it was applied by a stethoscope or an ophthalmoscope, and the impression was left that he was crassly ignorant.

The following list of signs, etc., may be useful ; many of the signs are, of course, very familiar, while some are almost obsolete, but should not be quite forgotten yet in medico-legal practice.

Argyll-Robertson Pupil.—A pupil which contracts to accommodate for near vision, but does not contract for increase of light. Found in locomotor ataxy (tabes), and general paralysis of the insane.

Babinski's Sign (see p. 67).—Extension instead of flexion of the great toe on tickling of the sole of the foot; indicative

292

EPONYMIC SIGNS 293

of organic disease, and never found in functional disorders. It is found wherever there is involvement of the crossed pyramidal tract ; its absence does not negative organic disease, as it is absent in lower neurone affections, such as tabes, peripheral neuritis, and infantile paralysis.

Banti's Disease.—Disease characterized by great enlargement of the spleen and anæmia. It is often associated with cirrhosis of the liver.

Bazin's Disease.—A tuberculous lesion of the skin of the legs, causing a series of very indolent ulcers, situate usually on the back of the calves.

Brown-Séquard Paralysis.—Paralysis of one side of the body with loss of the sense of position and muscular sense, and often exalted sense of touch and pain on the same side, with loss of sensation to heat and touch and pain on the opposite side ; found in lesions of one lateral half of the spinal cord, such as may be caused by the stab of a knife. It occurs often among Italians.

Burton's Sign.—The blue line along the edge of the gums, found in chronic lead-poisoning.

Calmette's Reaction.—A test for the presence of tuberculous disease. It is obtained by dropping tuberculin on to the eye. If positive, a conjunctivitis occurs within forty-eight hours. It is falling out of use, owing to severe inflammation being occasionally set up.

Cammidge's Reaction.—A complicated urine test, which, if positive, points to inflammation and active degenerative change of the pancreas. Found in acute and chronic pancreatitis.

Charcot-Marie's Disease.—See Tooth's Disease.

Charcot's Joints.—The degenerative arthritis found in cases of tabes and syringomyelia ; characterized by painlessness, by great and sudden effusion, and rapid disorganization. Found usually in one joint only, and that the knee, shoulder, or hip.

Chvostek's Sign, or Weiss's Sign.—Contraction of the facial muscles, obtained by tapping them, significant of tetany, neurasthenia, and hysteria.

Corrigan's Line.—The red-brown line of the gums found in chronic copper-poisoning.

Corrigan's Pulse.—The water-hammer pulse of aortic regurgitation.

MALINGERING

Dalrymple's Sign, or Stellwag's Sign.—More or less loss of winking of the eyelids, and increased width of opening between them ; seen in Graves's disease.

Dietl's Crisis.—Attacks of acute pain in the abdomen, met with in some cases of movable kidney.

Duchenne's Palsy.—An upper-arm palsy, caused by injury at birth, and very similar to Erb's palsy.

Erb's Palsy.—A palsy involving the deltoid, biceps, supinator longus, and brachialis anticus ; often the supinator brevis, sometimes the supraspinatus and infraspinatus, rarely the subscapularis. It follows injury to the brachial cord derived from the fifth and sixth cervical nerves. In adults it is caused sometimes by heavy blows on the shoulder ; it is often associated with loss of sensation, and is persistent. In infants it is caused by pulling on the neck during labour, and is often temporary.

Fauchard's Disease.—See Rigg's Disease.

Flint's Murmur.—A presystolic apical murmur indicative, not of mitral stenosis, but of aortic regurgitation and dilatation of the left ventricle.

Friedreich's Ataxia.—An hereditary and family ataxia, associated with talipes equino varus and nystagmus.

Friedreich's Disease (Paramyoclonus Multiplex).—An hereditary disease, characterized by rapid clonic contractions of the extremities, either continuous or coming on in paroxysms.

Friedreich's Sign.—The diastolic collapse of the jugular vein found in adherent pericardium.

Gellé's Test for Hearing.—In this the normal pressure on the tympanum is increased by means of a Siegle's apparatus or Politzer's-bag, when the power of hearing is normally diminished. If it remains the same, it signifies fixation of the stapes, as found in otosclerosis.

Head's Areas.—The areas of skin in which referred pain, due to inflammation of underlying organs, is felt.

Heberden's Nodes.—The nodules which form at the bases of the distal phalanges of the fingers in chronic arthritis deformans.

Hegar's Sign (of Pregnancy).—A sign of early pregnancy, in which the softening of the upper part of the cervix makes the uterus feel as if the body and cervix were separated from one

EPONYMIC SIGNS

another. It is one of the earliest signs, and can be obtained about the seventh week.

Holmgren's Test for Colour - Blindness.—This consists in giving the patient a number of various shades of coloured skeins of wool, which he is asked to match.

Hutchinson's Teeth.—Peg-shaped, permanent upper central incisor teeth, notched at the cutting-edge, and found in congenital syphilis.

Jaw-Jerk Test.—A reflex contraction of the biting muscles, produced by suddenly depressing the lower jaw when the mouth is open. Rarely found in health, but increased in lateral sclerosis.

Kernig's Sign.—Inability to fully extend the leg on the thigh when the hip is flexed on the abdomen ; indicative of meningitis.

Klumpke's Palsy.—This involves the flexors of the wrist and fingers, and the intrinsic muscles of the hand, with sensory and oculo-pupillary disturbances. It follows injury to the trunk of the brachial plexus, formed by the seventh and eighth cervical and first dorsal nerves.

Koplik's Spots.—The small white buccal spots found at the bases of the molar teeth, and sometimes on the mucous membrane of the lips, about the second day of measles.

Landouzy-Déjérine Disease.—A primary muscular atrophy involving the muscles of the face, shoulder, and upper arm.

Landry's Paralysis.—An acute spreading paralysis, beginning in the legs, and eventually involving all the muscles of the body, including at last those of respiration, but without sensory manifestations.

Ludwig's Angina.—An acute, dangerous, spreading cellulitis of the neck, often associated with some œdema of the larynx, and due to a deep-seated form of suppuration.

Opsonic Index.—A fraction expressing the relative (measured) resistance of a patient to a particular organism as compared with that of a normal person. For example, if a mixture of (1) white blood-cells, (2) patient's blood-serum, (3) tubercle bacilli, are incubated fifteen minutes at 37° C., it will be found after staining and examining that, say, 100 cells have taken up, say, 1,000 bacilli. If, now, the same thing is done, except that for the patient's blood-serum is substituted the serum of a known normal person, or a mixture of serum

MALINGERING

from healthy people, it will be found that perhaps 1,200 bacilli have been taken up. The patient's opsonic index of the tubercle bacillus is therefore $\frac{1000}{1200}$—*i.e.*, 0·83.

Parrotts Nodes.—The thickening of the bones of the skull round the anterior fontanelle found in inherited syphilis.

Pawlik's Grip.—In diagnosing the presentation of the fœtus, the hands are pressed deeply down into the pelvis to feel for the head. This is known as " Pawlik's grip."

Rigg's Disease, or Fauchard's Disease.—Another name for pyorrhœa alveolaris. A pyogenic affection due to spread of septic infection to the tooth-roots. The teeth are thereby loosened in their sockets, the gums are diseased, bleed easily, and become detached from the teeth, and the breath is foul.

Rinné's Test for Hearing.—This depends on the fact that in the normal ear a tuning-fork can be heard in front of the meatus after it has ceased to be audible when applied to the mastoid. If this is *not* the case, it points to obstructive deafness —*i.e.*, to a condition in which bone-conduction is better than air-conduction.

Romberg's Sign.—The swaying and unsteadiness of the body when the eyes are closed, and the feet placed close together. Seen in tabes and some other degenerative diseases of the spinal cord.

Stellwag's Sign.—Same as Dalrymple's sign.

Skodaïc Resonance.—The area of hyper-resonance near the apex in some cases of pleuritic effusion and basal pneumonia.

Still's Disease.—A form of osteo-arthritis found in children.

Tache Cérébrale.—The red line produced by drawing the finger-nail over the skin in some cases of meningitis.

Tooth's Disease, or Charcot-Marie's Disease.—The name given to the peroneal type of progressive muscular atrophy.

Trousseau's Sign.—The production of paroxysmal muscular contractions by pinching the nerve or bloodvessels of a limb ; found in tetany.

Volkmann's Contracture.—This is the contracted, paralyzed state of wrist and fingers caused by the too long and too tight application of splints.

Von Graefe's Sign.—Failure of the upper lid to follow the downward movement of the eye when the patient looks to the

EPONYMIC SIGNS

floor, so that a line of sclerotic is seen between the cornea and the upper lid ; found in exophthalmic goitre.

Von Pirquet's Reaction.—A cutaneous reaction obtained by vaccinating the skin with tuberculin. For purposes of comparison, an adjacent portion of skin is vaccinated with normal saline. A positive reaction is shown by the occurrence of vesicles and erythematous blush, and is indicative of the presence of tubercle in the body.

Wassermann's Test.—A complicated serum reaction which, if positive, indicates the presence of syphilis.

Weber's Test for Hearing.—This depends on the fact that if a tuning-fork is applied to the middle of the forehead it should be heard equally in both ears, but in cases of obstructive deafness it is heard more loudly in the deaf ear.

Weiss's Sign.—Same as Chvostek's sign.

Widal's Test.—The agglutination-test given by the blood of patients suffering from enteric fever ; obtainable from the twelfth day onwards.

CHAPTER XXVI

ELECTRICAL TESTING

A DESCRIPTION will be found in Chapter XII. of the use to which electrical reactions may be put in the detection of malingering.

At the end of this Chapter will be found a short description of the apparatus for those who are not familiar with its use.

It is proposed here to give a brief description of the method of electrical testing adopted when a patient is thought to be suffering from some definite nervous affection.

It must be clearly understood that it has not been possible within the limits of this work to do more than indicate the general principles which guide us in this branch of the subject. Sufficient has, however, been included to enable a practitioner who follows the directions to detect the reaction of degeneration, and in a straightforward case to localize the lesion.

Method of Electrical Testing.

Test with the Faradic Battery.—Start the current in the primary coil, and see that the rate of interruption is satisfactory.

Join up the electrodes by wires to the secondary coil, the large or indifferent one to be placed at some distant part of the body, and the other, with a make key in its handle, to be used as the testing electrode.

Have a bowl of warm water at hand, and freely moisten the electrodes themselves, and the skin of the patient over the muscles to be tested, and also, if possible, over the corresponding muscles on the other side of the body. The skin and electrodes must be kept moist throughout the experiment.

The Reaction of Degeneration.—The test for this condition is first by means of the faradic, and, later, if necessary, by the

298

ELECTRICAL TESTING 299

galvanic current. First test the strength of the faradic battery on oneself.

Test with a weak current the corresponding muscles on the other side of the body. If these respond by a moderate but quite definite contraction, test with the same strength of current the muscles under examination. If they respond as briskly as those on the other side, there is no *reaction of degeneration* (R.D.). In such cases it is not necessary to proceed further with electrical tests.*

If, however, the reaction of the muscles under examination differs from that on the other side of the body, either in character or in strength, a nervous lesion must be suspected, and it is wise to proceed to test the muscles in question with the galvanic current.

* When a motor impulse is sent from the brain to a voluntary muscle, it passes through two motor cells (or what are called neurons) and their processes. One cell is situate in the cortex of the brain, and the impulse passes through it and its main branch (the axon), which ends in a fine meshwork of fibrils round the other nerve cell situated in the spinal cord. The impulse passes across from the meshwork to the spinal motor cell, and through its axon, to end in a specialized organ in the substance of the muscle itself—the muscle spindle.

If a lesion occurs to the former of these cells or its axon, the muscle will not receive the impulse. It will therefore be paralyzed, but its nutrition *will not* suffer. It will therefore not waste more than can be accounted for by disuse, and its electrical reactions will be unchanged. If a lesion occurs to the latter of these cells—namely, the motor neuron in the anterior horn of the spinal cord—the muscle will, as in the former case, fail to receive the impulse, and will, therefore, be paralyzed, but its nutrition *will be* affected, causing it to waste rapidly, and its electrical reactions will be changed. This alteration is known as the " reaction of degeneration " (R.D.).

R.D., then, indicates the presence of a lesion in the lower motor neuron ; and this may be in the cell itself, the anterior horn of the spinal cord, or in any part of its nerve process to the muscle.

It should be noted that the interruption of the impulses is the essential thing, and that the lesion may be one of partial or complete severance, or severe pressure, or, in fact, any lesion causing physiological interruption of the axon of this trophic neuron.

It is the nerve which responds to faradic stimulation, and although the muscle responds by a contraction, it in all probability receives the stimulus only through its nerve. When this has been so injured that impulses cannot reach the muscle through it, some response to faradic stimulation can generally be obtained for one or more days afterwards by direct application of the current over the belly of the muscle (see R.D.). This reaction is, however, probably still due to nerve fibrils in the substance of the muscle whose nutrition has not yet suffered from the accident.

The galvanic current causes a contraction through direct stimulation of the muscles themselves, the nerve exercising only a controlling influence.

It may be noted in passing that—

The reactions to the faradic current are occasionally exaggerated. This may indicate any state of :

1. Undue irritability, such as chorea and the early stages of spastic paralysis.

2. Disease characterized by profuse sweating (which diminishes the resistance of the skin to the electric current)—*e.g.*, Graves's disease.

3. Hysteria. The reactions in this affection are variable, but in some forms there is an increased susceptibility to faradic stimulation.

The reactions to the faradic current may be diminished or absent. It is this condition which would make one suspect reaction of degeneration, and therefore makes it necessary to proceed to testing with the galvanic battery.

The Galvanic Current.—These tests need only be undertaken where the reaction obtained with the faradic current is diminished or absent.

The conditions here are somewhat different. The current is a constant one, and as contractions only occur when the circuit is closed (*i.e.*, " made ") or opened (*i.e.*, " broken "), and not while the current is passing steadily through the muscle, it is necessary for the operator, in order to observe the character of the contractions, to close or open the circuit himself.

The galvanic battery should be tested on oneself, and if found in good working order the electrodes *and* the skin of the patient are moistened as in the case of the faradic battery.

The Reaction of Degeneration.—It is convenient to begin the examination by connecting the testing electrode with the negative pole of the battery.

As in the case of the faradic current, *test first the corresponding muscles on the other side of the body* until the strength of current required to cause a *minimal contraction* under normal conditions has been ascertained.

Now apply the testing electrode with the make key to the muscles under observation, and note the following points :

1. Amplitude of response.
2. Mode of reaction.
3. Polar susceptibility.

ELECTRICAL TESTING 301

1. **Amplitude of Response.**—The reaction of the galvanic current may be either (a) increased or (b) decreased.

2. **Mode of Reaction.**—The changes observed in the mode of reaction are the most characteristic of all in R.D. Whereas normally a muscle reacts to galvanic stimulation by a quick reaction quickly terminated, when R.D. is present the reaction to be obtained is a sluggish one, starting slowly, of long duration, and *sometimes*, in the early stages, of greater amplitude than that to be obtained under normal conditions.

3. **Polar Susceptibility of Muscle.**—Under normal conditions a muscle responds—

To the Kathode (negative pole) at Closure (make) of Current most readily = K.C.C.

Then to the Anode (positive pole) at Closure (make) of Current next = A.C.C.

Then to the Anode (positive pole) at the Opening (break) of the Current = A.O.C.

And to the Kathode (negative pole) at the Opening (break) of the Current least readily = K.O.C.

This is generally stated shortly as follows :

$$K.C.C.>A.C.C.>A.O.C.>K.O.C.$$

the sign > signifying " greater than."

When, however, there is a lesion in the lower motor neuron, the order of susceptibility becomes—

$$A.C.C.>K.C.C.>K.O.C.>A.O.C.$$

In practical testing it is the first two of these (viz., the closing contractions) on which the attention is usually centred, for, if A.C.C. is greater than K.C.C., that in conjunction with the other evidence is sufficient to indicate abnormal reaction without troubling about the opening contractions.

When the nutrition of the muscle has been very seriously impaired, the reactions to the galvanic, as well as to the faradic, current become extremely slight, and ultimately entirely cease, because there is no muscle to respond. The last, or complete, stage of R.D., then, consists in the entire failure of the muscle to respond to either form of electric stimulation.

When does Reaction of Degeneration show Itself ?—It is impossible to give exact time limits for these stages, but,

302 MALINGERING

roughly speaking, it may be said that no change in electrical reaction can be noted for about forty-eight hours, or sometimes longer, after the occurrence of the lesion.*

The typical reaction of degeneration is generally established between a week and ten days after the accident, and will last for a good many weeks—six or more.

If complete severance of the nerve has occurred, the condition will, of course (unless remedial measures are adopted), go on until there is complete muscular atrophy. If, however, the cause of the physiological interference can be removed, gradual recovery will take place.

R.D. may be considerably postponed by passive exercises of the muscles at the earlier stages, either by massage and passive movements of the limbs, or by directly stimulating the muscles to contract with the electric current.

It is important to bear in mind the curious truth that, as recovery progresses, voluntary power is first re-established, and is then followed by normal susceptibility to electric stimulation.

To aid facility in diagnosis, a table of the reactions is appended, and it is very important to remember that with the galvanic current the change in *mode* of reaction is the most characteristic sign.

Electric Reactions of Muscles.

1. If reactions of nerve or muscle to both faradic and galvanic stimulation are exaggerated :	1. Patient is probably not suffering from an organic lesion, but from either— (*a*) Some condition of irritation of the nervous system—*e.g.*, chorea. (*b*) Disease characterized by profuse sweating — *e.g.*, Graves's disease. (*c*) Hysteria.

---

* As the reaction to faradic stimulation is almost certainly that of the nerve, and not of the muscle itself, this at first appears contradictory ; but it is probably explained by the fact that this reaction, which occurs for several hours after the nervous lesion, is due to the nervous elements in the muscle itself, whose nutrition is at first sufficiently good to yield a response.

ELECTRICAL TESTING

2. If reactions of nerve or muscle to both faradic and galvanic stimulation are normal :

2. Patient is either—
   (*a*) Normal ; or
   (*b*) Suffering from
   (1) A lesion of the nervous system not involving the lower motor neurons of the muscles tested.
   (2) A lesion of the nervous system involving the lower motor neurons, but of such recent occurrence that the nerves have not yet suffered in their nutrition (one or two days).

3. If reactions of nerve or muscle to faradic stimulation are reduced or absent :
Of nerve to galvanic stimulation are reduced :
Of muscle to galvanic stimulation are—
   (*a*) Increased in amplitude :
   (*b*) Sluggish in character :
   (*c*) A.C.C. > K.C.C. :

3. Patient is suffering from a lesion of the nervous system involving the lower motor neurons of the muscles concerned, which is of recent origin (about two to ten days).

4. If reactions of nerve or muscle to faradic stimulation are absent :
Of nerve to galvanic stimulation are absent :
Of muscle to galvanic stimulation—
   (*a*) Increased in amplitude :
   (*b*) Sluggish in character :
   (*c*) A.C.C. > K.C.C. :

4. Patient is suffering from a lesion as under heading 3, but of several weeks' duration.

5. If no reaction of nerve or muscle to faradic or galvanic stimulation is obtained :

5. Patient is suffering from the same lesion, but of such long duration that the muscles have wasted completely.

Practical Considerations.—Several practical points with regard to the application of these tests need to be mentioned.

1. If at first too strong a current be used, no reliable information can be obtained, as the resulting contraction, owing to the spread of the current to the surrounding muscles, is massive, and the reaction of any particular muscle or group of muscles, is lost in the general effect. The unpleasant sensation causes the patient to lose confidence, making further testing difficult.

MALINGERING

2. The farther away the muscle under observation is from the central axis of the body, the greater (even under normal conditions) is the strength of the current required to produce a reaction. Thus, in a perfectly healthy subject, the small muscles of the hand will only react when a much stronger stimulus is used than need be applied in the case of the biceps.

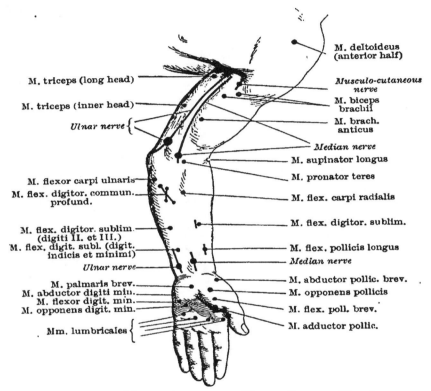

FIG. 27.—MOTOR POINTS OF UPPER LIMB. (ERB.)

The standard of comparison should then be, whenever possible, the corresponding muscle on the unaffected side of the body.

3. The resistance of the skin to the passage of an electric current is very great. Some attempt to diminish this is made by moistening and warming the skin by warm water. Also in actual practice it is found that the mere passage of the electric current itself rapidly diminishes the normal resistance of the skin. When, therefore, repeated testing of one muscle is to be carried out, the current will in all probability have to

ELECTRICAL TESTING

be reduced during the progress of the examination to counteract this increased susceptibility.

4. Motor Points.—If the reaction of degeneration (R.D.) be discovered, it is important to ascertain the extent of the lesion.

This is done by carefully testing all the muscles in the affected area, with a view to discovering which nerve is injured. It is found that each muscle responds more readily to either

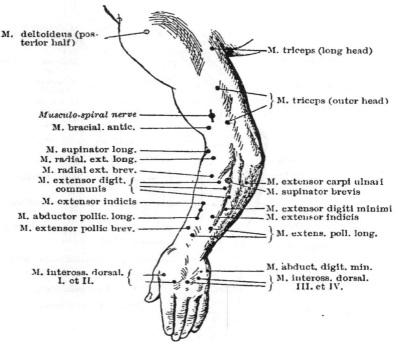

FIG. 28.—MOTOR POINTS OF UPPER LIMB. (ERB.)

form of the electric current when stimulated at one particular spot than at any other. This is at the neuro-muscular spindle, and is known as the " motor point " of the muscle.*

It is necessary, then, in carrying out these finer tests, to apply the current over the motor point of each muscle tested. These points have been carefully worked out by several investigators, and those for the limbs are reproduced here (Figs. 27-31).

* A neuro-muscular spindle consists of a bundle of fine muscular fibres enclosed in a thick sheath of connective tissue. It varies in length from $\frac{1}{8}$ to $\frac{1}{3}$ inch, and is about $\frac{1}{125}$ inch in diameter. Each receives a nerve fibre. It is believed that these are the end-organs of the nerves.

5. With these before one, and bearing in mind the nerve-supply of the muscles under observation, it is now necessary carefully to work over the affected area.

It is well to remember that the injury may involve—

(1) One or more of the peripheral nerves.
(2) One or more cords of a plexus.
(3) One or more nerve trunks as they emerge from the spinal column.
(4) A group of motor neurons in the anterior horn of the spinal cord.

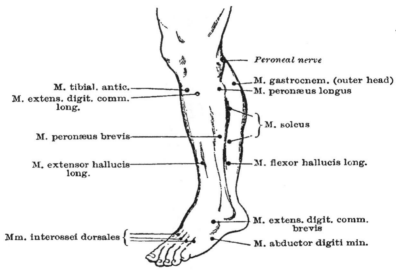

FIG. 29.—MOTOR POINTS OF LEG. (ERB.)

6. When drawing conclusions, one should remember that where a muscle receives fibres from more than one nerve, R.D. will not be obtained unless the nerve injured is the one mainly responsible for maintaining the nutrition of the muscle.

This varies slightly in different individuals, but a diagnosis seldom depends on the reaction of one muscle alone.

7. Difficulty may be experienced when muscles are closely grouped together in ascertaining which muscle has responded or failed to respond. This may be decided by attention to the following points :

(1) Whether the current is applied to the motor point of a muscle.

ELECTRICAL TESTING 307

(2) Whether the contraction obtained corresponds with the known action of that muscle.

(3) Whether the contraction passes in the direction of the fibres of that muscle.

In deciding the question of the localization of the lesion, it is also important to bear in mind the fact that reaction of degeneration only gives us information as to the condition of

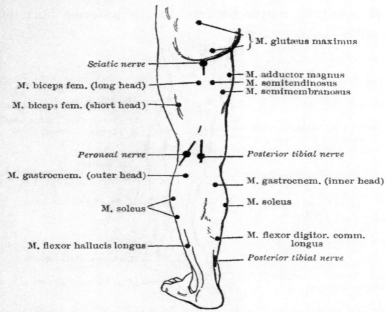

Fig. 30.—Motor Points at Back of Thigh and Leg. (Erb.)

the motor nerves; for the condition of the sensory fibres other tests are necessary, such as for the presence of anæsthesia, etc.

To take some practical examples of the way in which these tests may be applied:

Injury to Median Nerve.—The median nerve supplies the following:

> Pronator teres.
> Flexor carpi radialis.
> Palmaris longus.
> Flexor sublimis digitorum.
> Pronator quadratus.
> Flexor longus pollicis.

MALINGERING

Flexor profundus digitorum (outer half).
Abductor pollicis.
Opponens pollicis.
Flexor brevis pollicis (outer head).
Lumbricals of two outer fingers.

Result of injury : Loss of power of—

Pronating forearm.
Flexing wrist (this loss is almost complete).

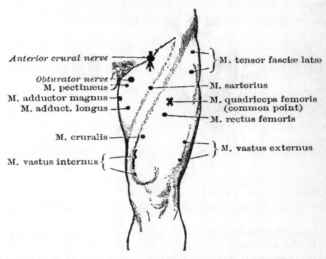

FIG. 31.—MOTOR POINTS OF ANTERIOR THIGH MUSCLES. (ERB.)

Flexing fingers firmly.
Opposing or abducting the thumb (flexion also much reduced).
Flexing the first phalanx of the two outer fingers.

N.B.—If the nerve is injured at the wrist, the first seven of the above muscles are not affected.

Deformity :

> Forearm held in position of supination.
> Wrist extended.
> Wasting of thenar eminence.

N.B.—It will be noticed that when the nerve is injured at the wrist, the deformity is slight.

A malingerer feigning loss of power in the hand not infrequently holds it in a position similar to that produced by injury to the median nerve. The electrical reactions of the muscles which appear to be paralyzed will clear up any doubt as to whether the disability complained of is genuine or not. The contractions so obtained in the long flexors of the forearm are very easily observed.

It must be remembered that a current of considerable strength will be required, even under normal circumstances, to produce a reaction in the small muscles of the hand.

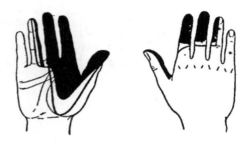

Fig. 32.—Shows the Area of Loss of Sensation following Lesion of the Median Nerve. (After Head.)

The total area of loss is contained within the continuous thick line. The black is the area of protopathic and epicritic loss. The zone between the black area and the continuous line is the area of epicritic overlap.

Protopathic sensibility signifies the recognition of painful cutaneous stimuli and extremes of heat and cold. Epicritic sensibility signifies the recognition of light tactile stimuli and intermediate degrees of heat and cold.

(From Turner and Stewart's "Nervous Diseases.")

Injury to Ulnar Nerve. — The ulnar nerve supplies the following :

    Flexor carpi ulnaris.
    Flexor profundus digitorum (inner half).
    Intrinsic muscles of little finger and palmaris brevis.
    Interossei.
    Lumbricals of two inner fingers.
    Adductors transversus and obliquus pollicis.
    Flexor brevis pollicis (small inner head).

310 MALINGERING

Result of injury : Loss of power of—
  Flexing wrist (this loss is very slight, see Median Nerve).
  Adducting the thumb.
  Adducting and abducting all the fingers.
  Flexing the first phalanx of the two inner fingers.
  Moving the little finger.

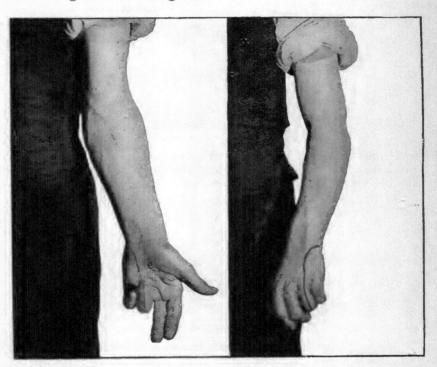

FIG. 33.—ULNAR PARALYSIS FROM A WOUND OF THE NERVE BEHIND THE INTERNAL CONDYLE OF THE HUMERUS.

The area within the black line is anæsthetic.

(From Purves Stewart's "Diagnosis of Nervous Diseases.")

Deformity :
  Wasting of the hypothenar eminence of the hand.
  Apparent prominence of the bones and tendons of the hand owing to the wasting of the interossei.
  Hyperextension of the first phalanx of the two inner fingers owing to the action of the extensor unchecked by the long flexor, the interossei, or the lumbricals.

ELECTRICAL TESTING

Flexion of the second and third phalanges of the two inner fingers, due also to the paralysis of the lumbricals. Hyperextension of the thumb at the first joint.

Sensation is affected in the areas marked in the figures.

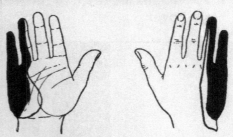

FIG. 34.—SHOWS THE LOSS OF SENSATION FOLLOWING A LESION OF THE ULNAR NERVE. (AFTER HEAD.)

The total area of loss is contained within the continuous thick line. The black is the area of protopathic and epicritic loss. The zone between the black area and the continuous line is the area of epicritic overlap.

(From Turner and Stewart's "Nervous Diseases.")

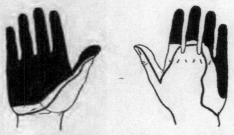

FIG. 35.—SHOWS THE LOSS OF SENSATION FOLLOWING LESION OF BOTH THE ULNAR AND MEDIAN NERVES. (AFTER HEAD.)

The total area of loss is contained within the continuous thick line. The black is the area of protopathic and epicritic loss. The zone between the black area and the continuous line is the area of epicritic overlap.

(From Turner and Stewart's "Nervous Diseases.")

Musculo-Spiral Nerve.—Supplies :

From its main trunk—

    Triceps—long head, inner head, outer head.
    Anconeus. (Supplied also by posterior interosseous nerve).
    Supinator longus.

Extensor carpi radialis longior.
Brachialis anticus (this muscle, however, receives its main nerve-supply from the musculo-cutaneous).

Through its branch, the posterior interosseus—
Extensor carpi radialis brevior.
Supinator brevis.
Extensor communis digitorum.
Extensor minimi digiti.
Extensor carpi ulnaris.

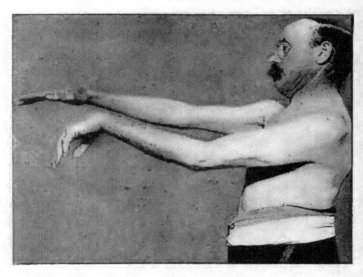

Fig. 36.—Left-Sided Musculo-Spiral Paralysis, showing Drop-Wrist and Atrophy of Supinator Longus.

(From Purves Stewart's "Diagnosis of Nervous Diseases.")

Extensor indicis.
Extensor ossis metacarpi pollicis.
Extensor longus pollicis.
Extensor brevis pollicis.

Result of injury : Loss of power of—
Extending forearm.
Supinating forearm.
Extending wrist.
Extending thumb and fingers.
Weakness in flexing forearm.

ELECTRICAL TESTING

Deformity :

Very characteristic position known as " drop-wrist " (hand flexed and pronated on forearm).

Sensation sometimes impaired at base of index-finger and thumb on dorsal aspect.

Circumflex Nerve.—Supplies—
> Deltoid.
> Teres minor.

Result of injury : Loss of power of—
> Abducting arm.

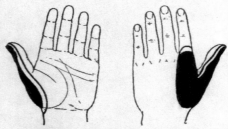

FIG. 37.—SHOWS THE LOSS OF SENSATION FOLLOWING A LESION OF THE RADIAL AND EXTERNAL CUTANEOUS NERVES. (AFTER HEAD.)

The total area of loss is contained within the continuous thick line. The black is the area of protopathic and epicritic loss. The zone between the black area and the continuous line is the area of epicritic overlap.

(From Turner and Stewart's " Nervous Diseases.")

Deformity :

Only that caused locally by the wasting of the muscle.

Sensation affected in area over the insertion of the deltoid muscle.

External Popliteal Nerve.—Supplies—

Through its branch the musculo-cutaneous :
> Peroneus longus.
> Peroneus brevis.

Through its branch the anterior tibial :
> Tibialis anticus.
> Extensor longus digitorum.

314 MALINGERING

Extensor proprius hallucis.
Peroneus tertius.
Extensor brevis digitorum.

Result of injury : Loss of power of—

Dorsal flexion of foot.
Extension of toes.
Eversion of foot.

Deformity :

Toes drop and are flexed, and the foot is raised high above the ground to prevent tripping.

Sensation impaired on outer side of leg and dorsum of foot.

Even if the reaction of degeneration be detected and localized, the problem is not completely solved, as a further point remains to be investigated—namely, whether interference with the passage of the nervous impulse is *completely* or only *partially* interrupted, and this it is often extremely difficult to determine.

The best way to arrive at a decision is to consider the amount of the reaction of degeneration (that is, whether partial or complete) in conjunction with the length of time since the occurrence of the lesion. The practical value of this point is chiefly in deciding whether, after an accident, complete or only partial physiological interruption has resulted.

The prognosis is very difficult in these cases. If complete severance of the nerve has taken place, complete loss of power of the muscles supplied thereby will occur, unless, by operation, the two cut ends of the nerve are sutured to each other, so that the new fibres as they grow from the central portion of the cut nerve may find their way into the old sheath.

If only partial severance of the nerve has occurred, the remaining portion, if uninjured, even though quite small, is sufficient to keep the two ends together, and therefore regeneration will usually take place without any operation.

It is frequently impossible to be perfectly certain what has occurred by simply testing on one occasion. Repeated examinations have to be made before it is possible to come to a decision.

These cases require considerable judgment and experience, and it is wise, if possible, to obtain the advice of an expert.

ELECTRICAL TESTING

Treatment.—With regard to the use of electricity in the treatment of motor nerve lesions, the tendency is generally to credit the electric current with much more power than it really possesses. Electricity will not generate nerve, nor will it even hasten its regeneration.

Its great use is to prevent the muscles from degenerating while their nerve-supply is temporarily in abeyance. By applying the current, such muscles may be thrown into action frequently, thus maintaining their nutrition and efficiency, until the course of the motor nerve is re-established. Massage and passive movements are important adjuncts to the electric treatment, and should always be used along with it to promote the circulation through the affected muscles. If, in such cases, neither electricity nor massage has been employed, when the nerve impulses are again enabled to reach the muscles in question, they find the latter shrunken and flabby from non-use, thus causing much delay in the recovery of full power.

A Short Description of the Apparatus.

These tests are carried out with (1) the faradic intermittent current, and (2) the galvanic or constant current.

1. The Faradic Battery.—This may be obtained in a very convenient and light form, and without great expense. The apparatus here illustrated is recommended from personal experience. If the battery is likely to be little used, a smaller and less expensive form will do, or one may be hired.

It consists essentially of a primary coil (Fig. 38), through which a current passes either from one or more (battery) cells or from the main (after modification by a transformer), and a secondary coil (Fig. 38) surrounding the primary one.

By means of binding screws two wires are inserted into this secondary circuit, which terminate in electrodes through which the current is applied to the point.

When the current is started, it passes in the direction shown by the arrows. Passing through M it makes it magnetic, and this attracts K (Neef's hammer), thus causing it to descend in contact with M. When this happens, contact with the point of the screw T is broken and the current interrupted. M then ceases to be magnetic, and the hammer K being attached to a spring resumes the position of rest. This starts the current again by remaking contact at the point of the screw *T*.

When the current is *started* in the primary coil, it induces a weak current in the secondary coil in the opposite direction to itself.

When the current is *interrupted* in the primary coil, it induces a stronger current in the secondary coil in the same direction as itself.

Owing to the presence of the interrupting key (Neef's hammer, *K*; see Fig. 39, p. 317) the current in the primary

FIG. 38.—BATTERY FOR FARADIC CURRENT ONLY.
P, Primary coil; *S*, secondary coil.

coil is started and interrupted many times a second. The stimuli to the nerve are therefore so frequent that the muscular contractions resulting from them fuse in a form of tetany.

For this single continuous contraction to be obtained, the primary circuit must be interrupted at least twenty times a second. The strength of the current in the secondary coil increases and decreases directly with that of the current in the primary coil, but may also be varied by the following means : By varying the proximity of the two coils. When the secondary coil immediately surrounds the primary coil (see Fig. 40), the induced current is strong ; when, on the other

ELECTRICAL TESTING

hand, the secondary coil is partially withdrawn from around the primary coil (see Fig. 41), the induced current is proportionally weakened. In many batteries the current strength may further be varied by a magnetic iron core (*C*), which, when inserted within the primary coil, increases its current strength, and consequently that of the secondary coil. Still another

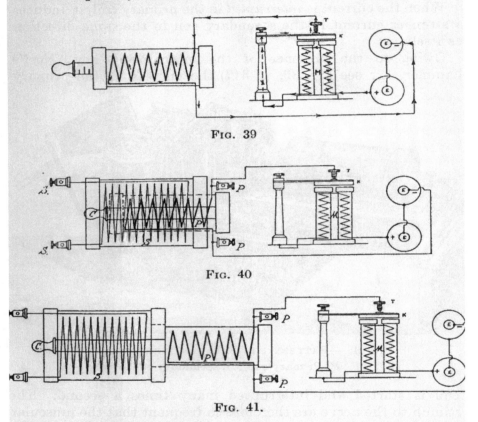

Fig. 39

Fig. 40

Fig. 41.

way of varying the strength of the current in the primary coil is by adjusting the rate of the interruption of the current by Neef's hammer.

Electrodes.—These are of different materials, forms, and sizes. One is rather the larger, and is applied to an indifferent part of the body; the other is smaller, and applied exactly to the region or structure to be tested. The intervening portion of the patient's anatomy completes the circuit.

318 MALINGERING

The Indifferent Electrode.—This is used simply for the purpose of completing the circuit, not for the purpose of testing neighbouring structures, and is placed as far as possible away from the point to be tested, in order that the result at the two poles may not be confused, and because the unpleasant effects of the current are minimized if, owing to a long course through the body, it is somewhat dispersed in transit.

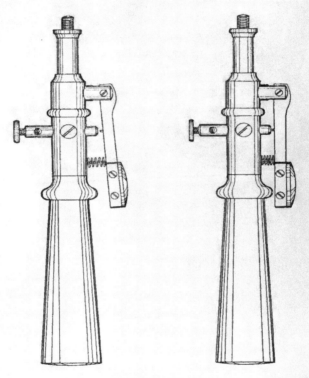

FIG. 42.—TESTING ELECTRODE HANDLE WITH MAKE KEY.

This indifferent electrode is most conveniently made in the form of a flat piece of flexible metal covered with flannel or wash-leather, as this can be placed at the back of the neck, over the sternum, over the sacrum, or at any fairly central part of the body.

The Testing Electrode.—This should consist of a small round pad fixed to a handle several inches in length, and in this handle there should be a make key by which, upon pressure

ELECTRICAL TESTING

with the thumb, the current in the secondary coil may be made when required for use.

Make Key.—In this form the current is interrupted when the key is at rest, and it can only be completed by throwing the key into action by depression of the thumb. The advantage of this key in testing is that while it is at rest the electrode can

FIG. 43.—BATTERY FOR CONTINUOUS CURRENT ONLY.
N, Normal; *R*, current reversed.

be moved freely over the skin without causing any stimulation, and the current therefore can be applied just when and where it is desired.

2. **Galvanic or Constant Battery.**—Electrical power for this can, if desired, as in the case of the faradic current, be obtained by a suitable transformer from the main supply, if the current is a continuous one; but if cells are to be used, a battery of

not less than thirty cells should be employed, as considerable strength of current is necessary in some cases to demonstrate reaction of degeneration.

Fig. 44.—Battery for Combined Continuous and Faradic Currents.

To the left, faradic battery: *P*, primary circuit; *S*, secondary circuit. To the right, galvanic battery: *G*, galvanic terminals; *F*, faradic terminals; *R*, reversed direction of galvanic current; *N*, normal direction of galvanic current—*i.e.*, + and − terminals as marked.

A galvanometer should be inserted in the circuit to show that the current is properly established, and also to indicate its strength.

It is also advisable to have the cells joined up in such a way that either end of the series can be used as desired. If such an arrangement is not made, the first cells in the series get

ELECTRICAL TESTING

exhausted, while those at the far end have perhaps hardly been used, thus necessitating very frequent renewal, with its accompanying waste of time and other inconveniences.

The current being a continuous one, muscular contractions are only produced if the examiner himself makes or breaks the circuit ; therefore, polar effects can be observed, and are of considerable importance. It is therefore necessary to have the anode and kathode clearly marked, and it is convenient to have some arrangement for automatically switching the current from the anode to the kathode cord, and *vice versa*, thus reversing the current without having to remake the connection.

The electrodes should be the same as those described for the faradic current.

It is possible to have the batteries for these two kinds of currents (the faradic and galvanic) combined in one instrument, and this is a very convenient arrangement if the tests are to be invariably carried out in one's own consulting-room ; or the power may be used from the main, through a suitable transformer, if the current is a continuous one.

INDEX

Abdomen :
    Aorta, palpitation in neurasthenia, 83, 90
    Injury to alleged, 131, 233
Abortion, criminal, accident alleged, 35
Abrasions. See Wounds
Acceleration. See also Accident, pre-existing conditions ; Disease ; and Chapter XVIII.
    of disease, by accident, 209, 220, 221
Accident. See also Disease, Workmen's Compensation Act
    Age, effects of, 20, 94, 100
    Cases decided upon application to revise or terminate weekly payments. See Chapter XXII.
    Compensation for, an obsession, 108
    Concealment of, from doctor, 144
    Feigned, 3, 126
    Fraud, compared with disease, 7, 281
    Genuine, complicated by fraud, 157
    History of important, 203. See also Chapter XVIII.
    Law, French, 1898, effects of, 107
    Mental influence of, 9, 265, 270
    Nervous system, alleged consequence to, 61, 265
    Notice of, 150
    Pension anticipated, influence of, 158. See also Pension
    Periodic, arranged by impostor and accomplice, 30
    Pre-existing conditions, 219 :
        Alcoholism, 220 ; aneurism, 221 ; asymmetry, 167, 174 ; cancer, 271 ; gonorrhœa, 221 ; hereditary degeneracy, 220 ; rheumatoid disease, 126, 135, 221 ; rupture, see Chapter XIII. ; syphilis, 220 ; tabes, 220 ; tuberculosis, 221 ; see also Acceleration, and the above diseases under their names

Accident (continued) :
    Psychical, 133
    Publicity, effects of, 265
    Rehearsals of details by patient, 11, 96
    Results of past, alleged due to subsequent accident, 157
    Results of permanent, but not incapacitating, 275
    Street statistics, 287
    Syphilis, diagnosed after trivial, 63
Age :
    And intercurrent disease in accident claim, 283
    Children, malingering by, 56
    Effects after accident, 20
    Excuse of, by able-bodied, 155
    Increased premium for insurance, 20
    Misstatement by patient as to, 52
    Old Age Pension Act, 281
    Presbyopia alleged due to accident, 117
    Rheumatoid disease, 134, 135
Agricultural workers, rheumatoid disease in, 134
Albumen. See Urine
Albuminuria, functional, 24. See also Urine
Alcohol :
    Effects of accident accelerated by, 234
    Examination of patient under, should be declined, 56, 57
    General paralysis of the insane, diagnosed from, 65
    Insanity, traumatic, diagnosed from, 212, 213
    Mental effect of accident received under, 82
    Muscular degeneration in, causes liability to injury, 152, 220
Alien :
    Brown-Séquard disease in Italians, 293
    Examination of, 4, 151
    Malingering by, excused, 159

324 MALINGERING

Amputation. See parts concerned under their names

Anæmia, fall alleged cause of, 18

Anæsthesia. See Sensation, loss of

Anæsthetic :
Death under, 261
Operation for hernia under, declined by man with constitutional disease, 262
Hysteria, use in, 84, 86
Incisions under, for septic wound refused, 263
Knee alleged stiff bends at proposal of, 163
Stiff joints, use of, for, 273

Aneurism :
Alleged due to strain by syphilitics, 220
Aortic, inequality of pupil in, 66
Internal rupture, alleged traumatic, 234
Neurasthenic symptoms in, 83

Ankle :
Ankle clonus. See Reflex, ankle clonus
Death after injury to, in subject of heart disease, 234
Injury alleged to, 4
Sprain of, alleged to incapacitate eight months, 16 :
Locomotor ataxia diagnosed, 27

Ankylosis, spine, 134, 137

Apoplexy, cerebral, alleged due to heat-stroke, 207

Appendix and Appendicitis :
Dilatation of pupil sign of pain, 76
Scar, detection of operation by, 44
Traumatic origin, 234

Appetite, loss of, alleged after injury, 137, 141

Approved societies. See Clubs and National Insurance Act

Arbitration. See also County Court actions, Workmen's Compensation Act
Postponement of, by Judge to suit plaintiff, 19

Argyll-Robertson pupil. See Pupil

Arm. See also Clavicle, Radius, Ulna
Asymmetry in, 174
Atrophy. See Muscular atrophy
Contractures and spasms, hysterical, 86
Fracture, alleged neurasthenia following, 101
Palsy of, 294
Raise, inability to, alleged after accident, 6, 102, 150, 151

Army :
Artillerymen, deafness of, 120
Methods of malingering in, 1

Arthritis deformans, results of, alleged due to accident, 176

Assessors, medical. See Workmen's Compensation Act

Asymmetry :
Causes of, 168
Frequency of, 167
Importance of knowledge of, 167
Measurements for, 168-174
Results of congenital, attributed to accident, 148, 167, 174

Ataxia. See Friedreich's ataxia, Locomotor ataxia

Atropine, use of, 65, 116

Auto-suggestion. See also Neurasthenia
Co-operating factors in, 11, 92
Effects of, 7, 96, 107
Hysteria in, 87, 89. See also Hysteria

Babinski sign. See Reflex, Babinski

Back. See also Muscles, Spine
Arthritis, 134
Bending of, persistent, 104
Examination difficult, 126
Idleness after injury to, 99
Injury to, 128 :
Alleged cases, 95, 131, 138, 270, 282
Kidney, traumatic displacement of, alleged, 127
Lumbago in, accident alleged cause of, 126, 127
Pain in :
Compensation for, 126 ; congenital asymmetry cause of, 166 ; diagnosis of, 126 ; mental, not physical, 140 ; psychotherapeutic treatment of, 129 ; referred, 128
Pain in, tests for :
Attention distracted, 130 ; battery, see Chapter XII. ; coal-scuttle, 132 ; horizontal position, 40 ; lateral movement of body, 33 ; location, 129 ; Dr. Hanson's location, 130 ; stethoscope, 129 ; stretching vertebral muscles, 129 ; spinous processes, 94, 139, 282
" Railway spine," 133
Rheumatoid diseases, 134
Sciatica, 140
Spondylitis deformans, 135. See also Spondylitis
Sprain of :
Admitted due to lumbago, 127 ; alleged, cured by hospital observation and firmness, 104 ; frequency of alleged, 128

INDEX

325

Back (continued) :
    Stiffness, 139. See also Spine, rigidity of
        Alleged, 95, 184 ; examinee alleged unable to stoop laces up boots, 131 ; nimbly picks up pencil, 130
        X rays, use of, 129. See also X rays
Backache. See Pain and Back
Banti's disease, 293
Battery. See Electricity
Bazin's disease, 293
Benefit societies. See Clubs
Biceps, dislocation of long head of, 151
Bladder, urinary, male, pain alleged, 143
Blake Odgers on slander and libel, 236
Blood. See Hæmorrhage
Blood-poisoning and traumatism, 231
Boiler-makers, deafness of, 120
Bones. See under their scientific names
    Injury or disease in, diagnosed by X rays, 175
Bowel, blood from. See Hæmorrhage
Brain. See also Nerves.
    Apoplexy, 208
    Concussion of, and spinal concussion, 133
    Giddiness in disease of, 70
    Organic disease of, feigned, 61
    Pain originating in, 96
    Tumour of, hystero-neurasthenia diagnosis, 93
Breathing :
    Unrestricted, in alleged chest injury, 77
    Tremor in, increased rate of, 69
Bright's disease. See Kidneys
Brissaud on sinistrosis, 107
Brown-Séquard paralysis, 293
Burns, 223. See also Wounds
Burton's sign, 293

Calmette's reaction, 293
Cammidge's reaction, 293
Cancer :
    Accident claims and, 127, 217, 241, 271
    Breast, symptoms alleged due to needle in hand, 27, 56, 270
Carbuncle, alleged traumatic, 223
Cartilage, semilunar, test for displacement of, 162
Casual labour. See Work, casual
Certificates, medical. See also Medical examiner and Medico-legal examination
    Club doctor, dependent position of, 11, 14
    Fraud carried on, 49

Certificates (continued) :
    Granted too easily, 15, 51, 54
    Obtained for sixpence, 16
Charcot's joints, 293
Charcot-Marie's disease. See Tooth's disease
Chest :
    Injury to, alleged, 76, 185, 233
    Pain in, alleged, 94
    Percussion of alleged painful area of, 53
Children :
    Babinski sign in, 68
    Eye, injury to alleged, 113
    Head injury alleged, 56
    Honesty of, 56
    Mental and physical symptoms alleged, 41
    Still's disease in, 296
Chvostek's sign, 293
Claimants, varieties of :
    Accident feigned, 3, 39
    Astuteness, 160
    Exaggerated expression of suffering, 50
    Garrulous, 37
    Illness feigned, 3, 15
    Illness prolonged, 3
    Insolence, 4, 37, 46, 142
    Non-committal and taciturn, 50
    Personation, 29
    Refractory, 37
    Stubborn, 37
    Symptoms exaggerated, 3, 43
    Unintelligent, 37
    Work, unwillingness to return to, 3, 4, 127, 134. See also Work
    Works in house whilst·wife goes out to hard work, 52, 54
Clavicle. See also Shoulder
    Fracture, disproved by X rays, 6 : feigned inability to raise arm, 151 ; normal period of recovery after, 6
Clubs and friendly societies. See also National Insurance Act
    Actuarial estimates for sickness greatly exceeded, 21
    Allowance from, compensation under Workmen's Compensation Act augmented by, 9, 50, 94 :
        Disability prolonged owing to, 94 ; equal to or more than when at work, 9 ; reluctance to disclose, 50, 139
    Lay inspectors of sick workmen appointed, 29
    Medical examiner should know number patient belongs to, 49
Coal-scuttle test, 155, 159
Cocaine, use in malingering, 116

MALINGERING

Coccydinia, coccyx. See also Spine
   Pain in, alleged, 141
Collar-bone. See Clavicle
Colotomy scar, concealment of, at life
   insurance examination, 2
Common law :
   Development of malingering, 1
   Medical examination not obliga-
     tory, 38
   Perjury of malingerer, 12
Compensation. See also Workmen's
   Compensation Act and Chapter
   XXII.
   Augmented by other payments, 9,
     48, 94, 95, 99, 135
   Exaggeration to obtain continuance
     of, 101, 137
   Expert swimmer draws, for seven
     and three-quarter years for
     alleged hand and leg injury, 46
   False pretences, conviction for, 13
   For accident which never hap-
     pened, 40
   For giddiness, 71
   For hernia in fraudulent claims, 188
   For traumatic neurasthenia, 105
   Idleness with, preferred to wages
     and work, 103
   Lump sum desired, 158, 160
   Misstatement as to, by malingerer,
     144
   Obsession of, 106
   Work, award to man at full, 5
Concussion. See Head injury
Contracting out, 22. See also Work-
   men's Compensation Act
Contractures, hysteria in, 86, 90
Copper-poisoning, 293
Cordite, chewing, by malingerer, 1
Coroner's jury, findings of, 234
Corrigan's line, copper-poisoning in, 293
Corrigan's pulse, 293
County Court actions. See also Work-
     men's Compensation Act, Evi-
     dence
   Cost of disputing, 21
   Court of Appeal. See Chapter
     XXII.
   Decision rests with Judge or Arbi-
     trator, 267
   Genuine accident complicated by
     fraud, 157
   Sympathy of Arbitrator to work-
     men, 138, 139, 143, 233
   Unsatisfactory results of, 20
   X-ray results overestimated by
     Judge and jury, 136. See also
     Electricity, Chapters XI. and
     XXII.
Criminal law, liability of malingerer
   under, 13
Cyst, traumatic origin of, alleged, 189

Dalrymple's sign, 294
Dark, fear of, after accident, 42
Deafness. See Ear
Death :
   Precipitated by pre-existing dis-
     ease in accident claim, 64
   Reports on probable causes of,
     after the event :
       Empyema in pleurisy of
     alleged traumatic origin, 230 ;
     fractured thigh in man with
     heart disease, 232 ; injury to
     ankle in subject of heart dis-
     ease, 234 ; internal rupture
     and alleged traumatism, 233 ;
     septicæmia following car-
     buncle, alleged caused by in-
     jury, 222 ; syncope and fall
     in man with heart disease,
     224 ; tuberculosis and trau-
     matism, 226
Deformity. See also Asymmetry
   Previous to accident, 100
Dermatitis, self-induced, 165
Detection. See Recognition
Diabetes. See Urine
Diagrams :
   Laity assisted by, 60
   Location of pain shown by, 45
   Measurements depicted on, 45
Diaphragm test (Harman), 111
Diarrhœa, hysteria in, 52
Dietl's crisis, 294
Diphtheria, loss of pupil contraction, 66
Disease and Accident :
   Existing before accident, 219-221
   Examination prior to employment,
     20
   Intercurrent in accident, typhoid,
     32
   Recognition of, 27, 64, 65 :
       Articular disease, 165 ; gen-
     eral paralysis of the insane, 64 ;
     gumma of leg, 240 ; heart, 33 ;
     hydrocele, 283 ; rheumatoid
     conditions, 126 ; spinal de-
     formity, 100 ; varicose veins
     and ulcers, 164 ; venereal
     disease, 165
Disfigurement :
   Compensation for, 114
   Loss of milk-tooth, 42
Dislocations. See also Joints, under
   their scientific names
   Stiffness following, due to lack of
     mental stimulus, 105
Disseminated sclerosis :
   Hysteria, resemblance to, in early
     stages, 79
   Hystero-neurasthenia diagnosed
     from, 93
   Spinal cord jar, 133

INDEX

District Medical Officers. See Medical examination, periodic, of employees

Doctor. See Medical examiner

Dog-bites, hysteria following, 87

Dreaming, and fear of dark, after accident, 42

Drugs, nerve-deafness after use of, 122

Duchenne's palsy, 294

Dupuytren's contraction, 155-160, 284

Dynamometer, use of, in feigned weak grasp, 152

Ear :
    Deaf mute, supposed, detected in "Peveril of the Peak," 75
    Deafness :
        Cerumen (wax) the cause of symptoms alleged due accident, 72, 119 ; contracting out under Workmen's Compensation Act, 22 ; Galton's whistle, 122 ; Gelle's test, 294 ; Hawkesley's clay, 123 ; hysteria, in, 89 ; nerve, 119, 121 ; Rinne's test, 122, 296 ; routine examination for, 118 ; stethoscope test, 123 ; tuning-fork test, 119, 122 ; total, detection of feigned, 122 ; voice, diagnosis by, 119 ; Weber's test, 122, 297
    Discharge from, 42
    Giddiness in disease of, 70. See also Giddiness
    Noises, sensitiveness to, in neurasthenia and traumatic neuroses, 82, 90, 96
    Petrous-temporal bone, fracture of, 121
    Tympanum (drum), rupture of, causes, 119, 120 :
        More common in disease than accident, 120 ; recent compared with old-standing, 121

Education :
    Exaggeration may be due to lack of, 4
    Incomplete, 9, 50, 136

Elbow :
    Feigned inability to bend, 152
    Incapacity due to age and hydrocele, 283

Electricity, use of :
    Amplitude of response, 301, 306
    Circumflex nerve, 313
    Electrodes, 182, 317, 318
    External popliteal nerve, 313
    Faradic battery, 299, 315, 316
    Galvanic current, 300, 319, 320, 321
    Make key, 319

Electricity, use of (*continued*) :
    Malingerer's dislike of, 5
    Median nerve, 308, 309, 311
    Motor points : Arm, 304, 305 ; thigh, 308
    Muscles tested, 147, 160, 304
    Musculo-spiral nerve, 311, 312
    Nerves involved in injury, 306
    Pain alleged when no current flowing, 19, 102, 132
    Pain " cured " by, 28
    Polar susceptibility of muscle, 301
    Pressure-test whilst applying, 77, 127
    Reaction of degeneration, 299, 300, 302, 306
    Reaction, mode of, 301
    Reactions, table of, 302
    Resistance of skin, 304
    Strength of current, 303
    Treatment of motor nerve lesions by, 315
    Ulnar nerve, 309, 310, 311
    Untruthfulness proved by, 94

Employers. See Workmen's Compensation Act

Employers' Liability Act, claim under, 27

Empyœma, traumatic origin alleged, 230

Enteric, nerve-deafness after, 122

Environment, working class, 9, 187

Epilepsy :
    Atropine used to dilate pupil in simulated, 116
    Feigned : diagnosis of, 204 ; case of, 206
    Traumatism forerunner of, 220

Eponymic signs, list and description of, 292-297

Erichsen, "railway spine," 133

Eserine, use of, 65, 116

Evidence, expert. See also Medico-legal examination, Medical examiner, Workmen's Compensation Act
    Accusation, danger of, 35, 62
    Conflicting, by doctors in Court, 22, 276
    Deafness simulated, 119
    Eponymic signs, familiarity with, 292
    Germany, specialists in, 35
    Giving of, 35, 239, 240
    Lay tribunal, 18
    Libel and slander, 237
    Neurasthenia and hysteria, differentiation in Court, 88
    Neurasthenia pretended under cross-examination, 82
    Privileged, 17, 238
    X rays, use of, in Court, 175-181

328 MALINGERING

Evidence, false, by claimants. See Perjury

Ewald on functional nerve disease in Germany, 106

Exaggeration. See also Incapacity, Work

Club doctor's dependent position helps, 14

Deliberately fostered, 100

Doctor should not countenance, 6

Effects of, 8, 93, 100

Functional nerve disease, kinship with, 97

In Germany, 106

Intentional and unintentional, 8, 17, 50, 61, 96, 101

Laborious work, means of escape from, 10, 100

Memory, good, required for success in, 44

Neurotic basis of, 62, 94, 96, 108

Original disability must not be ignored, 55

Personality in, 4

Suffering, cause of, 41

Symptoms of (case), 137

Examination. See Medical examination, periodic, of sick employees; Medical examination prior to employment; Medico-legal examination

Expert evidence. See Evidence, expert

Eye :

Accommodative asthenopia in neurasthenia, 82, 92

Atropine, use of, 65, 116

Binocular test for vision, 86, 110

Cocaine, use of, 116

Colour blindness, 295

Conjunctivæ, congestion of, in vertigo, 71

Cornea, sensitiveness of, 116

Diaphragm test (Harman), 111

Eserine, use of, 65, 116

Field of vision: Tests, 115, 116; restrictions of, 85, 115

Glaucoma, inequality of pupils in, 66

Hemianopia, 78

Hypermetropia, congenital, accident alleged cause of, 102, 117

Hysteria, alleged loss of sight in, 86, 89, 92

Iris, adhesions of, 65, 78

Iritis in examination of pupil reflex, 65

Monocular vision :

Coloured-glass test for, 86, 115; contracting out of Workmen's Compensation Act, 22; genuine, characteristics of, 109; method of testing, 109; pin-and-hole test, 114; prism

Eye (continued) :

test, 86, 114; stereoscopic vision lost in, 114

Morphia, use of, 116

Movements of, 66

Myopia, alleged result of accident, 72, 117

Nerve atrophy inconsistent with functional disease, 78, 79

Neutralizing lenses for alleged visual defects, 102

Nystagmus : Concealment of, by claimant alleging rupture, 33; disseminated sclerosis in, 79

Optic nerve severed, due to fall on head, 117

Pilocarpine, use of, 116

Perimeter test, 115

Presbyopia, accident alleged cause of, 72, 117, 119

Ptosis, feigned, 116

Pupil reflexes, examination of, 65, 66. See also Pupil

Refraction differing in each eye, 66

Self - inflicted injury alleged due accident, 14

Sensitiveness in neurasthenia, 82

Snellen's test types, 113

Squint, 108

Trial spectacle frames, 114

Von Graefe's sign, 296

Face :

Blackened to give realistic effect to alleged " fits," 28

Capillaries, congestion of, facial, in vertigo, 71

Chvostek's sign, 293   [150

Expression, indication of pain, 47,

Flushing, indication of pain, 74

Nerves of, rarely affected in functional disease, 79

Fœces, incontinence of, inconsistent with functional disease, 78

False pretences, conviction for, 13

Faradic current. See Electricity

Fauchard's disease. See Rigg's disease

Fear :

Of dark, and dreaming, after accident, 42

Future developments of, after idleness, 96

Types of, in neurasthenia, 83

Ferrier on organic disease following jar of spinal cord, 133

Fibula :

Fracture : Compensation drawn for, 14; compound, 138

Finger :

Amputation : Stump alleged tender, 159, 160; work refused after, 258, 268

INDEX

329

Finger (continued) :
    Permanent stiffness of, in relation to work, 275
Fire brigade, hernia in, 202
Firmness :
    Effects of, in hysteria, 86
    Cures exaggeration, 27, 50, 88, 157, 162
    " Fits," alleged, cured by, 28
    Refusal of assistance to undress, 54
Fistula, operation wound made pretext of alleged accident, 31
Flint's murmur, 294
France, malingering in, 108, 281
Fraud :
    Genuine accident complicated by, 159
    Intimate connection between hysteria and, 87
Fraudulent claims, cost of disputing, 21
Friedreich's ataxia, 294
Friedreich's disease, 294
Friedreich's sign, 294
Friendly societies. See Clubs, National Insurance Act
Functional nerve disease. See also Hysteria, Neurasthenia
    Accident laws, influence upon, 100, 101, 103
    Description of, 97-108
    Examples of, 96, 142
    Organic, diagnosis from, 78, 92
    Physical signs inconsistent with, 78
    Relation to malingering, 98
    Treatment of : Abroad, 103, 106, 107, 108 ; in hospital, 78, 105

Gait. See also Leg
    Feigned loss of power in, 148
    Hysterical, characteristics of, 91
    Nerve disease in, 61
    Sciatica, genuine, in, 140
Galton's whistle, deafness tested by, 122
Galvanic current. See Electricity
Gardeners, rheumatoid disease of, in relation to accident, 134
Gastric ulcer, traumatic origin, 234
Gastro-enterostomy, scars of operation for, 44
Gelle's test for hearing, 294
General paralysis of the insane :
    Argyll-Robertson pupil, 65, 292
    Diagnosed at examination for cut hand, 27
    Insanity, traumatic, diagnosed from, 212
    Pupils, inequality of, 66
    Symptoms of, alleged due to accident, 64, 220

Genital organs, female :
    Abortion, criminal, 35
    Diseases of, examination in accident claims, 127
Genital organs, male. See Venereal disease
Germany, malingering in, 106, 280
Giddiness. See also Romberg's test
    Back injury, alleged cause of, 136
    Compensation for, in painters, 71
    Fall, alleged cause of, 19
    Neurasthenia associated with, 72, 82, 90
    Organic, cannot be simulated, 70
    Tests for simulation of, 70, 71, 102
    Traumatic neuroses in, 96
Gingivitis, frequency and effects of, in working classes, 138
Gland, swollen, in groin, alleged traumatic origin, 165, 188
Glaucoma. See Eye
Gleet, nuclear albumen due to, 23
Gonorrhœa, effects of, alleged due accident, 22, 131
Gout, nerve deafness due to, 122
Grasp, power of, in hysteria, 84
Graves's disease, Dalrymple's sign in, 294
Gunpowder in self-inflicted wounds, 1

Habit :
    Asymmetry, 168
    Idleness, 137. See also Idleness
Hœmorrhage :
    From bowel, causes of, 217
    From ear, 120
    From lungs :
        Acceleration by accident alleged (case), 227 ; accident alleged cause of, 19, 142 ; anatomical causes and results of, 228 ; tubercle bacillus not present in alleged accident, 144. See also Tuberculosis
    From mouth, causes of, 216
Hœmorrhoids, accident alleged cause of, 19, 217
Hand :
    Dupuytren's contraction, 155. See also Dupuytren's contraction
    General paralysis of the insane diagnosed at examination for slight injury to, 27
    Needle in, and cancer in breast concealed, 27, 155, 271
    Operation upon, death under anæsthetic, 261
    Power, loss of, in, 152, 153, 154, 155, 276, 283
    Tendon, fraudulent misrepresentation of old injury to, 157

MALINGERING

Harman's diaphragm test, 111
Hawkesley's clay for testing deafness, 123
Headache :
    Neurasthenia in, 82, 92
    Subjective symptom, 42
Head injury :
    Blindness of one eye after, 117
    Deafness: After blow on outside ear, 120 ; after fracture of skull, 120
    Death after, in subject of heart disease, 226
    Example of, 99
    Giddiness after, 70, 72
    Locomotor ataxia diagnosed, 27
    Memory : Loss of, 42, 51, 56 ; unimpaired, concussion unlikely, 51
    Mental symptoms which ensue upon, 215
    Neurasthenia, traumatic, alleged following (case), 101
Head's areas, 294
Hearing. See Ear
Heart :
    Aortic regurgitation diagnosed at examination for slight injury, 27
    Beat, neurasthenia in, 82
    Death after injury in subject of disease of, 226, 232, 234
    Flint's murmur, 294
    Giddiness in disease of, 70
    Incapacity for work in disease of, 33
    Operation for rupture under anæsthetic declined by man with disease of, 262
    Palpitation in neurasthenia, 83, 90
    " Stopping " of, alleged, 102
Heatstroke, alleged, really due apoplexy, 207
Heberden's nodes, 294
Hegar's sign, 294
Hemianopia. See Eye
Hemiplegia. See Paralysis
Heredity :
    Neurotic, in traumatic neuroses, 94
    Results of, alleged due to accident, 167, 220
    Spinal rigidity due to, 134
Hernia. See Rupture
Hiccough, spasmodic, after seeing accident, 81
Hip :
    Free flexion negatives disease of, 131
    Rheumatoid disease in, 135, 176
Holmgren's test for colour-blindness, 295

Hospital :
    Attendance, constant, gives official stamp of invalid, 48
    Compulsory treatment, 104
    Functional nerve disease treated, 78
    Hysteria treated, 87
    Observation, benefits of, 28, 104
Hutchinson's teeth, 295
Hydrocele, old-standing, in accident claim, 283
Hyperæsthesia. See Sensation
Hysteria. See also Neurasthenia ; Neuroses, traumatic
    Contractures, 86
    Definition of, 84
    Disseminated sclerosis in early stages resembles, 79
    Education into invalidism, 98
    Field of vision, 66, 116
    Incapacity due to, after dog-bite, 87
    Law Courts, in, 101, 266, 267
    Neurasthenia, diagnosis of, 88, 90
    Onset, after traumatism, 88
    Paralyses, 85
    Self-mutilation, 83
    Sensation, loss of, 78, 84
    Spasms, 86
    Symptoms, 83, 84
    Treatment by firmness, 86, 87
    Vomiting, 52
Hystero-neurasthenia, 92, 93, 96. See also Hysteria and Neurasthenia

Idleness, effects of, 142, 158, 187, 272
Incapacity. See also Work, and Chapter XXII.
    After-effects of accident, 266
    At expense of community, 11
    Detection of feigned, 148, 158
    Fear, cause of, 10, 268
    Giddiness alleged cause of, 71
    Neurasthenia, mental and physical, 82
    Obsession as to compensation cause of, 108
    Physical signs of, absent, 144
    Rupture alleged cause of, due blindness, 33
    Suggestion, cause of, 8, 87
    Unconnected with accident, 32
Incontinence of urine. See Urine
Infectious diseases, nerve deafness after, 122
Influence :
    Intimidation attempted, 162
Influenza :
    Fall alleged cause of, 18
    Nerve deafness after, 122
Injury self-inflicted :
    By elastic bands, 159
    Dermatitis, artificial. 164

INDEX

331

Injury self-inflicted (continued) :
    Eye, 12
    In hysteria, 83, 84
    In syringomyelia, 84
    Wounds, 158
Insanity :
    Delirium alleged after injury to coccyx, 142
    Delusional insanity feigned, 215
    Dementia feigned, 215
    Feigned and genuine, compared, 211, 212
    Feigned, investigation of causes, 213
    General paralysis in connection with injury and syphilis, 65
    Heart disease probable cause of, 235
    Melancholia: Feigned, 214; hystero-neurasthenia diagnosed from, 93
    Mental symptoms which may follow accident, 215
Insomnia. See Sleeplessness
Inspection, lay, 29
Insurance companies (accident) :
    Dislocation of biceps muscle, claims for, 151
    Hernia, claims for, 188
    Hospital treatment paid for by, 87
    Hysteria, claims for, 86
    Impartial attitude, to claimants, 12
    Libel, position of medical man reporting to, 18
    Premiums in progressive ratio to age, 19
    Robbery of, considered justifiable, 11, 12
Insurance (life). See also Medical examination prior to employment
    Concealment of colotomy scar, 2
Intelligence. See Education ; Memory
Introspection. See also Hysteria ; Neurasthenia ; Neuroses (traumatic) ; Suggestion
    After accident, 9, 96, 98, 107, 133, 187, 268
    Idleness encouraged by, 107. See also Idleness
    In rheumatoid disease, 135
    Medical examination, frequent, encourages, 96
    Patient, encouraged by, 142

Janet on field of vision in hysteria, 84
Jaw-jerk test, 295
Jewish race, effects of accident on, 96. See also Women
Joints. See under their names
    Charcot, 293
    Stiffness of : Result on muscles, 149 ; relaxes under anæsthetic, 273. See also Anæsthetic

Kernig's sign, 295
Kidney :
    Bright's disease, operation under anæsthetic on subject of, 262 :
        Carbuncle, alleged traumatic, in subject of, 223 ; giddiness in, 70
    Traumatic displacement of, 128, 294
    Urine. See Urine
Klumpke's palsy, 295
Knee :
    Injury to, serious in working man, 161
    Knock-knees due to rickets, alleged result of accident, 42
    Rigidity of, assumed, 163
    Semilunar cartilage displaced, 162
    Swelling of : Intermittent, 42 ; alleged, detected by measurement, 162
    Synovitis, 162
    X rays, use of, in alleged injury to, 163
Knee-jerk. See Reflex knee-jerk
Koplik's spots, 295

Labourers :
    Mental effects of injury to, 265
    Spondylitis in, 137
Landouzy-Déjérine disease, 295
Landry's paralysis, 295
Lead-poisoning, 187, 293
Leg. See also Bones under their names
    Asymmetry. See Chapter X.
    Ataxic gait, 79
    Fracture : Incapacity alleged after, 163 ; X rays in diagnosis of, 175
    Kernig's sign, 295
    Limping : A habit, 79 ; soles of shoes an indication of, 55
    Spasticity, 79
    Ulceration of, disease diagnosed from accident, 164
Legal aid societies :
    Malingering encouraged by, 291
    Methods of, 287, 289
    Profits of, 288, 289
    Rise and status of, 286
    State provision of poor man's lawyer advocated, 291
    Treatment of workmen by, 290
Leon Gallez dynamometer test, 152
Libel. See Evidence, expert
Light, perception of, in hysteria, 89
Litigation. See also Workmen's Compensation Act
    Moral degradation resulting from, 15
    Non-litigious cases, 27

332 MALINGERING

Litigation (continued) :
  Recent, effect on elderly workmen in accident, 20
  Perpetuates incapacity, 8
Locomotor ataxia :
  Argyll-Robertson pupil in, 292
  Babinski sign absent in, 68
  Diagnosed at examination for trifling accidents, 63 ; for head injury, 27 ; for sprained ankle, 27
  Jar of spinal cord after, 133
Ludwig's angina, 295
Lumbago. See also Back, Rheumatoid disease
  Spondylitis, relation to, 135
Lungs. See Hæmorrhage, Tuberculosis

Massage :
  Electrical treatment in conjunction with, 315
  Unskilled, useless, 105, 138
Measurements, 45, 47, 240. See also Asymmetry, Medico-legal examination
  Congenital defect detected by, 148
  Swelling, feigned, detected by, 162
Medical assessors. See Workmen's Compensation Act, Assessors, medical
Medical certificates. See Certificate, Report
Medical Defence Union, 18
Medical examination, periodic, of sick employees :
  Advantages of, 27, 64
  District medical officers, organization of, 25
  Home Office system advocated, 25, 26
  Serious conditions revealed by, 27
  Statistics showing reduction in sickness by, 26
  Systematic, 25
  " Twenty-eight day " rule, results of, 25
Medical examination prior to employment :
  Advantages of, in public bodies and private service, 19, 20, 188
  Alertness at necessary, 25, 159
  Certificate form, 22
  Neurasthenia, pre-existing, concealed, 23
  Urine. See Urine
Medical examiner (club doctor and general practitioner) :
  Certificates of incapacity given without efficient examination, 49
  Family doctor not called at trial, 156
  Independence of, difficult, 15, 17, 284

Medical examiner (club doctor and general practitioner) *(continued)* :
  Treatment of auto-suggestion, 11
  Work and fees, 15, 51
Medical examiner (medico-legal cases).
  See also Evidence, expert ; Medico-legal examination ; Report of medico-legal examination
  Assault attempted on, 5
  Compensation, amount of, should be ascertained by, 9, 49
  Doubtful cases, 16, 61, 285
  Firmness. See Firmness
  Impartiality, 35, 39
  Party to exaggeration, 16,17,88,97
  Qualifications, 32
  Recognition of malingering, 1, 2, 14, 15, 97
Medical report. See Report of medico-legal examination
Medico-legal examination (conduct of).
  See also Evidence, expert ; Medico-legal examination ; Report of medico - legal examination ; Workmen's Compensation Act
  Avoidance of, 164
  Children. See Children
  Demeanour prior to and during, 37, 42, 150
  Difficulties of, 31
  Firmness cuts short incapacity, 136. See also Firmness
  Hysteria and malingering, differentiation of, 83
  Impartiality inspires confidence, 39
  Important points in, 136
  Instruments required, 60, 119
  Introspective, results on the, 10
  Lapse of time between accident and, 40
  Legal aspect of case, 39
  Location of pain, 45. See also Pain
  Measurements, 45. See also Asymmetry
  Nervous system. See Nervous system, examination of
  Obligation to submit to, under Workmen's Compensation Act, 34, 38, 54, 256-264
  Observation, dressing and undressing, 44, 46, 54, 130
  Obstruction, voluntary, 47
  Patient under alcohol, 56, 57
  Present condition, 40
  Presence of patient's doctor, 38, 244
  Presence of solicitor, 38, 244
  Questions by examiner, diagnosis assisted by, 39, 43, 44, 51, 93, 140, 157, 162, 206
  Refusal to visit examiner, 127, 144, 283

INDEX

333

Medico-legal examination (*continued*) :
Relatives and friends excluded from, 37 ركب
Statements of examinee :
Age misstated, 52 ; clear and consistent, if honest, 45, 137, 143 ; coached, before examination, 130, 186 ; evolution of symptoms detailed, 43 ; legal statement of claim compared with, 41 ; notes of, 41, 123 ; present complaints, 44 ; "suggestio falsi," 34 ; "suppressio veri," 34 ; verbal, of other doctors' views should not be encouraged, 50
Thoroughness, 41, 46, 119
Women, difficulty of, 55, 56. See also Women
Memory :
Accident, cause of continued disability, 101, 270
Loss of, in head injury, 42, 51, 56
Ménière's disease, relation to neurasthenia, 83
Micturition. See Urine
Migraine, 42
Miscarriage. See Abortion
Monocular vision. See Eye
Morphia, use of, 116
Mouth :
Blood from. See Hæmorrhage
Septic condition of, contributory cause of rheumatism, 138
Mucous membrane, anæsthesia of, in functional nerve disease, 79
Muscle. See also Chapter XXVI. for details of electrical testing
Biceps, dislocation of, 151
Co-ordination of, failure in vertigo, 71
Debility of, in neurasthenia, 82
Lumbar sacral, tearing of, 128
Tests for, 153
Trophic changes in, 149
X rays, injury diagnosed by, 179
Muscular atrophy (wasting). See also Asymmetry
Absence of, in alleged loss of power, 6
Arthritis deformans alleged due to traumatism, 176
Babinski sign absent in peroneal type of progressive, 68
Co-ordination normal when attention distracted, 91
Disease, not accident, the cause of, 158
Feigned, detected, 48, 102, 147, 148
Frequence of, feigned, 146
Functional disease inconsistent with, 78

Muscular atrophy (*continued*) :
Landouzy-Déjérine disease, 295
Measurements disprove, 47
Pain not confirmed by, 48
Progressive, after jar spinal cord, 133
Sciatica, in, 140
Tooth's disease, 296
Traumatic coccydinia, in, 131
Want of use a cause of, 14. 148, 272, 283

National Insurance Act :
Accident claims, age, and intercurrent disease in, 283
Additional sources of income, 135, 282
Amount of allowance under, 281
Approved societies : Insurance in more than one illegal, 35 ; protection of, 2, 285
Clinical aspect of case when no claim under, 62
France, malingering and sickness insurance in, 281
Fraud, possibilities of, under, 1, 61, 62, 280-285
Germany, malingering and sickness insurance in, 280
Illness : Simulated more easily than accident, 280 ; prolonged in advancing age, 281, 283
Medical referees for doubtful cases, 285
Old-Age Pension Act and malingering, 281
Persons insured under, 135, 280
Prevention of malingering under, 284
Unearned increment, 9
Navy. See also Army
Methods of malingering in, 1
Nerve, Nerves. See also Chapter XXVI. for electrical testing of
Brachial plexus injury to, Erb's and Klumpke's palsy, 294, 295
Deafness, nerve, 119, 121
Pain, alleged, follows no group of, 39
Sciatica, tenderness in, 140
Sensory, distribution of, 73
Nervousness :
Alleged, but no signs of, 42]
Diarrhœa and vomiting alleged due to (case), 52
Nervous system, examination of :
Diseases of :
See Disseminated sclerosis ; Epilepsy ; General paralysis of the insane ; Locomotor ataxia ; Tabes
Exaggeration of symptoms in, 63

334 MALINGERING

Nervous system, examination of (continued) :
Frequency of injury to, 61
Gait in disease of, 61
Reflexes. See Reflexes
Syphilis, 220. See also Syphilis
Traumatism, effects of, in labourers and cultured classes, 265
Urine, feigned incontinence, 144
Neuralgia :
Dilatation of pupil, 76
Nerve tenderness, 74
Neurasthenia, frequency of, 82, 92
Neurasthenia and traumatic neurasthenia. See also Hysteria ; Nerves ; Nervous system
Accident, after, 81
Allegation of, disproved (cases), 51, 137
Concealment of, attempted prior to employment, 23
" Cured " by damages, 62
Environment, change of, 62
Feigned, 53
Giddiness, after head injury, 72
Hospital observation cures alleged, 104
Hysteria, diagnosed from, 88
Incapacity alleged, 137
Induced by witnessing accident, 81
Law Courts, in, 101, 266, 269, 272, 276
Malingering, combined with, 142
Mental and physical capacity diminished in, 82
Psychic origin, 81
Symptoms of, 82
Time of onset after accident, 81
Traumatic neuroses, 92-97
Woman, fright alleged cause of, in, 98. See also Women
Working classes, prevalence in, 93
Neuritis :
Optic, inconsistent with functional disease, 78
Peripheral, Babinski sign absent in, 68, 293
Neuroses, traumatic, 92-97. See also Hysteria, Neurasthenia
Nystagmus. See Eye

Occupation :
Agricultural, rheumatoid diseases, 134
Artillerymen. See Army
Boiler-makers, deafness of, 120
Carmen, spinal rigidity, 135
Deafness caused by certain, 120
Exposure, results of, 135
Labourers, spondylitis apart from injury, 137
Painters, giddiness in, 18, 71

Old Age Pension Act, 281
Operation :
Hernia. See Chapter XIII.
Refusal of workman to undergo, 256-264
Scars should be looked for at examination, 44
Urgency of, 157
Opsonic index, 295
Organic nerve disease. See also Neurasthenia
Functional, diagnosed from, 78, 130, 293
Insidious in onset, 78
Osteophytic outgrowths, 134. See also Spine

Pain. See also Back, Sensation, and Chapter XII. for use of electricity in diagnosis
Anatomically inconsistent, 39, 47, 142
Anæsthesia, feigned, 77
Diagnosis, methods of, 74
Facial expression, 47
Genuine, may cause exaggeration, 41
Disproof of, difficult, 46, 73
Introspection fosters, 17
Location of, 5, 33, 47, 53, 73, 74, 129
Manifestation of, before test applied, 141
Movements free, in spite of alleged, 77
Psychic, after accident, 7, 10, 92
Pressure test, 76, 95, 140
Recognition of, 73
Sleeplessness caused by, 76
Stethoscope test for, 53, 77
Stooping alleged caused by, 40
Subjective, 101
Suggested by doctor, 43
Superficial touch said to produce, 53, 73, 127, 129, 156, 200
Variation in, suspicious, 76, 77
Painters :
Giddiness in, 18, 71
Heatstroke alleged, 207
Palate, 66
Pallor :
Indication of pain, 74
Vertigo, in, 71
Palsy :
Duchenne's, 294
Erb's, 294
Klumpke's, 295
Paralysis agitans :
Diagnosed at examination for fractured radius, 27
Spinal cord, jar of, 133
Symptoms of, 69

INDEX

335

Paralysis :
  Brown-Séquard, 293
  Extensive lesions seldom feigned, 146
  Feigned (case), 17, 141
  Fracture of petrous - temporal bone, 121
  Hemiplegia, functional and organic, 147
  Hysteria, 85, 90, 91, 92
  Infantile, Babinski sign absent, 68, 293
  Landry's, 295
  Lead-poisoning, 187
  Spasticity, 79
Paraplegia. See Paralysis
Paris, plaster of, in detection of malingering, 166
Parrot's nodes, 296
Pawlik's grip, 296
Penalty for malingering, 12, 13, 159. See also Perjury
Pension :
  Prospective, encourages incapacity, 28, 158
  Workmen's Compensation Act, 277
Periodic medical examination. See Medical examination, periodic
Peritonitis, traumatic origin, 234
Perjury by claimant :
  Conviction for, under Workmen's Compensation Act, 12, 13
  Evidence, perjured, 37
  Facts and symptoms wilfully misrepresented, 49
  Punishment for, 13
Personation by impostor and accomplice, 29
" Peveril of the Peak," deaf mute detected in, 75
Phthisis. See Tuberculosis
Pilocarpine, use of, in malingering, 116
Plantar reflex. See Reflex, plantar
Pleurisy :
  Dilatation of pupil in, 76
  Traumatic, alleged, 231
Post-mortem, brain laceration at, 133
Power, loss of. See Muscular atrophy
  Electrical testing of, 186
  Trapeze test for, 149
Prevention, best means of, 30
Privilege. See Evidence, expert
Professional valetudinarians, 97
Prostate gland, enlargement of, 131
Psychology of fraudulent mind, 7-12
Public Prosecutor, Judge sends case to, 6
Public service :
  Diabetes concealed at examination, 25
  Medical examination prior to employment in, 23
  Proportion of gross malingerers in, 3

Pulse :
  Pain indicated by, 74, 75
  Tremor and, 69
  Vertigo, in, 71
Pupil :
  Argyll-Robertson, 65, 78, 103, 292
  Hysteria, in, 84
  Pain, in, 74, 75, 76
Pyorrhœa in working classes, 138

Radius :
  Fracture : Paralysis agitans diagnosed at examination for, 27 ; return to work postponed after, 157
Railways : "Railway spine," 22, 133
Rawitsch on asymmetry, 173
Reaction of degeneration. See Electricity
Recognition. See also Medico-legal examination ; Examiner
  Difficulty of, 62
  Disease pre-existing, 64
Recovery. See also Work, return to
  Gradual, 3, 100, 270
  Mental attitude towards, 8
  Not admitted after slight genuine disability, 140
  Postponed by delay in litigation, 97
  Prolonged unduly, 3
  Rapid, when no compensation, 106
Referee, medical. See Workmen's Compensation Act ; Assessors, medical
Reflexes. See also Nervous system, examination of,
  Abdominal, absence of, 67
  Ankle clonus, description of, 68 :
    Routine examination of, 53 ; true and false, 69
  Babinski sign, description of, 67, 68, 293 :
    Functional nerve disease, inconsistent with, 78 ; relation to increased knee-jerk and ankle clonus, 69 ; significance of, 67
  Hysteria, 84
  Knee-jerk, absence of, inconsistent with functional disease, 78 :
    Description of, 66, 67 ; examinee's deductions from former examination of, 53 ; neurasthenia in, 83, 90 ; "reinforcement," 67 ; relation to ankle clonus, 68, 69 ; significance exaggerated, 67 ; simulation easy, 67
  Plantar : Relation of, to other reflexes, 69 ; routine examination of, 53

MALINGERING

Reflexes (continued):
  Pupil: Description of, 65, 66 ; routine examination of, 53. See also Pupil
  Routine examination, in medico-legal cases, 45
Report of medico-legal examination :
  Comprehensive and brief, 79
  Drawings. See Diagrams
  Formula for head of report form, 57
  Grounds of opinion should be stated, 57, 229
  Impartiality, 57
  Independent and reliable, aids return to work, 15
  Privileged if no malice, 17, 57
  Probable causes of death. See Chapter XVIII.
  Technical terms, abuse of, 57, 227
Rheumatism. See also Back ; Lumbago; Rheumatism ; and Spondylitis sciatica
  Accident alleged cause of, 126
  Exacerbation and acceleration by accident, 135, 221
  Nerve deafness after, 122
Rheumatoid disease. See also Lumbago ; Rheumatism ; Spondylitis deformans ; and Sciatica
  National Insurance Act, and, 281, 283
  X rays in diagnosis of, 179
Rib, fracture of, 99
Rickets, effects of, 42
Rinne's test for deafness, 122, 296
Riveters, deafness in, 120
Romberg's sign, and malingering in, 53, 69, 70, 103, 296
Rupture, or Hernia :
  Alleged traumatic, in man discovered to be blind, 32
  Attributable to traumatism, 190
  Complaints after radical cure, 198
  Examination for descent of alleged, 32
  Fraudulent claims for, 188
  Frequency of, 198
  History of accident in, 192
  Not attributable to traumatism, 191
  Operation for, under anæsthetic, declined, 262
  Origin uncertain, 192
  Truss : Marks of, 44 ; capacity to work with, 32, 196

Scars, operation, concealment of, 2, 44
Sciatica. See also Back
  Asymmetry, congenital, cause of alleged, 167
  Feigned, 140

Sciatica (continued) :
  Pain in back in, alleged accident due to, 39
  Posture and pin-prick test, 141
  Spondylitis in relation to, 135
Sclerosis, lateral, jaw-jerk in, 295
Secrecy, professional. See Evidence, expert
Sensation :
  Anæsthesia (*i.e.*, loss of), Brown-Séquard disease, in, 293 :
    Functional and organic compared, 79 ; hysteria, in, 89, 92 ; pin-prick test for, 7, 77, 91 ; rheumatoid disease, in, 135
  Hyperæsthesia (excessive), hysteria, in, 73, 87 : Neurasthenia, in, 82, 90 ; sciatica, in, 140 ; spine, of, 133. See also Chapter XXVI. for electrical testing
Sensory nerves, distribution of, 73. See also Nerves
Shock :
  Back injury alleged cause of, 91
  Death alleged caused by, 232
  Fall alleged cause of, 19
  Pathological changes arising from, 106
  Rare, after severe operation under anæsthetic, 107
  Repeated examination reproduces effects of, 96, 106
Shoulder :
  Arthritis of, 149
  Asymmetry in, 173
  Dislocation of, 157
  Paralysis feigned, 150
  Phthisis pre-existing, 27
  Rheumatoid disease of, 135
Sight. See Eye
Sinistrosis, 108
Skodaic resonance, 296
Skull, fracture of, 120, 122
Slander. See Evidence, expert
Sleeplessness :
  Back injury, alleged cause of, 137
  Hysterical contractions disappear in, 84, 86, 90
  Neurasthenia in, 82, 90, 92
  Genuine pain causes, 76
  Physical appearance inconsistent with alleged, 94, 95
Snellen's test types, 108
Spasms, hysteria in, 86
Speech :
  Alterations in, 79
  Deaf mute detected, 75
Spinal cord :
  Accident and, 127, 131
  Obsession as to progressive ascending degeneration of (case), 91

INDEX

Spine. See also Back
Base of skull, fracture of, 120
Battery, use of, 28. See also Electricity
Compensation for two years in alleged injury to, 27
Concussion, 133
Constitutional causes real basis of alleged injury to, 19
Hysterical, 133
Injury alleged, 34, 39
Irritation, 22
Micturition, abnormalities in, alleged due to injury of, 145
Myelitis alleged, 28, 61
Organic disease of, alleged, 61, 130
Ossification, varieties of, 134
" Railway " spine, 133
Rigidity, causes of, 134 :
Cured speedily in slight traumatism, 136 ; frequency apart from rheumatism, 136 ; intermittent, 39, 139 ; pain alleged due to, 129 ; persistently held bent, 22, 61 ; test by rotation of body, 140
Syphilis pre-existing, 133
Tests for, 95, 139
Spondylitis deformans :
Commencement of, concurrent with accident, 137
Pre-existing, accelerated by accident, 135
Symptoms, 135
Sprains. See under names of parts concerned
Statement of claim :
Discrepancies, 41
Exaggeration, 41
Statistics :
France, compensation for sickness in, 281
Hernia : Fraudulent claims, 188 ; frequency of, 198
Proportion of gross shammers, 3
Results of 10,000 examinations, 22
Reduction in sickness due to periodic examination, 26
Street accidents, 287
Stellwag's sign, 296
Stethoscope :
Deafness tested by, 123
Pain tested by, 53, 77, 129, 185
Stereoscope, use of, in sight-testing, 114
Still's disease, 296
Stricture, effects of, alleged due traumatism, 131
Subjective symptoms. See Symptoms, subjective
Sugar. See Urine

Suggestion. See also Auto-suggestion
Hysteria in, 87
Spinal rigidity increased by, 139
Sunstroke. See Heatstroke
Surprise visit :
Lay inspectors, 29
Legal position as to, 246
Medical examiner, 29
Sweating :
Pain indicated by, 74
Vertigo, 71
Symptoms :
Diagnosis of functional nerve disease combined with malingering, 61
Exaggeration of, in statement of claim, 41
Feigned, 43, 45
Nerve disease alleged due to trifling accident, 63
Past and present, 50
Suggested by doctor, 43, 93
Unconscious simulation of, by neurotics, 62
Unlikely, complained of, 44
Symptoms, objective, can be verified, 71
Symptoms, subjective :
Auto-suggestion causes variation in temperature, 99
Dependent on patient's statements, 101
Frequency of, 50
Giddiness, 70. See also Giddiness
Influence of mind on body, 42, 99
Proof difficult, 71
Reproduction of, illustrated in case of Napoleon's operation for stone, 107
Synovitis, knee, 162
Syphilis :
Congenital : Hutchinson's teeth in, 295 ; Parrot's nodes in, 296
Diagnosed at examination after accident, 63
Hystero-neurasthenia, diagnosis of, from parasyphilitic nervous affections, 93
Insanity, traumatic, diagnosed from results of, 212
Nerve deafness after, 122
Pre-existing, results of jar of spinal cord, 133
Pupil, loss of reflex after, 66
Results of alleged, due to accident, 219, 220
Rigidity of spine due to, 134
Wassermann test, 65, 297
Syringomyelia, Charcot's joint in, 293

Tabes :
Babinski sign in, 293
Charcot's joints, 293

338 MALINGERING

Tabes (continued) :
    Hystero - neurasthenia diagnosed from, 93
    Inequality of pupils in, 66
    Loss of pupil contraction in, 66, 292
    Romberg's sign in, 296
Tache cérébrale, 296 ·
Talipes equino-varus, 34
Temperature :
    Hysteria, in, 84
    Variation in, due to auto-suggestion, 99
Tests. Various tests are referred to under parts tested
    Delicate, cannot be applied to examinee under influence of alcohol, 57
    Methods of application, 155
    Reaction, by hysterics, 86
    Simple, yet effective, 155
Teeth :
    Disfigurement by loss of milktooth, 42
    Loose by disease alleged due accident, 138
    Rheumatoid disease caused by condition of, 138
Tenderness. See also Pain, Sensation
    Location of, alleged, 53
Tendo-Achillis, 68
Thigh :
    Fracture of, and heart disease, death resulting, 232
    Fracture of, return to work after, 274
Third party claims, no obligation to submit to medical examination in, 38
Thumb :
    Dislocation, 46
    Sprain, 28
Tibia :
    Compound fracture of, 138
    Rotation of, test for pain in knee, 162
Toe :
    Tiptoe test, 16, 47, 148, 161, 163
    Refusal to work after amputation of, 259
Tongue :
    Movements of, 66
    Rarely affected in functional nerve disease, 79
Tooth's disease, 296
Trade unions :
    Claims on, 269
    Funds saved at expense of employers, 94
Trapeze test, 149, 154, 207
Traumatic neurasthenia. See Neurasthenia

Traumatism. See Accident
Treatment. See also Operation
    Avoidance of, 51, 72, 158
    Co-operation by patient, 129
    Electricity. See Chapter XXVI.
    Environment, change of, 97 ·
    Firmness. See Firmness
    Hospital, in, 103
    Isolation, 97
    Massage, 104
    Mental conditions, 144
    Painful exercises, perseverance in, 136
    Personality, 88
    Psychical conditions, 133
    Psycho-therapeutic, 104, 129, 133
    Spinal rigidity, 136
    Strong measures for shammers, 6
Tremor :
    Intentional, stopped by firmness, 52
    Paralysis agitans, 69
    Simulated and genuine, 69
Trousseau's sign, 296
Tubby on asymmetry, 168
Tuberculosis :
    Acceleration by traumatism, 220, 226, 229
    Bazin's disease, 293
    Calmette's reaction, 293
    Caused by traumatism, 220, 226
    Diagnosed in examinee with injured shoulder, 27
    Opsonic index, 295
    Von Pirquet's reaction, 297
    Workmen's Compensation Act, 144
Typhoid fever, intercurrent, concealed, in accident claim, 32

Ulcer :
    Concealment of, attempted, 34
    Varicose. See Veins, varicose
Ulna, fracture of, 157

Unearned increment :
    Club money, 29. See also Clubs
    Moral degradation resulting from, 16
Urethra, nuclear albumen from deposit in, 23
Urine :
    Author's experience of 10,000 examinations of, 25
    Albumen :
        Accident, alleged cause of, 45 ; adolescent, 24 ; epithelial casts, 24 ; functional, 24 ; hyaline casts, 24 ; microscopical examination of, 23 ; temporary, 23
    Cammidge's reaction, 293

INDEX

Urine (*continued*) :

Micturition :

Difficult : Traumatism alleged cause of, 131 ; entrance, examination, at, 24 ; nerve disease, in, 145

Incontinence : Feigned, 142, 144 ; inspection of clothes disproves, 95, 143 ; functional disease, 78

Retention : Nerve disease, 145

Passing of, in presence of examiner, 25

Sugar :

Accident, alleged cause of, 45 ; concealment of, attempted at examination, 25 ; temporary, 24

Varicose ulcer. See Ulcer, varicose ; Veins, varicose

Veins, varicose, traumatism complicated by, 163

Venereal disease. See also Gonorrhœa, Syphilis

Results of, alleged due to accident, 165

Vertigo. See Giddiness

Volkmann's contracture, 296

Vomiting :

Complaint of, after alleged back injury, 136

Intentional or hysterical, 52

Von Graefe's sign, 296

Von Pirquet's reaction, 297

Walk, inability to, alleged, 141

Wassermann. See Syphilis

Wasting. See Muscular atrophy

Weakness. See also Muscular atrophy

Asymmetry may be the cause of alleged traumatic, 167

Feigned, indefinite, 147

Weber's test for deafness, 122, 297

Weight, loss of, alleged, 141

Weiss's sign, 293

Widal's test, 297

Women. See also Medico-legal examination

Abortion alleged due accident, 36

Displaced kidney in accident claims, 128

Fright alleged cause of traumatic neurasthenia, 98

Generative organs, diseases of, 127

Hysteria, proportion of, in, 89

Jewish, and traumatic neuroses, 96

Postponement of settlement of claim retards recovery, 97

Work. See also Recovery

Casual : Need of medical examination prior to employment, 20

Full : Compensation demanded and paid during, 5 ; refusal to return to, 163

Light : Functional neuroses cured by, 142 ; provision of, 19, 96 ; refusal to return to or continue, 137, 161, 267 ; workman makes no attempt to obtain, 274, 275

Return to. See also Chapter XXII. :

Causes of postponement, 14, 95, 96

Age increasing, 281 ; dislike of labour, 97, 281 ; half wages and idleness preferred, 103 ; income when ill nearly equal to or more than wages, 50, 94, 184 ; independent medical certificate, 15 ; indifference to, 107 ; medical advice disregarded, 39, 273 ; muscular degeneration owing to idleness, 272 ; obsession of injury, 136, 268 ; offered and refused, 100, 158 ; Old Age Pension Act, 281

Compulsory, on recovery, 11 ; dismissal without compensation for failure to, 27 ; duty to endure slight inconvenience on, 115, 136, 158 ; effect of, on character, 17 ; facilitated by personal interest of employers, 15 ; fitness for, 3 ; insurance cases unwilling to, 3; mental attitude towards, 8, 34, 95, 105, 146 ; obsession cured by, 156 ; operation preferred, 201 ; periodic examination, 26 ; psychological moment for, 101 ; public bodies, employees of, willing to, 3 ; resentment at suggestion by doctor, 138 ; stimulus of necessity, 9, 94, 95

Workmen's Compensation Act. See also Compensation ; County Court Actions ; Work

Accident prior to, 27

Assessors, medical, need and use of, under, 21, 154, 233

Cases decided upon application to revise or terminate weekly payments, 265-279

Clinical aspect of case if no claim under, 62

Comparison of cases settled in and out of Court, 21

340 MALINGERING

Workmen's Compensation Act (*continued*):

Compensation augmented by other payments, 9, 48, 94

Desire for lump sum settlement, 103

Development of malingering under, 1, 280

Effects of, on elderly workmen, 20. See also Age

Employer liable only in respect of inability to earn wages, 27

Employers not liable for results on nervous system of introspection, 268, 270

Employers' right to medical examination under, 242-245

Fees, employers not liable for those of claimant's doctor at examination, 244

Legal aid societies, 287

Obligation to submit to medical examination under, 38, 54, 142, 246-256

Pension disregarded under, 277

Place of examination, 244, 245

Proportion of community affected by, 106

Refusal to undergo operation, 256-264

Solicitor not entitled to be present at examination under, 244

Stimulus for work lessened by, 100

Third parties should be excluded from medical examination, 37

Traumatic neuroses increased by, 94

Tuberculosis and traumatism, 44, 226. See also Hæmorrhage and Tuberculosis

Visit, surprise, 246

Workmen convicted of perjury in proceedings under, 13, 14

Workman no absolute right to have his doctor present, 244

Wounds :

Dog-bite followed by hysteria, 87

Dressings: Elaborate, over-minute, 28 ; discarded after examination, 45

Exaggeration of trivial, 42, 87

General paralysis of the insane diagnosed at examination for slight, 64

Intentionally kept open, 158

Self-inflicted, 1, 158

Septic poisoning : Alleged muscular weakness after, 154 ; operation under anæsthetic refused, 263

Wrist :

"Drop wrist," 312

Fracture of, alleged, and disproved by X rays, 273

Writer's cramp, concealment of, attempted at examination, 23

X rays. For details of how to use, 175-181

Ankylosis of spine shown by, 137

Disability disproved by, in hysterical case, 87

Expert not called at trial, 139

Fracture of clavicle disproved by, 6

Fracture of wrist disproved by, 273

Ill-understood by Judge and jury, 136

Needle, position in hand shown by, 156

Obstruction, voluntary, under, 49

Organic disease disproved by, 142

Osteophytic outgrowths, 135, 139

Refusal to submit to, 5

Rheumatoid disease, use of, in, 134

Spinal injury alleged, disproved, by, 22

Torn muscles of back revealed by, 129

THE END

BILLING AND SONS, LTD., PRINTERS, GUILDFORD.

University of California
SOUTHERN REGIONAL LIBRARY FACILITY
Return this material to the library
from which it was borrowed.

W-
783

F. W. Brown

University of California
SOUTHERN REGIONAL LIBRARY FACILITY
Return this material to the library
~~from which it was~~

```
MSG#:Q07864
  IN#:   837    SRLF   OCT 01 1990
   TO: UCSRLF  QL
FROM: CLASS      UCDMCL
SENT: 23 APR 90 14:46:39
READ: 24 APR 90 12:07:01
SUBJ: ILL REQ
```

UCD Medical Center Library
4301 X St., Rm. 1005
Sacramento, CA 95817

To: UCSRLF
From: UCDMCL 4-23-90

G. Hutchinson, PhD Psychiatry faculty

Collie, John.
   Malingering and feigned sickness.

Ver: Melvyl. Your number = A 00036096

M. Clopton/UCDMCL/ILL
CCG

W—
783
C691m
1913

F. W. Brown

UC SOUTHERN REGIONAL LIBRARY FACILITY

A 000 360 964 1

ImTheStory.com

Personalized Classic Books in many genre's

Unique gift for kids, partners, friends, colleagues

Customize:
- Character Names
- Upload your own front/back cover images (optional)
- Inscribe a personal message/dedication on the inside page (optional)

Customize many titles Including
- Alice in Wonderland
- Romeo and Juliet
- The Wizard of Oz
- A Christmas Carol
- Dracula
- Dr. Jekyll & Mr. Hyde
- And more...

CPSIA information can be obtained at www.ICGtesting.com
Printed in the USA
LVOW011014190613

339270LV00011B/880/P